Calling on the Presidents:
Tales Their Houses Tell

Clark Beim-Esche

Published by FastPencil Publishing

*To
Trude
Harper —
Longtime friend
and compatriot.
Hope you enjoy
our travels, Trude!*

Second Edition

Table of Contents

Prologue

Calling on the Presidents is a book written **by** an enthusiast **for** other enthusiasts, a book of memories and guesses, a book of speculations and revelations. It is a personal journey, yet it is grounded in both historical fact and in actual visits to the locations identified and described in its text.

Fellow enthusiasts Clark and Carol Beim-Esche

Authors are often encouraged to define for themselves the audience for which they are writing. I find this easy to do.

I am writing for any reader who is interested in learning more about the men who have served as President of the United States. I am writing for any reader who has enjoyed, or who anticipates the enjoyment of, visiting the homes where Presidents have lived. I am writing for readers who believe, as I do, that these residences can provide a means of deepening their understanding and appreciation of these leaders. And I am also writing for the reader who is willing to entertain the notion that an ordinary American citizen can have worthwhile insights that may not always correspond to the current scholarly opinions regarding the Presidents whose homes he has visited.

Many of my conclusions have little or no relationship to current lists of "The 10 Best (or Worst) Presidents" that are so popular these days. I have particularly enjoyed finding angles or aspects of our most maligned Chief Executives that suggest the need to reassess, even to completely revise, the prevailing opinions regarding the worth of their lives and their administrations.

In writing this narrative account of Carol's and my travels to presidential homes, I often quote directly both from our own conversations and from what guides, docents, National Park Rangers, and other travelers have said to us. Occasionally I have mentioned these folks by name. As I have never used a recording device with which to take notes, I openly confess that any conversations set down here are reconstructions of these moments and not actual transcriptions of anyone's remarks. I have always asked Carol to confirm these recollections, and I have never intentionally misrepresented an idea or an insight that has been shared with us by any of the multitude of wonderful guides we have encountered in our travels. But since I have been a teacher for over 40 years (and on occasion have been misquoted myself), I am also quite aware that a docent or National Park Ranger who recognizes him or herself in this text might say, "I don't recall saying that." Please forgive any lapses of memory or inaccuracies of statement on my part. I have employed this technique of remembering conversations only with the intent of helping readers to relive the discoveries Carol and I experienced in coming to know—and appreciate more fully—the Presidents we were studying.

And what a joy it has been! The project has led us down many roads we would never have otherwise traveled, toward many surprising locales it would have been impossible to anticipate. I am happy to record what has revealed itself to me as a result of my thinking and reading about the lives of these Presidents, together with many hours of wonderful conversations with my wife, brilliant trip planner, and co-enthusiast, Carol, to whom I lovingly dedicate this book. We both encourage you to join us, to become our companions, as we begin *Calling on the Presidents*. Their homes have many fascinating tales to tell.

One final thought. Although the Presidents in this book are arranged chronologically, I would recommend reading the chapters in *any* order, according to your interests and/or travel plans. Above all, I hope that you will find your reading experience both enjoyable and thought provoking.

Clark Beim-Esche

Introduction

Perhaps it was my afternoon visit to the Harding Memorial. Or maybe it was because I had seen a current edition of *The Marion Star* outside the Applebee's restaurant where Carol and I had just finished dinner. *The Star* had been the local paper that had launched Warren G. Hard-

2009 Issue of Marion Star

ing into financial prosperity and a political career, and here it was, still being published in 2009. Whether these, or some other more esoteric, motivations were building up within me, less than a week later I found myself urged, even compelled, to write. As my earlier efforts had taught me, the only way I could really enjoy writing ex-tendedly was under the compulsion of *needing* to record my think-ing and experiences.

So why was I here at my computer beginning this book? Because of something that I have found to be of increasing importance to my life: a deeper, more sympathetic, more complex understanding of the men who have served as President of my country, the Unit-ed States of America. There is, of course, an obvious reason **not** to write about this topic. So much information already exists about the Presidents that one could spend an ample lifetime trying to read it all and still not do much more than peruse a small portion of the available information. What could I, admittedly an amateur his-tory enthusiast, have to add to this tsunami of data? My answer is actually quite simple: I have visited the places where the Presidents have lived. Nowhere in my research has anyone used the presiden-tial homes as a touchstone on which to base an understanding of the men who have occupied the vital office of President of the Unit-ed States.

In the past whenever Carol and I had been traveling, we would frequently stop to visit the homes of past Presidents if these locales did not take us too far off the routes toward the other destinations to which we had been journeying. Over time, however, this casual practice morphed into an activity more consequential and more central to our thoughts and interests than I would have imagined possible in earlier years.

Then for the first time, in the summer of 2009, Carol and I took a trip to Ohio for no other reason than to visit four presidential homes. Our route was comprised of a loop around Ohio, from the home of Rutherford B. Hayes in Fremont, to the renovated farmhouse of James A. Garfield in Mentor, near Cleveland, down to the one surviving home associated with William McKinley in Canton, and then back across the state to Marion and the home of the universally disparaged Warren G. Harding. Clearly these visits had begun to assume a larger significance to both Carol and me. But significance regarding what?

In recent years the political landscape of the United States has reflected some serious disillusionment. From both the political left and the political right we are almost daily presented with an endless litany of displeasure with nearly every decision any President makes.

The negativity feels pervasive. But the presidential homes Carol and I have been visiting over these years, attest to a very different truth, and we never leave any one of them with a sense of deflation or disappointment. Time and again, the predominant feeling Carol and I have experienced in these locations is a quiet gratitude for the dedication and efforts of the men who have been willing to serve their country as Chief Executive. Each of these leaders has been unique. Some have even been personal friends, though most came from substantially dissimilar backgrounds. But all the Presidents have been linked together by a few indispensable characteristics: each felt a humbling responsibility in becoming President; each worked tirelessly to leave the country better off than he found it; and each both succeeded and failed in bringing about the improvements and programs he wished to see enacted.

And for all this, I have concluded, these men deserve to be understood and to be remembered by all of us who have been the beneficiaries of their efforts. Just as *The Marion Star* continues to be published more than eighty years after Harding left his position as its owner and editor, Harding himself, together with all the other men who have captained the United States' ship of state, deserves an honored place in our hearts. This book is my attempt to chronicle the silent testimony regarding their tragedies and triumphs, their mistakes and their successes, and, most importantly, their individual perspectives on the world to which their homes often bear eloquent witness.

Note: All photographs in *Calling on the Presidents: Tales Their Houses Tell* were taken by the author, his wife, or their son, Andrew.

1

George Washington: The President in absentia

1st President George Washington (1789-1797): Mount Vernon in VA

To his most noted biographer, James Thomas Flexner, he was the "indispensable man." To a more recent historian, Joseph Ellis, he was "...a mysterious abstraction ... aloof and silent ...." (x). Richard Brookhiser has suggested that many Americans view him as if he "...had been carved of the same stone as his monument" (6). Yet year after year, thousands of us come to the places associated with his name, reverently, gratefully, searching for insights into—and perhaps even hoping for a closer connection with—the irreplaceable George Washington, our first President and the Father of his Country.

Gaining such insights and forging such a connection turns out to be more difficult than one might expect, however. Why? One answer can be found in the National Park Service brochure visitors receive upon entering the George Washington Birthplace National Monument at Pope's Creek in the Virginia tidewater. It identifies a challenge awaiting any guest attempting to understand Washington more completely:

> *George Washington is the most elusive of national heroes. His great achievements and the strength of his character led a grateful nation to elevate him to the level of myth. As his life was magnified with legend and held up as an example to schoolchildren, Washington the man began to disappear behind the model. 'The Father of his Country' is, like the monument built to him, an emblem of the nation. But for many the historical person has become as abstract as the monument, as unreal as the marble statues.*

What hope, then, is there of getting closer to Washington, the real Washington, and not merely to a mythologized ideal nor, equally dissatisfying, to some revisionist devaluation of his genuine greatness? And furthermore, who or what had actually determined to "elevate him to the level of myth" in the first place? The Pope's Creek site begins to offer some interesting answers to such questions.

By the early 19th century, the home where George Washington had been born had long since disappeared. Touring the farm site in 1815, Washington's step-grandson had placed a stone marker on the spot he believed to be the location of the original house, but nothing of consequence was done to materially preserve the site for over fifty years. By the early 20th century, however, as the bicentennial of Washington's birth approached, an organization styling itself the "Wakefield National Memorial Association" worked to have the location designated as a national monument and, furthermore, this group funded the building of a house on the original home site that would give Americans a clearer sense of the sort of environment into which Washington had entered the world. They constructed the Memorial House in time for the 1931 celebration of the two hundredth anniversary of Washington's birth. But in doing so, they participated in creating some of the tendency "to elevate him to the level of myth" to which the current park brochure refers.

As our docent, a knowledgeable young man named Alan, informed us, the Memorial House had not been placed on the actual site of the Washington home. The ground chosen for the reconstruction was closer to the water, commanding a more stately view of the confluence of Pope's Creek with Chesapeake Bay than had been afforded to the original house. Also, the recreated structure was much larger than the

George Washington's Reconstructed Birth House in Pope's Creek, Virginia

Washington plantation house had been and possessed considerably more touches of affluence than the Washington family had ever enjoyed.

The true farmhouse site was discovered in the years following the bicentennial celebration. Today its foundation stones are visible and indicate that the extent of this original home measures approximately half the scale of the reconstructed Memorial House.

Clearly, then, the goal of the Wakefield National Memorial Association had been twofold: first, to create a lasting national park site commemorating the birthplace of our first President, and second, to present an iconic symbol of Washington's world that would reflect the elevated stature of his reputation. Even the separate kitchen building constructed near the Memorial House is twice the size of the original structure that had been located there.

These amplifications, I firmly believe, were never the result of any intentional efforts to mislead the public. The buildings were not conscious fabrications. This glorification of Washington's earliest years had occurred naturally and was an understandable result of a 20th century appreciation of the scope of his career and of the meaning of his success, a meaning that not even the most prescient 18th century colonist could have imagined. Nevertheless, the "Washington myth" is clearly in evidence here at Pope's Creek, and, I have discovered, it is equally, if not increasingly, present in other sites connected with his name.

About thirty-eight miles west of the birthplace locale, on the eastern bank of the Rappahannock River just opposite Fredericksburg, is Ferry Farm, Washington's boyhood home where, this site's introductory leaflet informs visitors, "...Washington grew to manhood and developed the remarkable traits that helped him lead the Continental Army, become the first U.S. President, and guide a fledgling nation to its place in history."

What one actually encounters at Ferry Farm, however, falls considerably short of the impressive rhetoric quoted above. This site is essentially a field with its western edge sloping down to the Rappahannock River, now nearly invisible because of a variety of unkempt foliage blocking the view. Yet in this place, once again, we see the Washington myth being set forth, even as it identifies itself as myth.

For instance, although the Ferry Farm leaflet admits, honestly enough, that Parson Weems's anecdote of George Washington chopping down the cherry tree is probably only a "legend," it quotes the Weems account in full and uses as the leaflet's cover graphic an image of a cherry tree beneath which lies a discarded hatchet. Similarly, although archeological research has revealed that the so-called "Surveyor's Shed" dates from the late 19th century and, thus, is completely unrelated to Washington's boyhood years, The George Washington Foundation of Fredericksburg maintains the shed on the property to remind visitors that "Washington did learn to survey during his years at Ferry Farm and practiced in the fields and pastures." Finally, when referring to the legend of Washington throwing a stone (some accounts identify it as a silver dollar) across the Rappahannock, we are assured that "In his [Washington's] day, the river would have been much wider than it is today." Reality, it seems, is not quite enough when it comes to our appreciation of George Washington. He needs to be seen as larger than life, regardless of historical accuracy. It is a point of view that George Washington himself may have come to share. But for evidence of that, we need to drive north to Alexandria, Virginia, just south of the nation's capital.

Here we find the location that attracts more people to experience the world of our first President than all the other Washington sites combined. It is Mount Vernon, America's Versailles.

Over a million tourists each year find their way here to what is one of our greatest and certainly most venerated American "palaces." Compared to Versailles it doesn't measure up, but most Americans have never visited Versailles, and, consequently, the expansive acreage and exquisite placement of Mount Vernon on the rising hills above the Potomac still communicate the sense of affluence and elegance that we all associate with palatial grandeur.

George Washington himself fully appreciated the beauty and value of his plantation. Writing to a friend in 1793 in a rare moment of boastfulness, he noted, "No estate in United America is more pleasantly situated than this. It lies in a high, dry and healthy Country 300 miles by water from the sea ... on one of the finest Rivers in the World" (Haas 12).

Pilgrimages here are nothing new. Even in Washington's day, Mount Vernon had a staggeringly large number of visitors. In one year alone, a docent informed our tour group, George and Martha Washington had entertained 677 overnight guests.

What had brought them? Not, I think, the healthy air nor even the splendid view of the Potomac River winding its way to the sea. Some, of course, had come with the prospect of political gain, but most made this trek, I suspect, for reasons very similar to today's travelers: to feel closer to this great man, to connect to a person whose life decisions had approached an ideal that very few have any hope of equaling.

In this way Mount Vernon is more than a presidential home; it is an ideal, and it is that ideal that is on display today in pastoral Virginia. As I have toured the site with Carol on several occasions, I have invariably been struck with the panoramic loveliness of the piazza overlooking the Potomac, the unexpectedly bold aqua color of the walls of the "Great Room" with its 16 foot tall ceiling, and the pieces of genuine history which adorn the walls of the central entrance hall. (Displayed here, for instance, is an unprepossessing frame which houses a large key. "That arrived in late 1789," docents inform us. "It was one of the keys of the Bastille sent by Lafayette with the accompanying note, 'A symbol of liberty to the Father of liberty.'") Even the historical reality of slavery pales here, in no small part, perhaps, because of Washington's ultimate decision to free those men and women who had served him.

One might expect, then, in traveling to this beloved place which Washington had called home for over forty years, that an earnest seeker would gain many meaningful insights into the illustrious personage who had designed so many of its features and reveled in its graceful beauty.

Yet even after ascending the wide wooden stairway up to the second floor and standing quietly and patiently outside the doorway of Washington's bedroom for a chance to look at the bed on which the President had died in 1799, I have found it nearly impossible to envision George Washington here. And my subsequent research has revealed to me that, in this, I am not alone. As one of Washington's most esteemed biographers, Marcus Cunliffe, observed,

> *Innumerable tourists visit Mount Vernon. It is a handsome place, as they can testify, refurbished with taste and maintained in immaculate order. But the ghosts have been all too successfully exorcised in the process; Mount Vernon is less a house than a kind of museum-temple. We know that George Washington lived and died there; we do not feel the fact ....* (2)

It is important that such comments not be construed as criticism of the loving conservation of this site, provided so ably by the Mount Vernon Ladies Association. Mount Vernon is arguably the most completely perfect example of presidential home restoration and conservation in the United States. It is just that I have been unable to find much of Washington the man in this place.

That is, until the spring of 2012. On this most recent of my tours of the Mount Vernon property, I thought I glimpsed, however momentarily, an aspect of General Washington's humanity that related directly to the mythic stature he has assumed over the years. But then again, I may have been wrong. Walk with me down the pathway toward the river to visit Washington's tomb. Or tombs, I should say, for it is their plurality that provided me the insight to which I am referring.

In fact, it had not been my initial intent to stop at the Washington tomb(s) when I had begun the long walk down the steep hillside from the plantation house to the wharf on the Potomac. I had chosen to make the descent only because Carol and I had arrived at Mount Vernon nearly an hour before our scheduled house tour, and we needed something to do to pass the time prior to our entry to the home. Carol had chosen to enjoy the site's new state of the art Educational Center and Museum, and I had decided to see the riverside wharf and landing area which I had never taken the time to visit in my earlier trips here.

As I was about halfway down the hill, my attention was caught by a sign identifying Washington's "Old Tomb." As no one was heading down the brick pathway indicated by the sign, I wondered where it would lead. Why weren't there crowds of people wending their way to pay their respects to Washington? And why "old" tomb? Wouldn't any tomb containing the remains of the first President of the United States be old?

The pathway ended in a landing which spread out before a plain, square brick structure with a closed wooden door in the middle. Beside this small edifice was an explanatory sign which contained a quotation from Washington's Last Will and Testament: "The family vault of Mount Vernon requiring repairs and being improperly situated besides, I desire that a new one of Brick and upon a larger scale may be built at the foot of what is commonly called the Vineyard Inclosure."

George Washington's Old Tomb
at Mount Vernon

Although several other family members had already been laid to rest here, had Washington begun to question whether or not such a humble family vault was worthy of the "Father of his Country"? Was he realizing the importance of elevating himself "to the level of myth" in order to assure himself a permanent place in the hearts and minds of those who would come after him? As I wondered about all this, I became determined to see the newer tomb that had been erected in place of this original crypt.

George Washington's New Tomb
at Mount Vernon

The second tomb was a bit further down the hill, and it *was* deluged with reverent visitors who passed its door respectfully and solemnly. Its architecture was a striking contrast to the "Old Tomb." It was several times larger than the original vault. This, of course, had been in accordance with Washington's instructions regarding a "larger scale." The building also featured an elegant, brick Gothic arch, and, on either side of the path leading to the tomb, were impressive stone obelisks reminiscent of the monument that would later be erected in Washington's name on the mall of the capital city. Finally, I thought, here was a distinct glimpse of Washington, the man. After all his deprivations, his sacrifices for his country, his years of selfless service, here was concrete evidence that George Washington had desired glory and national reverence. I couldn't blame him. Certainly, if anyone in American history had earned such adulation, he had. But it also made him human, perhaps even understandably fallible, in a way that nothing else I had seen here quite matched. I had received my insight, my revelation.

Or so I thought. But, as I was to learn, quotations are tricky things. After I had returned home and was conducting some research into the design of the newer tomb, I came upon the complete text of the portion of Washington's Last Will and Testament relating to his burial site. The words that had been quoted on the sign by the "Old Tomb" were not all he had written. The next, concluding, sentence was vintage Washington: "And it is my express wish that my corpse may be interred in a private manner, without parade or funeral Oration." These were hardly the words of a man who, at the last, had wished for the lionization of his memory. The figure I believed that I had grasped, however momentarily, was once again becoming elusive.

Why was it so difficult to find evidence of Washington's human characteristics, his faults as well as his virtues, in this place? Perhaps Mount Vernon has remained distinct from Washington's personal character because, even for him, it had always been both more and less than an actual home.

It had been less than a home because, as much as he had thought about it and loved it, Washington was seldom present here for any extended period of time. From the moment he had officially acquired the estate in 1754, he had been constantly called away to service, first in the British nine year war with France and later in the colonies' eight year struggle for independence from Britain. Even with that remarkable victory achieved, Washington had been called away again—this time for eight more years—to serve as his country's first President. Finally, in 1797 he had been able to return to his beloved Mount Vernon, only to die two years later.

But Mount Vernon had always been more than a home, even more than the "museum-temple" referred to by Marcus Cunliffe. From its earliest days, it had been a kind of secular Mecca, a place of pilgrimage for the American people. And thousands of visitors still line the avenue each day, waiting for their tours to begin, waiting for their chance to witness for themselves this model of a perfect plantation life so clearly present and beautifully maintained here. This Mount Vernon was an ideal which Washington himself had never been fully able to inhabit, but it remains a powerful and important symbol for our national psyche. Almost literally, it was George Washington's "city on a hill," his ideal life that he was creating out of the promise and potential of the new world. But it was a life that future generations would enjoy more than he, for it was a life that could only be realized as a result of sacrifice and travail.

Washington's experiences away from this place, in the wilderness of western Pennsylvania and on the frigid heights of Valley Forge, on battlefields in New York and on a frozen river in New Jersey, would carry with them many essential lessons. He would learn to model a selfless devotion to duty for which he would receive no reward but honor, he would learn humbling lessons about what he could and could not accomplish as a soldier and a leader of men, and he would learn to dedicate himself tenaciously to his cause, regardless of personal cost or length of duty. More than anything else, these lessons—and his willingness to learn them—made George Washington the "Father of his Country."

And this, I suspect, is what brings us here by the thousands upon thousands. We come to appreciate his sacrifice, to acknowledge our debt of gratitude for his leadership, and to pay homage to his tireless efforts to achieve the ongoing ideal which became the nation he was so instrumental in founding.

2

John Adams and John Quincy Adams: Like Father, Like Son

2nd President John Adams (1797-1801) and 6th President John Quincy Adams (1825-1829): Peace field in Quincy, MA

[This chapter is unusual in that it treats two Presidents instead of one. It does so because our second and sixth Presidents were father and son. Even more unusual is the

*fact that so many key events in the lives of both Pres-
idents have taken place in the same three houses. John
was the first Adams to own all three of them. He had been
born in the first house; he and Abigail had celebrated the
birth of their first son, John Quincy, in the second house;
and he and Abigail lived the remainder of their lives in
the third house, the so-called "Old House" at Peace field
where he died on July 4, 1826.*

*As early as 1803, John Adams's eldest son, John Quincy
Adams, purchased the houses where he and his father had
been born. After the death of his father, John Quincy and
his wife, Louisa Catherine, came into possession of the
third home as well, The Old House at Peace field. Here
they would spend many of their remaining summers. It
would be here at The Old House in 1840 that John Quincy
would meet with Lewis Tappan, one of the founders of the
American Anti-Slavery Society, to plan the defense of the
Amistad prisoners before the Supreme Court of the United States.*
*Add to all this, the fact that the furnishings at The Old
House at Peace field are almost entirely original to the
four generations of Adams families who lived there, and
it becomes clear that attempting to separate the lives of
the two Presidents as they relate to these homes would be
an exercise in futility. Hence, the combination chapter.*
*Also, I must note that, as our family's first trip to the
Adams National Historical Park was, in some ways at
least, the most memorable, I have combined incidents
from our two later visits to this site into the narrative of
that initial journey.]*

In July of the summer of 2003, our family had just concluded
an enjoyable vacation with relatives on Long Island near New York
City. I had recently finished reading David McCullough's illuminating biography of John Adams, and I suggested to Carol and to our

two children, Katie and Andy, that this trip to the east coast might also afford us the opportunity to drive up to Quincy, Massachusetts, in a leisurely fashion (the map suggested it would be quite possible to do so in a morning) and tour the three Adams homes there. We would arrive, I assured everyone, by midday, check in at our hotel, eat a quick lunch, and proceed to visit the historic sites. Carol, Katie, and Andy all knew about my interest in such side trips, and everyone was gratifyingly willing to go along with my plan. We set off soon after breakfast. Unfortunately, our travels didn't work out exactly as I thought they would.

First, there was a drizzling rain. Then, a heavy, pelting, relentless torrent, a "monsoon season in the tropics" kind of downpour that began as soon as we patiently wended our way from Long Island onto interstate 95 and headed north toward southern Connecticut. Finally the storm settled in in earnest, waves of water lashing our rental car's windshield until visibility was so limited that I felt the fear rise in the gorge of my throat.

After what seemed like hours, hazy, briefly discernible road signs suggested that we had passed through Connecticut and were headed into Rhode Island, but all I could see with any clarity was the gray wash of fog and the interminable spray of trucks and impassioned motorists, all more eager than I to hurdle themselves into eternity.

By the time we finally arrived in Quincy, all that any of us had the energy to do was check into our hotel, order some pizza to be delivered to the room, and collapse into a heavy slumber to rest our jangled nerves and taut muscles. Tomorrow, as Scarlett O'Hara would invariably observe, would be "another day."

And, happily enough, tomorrow came, still cloudy but dry, and, with it, our adventurous spirits returned as well. We called a cab and had it deliver us to the Adams National Historical Park. After purchasing our tickets and briefly perusing the interior of the small but well-appointed Park Center shop, we were called to board a trolley-car tram that would take us to our desired destinations: the three Adams homesteads.

The fact that these three homes are still in existence suggests the wonderful foresight of several generations of the Adams family.

They must have realized that, in providing two of the first six Presidents of the United States, the family needed to be remembered, their world safeguarded for future generations to revere and savor. Perhaps the Adamses themselves, in taking special care to prosper as well as govern, had insured by their persistent efforts the longevity of their legacy.

As the Beim-Esches disembarked from the tram at its first stop, we found ourselves facing a triangular shaped section of land, itself surrounded by roadways and more modern buildings, but sitting comfortably within its boundaries, two large historical structures.

John Adams Birth House in Quincy, Massachusetts

The further building of the two, but the one toward which our guide first led us, was a two story, simple, brown, weathered, saltbox home with a central door and two ground floor windows, one on either side, surmounted by a second story with three windows, two placed directly above the ground floor windows, and a third positioned over the front door.

This home, the oldest of the three sites we would see today, was the "John Adams Birthplace" house. Owned by his father, Deacon John Adams, it was the home where the future second President had been born in 1735.

Like Adams himself, the house was unpretentious and direct, yet even in its advanced years, unmistakably sturdy and useful. There was no front hall to speak of, only a small landing at the foot of a narrow wooden spiral stairway leading to the upstairs bedchambers. Immediately to the right was the "Great Room," or "Winter Kitchen," including a fireplace at least seven feet wide. Beyond this room lay the largest space in the house, the "Summer Kitchen," an addition created by Deacon John. It provided an area where he could hold political meetings as well as oversee the ecclesiastical councils that were an important part of his duties as a Deacon of the church. The space included a long table that still stood, drawn up against the wall of that room, where, we were informed, the young John Adams would have listened to the wranglings and disputations regarding the politics of his father's age. The head spokesman of any such political meeting was denominated the chairman of "the board" that we saw literalized before us.

Our guide, Rick, informed us, however, that it would be a meeting of the ecclesiastical council held in this room, more than any political gathering that had taken place here, that would forever change the direction of John Adams's young life.

Lemuel Briant, a young minister in the nearby Quincy church, had embraced the liberal religious ideals of the Great Awakening. In doing so, he had angered many in his more conservative congregation. An ecclesiastical council meeting had been called to examine his worthiness to continue in his position. As Adams had listened to the acrimonious give and take, he quickly realized that his own temperament would never be suited to having to amend his ideals to please the opinions of a church congregation. Very soon thereafter, he had altered the course of his studies toward the law rather than theology, and, upon passing the bar, he set up his first law office in the second front room of the home, his mother's parlor or "Best Room" as she had called it.

I find it both meaningful and illuminating that John Adams, even after his parents had passed on, had chosen to keep this original house intact as a part of his estate. There is a powerful reverence for one's roots implicit in that decision. Also an impressive humility. This very plain structure with its rudimental floors and unornamented utilitarian rooms bespoke a modest origin and a rather obscure heritage that many successful people might have wished to have put behind them rather than retain. John Adams, an admired lawyer and defender of rights, even those of the British soldiers involved in the so-called "Boston Massacre"; John Adams, a signer of the Declaration of Independence; John Adams, a key member of the Second Continental Congress, a minister to three foreign governments (France, Holland, and Great Britain), a Vice President to George Washington, and himself the second President of the United States after Washington's two terms of office had been completed; this remarkable man, John Adams, appears to have been completely at peace in acknowledging his connection to his humble roots.

John Quincy Adams Birth House in Quincy, Massachusetts

Our next stop was just a few steps away: the home where, in 1764, John and Abigail had begun their married life together. Here they would ultimately have five children including, in 1767, their first son, John Quincy. And here Abigail and her young family would weather the storm of the Revolution as her husband labored to gain the essential European aid that would help insure a victory for the colonies.

Of the three homes we would visit here, this one seemed the most tinkered with and, as a result, in a strange way, the least genuine. We entered to the rear of the house into a distinctly lighter and airier room than any we had seen in the John Adams Birthplace house. The interior rooms had been quite consciously cleared to make room for tourists, and the pristine, newly—it felt—plastered walls gave this home a sense of having been emptied of its Adams memorabilia (which, of course, it HAD been when the Adams themselves had moved to "The Old House" at Peace field). Its lack of decoration made it hard to conceive of John and Abigail living and working here while their family and their country grew noisier and more aggressively active around them. This house's proximity to the road, however, was a most apt development for John Adams. It would have been impossible to feel very isolated here, as the bustle of wagons and passersby occurred literally just outside the front windows and doors of this pleasant home. Although this structure, in terms of space and size, was very similar to the John Adams Birthplace house, it was significantly newer and, for the Adams family I'm sure, was invested with the additional happiness of being theirs alone.

The one key alteration in this second home's saltbox design, aside from the cream-colored siding that made this structure visibly more attractive from the outside than had been the John Adams Birthplace house, was an exterior door cut in the side wall of the bottom left front room. I had read about this structural decision as Adams had established his law practice and had used this front room as his office. This door, so convenient to any street traffic, had enabled him to consult with clients who could enter and exit the home without disturbing the family. Clearly Adams had desired to keep his home—and the activities that characterized it—separate from the necessities of his active legal practice. This additional street side door had been his solution to the dual demands of career and home life. It was a simple and practical answer. Very Adams-like, I thought.

It also deserves mention that, in addition to being his law office, this front room had been the setting for one of John Adams's most lasting political legacies. Here, having been delegated to the task by his firebrand cousin, Samuel Adams, and James Bowdoin, President of the state constitutional convention, John had drafted the Constitution of the Commonwealth of Massachusetts, "the oldest functioning written constitution in the world," David McCullough notes in his definitive biography (225).

After our brief tour, we boarded another tram that had pulled up outside the second Adams home and were shuttled off for a somewhat longer drive toward our final destination: the Old House at Peace field. This last Adams home, however, had the extraordinary advantage of having been kept in precisely the same state and condition the Adams family had left it in when they ceded the property to the National Park Service in 1946. Included in this munificent gift were all the home's original furnishings. And this would be the setting where the reality of this extraordinary family, including two of our nation's Presidents, would come most thrillingly to life.

"When the 1731 front door to the Old House opens, one is immediately immersed in the world of the Adamses," reads the Adams National Historical Park guidebook on sale at the Visitor's Center. That is an understatement. I found myself reminded of the moment when, as a freshman in high school, I had first stood before Westminster Abbey in London, thinking, "William Shakespeare could have stood on the very spot where I'm standing, looking at the same cathedral." The Old House at Peace field is like that: history is everywhere.

Even the rather ornate knocker on the entryway door, our site docent, Bob, informed us, was a historic relic, dating from John Adams's days in Philadelphia when he was serving as Vice President in the Washington administration. During one of his daily walks around town Adams had noticed the distinctive design of this door-knocker. He had stopped to inquire of the owner if the knocker was for sale and, learning that it was, he had purchased it and brought it here to his home in Quincy. Pausing a moment to gaze at it, we then moved into the original hallway of the Old House. It was like entering a treasure trove of American history.

Once inside, our tour's first stop was the famous "Paneled Room." This elegantly wood-paneled chamber, looking like a scholar's study, had been John and Abigail's whitewashed dining room. Here President James Monroe, Commodore Perry, and General Lafayette had, on separate occasions, dined with John and Abigail Adams. And here, years later, in the room then serving as a parlor, John Quincy Adams would meet with Ellis Gray Loring and Lewis Tappan of the Amistad committee as they urged the ex-President to use his considerable legal skills to argue for the defense in the case of the imprisoned Mendi people who were facing extradition to Cuba and from there into slavery.

The dining room (although it had originally served as John and Abigail's living room) was our next stop. This area felt low and rather dark, though the Edward Savage portraits of George and Martha Washington on the west wall and the Gilbert Stuart portrait of the aged John Adams on the east wall gave this setting a special importance.

Passing through the dining area, we stepped carefully down into the first major addition the Adamses had commissioned here at the Old House and crossed a hallway into the Long Room. Once again, we were to be presented with a cornucopia of historical moments.

This room, creating the only large gathering place on the first floor, had been added at Abigail's request, as she knew such an expansive area would serve an important function in the public lives she and her husband would be leading here. And how right she had been. In this room General Lafayette would stand before the fireplace, "saluting the ladies" of Quincy. Here, John and Abigail would entertain both President Monroe and the famous Transcendentalist writer and philosopher, Ralph Waldo Emerson, each of whom had come to congratulate the ex-President on the election of John Quincy to the nation's highest office.

Throughout the room are to be found furnishings which had been placed in the White House when John and Abigail lived there. Several Louis XV chairs and a matching settee, among other pieces, date from John's ministerial years in the Netherlands when he had had to decorate the new American embassy in The Hague. He had brought these pieces back with him when he had returned to America and had carried them to the presidential mansion when he had been elected to the Presidency. Thereafter, as was then the custom in Washington, he had returned with them to Quincy at the end of his term. These possessions lent a marked air of elegance, grace, and historical pedigree to the Long Room.

Passing back into the hall, Bob then led us up the straight staircase to what, for me, would be the most meaningful room in the house: the upstairs study. This was the room where both Presidents, John and John Quincy, had spent the most time, reading their beloved books and writing the letters that would come to form some of the most famous of American literary correspondences. Here, John Adams, seated in the floral wing chair which remains placed in the corner where he loved to sit, had uttered his last public pronouncement to a small delegation of town leaders who had asked him to give them a Fourth of July message that they might read to the citizens of Quincy. "I will give you ... Independence forever!" he had spoken (McCullough 645). Sitting right there in that corner. In that very chair.

Elsewhere in the room could be seen John Quincy Adams's W. Bardin terrestrial globe, a fitting possession for the most well-traveled diplomat in American history to that date. And then, almost nestled in the northeast corner of the study, stood John

Adams's secretary desk, the spot where he had written the 158 letters that constituted his side of the indispensable correspondence with Thomas Jefferson that had reunited the old friends and past adversaries. And everything was still here, still placed as the Adamses had seen fit. Remarkable, simply remarkable.

As we left the study and proceeded down the passage that John Quincy had added to the house in order to make the study more directly accessible from the President's bedroom, I was reminded of this second Adams President's most noteworthy characteristic: his passionate love of reading. The passageway is literally lined with shelves, each groaning under the weight of an astonishing assortment of books. No wonder that John Quincy had asked his son Charles Francis to build a library on the grounds as his contribution to the homestead. The Adams family's voluminous collection of tomes had begun to outstrip the capacity of the house to hold them.

Our guide, Bob, then led us to the presidential bedroom. A decorative touch that I thought particularly apt was the addition of the Sadler tiles surrounding the fireplace grate. John Quincy had purchased them in Liverpool, England, in 1801, toward the end of his stint as Minister to Prussia, and he had sent them home to his mother. The tiles had then been installed in the presidential bedroom. Surely their blue and white distinctly Dutch design must have brought to mind John Adams's courageous efforts in Amsterdam during the Revolution, when he had labored so tirelessly to negotiate a loan from the Netherlands that would help pay for the munitions and supplies necessary to support the American armies fighting the British. In light of his father's recent defeat in seeking a second term as President, John Quincy's gift must have been seen as a most thoughtful and appreciative reminder of this earlier, crucially important success.

Bob now led our group back downstairs, and we ended up in the Long Hall. Taking note of the portraits of Charles Francis Adams, as well as of First Lady Louisa Catherine, he drew our attention to a framed and beautifully preserved floral wreath, hanging between portrait busts of George Washington and John Adams.

"This wreath was sent to Louisa Catherine Adams in 1826," Bob told us, "at the time of John Adams's death. Of course Abigail had already passed on by this time, so the women of the Seminary for Female Education in Bethlehem, Pennsylvania, had sent it to the current First Lady, Louisa Catherine Adams. They had wished to express their gratitude for President Adams's support for female education, evidenced in his visit to their school during the Revolution." The wreath was a perfect reminder of the sentiment that Abigail had written to her husband in Philadelphia during the long, hot days of the debate concerning Independence, "Remember the ladies." Clearly he had done so, and the wreath bore beautiful evidence that the ladies, too, had remembered him.

As we left the Old House, I thought that the tour was over. Happily I was mistaken, for we had one more stop to make: Charles Francis Adams's Stone Library.

It had been the wish of John Quincy that his son, Charles Francis, would construct a library on the property at Peace field to house the now over 12,000 volumes the two Presidents had accumulated over the years. Charles Francis had been unable to comply with his father's wishes during his lifetime, due to the demands of his extremely active scholarly pursuits and the vital ministerial service he had performed in England during the Civil War. Yet in 1870 he finally succeeded in creating the quintessential memorial to his father and grandfather here at Peace field, the Stone Library.

Our new docent led us to the door of this wisteria covered, chapel-like structure, and then she invited us to enter into the library's cordoned-off space to view its interior. Once inside we were immediately surrounded by two stories of shelves filled with thousands of books. I remember feeling distinctly that Professor Higgins from *My Fair Lady* might appear at any moment to lecture us on correct diction.

"You have come on a special day," our docent informed us. "Today, July 11, is John Quincy Adams's birthday, and this is the day when we show this particularly interesting book to our visitors." She moved to the large table in the middle of the room, opened a closed box, picked up out of it a folio sized volume, and brought it over to us.

"This is the Mendi Bible. It was given to John Quincy Adams by the Mendi prisoners who had been taken off the ship *Amistad*. It was their expression of gratitude for his successful defense of their right to return to their homes in Africa, argued in the Supreme Court of the United States. Look here," she continued, holding up a laminated piece of paper, "Inside the front cover of the book, each one of the Mendi people made his mark. This is a photocopy of that page. Here is the mark of their leader, Cinque."

I believe my goosebumps had goosebumps of their own. I was standing here, not two feet away from the gift of the *Amistad* people to their liberator, ex-President John Quincy Adams. I felt that I was in the very presence of history.

And the rest of the room would only deepen the feeling. In the southwest corner of the room stood John Adams's law desk, upon which he had drafted the Constitution of the Commonwealth of Massachusetts. Standing before the library's north window could be seen John Quincy Adams's desk from the U.S. House of Representatives, from which, from 1831 until the day of his death in 1848, he had earned the name "Old Man Eloquent" because of his continuous, vociferous, and strident attacks on the presence of slavery within the United States. Everywhere here in the Stone Library there were to be seen crown jewels of early American history. It was a dazzling, unforgettable experience.

Since this first visit, Carol and I have returned here twice. With each succeeding tour we have noted and appreciated objects and aspects of the homes that we had missed in earlier years. But I will never forget that moment of wonder when the Mendi Bible was brought before me. It truly established for me the reality of this place, the reality of this father, and of his son, and of this indispensable family. I saw, as I had never seen before, the importance of visiting the homes of the Presidents, not simply as side trips stemming from a dutiful sense of patriotism, but as a means of discovering and appreciating the essence of the men who had molded and directed the United States. Their history was also my history. Their legacy has created my present, the America of today. I realized that understanding these men and the worlds they had inhabited could, in a very special way, open a door for every American to better understand both his country and himself. Taking the time and making the effort to do so has become a fascinating journey that has never ceased to inspire and enlighten me.

3

Thomas Jefferson: "...a work of art."

3rd President Thomas Jefferson (1801-1809): Monticello in Charlottesville, VA

Thomas Jefferson's Monticello may well be the most beautiful house in the United States. It is more than a presidential home. It is, as one writer has observed, "the visible projection of its resident" (Hyland xvi). And, since the first time I traveled here to see this architectural marvel, I have felt that the spirit of Thomas Jefferson is remarkably present in this place—not in any spiritualistic sense, of course, but rather in the vivid display of his kaleidoscopic interests, his restless intellect, and his unending pursuit of knowledge.

From the artifacts sent by Meriwether Lewis and William Clark in the front hall to the removable shelves of books in his study, from the dumbwaiters concealed in the dining room mantels to the polygraph machine that made ink copies of his letters, Jefferson has left an indelible impression here at Monticello of what it means to have been an inspired thinker in the Age of Enlightenment.

In the spring of 2012, Carol and I traveled to Virginia to revisit several of the great plantations owned by some of our early Presidents. Monticello was right at the top of our list of homes that I wanted to experience again before writing about Thomas Jefferson. But our first historical stop had the distinction of being a completely new site for us: Jefferson's Poplar Forest.

For many years I had known nothing of this house. Several of the books I had read about our third President had never mentioned the site, nor the fact that Jefferson himself had been its architect and had intended this locale to become a post-retirement haven for him, apart from the bustle and crowded conditions of Monticello. Only open to public view since 1998, this restored gem—the interior of which is still very much under construction—provides a wonderful glimpse into the mind of its creator.

As we turned off SR 661 into the entrance of Poplar Forest, a narrow unpaved road led us through dense woodlands for quite some time. Finally, as the road rose up a gradual hill, there on the left, Poplar Forest came into view. There could be no question as to the man who had conceived this home. It looked like a downsized Monticello: a brick

Thomas Jefferson's Poplar Forest
in Forest, Virginia

structure with Doric columns holding up an architrave and frieze, crowned with a classic Greco-Roman pediment. It was pure Thomas Jefferson. And if a building's design can truly be said to reflect the consciousness of its architect, then the simplicity and modest scale of this home illustrated a key quality that must have lain at his very heart: a deep desire for balance and order.

Oh! Blessed rage for order, pale Ramon
The maker's rage to order words of the sea,
Words of the fragrant portals, dimly-starred
And of ourselves and of our origins....

So wrote the great American poet, Wallace Stevens, in "The Idea of Order at Key West," and Poplar Forest immediately sent this verse coursing through my mind. This house is a hymn to symmetry, even more than Monticello, itself a most orderly structure.

Arranged around a central dining area that measures 20' by 20' by 20', the interior of Poplar Forest is comprised of a front entrance hall, flanked on each side by three octagonal bedrooms and, opposite the entryway on the other side of the dining room, a library sitting area, creating the building's external octagonal configuration. If ever a dwelling reflected a "Blessed rage for order," it is Poplar Forest, and, while its maker had no apparent interest in the "words of the sea," too far from this location to be heard, there is plentiful evidence of a desire for personal balance, equilibrium, and harmony. Nothing here is off center. The two chimneys on the right side of the home are counterbalanced by the two chimneys on the left side. The front porch is symmetrically echoed by the back porch, each with four columns set equidistant from each other, and each supporting a classic pediment. Both sides of the house feature identical projecting enclosed stairway pavilions with half arched windows to provide light for their interior passageways.

Nothing is out of place, no design element haphazard.

Throughout his life, Thomas Jefferson had experienced both great personal joy and agonizing tragedy. He had faced the rigors and stresses of foreign diplomacy as well as contentious political battles at home. Even his Presidency had yielded very mixed results. His first term had been a stunning success, the most notable achievement of which had been the Louisiana Purchase. His second term, however, had forced him to deal with both foreign and domestic treachery. Finally, in an effort to avoid a war, he had instituted an ill-advised and ineffective embargo that had made him extremely unpopular. By the end of his eight years as President,

Thomas Jefferson was exhausted. In a now famous letter to a friend, he wrote, "Never did a prisoner released from his chains, feel such relief as I shall on shaking off the shackles of power." Poplar Forest, he believed, would be his refuge, his harbor from the storms of life where he could enjoy, in his own words, the "solitude of a hermit."

Sadly, enough, it was not to be. Perhaps because of his advancing years, or, even more understandably, perhaps because of his deep desire to feel himself surrounded by his remaining family and friends, Jefferson would not retire here, but rather to his beloved Monticello. Poplar Forest, his octagonal monument to symmetry, balance, and classical grace, would pass into other hands and would burn in 1845.

Today, the restoration and preservation of Poplar Forest have kept intact Jefferson's dream of an ideal retirement, a world of perfect order. But the man himself is not to be found here. He resides, still, ninety miles north, in Charlottesville.

On many occasions I have had to search diligently for a revealing symbol or sign of a President lying undiscovered or unheralded in some artifact on display in his home. At other times the residence itself may have suggested subtle truths that a casual visitor might overlook. Monticello poses no such challenges. Thomas Jefferson is present almost everywhere in this place. The home is a living testament to his interests, to his achievements, and to his character.

This is all the more remarkable because, unlike some other presidential homes, Monticello has had to have been completely reconfigured and reconstituted over the years. Jefferson's accumulated debt at the time of his death in 1826 was estimated to have been in the vicinity of $100,000. This was a colossal sum, easily more than a million in 21st century dollars. As the result, "A dispersal sale [was] held in 1827 [that] included his slaves, crops, household items, and furniture" (Clotworthy 45). The estate at Poplar Forest was sold. Lastly, in 1831, Monticello itself.

Happily for future generations, a Navy Commodore named Uriah P. Levy purchased the property in 1834, and he, and later his son, Jefferson Monroe Levy, worked tirelessly to restore Monticello. When in 1923 the Levy family finally sold it to the newly established

Thomas Jefferson Foundation, this precious national architectural legacy had been saved from decay and destruction. Since that time the Thomas Jefferson Foundation has continued to maintain the home and has also worked to restore its interior and replace the long lost furnishings and objects d'art which records show had been present here with retrieved original pieces or authentic replicas. The result, as one book on presidential residences puts it, is that "Today Jefferson's Monticello is much as it was when he retired to enjoy his last years among his family and flowers" (Haas 29).

As Carol and I stood on the famous front porch of Monticello, together with a group of about twenty other guests, we listened closely to our articulate and entertaining docent, a man named Bill. He began our tour by informing us of the legacy that Jefferson had most wished to leave his nation: "Political liberty, religious freedom, and public education," Bill intoned. "These were the greatest, the most important values for Thomas Jefferson. These were the values that he chose to list on his tombstone, as he identified the accomplishments of which he was most proud—'Author of the Declaration of American Independence'—that's political liberty—'Of the Statute of Virginia for Religious Freedom'—that's religious freedom—'And Father of the University of Virginia'—that's education." Bill beamed at us, and I knew that we were in the hands of a docent who not only was knowledgeable, but who revered his subject as well. It would make for a most memorable visit.

We entered through the doors into the main hall, and Bill launched into descriptions that all docents of Monticello are obliged to give: identifications of various Lewis and Clark artifacts on display throughout the room; of peace medals given to a variety of Indian chieftains; of the famous weekly clock with the cannonball weights on its chains that pass through the floor. But then he drew our attention to some of the statuary in the room.

"Here in the main hall we see busts of Voltaire, Turgot, and Alexander Hamilton," he informed us. I would have expected Voltaire, a French philosophe with whom Jefferson had been ideologically in tune. But Hamilton? The man who had fought Jefferson's vision of America as an agrarian utopia? The man who had argued for the creation of a national bank and federal assumption of state debt following the Revolution? The man who had fought against Jefferson's election as President in 1800? I couldn't help asking Bill whether or not the presence of this marble bust was a subtle joke played on unsuspecting tourists.

"Actually," he answered me, "... we know that Mr. Jefferson **did** have a bust of Alexander Hamilton here in the main hall. Don't forget, despite their differences, it was Hamilton who had worked with Mr. Jefferson's friend, James Madison, to ensure the ratification of the Constitution by writing several of *The Federalist Papers*. And it was also Mr. Hamilton who tilted the final vote in the House of Representatives that broke the deadlock between Mr. Jefferson and Aaron Burr." All this was true, but nevertheless this bust represented to me an impressive indication of the extent to which Thomas Jefferson had been willing to forgive an old adversary.

Turgot was another matter. I had known that he, too, was a philosophe and a friend of Voltaire, so the pairing of these two sculptures was at least superficially logical. Also Turgot had admired the political impulse behind the American colonies' decision to separate themselves from Great Britain and create a new government based on republican principles. But Turgot had also vigorously opposed on economic grounds any French participation in aiding the colonies during the Revolutionary War. So why, then, place his image here when there were other Frenchmen, Lafayette comes immediately to mind, who had been more unreservedly supportive of the American cause? I believe Jefferson's decision may have been connected to the nature of Turgot's character.

History remembers Anne-Robert-Jacques Turgot as being dedicated to truth and fair play, and, like most French philosophes and Enlightenment thinkers, he was an ardent believer in the "natural rights" of all men. Furthermore Turgot's personality was frequently described as withdrawn, and he had difficulty expressing himself orally. As a writer, however, he was extremely compelling, and his words often led others to agree with his ideas. All this sounds strikingly similar to Jefferson himself. Perhaps the President had decided that it was only fitting that such a kindred soul as Turgot should be memorialized at Monticello.

After a brief first stop in the plantation office, we moved into the three chambers which comprised the President's private quarters: his library, study, and sitting room. It is here where the spirit of Thomas Jefferson is most conspicuously present. I also think it is important to observe at this point that each of these three rooms are both quite modest in size and are placed in a very close proximity to the public areas of the home, the main entrance, the formal parlor, and even the gardens right outside their windows. Bill assured us that, when Mr. Jefferson's doors were closed, no one was to disturb him, and, I'm sure, no one would have wanted to interrupt his reading, his researches, or his voluminous letter writing. But it should also be equally clear to anyone visiting this home that the President's rooms here at Monticello were very close to the constant activities of plantation life, particularly when one remembers that at the time of his sojourns here between political assignments, he was constantly surrounded by family and friends.

First, we entered the library. It was a marvelous scholar's nook with its reconstituted collection of over six thousand volumes. Of particular note to me was an octagonal table on which could be propped several books at one time (perhaps another example of Jefferson being ahead of his time: the original multi-tasker). Also, Jefferson's bookcases had hinges and handles which would allow them to be closed up and moved rapidly should the necessity arise. No more tragedies like the fire at Shadwell, his family home, that had destroyed his first library, I thought to myself. Here at Monticello, should an emergency occur, the books could be out the door in minutes. A scholar's invention, indeed, and another clear glimpse of the man who would also write, "I cannot live without books."

From the library our group passed into Jefferson's study. This sunny area was filled with scientific instruments and a swivel table (more multi-tasking here) on which, among other inventions, was the polygraph that had enabled Jefferson to make simultaneous copies of any of the nearly 19,000 letters he would write. Nearby, there was a telescope placed close to one of the windows, and next to it sat a portrait bust sculpture of Jefferson in old age. Was this Jefferson's reminder to himself that, as the 17th century poet Andrew Marvel had written, he had "heard Time's winged chariot hurrying near"? Bill would never have been so presumptuous as to have suggested an answer to such a question, but he did note that "Mr. Jefferson was fascinated with the natural world and had catalogued 330 varieties of nuts, vegetables, and fruits, planting many of them in his gardens here." A scholar's study and working laboratory indeed.

Jefferson's sleeping alcove, placed between this study and his sitting room with immediate access to each, featured a clock in the wall over the foot of the bed. "Mr. Jefferson was a self-proclaimed miser with his time," Bill reminded us. "There was always more to know, more to learn about the world, and his time was limited." As if to illustrate this point, Bill now reminded us that the President had died here on July 4, 1826. It had been fifty years to the day since his great Declaration had announced to the world the birth of a new nation, based on the revolutionary principle that a government's power, and even its legitimacy, rested squarely on the consent of its people.

We moved quietly into the sitting room and noted its simplicity as a place to dress for the day. Nothing else was particularly interesting about this room, and it led immediately into the hall before the formal parlor and dining room areas of the house.

The parlor was a gracious space which afforded beautiful views of the back gardens and walkways. Oil painted portraits of the Enlightenment luminaries, Bacon, Newton, and Locke, decorated the walls. The nearby dining areas also featured portrait busts, but here the theme was more strictly American, with images of Franklin, Washington, Lafayette, and John Paul Jones silently surrounding the tables.

The final room on our downstairs tour was directly opposite the plantation office. It was the so-called "Mr. Madison's room," named for its most frequent visitor, and I was fascinated to note that it was constructed in the shape of a perfect octagon. No wonder Jefferson had designed Poplar Forest as he had—the perfection and balance of that geometry had been a very conscious ideal for him.

The various gardens, the out buildings, including even the modest original almost Thoreauvian single room south pavilion where Jefferson and his wife Martha had begun their marriage, were all beautifully preserved and maintained, but for me it was the library and study that carried with them the most lucid insights into Jefferson the man. He had lived at a moment in history when the sum total of human knowledge could be contained in a single library, and Jefferson had made it his goal to learn as much of

Thomas Jefferson's One Room South Pavilion at Monticello

this accumulated wisdom as he could squeeze into a lifetime. He had also desired to add to this wealth of knowledge—to make his own discoveries and report them to the world. Monticello stands as a symbol of this goal and as irrefutable evidence of this desire.

Following our tour, Bill invited us to walk the grounds and visit the areas of the site for which no docents would be needed. There were informative displays in a number of these locations, many devoted to plantation life and the realities of slavery at Monticello. But it was my final stop at a lovely shop site which overlooked the plots of the vegetable and fruit gardens that would provide a lasting inspiration for me.

Like most tourists, I was interested in acquiring a two dollar bill (the only paper U.S. currency on which President Jefferson's image appears), and I knew that, if any place would have a supply of them, the shop at Monticello would. I was not disappointed, and, after a helpful worker had changed my two ones for a Jeffersonian two dollar note, I struck up a brief conversation with her.

"I love this home," I began. "It must be wonderful to work here." She was delighted with my enthusiasm and immediately assured me that, for her at least, it *was* a privilege and a joy. I continued, "Most Americans tend to think of it as some sort of plantation palace. But it's not that. Its rooms are small by comparison to European chateaux. It's **not** a palace, not even palatial!" She nodded as I spoke. "It's ... it's ...." My words were failing me. Very gently, she quietly finished my thought: "... a work of art."

"Exactly," I exclaimed. "That's it! A work of art." Monticello, designed and overseen by this man of the Enlightenment, was a gracious and elegant dwelling place. Like the house at Poplar Forest, it was also in its own unique way, a priceless work of art, well worth visiting, well worth preserving. And it is here, as John Adams said with his dying breath on July 4, 1826, that "Thomas Jefferson still survives."

4

James Madison: "Nothing more than a Change of Mind."

4th President James Madison (1809-1817): Montpelier in Orange, VA

Carol and I have visited James Madison's Montpelier three times now. And for good reason. The place keeps changing, both literally and figuratively.

The first time we stopped to see Montpelier, various architectural additions that had been made to the original home, additions commissioned by the duPont family who had owned the property most recently, were being removed in order to restore the house to its appear-

Montpelier in the Process of Reconstruction

ance at the time the Madisons resided there. The Montpelier we saw on this first visit, then, resembled a construction site, with large tarpaulins masking off the wings where the deconstruction was under way.

Nevertheless, our first tour of this site resulted in an important lesson for me, a lesson which can benefit any visitor to a historical location: always be sure to confirm questionable information imparted by an inexperienced docent before repeating it to others.

We had arrived in the late afternoon, and we were told at the Visitor's Center that, if we hurried, we could join the final group of the day. We hastened to the home site and joined a small crowd of tourists already gathered there. Moments later, we were being guided toward the house under deconstruction. Our docent—a dear young woman who was trying to make the best of a difficult situation—informed us that, regrettably, we would not be able to enter the home, as much archeological work, as well as the demolition of the duPont additions, made visiting the interior potentially hazardous. We would be able, however, she assured us, to enter one wing of the home at what had been the kitchen level, and we would thereafter be free to wander the expansive grounds until the closing hour.

Carol and I were disappointed, as might be expected, to learn that the house itself would not be open to us, but we had driven all the way here, and we decided to make the most of our time. Even from the outside, Montpelier was a spectacular setting with a dramatic view of the Blue Ridge on the western horizon and a manicured formal garden on its south side. We were led up a walk to the right wing of the house where there was a cellar entrance to the kitchen area.

As the members of our group entered this lower level, however, I stopped to look at the mansion. I was struck by what appeared to be a sunken walkway that ran completely around the home. It was about seven or eight feet deep and four feet wide, and, for the life of me, I could not understand what function it might have served the Madisons.

"Excuse me," I called to the docent who was waiting for me to follow the other members of our group. "Could you tell me what was the purpose of this walkway around the circumference of the house?"

The docent looked slightly uncomfortable at this question, but she motioned me to come over to her, and then she answered my query in hushed tones. "Mr. Madison never wanted to be reminded of the ..." she paused momentarily, "...workers who made his lifestyle possible. They could move from one end of the mansion to the other by using this walkway, and they would be invisible to anyone strolling around the grounds."

I nodded understandingly, and we both joined the others who were already waiting in the kitchen for the one room tour of Montpelier's lower level. Afterwards, as Carol and I circumnavigated the exterior of the house, I informed her of my question and the rather telling response I had been given by our docent. Sure enough, we both noted, the sunken walkway **was** completely invisible from both the front lawn area and from the beautiful classic temple that Madison and his friends had enjoyed frequenting. "He didn't want to be reminded of the slave labor necessary to enable his luxurious lifestyle," I found myself thinking. Like so many of the most thoughtful Virginians, and Madison was nothing if not that, he had found the reality of the slave culture of plantation life at odds with the idealism at the heart of his political vision. Quite an exercise in denial, I concluded.

Weeks later, when I returned to my classroom, I made much of this story. It was the perfect metaphor, I would tell my students, of the southern lifestyle which was at once the ideal of an Arcadian dream and also the reality of the misery of an enslaved labor force. Madison's solution to such a dichotomy, I noted, was simply to put slavery out of sight and, thus, out of mind. For me the matter was settled.

After two or three years passed, however, I became aware of the progress being made in the restoration of Montpelier. Furthermore, I determined that Carol and I should return in hopes of seeing the interior of the home in addition to our earlier appreciation of its impressive grounds.

This time, of course, we would know what to expect—at least on the outside.

As we arrived at the newly refurbished Montpelier, we were greeted at a well-appointed gatehouse where we purchased tickets while still in our car. Then we were directed to the newly constructed Visitor's Center where we were to join members of another tour group who were getting ready to view an informative film presentation chronicling Madison's life and political accomplishments.

Montpelier Newly Refurbished

One of my chief regrets about our first visit here, aside from not having been able to go inside the mansion proper, was the fact that I had neglected to take a picture of the sunken walkway. This time I was prepared and fully intended to get visual evidence to share with my students. But as we approached the home which looked beautifully restored to its Madisonian splendor, I was shocked to find the carpet of lawn graded right up to the foundation of the house. There was no evidence anywhere of the sunken pathway!

"Oh my," I thought, "not **architectural** revisionism! How could the renovators dare to erase this piece of history—however painful—simply to make Madison look more acceptable in the eyes of 21st century tourists?"

I was upset and confused, and I immediately questioned our docent about this alteration.

"I don't know what you are talking about, sir," he commented rather stiffly. "The restoration has put the mansion back into its exact state as the Madisons had it. There was no such feature at that time. I rather imagine that the archeological team that oversaw the restoration concluded that this feature, if it ever existed, was the addition of later owners."

"**If** it ever existed!" my mind shouted. "I saw it. Carol saw it. Does this fellow really think that the 20th century duPonts had had such a feature added to their estate?" Obviously not. This was, I concluded, nothing less than a cover-up promulgated by the Montpelier Foundation.

And if this disappointment had not been enough, Carol and I found that, although guests were now allowed to enter the mansion, its interior was almost completely still devoid of the Madisons' belongings. As I recall it, only one room, the downstairs parlor, was even partially furnished, though I do remember being struck by an ink stain on the floor of Madison's upstairs study. This, our docent assured us, was original and indicated the exact placement of Madison's desk as he had worked on his researches leading up to his writing of the Virginia Plan, prior to the Constitutional Convention of 1787.

There were also some archeological displays explaining and illustrating the work of the ongoing restoration of the mansion, but it didn't take us too long to realize that, if Carol and I were ever to see the completely recreated Montpelier, we would have to return some years hence.

I had my big story, however. Once again, upon returning to my classroom, I was able to tell my students and colleagues the tale of the disappearing sunken walkway and to emphasize the dangers of altering historical truth to suit contemporary preferences. It would be another few years before Carol and I, once again touring Virginia in search of presidential sites and dwellings, would make our way back to Montpelier. But this visit would be very unlike the first two and would carry with it a very important lesson for me.

In April of 2012, Carol and I drove north from Charlottesville and presented ourselves for the third time at the Visitor's Center at Montpelier. Again, we saw the Madison film, and again we joined an assembled group for a tour of the home. This time our guide was a gentleman named Bob who led us up on the front porch and began his tour by talking about Madison's horticultural interests. Very quickly it became apparent that Bob was significantly more knowledgeable about Madison than had been either of our earlier guides. And, as we entered the house, it became equally apparent that Herculean strides had been made to decorate its interior in the years since our last visit.

Carol particularly enjoyed the fact that the Madisons' Montpelier had been, in fact, a sumptuous duplex. Madison's mother had occupied the right hand wing of the house, while James and Dolley had lived in the central and left wings. Each side had only been accessible to the other by exiting out onto the front porch and walking to the opposite wing's entrance door!

The central parlor was now completely decorated as the Madisons would have recognized it, and Bob was quite thorough in identifying the variety of marble busts that were displayed around the circumference of the room. Images of Washington, Madison himself, Lafayette, Jefferson, Franklin, even Robert Livingston, one of the diplomats responsible for the Louisiana Purchase, were all present in this sculptural grouping. (Bob smilingly noted that Livingston had sent his own statue to Madison to add to his collection, subsequent to visiting here for the first time.) Appropriately enough, though, it was the spirit of Madison's best friend, Thomas Jefferson, that most clearly permeated the room. In addition to his marble bust, two oil painting portraits of the third President hung on opposite walls, and a Campeche chair, Jefferson's favorite, sat in one of the corners of the parlor.

Bob then led us into the formal dining area, another beautifully decorated interior, complete with a grass-green scalloped design wallpaper that perfectly matched the sample of the original wall covering that had been discovered during the renovation. Gathered around the extended table were life-sized cardboard images of some of the most famous persons who had dined here, including Jefferson, of course, and Andrew Jackson.

Next was the room which had originally been James and Dolley Madison's bedroom. It now contained objects which had been part of Madison's library, including a large fossil of prehistoric marine life. Also of interest here was yet another portrait bust, but unlike the statues in the parlor, this piece, Bob informed us, was the only sculpture original to the house. As I inquired about just who this image was, Bob replied with a laugh, "I know the name, but you've got me here. You'll have to do a bit of research yourself to find out his significance to Mr. Madison. The man was George William Erving. That's all I know."

Now, nothing gives a writer more joy than such a challenge, and in the days following our visit, I did learn more about this interesting man. George William Erving had been a diplomat during the Jefferson, Madison, and Monroe administrations, serving as U.S. Consul in London from 1801 to 1804, Charge d'Affaires of the United States in Madrid from 1804 to 1809, Special Negotiator to Copenhagen in 1811, and U.S. Minister to Spain from 1814 to 1819. But it was not until I dug deeper that I discovered why Madison might have wanted to have the sculpted bust of this personage prominently displayed in his home. In a long out-of-print volume entitled *Diplomatic Services* by J.L.M. Curry, I found the following passage:

> *Mr. Madison then told me that he never had a more capable and faithful minister in his service during his sixteen years' term as Secretary of State and as President of the United States, than George William Erving.* (6)

Any student of Madison's presidential years quickly discovers that he had been faced with daunting challenges, both from foreign quarters and from within regions of his own nation, sometimes even from within his own political party. It was telling to me that Madison had come to value so highly both the abilities and faithfulness of this now largely forgotten diplomat. Erving's marble image must have assured the now aging ex-President that his years as

Chief Executive, as arduous as they had been, had not lacked loyal and capable workers within his administration. There must have been comfort in that remembrance.

Our last stop on the first floor of the house was James Madison's final study and sitting room. Its walls were colored a deep aqua, and it was here that Bob recounted the story of Paul Jennings, Madison's slave who had served him to the very end. It was Jennings who had helped Dolley remove the famous Stuart painting of George Washington on the night in 1814 when British troops had captured the capital and burned its public buildings, including the White House. It was Jennings who had continued to care for Madison at Montpelier during his difficult post-presidential years. And it was Jennings who had been present to overhear Madison's last words. When a visible alteration had passed over the old man's countenance, he had been asked if everything was all right. His response, his last response, was simply, "Nothing more than a change of mind." A moment later he had slumped over, dead.

After a moment of stillness, Bob then led our group upstairs, and here the renovation of the home was very much an ongoing process. There were no bookcases in Madison's second floor library, though the ink stain on the floor remained quite visible. Overall, this tour had been such a marked improvement over my earlier visits to Montpelier, that, after Bob had finished his presentation and had encouraged us to go off and wander the grounds, I couldn't resist cautiously questioning him about the sunken walkway. He was immediately interested, and he told me that he had never heard about it.

"But I know the person you should ask about this," he added. "Carole White is in charge of all the docents. If anyone can answer your question definitively, she's the one. Come on, I'll find her for you and introduce you."

Before I had a chance to respond, Bob was rapidly heading downstairs, and I sprang after him. At the foot of the stairway, he told me to wait, and he exited out a door. In only a minute or two, the same door opened, and a pleasant woman greeted me.

"I hear you have a question that Bob couldn't answer," she began. "Maybe I can help."

I recounted to Ms. White the story of the sunken walkway and its disappearance. She listened carefully, then quietly shook her head.

"Oh dear," she sighed, "I do so wish that those early docents had simply been willing to admit it when they didn't know an answer. I **do** know exactly what you saw, but it's nothing like what you were told. When the deconstruction and restoration of Montpelier got underway, a careful examination of the foundation of the home revealed serious cracks and water damage that threatened to weaken the overall structure of the mansion. It was decided that, first off, the foundation needed waterproof sealant applied to the entire exterior of the foundation. The restoration team dug that sunken walkway around the circumference of the house so that the foundation could be correctly sealed. Once the moisture problem had been solved, the ground was graded up to the foundation just as it had been during Mr. Madison's time. The Montpelier Foundation accepts the facts of Virginia's plantation life, and we would never have tried to conceal an original architectural feature of this home. I hope this helps you," she gently concluded.

It certainly had. How wrong, how **eagerly** wrong I had been—both to assume that Madison had wanted to hide his slaves from view and, next, to believe that such a careful and painstaking restoration of a site could be complicit with a cover-up of a historical truth. I thanked Ms. White and went to find Carol who had already exited the house. After I told her the information that Ms. White had just given me, I realized that I would have some important phone calls to make when I returned home, particularly to colleagues to whom I had told the infamous story of Montpelier's vanishing sunken walkway.

And I had also learned an important lesson about anecdotal information conveyed by docents. Check the facts before repeating a tale.

In some ways, like Mr. Madison, I had experienced a profound "change of mind" regarding what I had believed to be true. But also like Madison, my error had been "nothing more" than that, only a misunderstanding. The truth had never been affected by what I had been willing to believe. And now that I had experienced a "change of mind," I understood the reality of the situation. I wondered if Mr. Madison, too, as he had experienced "nothing more than a change of mind," had reached a similar revelatory understanding, only, in his case, of the much grander matter of the nature of life itself.

5

James Monroe: "...getting things done."

5th President James Monroe (1817-1825): Ash Lawn-Highland in Charlottesville, VA

Every once in a while, my natural inclination to be chatty has stood me in good stead. This was certainly the case in March of 2012 when I first called Ash Lawn-Highland for advice about Carol's and my upcoming visit there. My chief concern had been whether or not we could fit in a meaningful tour of both Thomas Jefferson's Poplar Forest and James Monroe's Ash Lawn-Highland estates in a single day. My computer research had suggested to me that it would be possible, but I wanted the plan to be confirmed by someone "on the ground," as it were.

The telephone at Ash Lawn-Highland was answered by a woman with a pleasant voice who was happy to tell me that, because of Ash Lawn-Highland's late closing hour (6 pm at the season when we had scheduled our trip), this double site plan would be completely workable. She even reconfirmed the routing to Charlottesville from Poplar Forest that I had found online. I was most relieved by her assurances and thanked her for taking the time to give me this help. But before I hung up, I felt impelled to mention my book project to her.

"The last time I visited Ash Lawn-Highland, I hadn't begun to write yet, so returning this time will be an important step in my overall project. Nevertheless I remember that earlier visit with great fondness because of a book I purchased in your store."

"Really?" she responded. "Which book?"

"It was entitled *The Religion of the Founders*, and it helped me teach my A.P. American Literature and U.S History classes every year I taught thereafter, right up to my retirement. Its descriptions and definition of Deism constituted the clearest presentation of that difficult subject I had ever encountered. The author was David L. Holmes."

There was a very long pause, followed by a subdued chuckle. "Well," the lady continued, "my husband will be delighted that you liked his book so much. I'm Carolyn Holmes. It's safe to say you have made both his and my day, today." Then, very graciously, she continued, "Tell me a little more about the book **you** are writing. I imagine David would like to hear about it."

For the next ten minutes or so, I outlined to her the ideas behind *Calling on the Presidents*, and she indicated to me that she believed she would be on site at the time Carol and I would be visiting. "Ask for me when you get here," she urged me. "It would be a pleasure to meet you and your wife in person."

I put down the receiver and told Carol about my call. What a pleasant woman, I thought, and how generous she was with her time and advice. Carolyn Holmes, I would later learn, was the Executive Director of Ash Lawn-Highland, and she wanted to meet Carol and me!

On the appointed day, Carol and I arrived, just as Mrs. Holmes had said we would, around three o'clock, in plenty of time for an afternoon tour. Upon entering the Visitor's Center, I asked for her and was told to proceed toward the lower level of the home where the executive offices were located. Here we were greeted by Carolyn Holmes who invited us into her office. She was very complimentary of the manuscript of my book that we had brought for her perusal, and then we settled down for a brief chat. Knowing my interests, she wasn't surprised by my first question.

"What are the qualities of President Monroe that you most admire?"

She thought for several moments before responding. "I know you're interested in the house and what it reveals about the President who lived here," she began, "but the first thing that comes to my mind is his favorite name for Ash Lawn-Highland. President Monroe called it his 'cabin castle,' and I love that. It's unpretentious—in touch with reality—as he always was, and it's a perfect description of the plantation: small but elegant, modest but beautiful."

I was scribbling quickly as she next spoke about Monroe's various travels, so vital to our nation's history. Then she told of how Ash Lawn-Highland had had to be sold after Monroe's presidential years because of debts he had incurred in Europe while acting as an ambassador of the United States, debts for which he had never been fully reimbursed by the government. Finally there was a very long pause.

"You know," she observed thoughtfully, "as I think about it now, I believe that the quality I most admire in President Monroe is that he was so good at getting things done."

Indeed he was. In fact, it would be quite easy to make a case for Monroe as the most successful "getter of things done" in presidential history. To make that case more lucidly, however, I will turn to a contemporary, John Quincy Adams, who, in his inauguration speech of 1825, summed up the achievements of his immediate predecessor in office:

> *... in his [Monroe's] career of eight years the internal tax-*
> *es have been repealed; sixty millions of the public debt*
> *have been discharged; provision has been made for the*
> *comfort and relief of the aged and indigent among the*
> *survivors of the Revolution; the regular armed force has*
> *been reduced and its constitution revised and perfected;*
> *the accountability for the expenditure of public monies*
> *has been made more effective; the Floridas have been*
> *peaceably acquired, and our boundary has been extended*
> *to the Pacific Ocean; the independence of the southern*
> *nations of this hemisphere has been recognized, and rec-*
> *ommended by example and by counsel to the potentates*
> *of Europe; progress has been made in the defense of the*
> *country by fortifications and the increase of the Navy, to-*
> *ward the effectual suppression of the African traffic in*
> *slaves; in alluring the aboriginal hunters of our land to*
> *the cultivation of the soil and of the mind, in exploring*
> *the interior regions of the Union, and in preparing by sci-*
> *entific researches and surveys for the further application*
> *of our national resources to the internal improvement of*
> *our country.*

This is a very long list. Let's review quickly the accomplishments of the Monroe administration that Adams notes here. 1) Taxes are down. 2) National debt is falling. 3) Veterans' needs are being met. 4) The army has been both trimmed and improved. 5) Florida has been acquired and the nation's boundaries extended to the Pacific Ocean. 6) Various nations in South and Central America have been recognized, and Europe has been told to stay out of their internal affairs ("The Monroe Doctrine"). 7) Our coastal defenses have been strengthened. 8) The navy has made meaningful efforts to stop the slave trade. 9) American Indians have begun to learn farming and are becoming more educated. 10) Scientific methods are being applied to enable internal improvements throughout the country. While several of these issues were still far from being finally re-solved, is it any wonder that Monroe's Presidency had been labeled, even at the time, an "era of good feelings"? Or, even more extraordinarily, that he would be, along with George Washington, the only President to be re-elected to that office without opposition? And all this "doing" was after such earlier instances of taking action as volunteering to fight in the Revolutionary army under George Washington and helping to negotiate the nation's largest land deal in history: the Louisiana Purchase. Carolyn Holmes had put it most aptly: President Monroe had been awfully "good at getting things done."

Both his home and even the ongoing stewardship of the estate perfectly reflect this dynamic quality of commitment to action.

If one has come from the more palatial Virginia plantation homes of the earliest Presidents, Ash Lawn-Highland (or "Highlands" as Monroe called it) seems almost painfully small. Currently the Monroe-era portion of the house (a two-story addition was added in the late 19th century) is comprised of only five rooms on the ground floor, though recent research has revealed that the home's original front hall and an office had been present on the site where the later two-story addition now stands. The original Monroe structure contains, then, a modest drawing room, a somewhat larger dining room, a study, and two bedrooms. The kitchen area was located downstairs on a walkout level. The only two rooms which betray even a hint of presidential splendor are the drawing room and dining area, and each deserves a more thorough description, for they both do attest to the Monroes' superb taste and refined sensibilities.

In the home's current layout, visitors first step into the drawing room from the side where the front hall was originally located. Though the room was not large (perhaps no more than about 18 feet square), it's a quite evocative interior. Floor to ceiling decorative wallpaper, reminiscent of the tapestries the Monroes had brought from France, depicts a romanticized pastoral topography surrounding the visitor on every side. And, most interesting to me were two prominently displayed busts, one of which I recognized immediately. "This bust is of Napoleon Bonaparte," our guide explained, "and was a gift to President Monroe from the French emperor himself." A member of our tour group quickly asked a follow-up question: "Why would Monroe want the portrait bust of a dictator in his home?"

"Don't forget," our guide countered, "Mr. Monroe got Louisiana from Napoleon." She paused a moment. "And then, of course, Eliza Monroe, the Monroes' first child, went to school with Napoleon's step-daughter Hortense, the child of Josephine, while the Monroes were living in Paris, so there was a personal connection, too." My subsequent research regarding Eliza and Hortense made this postulate feel somewhat suspect. Henry Ammon, a noted Monroe biographer, records that, as a result of Eliza's French education and school companions, she "... had tended to develop exaggerated notions of [her] own importance..." (139). Such a development would hardly explain the bust of the man whose stepdaughter had helped turn his eldest child into a snob.

We were just about to leave this room, when I noticed the second bust, the image of a man I had never seen. "Excuse me," I called out to our docent. "May I ask who **this** person is?" She smiled broadly. "Certainly," she answered. "That is Charles James Fox, an English politician who sided with the colonies during the Revolution. He was also a friend of Wilberforce."

Our tour group moved on to the dining area, but mentally I was still in the drawing room. "Napoleon and Fox, Napoleon and Fox," I kept repeating to myself. Certainly an odd pairing of portrait busts in this small drawing room. And then Carolyn Holmes's phrase struck me again. As different as both these men were—and as distinct as each had been from James Monroe—all three shared that same essential quality of being "good at getting things done." Fox had courageously challenged the British Parliament during the American Revolution, going so far as to wear the colors of the continental army to sessions of parliament. He had also been outspoken on the issues of religious tolerance and individual liberty, even sullying his good name when he had come out in support of the French Revolution. Later he had worked tirelessly with Wilberforce to wipe out the scourge of human trafficking in African slaves. Napoleon, too, of course, had been an endlessly enterprising "doer" who had come very close to creating a new European empire with

Paris as its center. Monroe may have had his reservations about some of each of these men's personal failings, but it would have been impossible for him to deny that both men were thoroughly committed to action. Neither had been merely content to plan a future society—or world—for others to realize. As such they belonged here.

The dining room seemed almost out of place in such a humble dwelling—the decision to dedicate an entire room of the five to giving dinner parties appeared, on its surface at least, a questionable use of space. But then I recalled Carolyn's enjoyment of Monroe's phrase describing Highlands, "my cabin castle." This was the room that transformed the plantation into a "castle," suitable for entertaining the likes of Thomas Jefferson, who dined here often, James Madison, Lafayette, and other notables of the new revolutionary age. Though issuing from a much more unexceptional background than any of his Virginia political peers, Monroe was no less a representative of the aristocracy of merit about which his friend Thomas Jefferson had spoken so memorably. The elegance of the dining table, the refinement of the furnishings and dishware, all spoke of this new generation of republican worthies, of which James Monroe was an established member.

The last three rooms on our tour, two bedrooms and a rather cozy study, were serviceable and straightforwardly useful. There was no ostentatious display of wealth or possessions in any of them, but a small family could be most adequately housed in such a "cabin castle." The Monroes had loved this plantation site and had only put it on the market when their overall indebtedness had necessitated the sale.

Before we left the last room of our tour, the study, our docent pointed out several silhouettes of the Monroe family, framed and hanging as decorative touches on the walls of the room. Her chief interest in them was in the fact that, unlike most silhouettes, which are black paper cutouts mounted on white backgrounds, these silhouettes had been created by the cut out edgings of white paper. The black silhouette images we saw, then, were not cut out of black paper but were created by the white cut edgings, placed upon a plain black background. Her next observation, whether or not she had intended it as a continuation of her comments about these unique silhouettes, constituted a wonderful parallel to them. She noted that when James Madison had inquired of Thomas Jefferson about the character of James Monroe, Jefferson's answer had been immediate and unequivocal: "If you turn Monroe's soul inside out, you will find not a speck." Even Jefferson's portrait of James Monroe, then, was cut completely out of white paper.

The remainder of our tour of this beautiful farm/plantation took place outside, and I found it particularly interesting to note that Ash Lawn-Highland is committed to being a center of living history. The site's education department is dedicated to helping young people from nearby communities have a chance to experience life as it was lived in the early years of the 19th century. There is a sheep-shearing day where children can see where wool comes from and watch it being spun into material that will be used to create items for sale in the site's store. Hay mowing, egg gathering, and cooking classes that feature foods harvested from the Ash Lawn-Highland gardens give young students a window into the workings of a functioning plantation.

I couldn't help but think that James Monroe would have loved to see his plantation so full of activity. Of all the beautifully maintained and reverently presented presidential homes in Virginia, none was so dedicated, even more than 150 years after the passing of its President, to "getting things done."

6

Andrew Jackson: "Old Hickory" down Rachels Lane

7th President Andrew Jackson (1829-1837): The Hermitage in Nashville, TN

I have had the opportunity to visit Andrew Jackson's estate, the Hermitage, just east of Nashville, Tennessee, on three separate occasions in three separate years, and I have always come away with an appreciation of the extent to which this locale presents both the complexity and the worth of this great man. I also suspect that this first sentence may have already enraged some of my readers. "Complexity?" I can hear a voice repeat bitterly. "Jackson was the least complex, most stubbornly direct man who ever darkened the door of the White House." "Worth?" I can hear another scoff. "Tell that to the Supreme Court!" "Great? Only if you consider 'greatness' to be a tyrannical insistence on having one's own way regardless of the consequences to the nation."

So you see I am not unmindful of the controversies that still surround the legacy of our seventh President. But here at the Hermitage, one feels invited at almost every turn to contemplate the man more deeply, to appreciate more thoroughly both the world he inhabited and the world he envisioned, and to understand more completely why the political age he initiated still bears his name.

That such is the case is due, in no small part, to the continuing efforts of the Ladies' Hermitage Association, an organization that has curated and overseen the preservation of the Hermitage since 1889, rendering it, in the words of one guide to presidential homes, "...the most accurately restored early presidential home in the country" (Schaefer 41).

Nowhere is the complexity of Andrew Jackson more blatantly on display here at the Hermitage than in the fact that this site boasts two "Hermitage" structures: the original log cabin (or, at least, the second floor thereof) in which Andrew and Rachel Jackson lived for seventeen years, and the later "Hermitage," the

Andrew Jackson's First Hermitage

more familiar Mansion House, that was finally completed in 1821. The question worth asking, of course, is why did the President keep this first roughhewn reminder of the Jacksons' humble beginnings so near to the later and more impressive Mansion House? The pat answer that is frequently forwarded to this question is that Jackson's frugality had come to the fore and that he had simply used the upper story of what had been his home to accommodate slaves on his burgeoning plantation. While true in the most literal sense—the remaining structure did become a living space for some of the slave population of the Hermitage plantation—it doesn't explain why Jackson would have gone to the trouble of preserving it. To understand this decision, one needs to know the man more intimately.

Like the hickory wood to which he was so often compared, Andrew Jackson was tough, hard, and unbending. And, most significantly, he was a man who never pretended to be anything more or less than what he was—even when "what he was" might be unpolished or unadmirable. Jackson was proud of his frontier roots. Like the common people he so openly championed and worked to include more broadly in the democratic process, his rustic origin was simply the truth about his beginnings. Why hide such a heritage? Why regret it?

After all, the crucible of the frontier had been the backdrop of the rags to riches story of an orphaned son determined to get ahead. The harsh and brutal realities of the "far west" had made Jackson a fierce and tenacious Indian fighter and, all the same, had led him to the later chapters in his life: a successful law practice, political ascendancy, and, ultimately the supreme office of Chief Executive. Jackson never forgot, never wanted to forget, the origin from which he had sprung. But his sights were also set considerably higher than merely achieving personal comfort and affluence, and these aspirations serve to add complexity to the simple picture already considered of a homespun frontiersman who had made good. Jackson was a visionary as well as a fighter, and his expansive visionary dream is visible everywhere here at the Hermitage.

In an important sense, his beliefs about the potential of each man—and of the United States as a whole—were closely connected to the love of his life: Rachel Donelson. Much has been written about Andrew Jackson's romance with Rachel: his attraction to this unhappily married woman; his chivalry in rescuing her from her abusive husband in Kentucky; his gallantry in leading her to a safe haven in Mississippi, only to learn of her divorce; their hasty marriage and their need to remarry after it was discovered that the divorce had not yet been granted at the time of their wedding. But much of this oft-told tale misses the essence of what Rachel meant to Andrew Jackson. To fully comprehend the Hermitage requires an appreciation of that essence.

In the garden east of the Mansion House Hermitage is a lovely Greco-Roman grave site, the final resting place of both General Jackson and Rachel. President Jackson's stone is marked simply with the words "General Andrew Jackson" followed by the dates of his birth and death. Rachel's stone, next to the President's, was carved much earlier (she having died on the eve of her husband's Presidency) and includes President Jackson's assessment of his wife:

> *Her face was fair, her person pleasing, her temper amiable, and her heart kind. She was delighted in relieving the wants of her fellow creatures, and cultivated that divine pleasure by the most liberal and unpretending methods; to the poor she was a benefactor; to the rich an example; to the wretched a comforter; to the prosperous an ornament; her piety went hand in hand with her benevolence, and she thanked her Creator for being permitted to do good. A being so gentle and yet so virtuous, slander might wound but could not dishonor. Even death, when he tore her from the arms of her husband, could but transport her to the bosom of her God.*

This eulogy to the woman he loved is indicative of a side of Andrew Jackson that even his admirers tend to miss or discount. Certainly it illustrates the deep devotion of a grieving husband at the time of losing his best friend on earth, ironically at the very moment of his greatest personal triumph. But these words also relate to another of Andrew Jackson's great loves: the nation over which he had just been elected steward. Like Rachel, the United States possessed a limitless potential, a potential Jackson had seen embodied in his wife but which also encapsulated his vision of the possibilities of this new nation. Like Rachel, the United States was physically "fair" and "pleasing" with its endless forests and breathtaking vistas. Like Rachel, this new country could—and, Jackson believed, should—become a "benefactor" to the poor, an "example" to the rich, and a "comforter" to the wretched. In appreciating what Jackson most admired in his beloved wife, one becomes poignantly aware of what he most valued in his country.

It is no coincidence that tourists today reach the site of the Hermitage by traveling down Rachel's Lane. In many ways the structure one visits today is Andrew Jackson's architectural monument to the exemplary qualities he had enumerated on his wife's gravestone. For President Jackson, the fledgling nation that had emerged from two bitter wars with Great Britain was, like the Hermitage, a twofold creation. On one hand it was a roughhewn, primitive, unsophisticated experiment in democracy, huddled between an ocean and an untamed wilderness. On the other it was the promise of reclaimed Eden, a new opportunity for men to reach heights of virtue and achievement undreamt of in the world from which they had come.

To get a glimpse of the promise of this new Eden, one need only follow a costumed site interpreter into the front hall of the Mansion House Hermitage. Particularly by contrast to the unassuming simplicity of the first log Hermitage, the Mansion House seems like an Arcadian dream. Richly decorated ornate wallpaper depicting vistas of classical mythology surrounds the visitor as he enters this home. As the eye travels the length of the entry that spans the entire depth of the house, one is immediately taken by the elegant sweep of a grand circular stairway leading to the second floor.

The rooms on either side of this expansive entrance hall continue the ambiance of affluent generosity. The parlor with its spacious area and ornate furnishings invites the visitor to imagine the Hermitage's continuous stream of welcome guests amusing themselves with music and conversation throughout the long evenings. The dining room's enormous table, filled to overflowing with docent described course after course of superbly prepared delicacies, speaks of a gracious world of both refinement and honest pleasures.

Across the hall tourists are invited to view the President's private sitting room/office with its leather bound copies of the newspapers Jackson would read avidly throughout his life. Even here, and perhaps even more so in the President's nearby first floor bedroom with its elegant draperies surrounding the bed and the beloved portrait of Rachel hanging on the wall as the first sight that would greet President Jackson when rising, one senses a world made more ideal, more perfect through the efforts of its tireless builders and conservators.

And as a kind of architectural coup de grace, when visitors leave the Mansion House from the rear door, one particularly notable feature of the building becomes immediately apparent: its front display of white columns is a beautiful façade, not a structural component of the largely brick pediment-crowned home visible from behind the Man-

Andrew Jackson's Hermitage Facade

sion House. To the adversaries of President Jackson, here would appear to be proof positive of his vaulting ego and imperial ambitions. One can almost hear them observing, "Yes, that's King Andrew for you, always wanting to look better than he really is—lording it over everyone else." But the actual meaning of this architectural detail may be more subtle and ultimately more significant in coming to a full understanding of our seventh President.

Of course, the docents here at the Hermitage would be quick to note that this façade addition had been added to the home after the fire of 1834, but Jackson had approved the changes and had enjoyed the setting after returning to Nashville subsequent to his presidential years. The point, I believe, is that, like the wallpaper in the entrance hall, like the expansive garden with its Greco-Roman grave markers, like the manicured grounds surrounding the Mansion House, Andrew Jackson's Hermitage stands as a monument to the possibilities he conceived for the nation he had led—what the United States could become as well as what it was. The grand entrance to the Mansion House was that vision made visible and fashioned in no small part from the character of the woman he loved. The Hermitage, like Rachel, stands today as a "prosperous ornament" both to the city of Nashville and to the President whose home it was and whose aspirations it embodied.

Without question, Andrew Jackson was a frontier fighter, a man well acquainted with the dangers and challenges of pioneer life. He regarded with contempt those forces that made more difficult the task of transforming and refashioning the wilderness, whether they came in the form of indigenous natives or Eastern bankers whose fiscal policies had worked against western interests. Jackson would oppose—and ignore--even a Supreme Court ruling if it placed the intrepid men and women of the western regions into a purgatory of territorial indecision.

But as much as any of his predecessors in office, Andrew Jackson was also possessed of a prophetic image of what this new nation might become, a vision he had fought his entire life to bring to pass. He had bled twice in helping to establish his country's independence from England, and he had risen from a state of rustic poverty which he had chosen never to forget. But his ultimate dream, the promise realized most fully, perhaps, here at the Mansion House Hermitage, was the possibility of a people's republic where any man, with tireless effort and adamant resolve, could create a world for himself more beautiful and more prosperous than anywhere else on the globe. The combination of Old Hickory and Rachel's Lane defined for him the necessary ingredients of American success.

7

Martin Van Buren: Winning

8th President Martin Van Buren (1837-1841): Lindenwald in Kinderhook, NY

Martin Van Buren was not the first President to face the problem. Nor would he be the last. John Adams had already experienced it. Andrew Johnson, later in the 19th century, would come to understand as completely as anyone ever could the full weight of its challenge. In the 20th century, the careers of Presidents William Howard Taft and the first George Bush would illustrate that the problem had lost none of its daunting difficulty over the years. Why, all these men would come to question, was it virtually impossible to successfully follow in the footsteps of a charismatic leader who had become a political icon?

George Washington, Andrew Jackson, Abraham Lincoln, Theodore Roosevelt, Ronald Reagan. As uniquely individual as these men were, and as diverse as were the challenges they faced, each one of them had assumed a larger-than-life persona that had helped him guide the ship of state in the direction he believed would yield the greatest benefit to the nation. But these Presidents would have to be followed in office. There is a compelling logic in the assumption that the men whom such dynamic Presidents had specifically chosen to be their successors would be excellent candidates for the office of Chief Executive. Why, then, had it turned out to be so hard for these successors to govern well? Not one of them, from John Adams to the first George Bush, would be re-elected to a second term of presidential service. History would conclude that, in some way, all of them failed to provide the leadership necessary to effectively solve the problems which had arisen during their administrations.

In the case of Martin Van Buren, such a conclusion appears unduly harsh, both as an assessment of his historical significance and as a measure of his personal success. His home, Lindenwald, which he had acquired during his years as President, tells a much more positive story. Still it is a different tale than the one Van Buren must have envisioned for himself as a young lawyer looking for ways to get ahead in the world of state and, eventually, national politics.

One lesson he had learned early on, as he had served customers in his father's tavern and listened to the political banter that had attracted his interest from the start: in politics, everything came down to winning. A winner was revered; a loser was forgotten. It was a truth that he took to heart—a truth that ultimately would explain his own place in history.

Lindenwald, now run by the National Park Service, is a beautiful country estate surrounded by over two hundred acres of cultivated farmland. Ray, the park guide to whom I first spoke upon entering the Visitor's Center, made special note of that: "I love the fact that, after his Presidency, Mr. Van Buren returned here and became a

simple farmer. It's like what Thomas Jefferson did, and it's particularly appropriate because Mr. Jefferson was the first presidential
candidate that Mr. Van Buren had supported as a young man."

Well, yes and no. While still a teenager Van Buren had enthusiastically campaigned for Thomas Jefferson. And, like Jefferson, after leaving the Presidency, Van Buren had returned to this pastoral
estate in the Hudson River Valley. But Martin Van Buren had never intended to remain here. After losing his bid for re-election in
1840, the ex-President had lobbied energetically to recapture his
party's nomination for the Presidency in 1844. Failing that, he had
gone so far as to team up with Charles Francis Adams, the son of his
old adversary John Quincy Adams, and aligned himself with a new
political entity, the Free Soil Party, to make a then unprecedented fourth run for the Presidency in 1848. But the political tide had
turned against him. Van Buren was unable to win a single vote in
the Electoral College that year. The only real impact of his Free Soil
Party candidacy was to split the Democratic votes in such a way as
to insure the election of the Whig candidate, Zachary Taylor. It was
a bitter defeat, and Van Buren would never again run for political
office.

The Lindenwald estate stands as a kind of memorial to all this: to
Van Buren's aspirations and successes as well as to his final losses. As Carol and I have often found, the house illustrated the President's story most compellingly.

Our site guide was a pleasant young college student named
Rachel. We had arrived early and were the only guests for the 11:00
tour. We began toward the front of the house where Rachel recounted the tale of a youthful Martin Van Buren wending his way
up to the porch where Peter Van Ness, the family patriarch who had
built Lindenwald in the closing years of the 18th century, was reading.

"Mr. Van Ness," Rachel informed us, "was a Federalist, and he
knew Martin Van Buren was a Democratic-Republican. As the
young man approached, Mr. Van Ness refused even to acknowledge
his presence and continued to read." Rachel paused a moment. "But
as Martin Van Buren strode up to the door and knocked, Mr. Van

Ness couldn't help but smile at the persistence and resolve of this young visitor."

This is obviously an apocryphal tale, though Van Buren had become friends with two of the Van Ness sons, Peter and William (both of whom were also Democratic-Republicans). Rachel's point, however, wasn't concerned with his friendships. She was more interested in portraying Van Buren, even at this early moment, as a man not easily flustered or intimidated.

That point, history reveals, is undeniably true. The story of Martin Van Buren's steady rise to political prominence reads like a Horatio Alger tale. While still a young lawyer, he successfully defended his friend William Van Ness from the charge of "having willfully and with malice aforethought murdered [Alexander] Hamilton" as a result of acting as Aaron Burr's second in the infamous duel that had cost the life of the great Federalist (Fleming 351). Building on the reputation this victory afforded him, Van Buren thereafter became known as the "Little Magician" who so professionally engineered the dominance of the Democratic Party in New York, the so-called "Albany Regency," that he managed to get himself elected to the U.S. Senate and, after that, to the governorship of the state. Later, both as Secretary of State to the first elected Democratic President, Andrew Jackson, and as Jackson's Vice President in 1832, this small-framed tavern keeper's son, this "Red Fox of Kinderhook," had arrived at a pinnacle of power and prestige that few of his townsfolk would ever have imagined possible. In the national election of 1836, he would win the Presidency itself, carrying the election by a comfortable margin in both popular and electoral votes.

Then, in 1839, the second year of his term of office, and almost like an award acknowledging his ascendency, the old Van Ness estate, Lindenwald, had come up for sale. The President wasted no time in purchasing it, even though, over the years, the house had deteriorated into a state of serious disrepair. One can only imagine what its acquisition must have meant to Martin Van Buren. That forbidding porch, once presided over by the patrician Peter Van Ness, had now become Van Buren property. The front parlor with its elegant Ogee arch leading into the breakfast area, the spacious front hallway with its spiral staircase leading to the upstairs bed-rooms, all were now his to reconfigure and to redecorate as he pleased. After a two year restoration, Martin Van Buren took up residence here in 1841, just as his own political roof was about to cave in upon him.

Not that that had come as a complete surprise. Almost from the moment he had entered the Presidency, Van Buren had seen the nation plummet into the worst economic downturn of its young history. Despite his belief that his proposed Independent Treasury Act would do much to ameliorate the nation's financial problems, he knew that there would be formidable political battles ahead if he attempted to retain his office. But Martin Van Buren had never been a man to avoid a good fight. In fact, as Rachel led us into the large ground floor central hall of Lindenwald, one of the alterations he had insisted upon in the renovation spoke very clearly of his po-litical ambitions.

"The original structure had featured an impressively elegant winding staircase leading to the second floor," Rachel informed us. "Mr. Van Buren had that feature taken out so that the room could be extended to accommodate large political gatherings."

And in fact it had been here that the President had invited his friends and operatives to help him design each of the three re-election bids that would occupy him for the next twelve years.

Looking around the capacious interior of the room, complete with a banquet table that could easily accommodate over thirty people, it was hard not to notice, as well, the expansive wallpaper scene that illustrated various stages of an aristocratic fox hunt.

"It reminds me of the front hall of Jackson's Hermitage," I whis-pered to Carol. But I also saw an important difference. Jackson's wallpaper depicted an ideal and mythological vision of pastoral beauty. Here at Lindenwald, the hunt, while set in a verdant and bu-colic setting, was much more realistically rendered.

"And look at this," Carol gestured to me and pointed toward one of the scenes on the wallpaper just to the left of the entrance to the home's main parlor. There, astonishingly, was pictured a group of hunters enjoying a festive beverage as the pelt of a red fox hung from the limb of a nearby tree! Was this a piece of self-deprecating humor that Van Buren may have enjoyed to set a tone of convivial humility? Or, more seriously, had Martin Van Buren already guessed that his day had passed, that the "Red Fox of Kinderhook" had already run his last meaningful race?

The use to which he had put this large room would certainly suggest that, at least at the time he moved in, Martin Van Buren had missed the irony pictured on the walls of his political headquarters.

As Rachel continued to lead us through the back rooms of the house, it became increasingly apparent that much of what we were seeing had been the result of additions commissioned by Smith Van Buren, the son whose family had moved in with the ex-President in his later years.

The modernization of the kitchen areas, the elaborate Italianate tower that dominates the rear of the house, even the bright yellow paint of the building's façade, all were Smith's alterations of the original Van Ness structure that Martin Van Buren had purchased in 1839.

It was hard not to find in all these modifications a poignant parallel to Van Buren's political life. The party structure he had labored so intently to establish was now developing in new directions and backing new candidates. Commenting on his son Smith's many architectural improvements to Lindenwald, Martin Van Buren observed that "the idea of seeing in life the changes which my heir would be sure to make after I am gone, amuses me." Apparently it was more difficult to be amused by the changes wrought by his political heirs.

The final, and perhaps the most telling, insight into the life of Martin Van Buren that we were to encounter at Lindenwald came as Rachel welcomed Carol and me into the President's bed chamber. There, lying diagonally on the white bedspread, was a silver headed walking stick.

"This is one of my favorite pieces in the house," Rachel began. "It was a gift to Mr. Van Buren from Andrew Jackson. It's made of old hickory, echoing Mr. Jackson's famous nickname, and look at what the silver cap reads." She held up the cane so that we could make out its inscription: "Mr. Van Buren For the Next President."

Martin Van Buren's Walking Stick Gift From Andrew Jackson

"Isn't that great?" Rachel continued. "Right there Andrew Jackson was passing the baton of power to his chosen successor. And look down the shaft of the walking stick. There are thirteen silver discs placed around the stick, each carrying one visible letter: A-N-D-R-E-W-J-A-C-K-S-O-N. This gift must have made Mr. Van Buren very proud."

Well, again, yes and no. Certainly the stick was a clear indication of Jackson's approbation and support. But did it not also suggest that Van Buren would forever be leaning on the reputation and career of his illustrious predecessor? The verdict of most historians would appear to confirm both of these conclusions.

One of the most prominent of these historians, Joel H. Silbey, who wrote an acclaimed study of the significance of the Presidency of Martin Van Buren, identified four categories into which he believed the Presidents of the United States could be accurately grouped. The first was "the leader-statesmen" group, towering figures of national resolve; the second, Silbey labeled "prophets," men, often unappreciated in their own time, who foresaw problems the nation would have to face in later years; third in Silbey's categories were the "run-of-the-mill officeholders," essentially ciphers in political history; and fourth and lastly were "the organizers/managers of American political life," of whom, Silbey concluded, Van Buren was "a major example, perhaps the leading one..." (xi-xii).

Most other historians have accepted this vision of our eighth President: Martin Van Buren, the "Little Magician," the sly "Red Fox of Kinderhook." He is widely seen as the father of the political party machine, the organizing process of attaining and retaining power which has held national sway right up to the present day. This, historians have tended to agree, was his great legacy to his country. Yet this legacy may also be largely responsible for the negative light so often thrown on his achievements as a leader and as a President.

Why? Because it is an enigmatic truth that although Americans find politics a source of almost endless fascination and debate, they also tend to distrust and dislike politicians. Unless, of course, they win. Then, all is forgiven.

Martin Van Buren, as Silbey suggests, had played an essential role in creating the modern political party machine. He had ridden its influence all the way to the White House. But when he had lost his bid for a second term, the very machine he had been so instrumental in founding had cast him off for other more potentially attractive candidates. He would live long enough to find even at his beloved Lindenwald that his heirs and successors would amend and alter the estate to suit their own needs and tastes. He had lost the power to dictate the direction of his world.

The home here in Kinderhook, New York, then, stands as a somewhat curious combination of attained prominence and accepted defeat. As his country plunged into Civil War, the aging Martin Van Buren would persistently question both his family members and any visitors to Lindenwald about news from the front. Would the Union be saved? Were the Northern armies achieving victories? Had Southern forces threatened Washington? His family and friends repeatedly attempted to reassure the ex-President that the nation would withstand any adversity.

For Martin Van Buren, however, only absolute certainty could relieve him of his anxieties, and, during the first two years of the war, any such certainty was impossible to provide. He died here at his beautiful New York estate in July of 1862. Ironically it was a moment of history when nobody, not even one of the most astute politicians of his age, could be sure of just which side it was that was winning.

8

William Henry Harrison: No "LOG CABIN"... No "HARD CIDER"

9th President William Henry Harrison (1841): Grouseland in Vincennes, IN

President William Henry Harrison is more often cited as the answer to humorous trivia questions than for his considerable accomplishments prior to being elected our ninth Chief Executive. "What President gave the longest inauguration speech?" "What President served for the shortest time?" "What President's campaign slogan was, '...settle upon him a pension of $2,000 a year, and... he will be content to live in a LOG CABIN and drink HARD CIDER the remainder of his life.'" Yet, both his home in Vincennes, Indiana, and his birthplace, Berkeley Plantation, in the Virginia tidewater, reveal a very different and more substantial William Henry Harrison than do these often repeated quips. Each location speaks volumes to visitors interested in learning more about the man behind the trivia.

My first geographic encounter with the historical William Henry Harrison occurred at neither of the two above mentioned homes, but rather in a leaf-covered narrow plot of fenced-in ground in central Indiana. Our son had recently matriculated to Purdue University in West Lafayette, and, after a happy parental visit, Carol and I found our way to the nearby site of Tippecanoe.

As battlefields go, Tippecanoe is quite small: a long, narrow strip of forested land butting up to the steep bank of a meandering stream. But this seemingly inconsequential site would launch William Henry Harrison all the way to the Presidency. Here, in November of 1811, the most serious threat to American expansion into the so-called Northwest Territory had ended in a furious predawn battle that would rout the American Indian forces gathered at their capital, Prophetstown. Although Indians would continue to aid British forces in the upcoming War of 1812, no battle in the northwest would be fought this far south again. General Harrison and his army would go on the offensive, pursuing the British and their Indian allies into Canada before achieving final victory in Ontario.

By the time he fought at Tippecanoe, William Henry Harrison had served as Governor of the Indiana territory for twelve years. He had parleyed with, as well as campaigned against, various native tribes and leaders, and he had recognized the influence and power exercised over these peoples by charismatic chiefs like Tecumseh. The Governor's mansion that Harrison commissioned in the territorial capital of Vincennes stood as a powerful symbol of the ideals he was dedicated to bringing to the region under his charge. He named his new home Grouseland in acknowledgment of the abundant game fowl indigenous to the region.

Built in the first years of his governorship of the Indiana Territory (1803-04), Grouseland, or as it was also called, "The Great House," must have seemed like an architectural miracle to the people of the frontier. It is important to remember that at this period western Indiana was regarded as the far west territory of the fledgling United States of America. Yet here in Vincennes arose a two-story brick Greek revival home with a projecting porch of Doric and Ionic columns, crowned with a classic pediment. The left side of the home bowed out toward the river, creating a wall with a semicircular arch, and the front hall featured an elegant staircase that seemed to float in air as it made a twisting curve up to the second story of the home.

There are also evidences that this astonishing structure was created, fully mindful of the hostile wilderness which lay close by. The walls are over a foot thick and contain slit holes to accommodate rifle barrels. The long windows were fitted with heavy shutters that could be pulled over the glass in case of attack, and there was a powder magazine located in the basement area of the mansion. The resulting structure, then, is a curious mixture of elegance and fortification, both qualities Harrison wished to incorporate into the plan of his Grouseland.

On the day of Carol's and my visit to this beautiful home in Vincennes, I tried to imagine the scene in 1810, when Tecumseh, along with several hundred of his Indian allies, had arrived here to conference with the future President. Before these very walls, the two adversaries had wheeled and parried around each other's aims and intents. Yet even then, on some level, Tecumseh must have felt that his people's day was fading. Despite the adamancy of this great Indian leader of the confederation of tribes under his command, Tecumseh must have sensed that his people would be no match for the technological superiority of the new settlers who had created such an architectural phenomenon in the heart of Indiana. Grouseland remains today a metaphor and a reminder of what William

Henry Harrison knew all along: that the future belonged to the people of the United States and that the native Indian populations would someday and in some way have to accede to that fact.

Of course, none of this really explains how Harrison became, in later years, the "LOG CABIN" and "HARD CIDER" candidate of the Whig party in 1840. Certainly such a roughhewn image, aside perhaps from his pedigree as a frontier Indian fighter, was totally absent from the mansion he had established here in the territorial capital.

And visiting his birthplace in the Virginia tidewater offers no help in fathoming the Whig slogan either, for Berkeley Plantation is one of the truly grand Virginia homes, dating back fifty years before the Revolution.

Berkeley Plantation, about fifteen minutes west of Colonial Williamsburg, is a storied location. Here, in December 1619, on the banks of the James River, a year before the Pilgrims landed in Plymouth, Thanksgiving was first celebrated in the new world. Here, over two hundred years later, a young Union soldier, billeted on the grounds with thousands of other men, would compose "Taps." And here, in February of 1773, William Henry Harrison was born.

William Henry Harrison's Birthplace, Berkeley Plantation, in Charles City, VA

Berkeley Plantation, like Grouseland, is a brick structure, replete with Greco-Roman echoes and elements. Graceful pediments jut out over the front and back doors of the home. Expansive grounds spread out from this plantation centerpiece in all directions and to the south include manicured gardens that lead one down a gradual slope to a dock on the James River. In total, Berkeley stands as a prime example of settled, affluent, civilized power.

And, walking the grounds, Carol and I noted it was also clearly the inspiration for the Grouseland mansion Harrison would construct a thousand miles to the west.

So what explains the "LOG CABIN" and "HARD CIDER" moniker? Pure, undiluted politics. And even, with a terrible irony, these two homes suggest an explanation of the other hackneyed pieces of Harrison trivia: his extravagantly long inaugural speech and his short-lived Presidency.

In 1840, the Whig party was desperate for a viable presidential candidate. And, what is more, they were sure that, with the right man, they could win. For the Whigs, the Presidency of Andrew Jackson had been an extended nightmare. In fact the Whig party itself, rather than being any sort of a defined political organization, was a hodgepodge of various factions which could agree only on the need to oust the dominant Democratic control of the Presidency, personified first in Jackson and, more recently, in his chosen successor, Martin Van Buren.

Now, in the upcoming 1840 election, the Whigs saw their chance. The financial panic of 1837, caused largely as a reaction to Jackson's war on the Second Bank of the United States, had left his successor in a tight financial bind. Yet even this economic downturn, Whigs feared, might not be enough to woo American voters to abandon their beloved "General Jackson" and his minions. What the Whigs needed was another western, tough-as-nails, Indian fighting General. And William Henry Harrison appeared to fit the bill perfectly. But Harrison was also a gentleman from Virginia, the civilized builder of Grouseland, who hailed from one of the most prestigious patrician families of the Virginia tidewater.

"Forget all that," his political handlers counseled. "Let's make him out to be the Whig Andy Jackson: a down-to-earth western fighter, a man of the people." And so, with an early and brilliant example of political spin, William Henry Harrison was presented and touted as a relatively unlettered and unsophisticated man, upon whom a pension, a "LOG CABIN," and a barrel of "HARD CIDER" would suffice to render him content for life.

The result was a landslide electoral win for the Whigs, but a discontented victor. One gets the distinct impression that Harrison, though obviously gratified to have been raised to the highest position in the land, wanted, perhaps even needed, to let the American people know that, however hardened his life on the frontier might have made him, they had elected no bumpkin to the Presidency. After the election he returned to his ancestral home, Berkeley Plantation, and there crafted his inauguration speech, brimming with prolonged classical allusions and erudite phraseology.

What he hadn't counted on was the weather. On inauguration day in early March, a bitterly cold wind swept through the capital city. Regardless of the chill, Harrison spoke at length, even refusing to wear an overcoat or hat. He was, after all, old Tippecanoe, and thirty days later, he was dead of pneumonia.

It is hard not to feel an irony implicit in the two homes which are associated with this great man. If they could have spoken to him, one wonders whether or not they might have counseled the old soldier and territorial governor to insist on staying closer to his genuine lineage. William Henry Harrison was no unlettered backwoods figure, emerging out of obscurity and armed only with a smattering of common sense, coupled with militaristic gusto. He was the son of privilege (his openly aristocratic Vice President, John Tyler, resided only one or two plantations up from Berkeley on the same Virginia tidewater section of the James River). Harrison was a soldier of great cunning and courage. And, as the architecture of both his birthplace and the home he built in the western wilderness territory clearly attest, he also was a man of refinement and taste. There was nothing trivial about him except the political world which he, unwisely it turned out, had allowed to define his legacy.

9

John Tyler: A Party without a President

10th President John Tyler (1841-1845): Sherwood Forest in Charles City, VA

When John Tyler left the Presidency in 1845, he returned to a home he barely knew that was located on a peninsula where he had lived all his life. Originally named "Walnut Grove," the beautiful plantation to which Tyler and his second wife, Julia, retired was renamed "Sherwood Forest" after a spurious rebuke hurled at the exiting "President without a party" by his political adversary Henry Clay. It was Clay who had mockingly suggested that Tyler, now exiled from both the Whigs and the Chief Executive's office, should run off and hide like Robin Hood of yore. Tyler, unoffended, had enjoyed the allusion, and he and Julia would spend the rest of their lives living in and adding on to their impressive "Sherwood Forest" estate until, by the time of Tyler's death, the house would stretch 300 feet in length, though often only a single room in depth. It remains to this day the longest frame house in the United States.

As Carol and I drove into the plantation's parking area, I found myself wondering if "Sherwood Forest" would offer the sort of illuminating parallels with and insights into the couple who created it in its final form, as had so often been the case in our visits to other such sites. And, even more special would be the fact that President Tyler's grandson, Harrison Ruffin Tyler, would be our guide throughout this magnificent structure. Our visit in August 2009 would turn out to be one of the more memorable days of any of our many tours of presidential homes. But for reasons we could not have guessed before arriving.

President John Tyler, historians have often noted, was a man of many firsts. He was the first President who had changed political parties prior to serving as Chief Executive (he had begun his career as a Jacksonian Democrat and had become a Whig, in part, at least, to protest of some of Jackson's more "imperial" tendencies). Tyler was the first Vice President to become President as a result of the death of a President (William Henry Harrison). Tyler was the first to establish the fact that a Vice President coming to power under such conditions would, in fact, assume the full mantle of the Presidency for the duration of his term. Tyler was the first President to be officially expelled from his own political party during his administration. Tyler was also the first President to marry (after, in his case, being the first sitting President to be widowed) during his years in office. And he was the first President—and thus far the only President—to father fifteen children, eight with his first wife and seven with his second.

In addition to these "firsts," Tyler would enjoy a more controversial place in history as either the first President to become a citizen of another country, subsequent to his Presidency, or the first President to become a traitor to his nation, subsequent to his Presidency. The determination of which of these mutually exclusive "firsts" one accepts depends on the side one espouses regarding the American Civil War. Tyler, after a failed attempt to reconcile the interests of North and South in a peace commission held in 1861, allowed himself to be elected to the Confederate House of Representatives, dying before he had been officially sworn in to take his seat in that governing body. For some, his willingness to serve in the Confederate congress was an act of treason. For others it bore testimony to his lifelong dedication to state's rights and his willingness to serve what he saw as his new nation, the Confederate States of America. Whichever way one sees it, this was the final, most controversial "first" in Tyler's remarkable political life.

In many ways this larger than life list of "firsts" seemed beautifully reflected in the extraordinary scope of the Tyler home here in the Virginia tidewater region. But the political impulses of both John Tyler and of his second wife, Julia, remain difficult to discern behind all these "firsts." Their grandson, Harrison Ruffin Tyler, would be interested almost exclusively in the personalities of his famous forebears, and not so much in the public lives of his grandfather and grandmother. It would be the stories he told us, rather than any meaningful historical or political revelations, that would linger in the memory, after our visit here on this lovely summer day.

Harrison Ruffin Tyler, the President's grandson, born sixty-six years after his President-grandfather's death, was—and is—a marvelous purveyor of tall tales on a peninsula replete with them. (To illustrate such Tidewater propensities, let me simply note that on the very morning of the day we visited Sherwood Forest, Carol and I had toured William Henry Harrison's boyhood home, Berkeley Plantation, just ten miles or so from Sherwood. The tour guide there had suggested to his credulous listeners that a cannon ball lodged in the brickwork chimney had been shot there by a Confederate cavalry unit during the Civil War—this at the time when the entire Union army had been billeted on the grounds of Berkeley. Were we to believe this? "You'll hear a lot of silliness down here," we were quietly assured by a more forthright gift shop worker).

Cannon Ball Embedded at Berkeley Plantation

But Sherwood Forest, we were certain, would be different, if only because our "docent" would be an actual Tyler descendent, the youngest grandson of the tenth President. Here would be living history. In this we were not to be disappointed, for we would find Harrison full of engaging tales, but few presidential homes we have ever visited have been more devoid of insights into presidential life than Sherwood Forest plantation. Like the famous man/myth Robin Hood, Virginia's Sherwood was such a hodgepodge of credible history and fanciful tall tales that one quickly realized there would be no way to disentangle fact from fiction. All we were left with by the close of our visit were the stories told by their rather florid raconteur, but what stories they were!

We were welcomed by Mr. Tyler into the entry hall of Sherwood (after we had paid our $35 per person admission fee!), along with one other couple, and right from the start, we found ourselves entranced by the mellifluous voice of our octogenarian host.

"Good day, it's a pleasure to meet you. I'm Harrison Tyler," our host intoned in a soft, fluid, and cultivated Virginia accent that bespoke a heritage of gracious privilege. "Welcome to Sherwood."

We stood grouped together in the spacious front hallway which ran straight through to the rear of the home while Mr. Tyler spoke about a variety of paintings on display there. "This," he pointed to a portrait hanging on the wall," was my grandfather's first wife, Letitia. And this," he continued, gesturing to another portrait, "was my grandmother, Julia. My grandfather was widowed while serving as President, but his remarriage is a captivating story." Indeed it was, though it was a tale I had already known about from a variety of historical sources. Yet hearing it told from Harrison Tyler's perspective, even this initially grisly account took on a softer, much more genuinely romantic flavor. The tale involved the firing of a cannon, the barrel of which had burst, killing Julia's father. When she had seen her father's body, Julia had fainted literally into the waiting arms of President Tyler.

"He held her gently, gently," Harrison continued in his softest, most soothing voice, "and when she recovered the first face she saw was my grandfather's, gazing at her with tender affection."

How much of this had actually happened exactly as Harrison Tyler had narrated, none of us could say. Nevertheless, in a relatively short time after the tragic incident, President Tyler and Julia Gardiner had married and the nation had a new First Lady living in the White House. As Harrison led Carol and me, together with the other tourist couple, through the rooms in the central portion of the house, the anecdotes kept coming in a seemingly endless flow.

Story after story, tale after tale, issued from Harrison Tyler, some memorable, others too intimately involved with a line of family feuds and relations to be easily recalled, but none were dull. One that I especially remember involved a suitor-adversary of Harrison's who had, through a variety of means too complex to relate here, tried to steal a particularly beautiful girl from Harrison and had also laid claim to a set of presidential china rightfully belonging to the Tyler family. This rival had been a pilot, and one day by chance, Harrison noted, "his plane went up, and then went down." He added, after an appropriate pause, "and that was the end of him."

The girl in question, it turned out, had ultimately become Harrison's wife, and the china had been recovered by the Tyler family at an estate auction. "So you see," Harrison concluded, "in the end I got both the girl and the china." At this point he opened the door of a copious armoire to display the retrieved dishware.

Leading us back across the front hall, Mr. Tyler brought us into the parlor for more stories and, it turned out, a special treat. "I'm somewhat tired from a tennis match I had this morning," he noted. "Would you all mind if we just sat here in the parlor to talk?"

Before we had any chance to respond, Harrison was taking down the rope which cordoned off the precious furniture and objects of the room from normal tourist traffic, and we were being invited to sit on the museum quality settees and chairs on display there. But, I reminded myself, who better to do this than the man whose home this was?

The tales kept coming now. We learned about Julia's experiences during the Civil War (John Tyler had died in 1862) and how she had delicately kept hold of Sherwood Forest plantation by calling on the aid of Union generals as an ex-First Lady rather than as the widow of a rebel slave-owning Virginian. Harrison also reenacted in his inimitable way how the household slaves had saved the home from conflagration. Many of their newly freed slaves, Harrison explained, had remained at the plantation even after Julia had returned to the safety of her family estate in New York during the war. These servants had picked up burning pieces of wood that the retreating Union soldiers had thrown into the front hall and had rushed to the back door to throw them away from the house. (Harrison would later point out on the hall floor the clear evidence of charred floorboards to substantiate his story.)

When Julia had returned to Virginia after the conclusion of the war, Harrison told us, she had continued to live at Sherwood and had then happily paid for the labor of those who once had been her slaves (here he showed us her actual account book, indicating each worker's terms of employment). He also

Virginia Reel Parlor

rather gleefully confirmed, when questioned, that the Tyler family were descendants of John Rolfe and Pocahontas, and, as we got up to view the Grey Room (complete with its resident ghost) and the parlor President Tyler had had specially constructed for Julia as a venue in which to dance the Virginia reel, our heads were positively swimming with the tales told by our incomparable host.

After about an hour and a half, Carol and I thanked Harrison Tyler for his fascinating tour, and we went back outside to take a few photographs and familiarize ourselves with the outlying buildings of the estate.

But even more importantly, it gave us the chance to try to assess everything we had been hearing for the last hour or so.

"All this is almost hard to believe," I found myself thinking, "yet his memories are so clear and detailed that it's equally hard to call them into question." Upon further research after I returned home, I found evidence of the probability of the Rolfe/Pocahontas connection to the Tyler family. Perhaps all the stories were just as real as their narrator.

Sherwood Forest was the perfect name for this beautiful place for, like the more famous original in medieval England, this Virginia Sherwood had housed an almost mythic man of firsts, and the tales surrounding both him and his descendants simultaneously defied and inflamed the imagination. The stories we had been told seemed as tall and long as the home itself, yet those one hundred yards of white clapboard siding were undeniably real. We could see them before our eyes and photograph them with our cameras. If we had reached out our hands, we could have touched them. Although we had gained few new historical perspectives here at Sherwood, our visit had been an experience never to be forgotten: a delightful party replete with fascinating narratives, hosted by the grandson of a President.

10

James K. Polk: "Who is James K. Polk?"

11th President James K. Polk (1845-1849): Ancestral Home in Columbia, TN

Just North of Columbia, Tennessee, by the side of State Highway 31, near a grassy and tree-lined field, there stands a historical marker indicating the approximate location of the first Polk Tennessee homestead where the future President would spend his adolescent years. There is nothing here that remains from those days of the Polk family residence. Even the rather dilapidated house nearby, nestled in a grove of unruly and overgrown scrub brush, dates from a later era.

"I wish they would take down that sign," complained our docent at the Polk ancestral home Visitor's Center. "It just confuses people." Maybe so, but as a metaphor of our 11th President, it's not a bad match.

James K. Polk's Boyhood Home Location Sign

"Who is James K. Polk?" was the belittling Whig slogan adopted for the election of 1844, intending to suggest that the adversary of the Whig candidate, Henry Clay, was a nobody, out of his league when pitted against one of the most well-known politicians in the United States. Of course, when the votes were finally counted, this "nobody" had won the Presidency. But that fact alone had not made the answer to the taunting campaign slogan any clearer. In like fashion, when Carol and I paid a visit to Polk's ancestral home, it left us with many more questions than answers about this intriguing man, sometimes known as "Young Hickory."

For many, it is **that** appellation that stands as the passageway into a more full comprehension of the man. "To understand James K. Polk," a presidential video proclaims, "one must understand Andrew Jackson." But as simple a suggestion as that appears to be, the plain truth is that, both culturally and temperamentally, Jackson and Polk were almost polar opposites. Their goals were similar: both valued the increasingly democratic politics of their times, and both were dedicated to the expansion of the United States, but Jackson was a commander, a "general" in almost every sense of the word, whereas Polk was subdued and measured. Jackson was passionate. Polk struck many people as distant and cool, though his wife, Sarah, so loved him that she would spend more than forty years in mourning over his memory. Most significantly, Jackson was adored by the majority of the American people, winning the national popular vote in three consecutive presidential elections, while Polk would not be able to prevail in two of his three gubernatorial contests in Tennessee and failed to carry his state in his one campaign for the Presidency.

Although over the years I have often found presidential homes to offer revealing insights into the men who lived in them, Polk's ancestral home, while providing several helpful pieces of visual and historical data, would leave its most famous resident still swathed in mystery.

For one thing, the house is only tangentially a presidential home. As a helpful, and quite honest, sign identifies near the front door, Polk was 21 years old when his parents built the home in 1816. Upon his return from college in 1818, he lived here until his marriage to Sarah Childress in January of 1824. Of course, this house was the home of his parents, and, as such, both James and Sarah would have been frequent visitors. But this house cannot be said to have been formative or really indicative of Polk's tastes or character as he had had no real part to play in its construction or articulated ground plan.

Nevertheless, the home does stand as a memorial to the Polk family. It is "... the only surviving original residence of the eleventh president," a guidebook states—beside, of course, the White House itself.

It is located on a busy corner of downtown Columbia, Tennessee, though set back slightly from the bustle of traffic. The exterior is brick, sporting a rather pleasant coat of pale green paint, and a specimen tulip tree spreads its luxurious foliage to the right of the house. After entering the nearby Visitor's Center and seeing an introductory video on Polk's presidential accomplishments, Carol and I were led to the front door of the home.

We ascended the front stairs into the entrance hall, and I noted the spaciously high ceiling and the simple, straight staircase leading to the second floor. Just inside the front door was an elaborate wooden umbrella stand/coat hanger which housed an old mirror. It was hard not to be struck by the fact that, as I gazed into the mirror's depths, I was seeing myself reflected in the very glass that President Polk would have looked into when he had entered or exited this house.

Overall, the home was quite small. Aside from the front hall and staircase, there were only two rooms on its lower floor. Yet each contained a valuable collection of personal belongings from the Polks' White House years, objects that had never been housed here when the home was being used by the rest of the Polk family. Several pieces of vibrantly red upholstered furniture that James and Sarah had brought to the White House, an elegant dress worn by the diminutive First Lady, and an impressive circular table, picturing the American eagle sculpted from Egyptian marble, were among the most notable treasures of the front sitting room. Sarah's pianoforte stood close to one of the windows, and both James's and Sarah's White House portraits—the originals—stared down on us from the walls. All these artifacts were elegant and tasteful, but not particularly revelatory.

James K. Polk's Coffee Cup

This large sitting room gave onto a comparably sized dining room that featured a display of some of the Polks' presidential china. More interesting to me, however, was a glass fronted sideboard in which was to be seen a chipped red and white ornamented china coffee cup. Here, for the first time, I became aware of the man as well as the President. The cup seemed to speak of the hours of labor ("16 to 20 hours a day," the docent informed us) that had made President Polk, in his own words, "… the hardest working man in the country."

Passing back into the front hall and climbing the steep staircase up to the bedroom areas, we saw three modestly sized rooms, one decorated as a study, which comprised the remainder of the home.

The study had several items from Polk's presidential years, including a desk/chair piece of furniture where he had often sat both to read and to write. Nestled near the wall of the room was a rather uncomfortable looking day bed which, our docent informed us, had been placed in the President's office in the White House so that he could rest momentarily when the rare occasion to do so had arisen. There was also a small desk and selected legal volumes behind glass doors. But there was nothing particularly personal here, with perhaps the exception of a pair of dime-sized eyeglasses. Everything else could have been found in many mid-19th century American homes.

The bedchambers bore more evidence of Sarah's presence than of her husband's. Her sewing table was on display, as well as two golden lounge chairs that she had purchased for the White House and had brought back with them to Tennessee when the couple had left Washington after their four tumultuous years there. But here in Columbia, in a setting for which they had never been intended, these furnishings seemed sedate, mute, and curated rather than eloquent.

Leaving the upstairs, our docent pointed out the anachronism of a large, dark oil painting of Cortez, hanging over the stairway.

"This was a gift to the President from one of his generals at the conclusion of the war with Mexico," she intoned with the same sonorous Southern inflection with which she had conducted our entire tour. The painting seemed a completely incongruous addition to the simple home in which it was displayed.

In fact, nothing here in the ancestral home gave evidence of the determined persistence, expansive aspirations, and tireless management which characterize the descriptions of President Polk forwarded by so many of his biographers. Rather than reflecting the grandiose vision of a President determined to extend the territory of his country as an expression of divinely authorized "Manifest Destiny," the overall feeling of this beautiful but modest home was one of graceful, unpretentious comfort in a small country town. Polk himself remained an elusive presence, associated with, but hardly elucidated by, this locale.

We exited out a door at the back of the house into a garden area and then toured the separate kitchen building before circling around to the Visitor's Center to visit the small but well presented museum therein. It contained a few items of particular interest which would aid our efforts to understand Polk the man.

First, and most centrally, displayed, was a fan that Polk had presented to Sarah at the time of his inauguration festivities. Each panel of the fan pictured one of the ten Presidents who had preceded him in office, his own image occupying the final panel. Washington's portrait, appropriately enough, occupied the central, most prominent, panel, and then, starting from the left, came Adams through Quincy Adams, followed on the right half of the fan by images of Jackson through Polk. This fan, in and of itself, might be passed off easily enough as a piece of self-congratulatory fluff, but there were other hints in the museum that Sarah may have taken it more seriously.

In a frame that couldn't have measured much more than four by six inches in size, Sarah had placed a picture of the meager log cabin in North Carolina where her husband had been born. The distance between that homely cabin and the splendid, hand-painted inaugural fan must have felt almost incalculable.

And then there was the Pillow fan and sword.

Gideon Pillow, at least according to Polk biographer Walter R. Borneman, may have been one of the very few men that President Polk had misjudged and overvalued. A longtime lawyer friend from Columbia, Pillow had wheedled his way into a military command during the Mexican war and, although acquitting himself with honor, insisted on claiming that the American victory in that conflict was largely his own doing. Counterclaims had been leveled by other officers involved in the war, and an embarrassing, and ultimately inconclusive, court martial hearing had only made matters worse.

None of this story, of course, was told in the museum. What **was** on display were two gifts that Pillow had given the President and First Lady: a gaudy, ornamental sword and a gold encrusted fan. As Polk had never served in the army, the sword was an odd, and, frankly, inappropriate gift. The fan, while undeniably splendid, was so heavy that Sarah had never attempted to fan herself with it, only holding it "on state occasions." So why had the Polks kept these somewhat inappropriate and unwieldy mementos?

One final clue hung on the wall just at the point where visitors would be leaving the small museum. It was a photograph of Polk Place, the home to which the Polks had intended to retire. It was also the home where James Polk had died only three months after leaving office. The photograph had been taken sometime after his death, as his mausoleum, a prominent structure, had been erected in the front yard, only a few steps from the staircase leading to the main entryway. Why on earth would Sarah have placed her husband's gravesite there? Why this constant reminder of her widowhood, a reminder that would be paralleled in her 42 years of continual mourning?

Like the somewhat confusing sign by the side of Route 31, these markers of the lives of President and First Lady Polk have remained to challenge and pique the interest of visitors here to Columbia, Tennessee. Perhaps they tell an all too comprehensible story of a man and a woman who found their ascendency to the highest positions in the land almost too grand to believe. Polk's humble beginnings had ultimately led to showy swords, encrusted fans, and an elegant home, now destroyed. Only the fragments of their realized dream remain here in this quiet, modest place. Or perhaps James K. Polk was someone else entirely. His "ancestral home" gives only clues, no "Manifest" conclusions.

II

Zachary Taylor: "...devoted to the Union..."

12th President Zachary Taylor (1849-1850): Springfield in Louisville, KY

By 1848, the Whigs has learned to love generals. Their general-candidates had won the White House for them in two of the three most recent national elections. But this love affair with generals hadn't been easy for the Whigs. A decade earlier it had been their collective hatred of a general that had galvanized this rather disparate collection of sectional factions into creating a new political party, the fourth to emerge in the relatively young history of the United States of America.

In fact the only issue on which all their members could reliably agree was their uniform aversion to General, now President, Andrew Jackson. The Whigs labeled him, "King Andrew," and they despised both the policies and the person of "Old Hickory." Why?

For starters, because in his eight years in office, Jackson had vetoed more bills than had been vetoed by all six of the Presidents who had preceded him combined. In so doing, the Whigs concluded, this President had evidenced his willingness to overrule Congressional legislation whenever it suited him to do so. In addition, Jackson had shrugged off the rule of law, particularly in his reported quip regarding the verdict of the Supreme Court in the famous case of *Cherokee Nation vs. Georgia:* "Well, John Marshall [the Chief Justice of the Supreme Court] has made his decision: *now let him enforce it.*" And most troubling of all, the Whigs had despised Jackson for ignoring both common sense and the financial security of the nation in his unilateral determination to destroy the Second National Bank of the United States in favor of his own set of much less reliable regional "pet banks." The Whigs all agreed that "King Andrew" Jackson, together with his minions of the Democratic Party, had to be thrown out of office.

Doing so was easier said than done, however. The constituents of this new Whig party were so sectional and so diverse that in 1836, the first presidential election after their founding, they were unable to reach a consensus on any one candidate, fielding instead three Whig contenders against Jackson's chosen successor, Vice President Martin Van Buren. Against such a divided field, Van Buren won handily, and the Democrats retained the White House for another four years.

In 1840, the Whigs changed their strategy. If Americans wanted a general (or one of his followers) to be their Chief Executive, they reasoned, the Whigs would find a general of their own. William Henry Harrison, an Indian fighter and hero of the battle of Tippecanoe, became the Whig candidate in the election of 1840. His national popularity as a war hero, together with the country's malaise resulting from the economic depression which had characterized the years of the Van Buren administration, swept Harrison into office with a comfortable margin of over a hundred and fifty electoral votes. Finally the Whigs had hit upon the way to win the White House and take control of the rudder of the Ship of State.

For, it turned out, one month. The overall plan had been simple enough. Elect a Whig President, and then, Harrison being somewhat advanced in years, the most influential Whigs in the legislative branch of government (Henry Clay, Daniel Webster, and John Calhoun—the so-called "Great Triumvirate") would instruct him as to what he should do as Chief Executive.

Only it hadn't worked out that way. Perhaps because he resented the "Log Cabin and Hard Cider" theme of the Whig election campaign which, although it won him the Presidency, had characterized him as something of a backwoods rube, Harrison decided to write what is still the longest inaugural address in the history of the United States. Its language was filled with classical allusions and erudition. Three of its sentences will suffice to illustrate its tone:

> We have examples of republics where the love of country and of liberty at one time were the dominant passions of the whole mass of citizens, and yet, with the continuance of the name and forms of free government, not a vestige of these qualities remaining in the bosom of any one of its citizens. It was the beautiful remark of a distinguished English writer that 'in the Roman senate Octavius had a party and Antony a party, but the Commonwealth had none.' Yet the senate continued to meet in the temple of liberty to talk of the sacredness and beauty of the Commonwealth and gaze at the statues of the elder Brutus and of the Curtii and Decii, and the people assembled in the forum, not, as in the days of Camillus and the Scipios, to cast their free votes for annual magistrates or pass upon the acts of the senate, but to receive from the hands of the leaders of the respective parties their share

of the spoils and to shout for one or the other, as those col-
lected in Gaul or Egypt or the lesser Asia would furnish
the larger dividend.

History has been relatively mute regarding the popular response to this torrential display of verbiage, but the combination of its extreme length, the chilliness of inauguration day, President Harrison's decision not to wear appropriately warm clothing for the occasion, plus the numerous demands made on any newcomer to the office of the Presidency, proved lethal for the old general. His administration lasted only thirty days.

For the first time in the history of the United States, a President had died in office. Would this event necessitate a hastily called national election? Who would govern in the interim? What would be the role, if any, of the Vice President, Virginian John Tyler? Although no one in the Whig party knew for certain the answers to such questions, Tyler himself was quite confident regarding the matter. At the decease of the elected President, he maintained, the Vice President [namely he himself] assumed the full mantle of the office of President of the United States. And President Tyler wasted no time in asserting his rights in this regard.

Perhaps had he been as tractable as the "Great Triumvirate" had hoped President Harrison would have been, John Tyler's term in office might have gone more smoothly. But Tyler was no frontier general looking for political guidance. He was a Tidewater Virginian whose ancestors traced their lineage back to the very founding of Jamestown. He was no Jacksonian Democrat, but neither was he interested in any interference with his legislative and political goals—even from the most respected Whig members of his own cabinet. He informed them, "... I can never consent to being dictated to as to what I shall or shall not do .... I am the President .... When you think otherwise, your resignations will be accepted" (Pious 82).

Such pronouncements had driven the Whigs wild. Additionally, President Tyler abandoned some of the most cherished Whig financial and tariff programs. He crossed swords with the venerable Henry Clay over the issue of rechartering the Second National Bank of the United States. Before his first year as Chief Executive had passed, all but one of his cabinet ministers had resigned their posts, and the Whigs officially expelled the President from their political party. The result was a legislative stalemate for the remainder of his term of office.

The Democrats, of course, stood to benefit from all this political chaos. In 1844 they nominated and elected a "dark horse" candidate, James K. Polk, whose chief claim to fame was his devotion to and personal relationship with the aging Andrew Jackson. Polk was identified as "Young Hickory" to remind voters of his pedigree. He narrowly defeated his Whig opponent, Henry Clay, by less than 40,000 popular votes, and once again the Democrats regained the White House.

The Whigs weren't finished, however. As 1848 approached, they knew that they had learned what it took to capture the Presidency. All they needed was the right standard-bearer, and here, ironically enough, President Polk had helped them immensely. As far as the Whigs were concerned, Polk's recent war with Mexico, however politically—and even ethically—suspect it may have been, had provided them with a perfect candidate for the office of Chief Executive: General Zachary Taylor, the old "Rough-and-Ready" veteran of the second Seminole Indian war and the hero of Buena Vista in the war with Mexico. Though a complete stranger to politics—he had never cast a vote in a presidential election—Taylor won the Whig nomination with relative ease.

Once again, the formula worked like a charm. Although not a landslide victory, Taylor received over 100,000 more popular votes than his nearest competitor. The Whigs were back in power once again.

But who exactly had they elected? Not even the Whigs seemed to know for sure. He was a professional soldier, actually the first Chief Executive to have spent his entire adult life in the military. He was a Southerner and a slave owner whose youth had been spent in what was then the far frontier territory of western Kentucky. He had been an Indian fighter and a courageous participant in numerous battles. And he had been willing to run for office as a Whig. But beyond this, no one really knew just what it was that he would stand for as a President. Horace Mann, recently elected Whig Representative from the state of Massachusetts, commented somewhat wryly on the character of the new President:

> *He has the least show or pretension about him of any man I ever saw; talks as artlessly as a child about affairs of state, and does not seem to pretend to a knowledge of anything of which he is ignorant. He is a remarkable man in some respects, and it is remarkable that such a man should be President of the United States.*

Mann had been elected to fill the vacancy in the House of Representatives created by the death of John Quincy Adams, and one senses in his comment on the new President, his concerns for the country. The striking difference between the political expertise and scholarly intelligence of Adams when compared to the roughhewn and unkempt Zachary Taylor must have shocked the newly minted Congressman. Taylor was clearly honest and unpretentious, Mann was quick to admit, but would that be enough? Where was the "gravitas" one expected of a President?

President Taylor himself would soon make very clear to both his political party and to the nation at large just where his priorities lay. In his mercifully brief inauguration address, after promising to govern in such a way as to serve only "the best interests of the country," he quickly went on to identify just what, in his view, were those "best interests":

> *I shall look with confidence to the enlightened patriotism of [Congress] to adopt such measures of conciliation as may harmonize conflicting interests and tend to perpetuate that Union which should be the paramount object of our hopes and affections.*

The new Whig President was a Union man. His uncompromising commitment to this cause would come to characterize completely his brief term in office. And, once again, a Whig Chief Executive would find himself pitted against some prominent members of his own party, the party that had paved his way to the White House.

Southern elements of the Whig party had assumed that the new President, being a slave owner himself, would be at the very least a strong advocate of states' rights. John Calhoun may even have expected to find an ally in President Taylor regarding the expansion of slavery into the new western territories acquired as a result of the war with Mexico in which the general had played such a prominent role.

Henry Clay, similarly, must have been heartened by the President's inauguration promise to look to Congress for the "measures of conciliation" that would lessen the increasingly strident factionalism that was threatening to tear apart the young nation from within.

Yet both these important figures in the Whig party were to be disappointed in their hopes and expectations. President Taylor became a strong advocate for admitting both the territories of California and New Mexico as free states, thus upsetting the delicate balance of power in the United States Senate and infuriating the Southern Whigs who had supported his candidacy.

Even more inexplicable to the Whigs was Taylor's threat to veto Henry Clay's "omnibus bill" that included state sovereignty regarding the extension of slavery in the western territories, the abolishment of slavery in the District of Columbia, and a strengthened Fugitive Slave Law to placate southern interests. Why would the President threaten to reject such "measures of conciliation," compromises such as he himself had called for in his inaugural address?

Because, as he had also identified in that same address, President Taylor's primary concern was the preservation of the Union. He understood that the omnibus bill forwarded by Clay would have a difficult time getting through Congress, and even if it managed to pass, would only postpone, not solve, the larger problem of sectional dissent over slavery. History would ultimately prove him right in this assessment, though not in his lifetime.

In early July of his second year in office, Zachary Taylor suddenly became ill and died. Once again, the death of a Whig President resulted in making a Vice President, in this case Millard Fillmore, a staunch Whig, the new Chief Executive. President Fillmore would come to sign into law the so-called Compromise of 1850, a piecemeal version of Clay's earlier omnibus bill. And, just as President Taylor had feared, this "great" compromise proved to be ineffective in solving the civil tensions plaguing the nation.

In the years following his death, and with the notable exception of those conspiracy theorists who believed—wrongly it turned out—that he had been poisoned because of his resistance to the expansion of slavery into the western territories, the Presidency of Zachary Taylor faded into obscurity. His military record left a more lasting legacy than his abbreviated political life.

Today even Louisville seems to have largely forgotten their native son. The only surviving home associated with him is privately owned and is not open to the public. This plantation house named "Springfield" is where Zachary grew to manhood. It is now surrounded by a suburban subdivision of homes occupying land that was once the frontier location of the 700-acre Taylor family farm.

The white brick home, the older section of which juts slightly out from the expansive addition made by the Taylor family after Zachary had joined the army, sits gracefully but unobtrusively on a 3/4-acre lot. A small historical plaque has been placed on the street, identifying the site as the boyhood home of Zachary Taylor, the 12th President of the United States. Yet even this rather inconspicuous memorial is not exclusively dedicated to preserving his memory. The plaque's text ends by noting that President Taylor's daughter, Sarah, had married Jefferson Davis, and that their son, Richard, had served as a general in the Confederacy during the Civil War.

A short drive away, on what was once the edge of the Taylor family's acreage, the President and First Lady's gravesite and mausoleum stands as part of a larger national military cemetery. Here at least is a tall square cut column surmounted with a life-size statue of the general and President. Inscribed on the sides of the monument is a list of his most noteworthy achievements, together with a transcription of his last words: "I have endeavored to do my duty. I am ready to die. My only regret is for the friends I leave behind me."

So what is one to make of this second Whig general elevated to the Presidency? It is interesting that, even though a Southern slave owner, President Taylor had been such an ardent Unionist. Thomas Hart Benton, Senator from Missouri, summed up his praise of the President in glowing terms:

Zachary Taylor's Grave Monument

> *His death was a public calamity. No man could have been more devoted to the Union; or more opposed to the slavery agitation; and his position as a Southern man would have given him a power in the settlement of these questions which no President without these qualifications could have possessed. (Eisenhower, Taylor 137)*

Of course, this is pure speculation on Senator Benton's part. No one can assuredly know how successful President Taylor might have been in averting the coming crisis that would erupt into the disastrous carnage of the Civil War only eleven years after his death. There is something intriguing, however, about Taylor's adamant devotion to the Union. And it becomes particularly fascinating in the context of the other two Presidents who shared a similar dedication to the same ideal: Andrew Jackson and Abraham Lincoln.

What links these men is not the fact that they regarded themselves as "Southern men." Lincoln unquestionably would have rejected that description. Their common bond and their shared experience was life lived on the frontier of the nation. And this may well have forged in each of them an understanding of the absolute necessity of union. On the frontier, union was essentially synonymous with survival.

Wilderness settings had taught each of these men the importance of standing and working together. It had been the only way to insure the well-being of the communities of which they were a part.

All three of these men had worked to clear the land on which they had lived and farmed. They had all taken refuge in hastily constructed shelters and had learned to weather the sort of physical hardships that had already passed into history in Massachusetts and Tidewater Virginia. Jackson, Taylor, and even Lincoln for a short time in the Blackhawk war, had banded together with other settlers to fight the threat of Indian attacks. They knew intimately and personally, as Ben Franklin had stated in the early days of the colonies before the Revolution, that the choice of Americans on the frontier was simple: "Unite or Die." And, even more importantly, they understood that the meaning of that phrase applied as much to their nation as it did to the rigors of frontier or military life. If this great experiment in democracy, if this country governed by and for the people, was to survive, it would have to remain unified.

For Zachary Taylor then, as well as for Presidents Jackson and Lincoln, preserving the Union trumped all other concerns. If the nation were to be splintered and divided according to sectional differences, everything which each of them had fought for and devoted his life to would be lost.

In a eulogy written shortly after President Taylor's death, Abraham Lincoln, then a young Congressman from Illinois, wrote that the demeanor and bearing of the recently departed Chief Executive had illustrated "...the great truth that 'he that humbleth himself shall be exalted.' " But it was Thomas Hart Benton who had identified the essence of the man, when he said of the "rough and ready" career soldier and President from Kentucky: "No man could have been more devoted to the Union."

12

Millard Fillmore: "Now you see him...now you..."

13th President Millard Fillmore (1850-1853): *Millard Fillmore House in East Aurora, NY*

"One scoop or two in your waffle cone?" the girl asked me as Carol and I stood in an ice cream shop on Main Street in East Aurora, New York. "One is fine," I answered her. The late June day had become unseasonably warm, and the prospect of ice cream had been irresistible. We pulled chairs up to the small table near the counter, and the girl, whose name we later learned was Caitlin, brought us our cones.

No one else was currently in the shop, and we struck up a conversation with Caitlin. She was a recent high school graduate and was looking forward to college where she intended to go into nursing. Being a longtime teacher, I decided to give her a quick quiz.

"Do you know that this ice cream shop is located next to the spot where a President once lived?"

"No," Caitlin answered, her eyes widening a bit, "Really?"

"His house was once right next door on Main Street, where the Aurora theatre is now. Later, the house was moved to the back of the lot before it was relocated to Shearer Avenue where it stands today. And across the street there," we all looked out the front window of the ice cream shop, "right where Vidler's 5 and 10 store stands today, were the law offices where he worked before his career in politics."

"That's amazing," Caitlin responded. "Which President was this?"

"Millard Fillmore."

Caitlin's face clouded. "Millard Fillmore," she repeated, her forehead slightly furrowed. Then I saw a light in her eyes. "That's why they named the hospital Millard Fillmore Suburban! I hadn't known. Thanks for telling me."

Carol and I finished our cones and walked back out to our car. It wasn't as if our 13th President had been completely neglected by East Aurora. The next street over, behind the theatre lot, was "Millard Fillmore Avenue," and the 5 and 10 store did have a small plaque in a corner of its display window identifying the fact that Fillmore's law office had occupied that spot until the building had burned down in 1904. But our conversation with Caitlin did bring to mind one of the first pieces of information I had ever learned about Millard Fillmore. For a number of years, members of a group styling itself "The Millard Fillmore Society" had convened annually on the President's birthday to "celebrate his invisibility."

As a result of our travels, Carol and I have come to appreciate not only the humor of that event but also its odd accuracy in describing the man. More than almost any other American President, Millard Fillmore has indeed become "invisible." Why?

There are a number of partially true explanations. Like John Tyler before him and like other less well remembered Presidents after him (e.g. Andrew Johnson and Chester Arthur), Millard Fillmore was a so-called "accidental President," a man who became Chief Executive of the United States only because of the death of a President. In addition, he, like these other men, was not nominated by his party as their presidential candidate in the succeeding election. The Whigs chose war hero Winfred Scott as their standard-bearer in 1852. But perhaps most importantly, President Fillmore would come to be seen by later historians as having been on the wrong side of history, choosing to support a version of Henry Clay's Compromise of 1850, rather than running the risk of plunging the nation into a bloody civil war.

Indeed, his final State of the Union address to Congress in December of 1852 carries with it a sense of pungent irony, given a knowledge of the upcoming events of the next fifteen years:

> *...permit me, fellow-citizens, to congratulate you on the prosperous condition of our beloved country. Abroad its relations with all foreign powers are friendly, its rights are respected, and its high place in the family of nations cheerfully recognized. At home we enjoy an amount of happiness, public and private, which has probably never fallen to to the lot of any other people....We owe these blessings, under Heaven, to the happy Constitution and Government which were bequeathed to us by our fathers, and which it is our sacred duty to transmit in all their integrity to our children.... it is with devout gratitude in retiring from office that I leave the country in a state of peace and prosperity.*

Such an assessment of the condition of the nation in 1852 could have—and has—been seen as indicative of Fillmore's political naiveté. In truth, it constitutes the President's ardent hope that the problems facing the United States had, in fact, been resolved by the achievements of his administration. Those achievements deserve to be understood.

Although Fillmore's years as Chief Executive are frequently regarded solely in terms of the contentious issue of slavery, he oversaw several significant foreign policy successes to which he was alluding in this last State of the Union address. By sending Commodore Perry on a mission to open Japanese ports to American ships and American trade, President Fillmore initiated a vital foothold for his country's economic interests in Asia. He had also prevented France from forcibly acquiring Hawaii by informing French leader Napoleon III that the United States would not tolerate any such efforts to annex these vital mid-Pacific islands. Closer to home, the President had negotiated quite skillfully with England, Spain, and France to avoid going to war over Cuba after a Venezuelan adventurer, Narciso Lopez, had, with backing from a number of prominent Americans from southern states, made two abortive attempts to gain control of that important Caribbean island. These foreign policy successes led to his comments regarding the United States' "high place in the family of nations." No foreign powers were pushing around the American government or impinging on American interests.

Domestically, of course, the central debate of the day concerned the question of slavery—its expansion, its elimination, or its continuance. But in order to understand President Fillmore's stance on this problem, it is important to appreciate how Henry Clay's suggested compromise constituted a determined effort to address and, at least temporarily, to defuse this divisive issue.

The southern states had made it clear that any attempt by the federal government to abolish the institution of slavery would be seen as an attack on their economic lifeblood. The southern economy—dependent largely on the exportation of cotton—relied upon the slave labor system that had predominated in the South for over a hundred and fifty years, a system both acknowledged in and protected by the original Constitution of the United States.

The northern states, having eliminated the practice of slavery within their borders, saw involuntary servitude as an evil that should be rooted out of the country. Surely, they believed, it should not be permitted to expand into territories newly belonging to the United States, such as those most recently acquired in the war with Mexico.

Henry Clay's solution was an omnibus compromise bill intended to do for the 1850's what his earlier Missouri Compromise bill had done for the 1820's: allow each side a victory and provide a period of time for tempers to cool and for the nation to remain whole, despite its social and economic differences. Perhaps future legislators, Clay hoped, would be able to resolve the problems which appeared insoluble at the present moment.

In a speech lasting five hours Clay proposed a bill that had something for everyone. It protected the institution of slavery by strengthening the fugitive slave laws, enabling southern slave owners to recover runaway "property" found in non-slave states. The larger purpose of this portion of the bill was to assure the southern states that there would be no congressional attempt to circumvent the Constitution or outlaw slavery.

To appeal to the northern states, Clay's bill proposed both admitting the state of California to the Union as a free state and eliminating the slave trade in the District of Columbia. The larger intent here, of course, was to acknowledge the importance of a gradual elimination of slavery—including a limitation on its expansion—as the nation moved forward.

President Zachary Taylor had opposed Clay's plan, but Millard Fillmore, along with the famed Senator from Massachusetts Daniel Webster, had seen the bill as the only means by which the union could be preserved without bloodshed. Fillmore, as Vice President, had informed President Taylor that, if necessary, he would cast a tie-breaking vote in the Senate in favor of the bill. Now that he had become President, casting such a vote was no longer a possibility.

History, of course, shows that although Clay's omnibus bill initially failed to pass, Stephen A. Douglas, a young Senator from Illinois, had been able to break the bill into pieces and pass each section separately. Thus the components of Clay's Compromise of 1850 were ultimately enacted by Congress and signed into law by President Fillmore. History also informs us that these compromise measures would prove to be unsuccessful in placating either northern or southern interests. But to the legislators of 1850, the prospect of avoiding a devastating internal conflict by enacting a compromise generated by Henry Clay, a famed legislator whose earlier compromise had yielded thirty years of national prosperity and growth, was a measure not to be taken lightly. In signing these pieces of legislation into law, the President believed he had accomplished something very similar to what President Monroe had done thirty years earlier when he had signed the Missouri Compromise: guarantee another extended period of "good feeling" and prosperity.

None of this course of action was the result of political naiveté. President Fillmore knew exactly what he was doing and exactly what he was trying to save, as is evidenced in a letter he wrote to Daniel Webster in 1850:

> *God knows I detest slavery, but it is an existing evil, for which we are not responsible, and we must endure it, and give it such protection as is guaranteed by the constitution, till we can get rid of it without destroying the last hope of free government in the world.*

He also implied his thoughts on the matter in his State of the Union Address of 1851 in which he proposed architectural additions to the nation's capital buildings. Although purportedly referring only to the architect's designs, President Fillmore's words voiced a vital and far-reaching truth. His proposed plan for the redesign and expansion of the capital was modest, not radical. While it was clear that more space was needed in the legislative buildings, "It was also desirable not to mar the harmony and beauty of the present structure, which, as a specimen of architecture, is so universally admired."

The "harmony and beauty of the present structure," this "last hope of free government in the world" needed, above all, to be preserved intact. President Fillmore earnestly wished and hoped that this second great compromise would succeed in bringing about exactly that result.

It didn't. Fillmore was castigated by both North and South for his backing of the Compromise of 1850, and, at his term's end, that cloak of invisibility began to descend upon his memory. Everybody, it seemed, simply wanted to forget him.

But not Kathy Frost, Curator of the Millard Fillmore Home Museum in East Aurora, New York. From the moment I first heard Ms. Frost's recorded voice on her answering machine, I knew that Carol and I would like her. ("Hello, it's another beautiful day in East Aurora, so please leave me a funny and happy message, and I'll return the same. Bye now. Beep.") She is a most worthy keeper of the memory of our 13th President.

While there are two sites associated with Millard Fillmore, only one of them actually boasts a home that had been lived in by the President and his wife, Abigail: the small frame dwelling on Shearer Avenue in East Aurora, New York. Here the Fillmores had begun their married life in 1826 and here, two years later, their first child had been born. Although the home is usually open only three days a week during the vacation months, Kathy was quite willing to have us come on an off day for a separate tour. Happily we didn't need that special dispensation, but her ready willingness to provide it was typical of her eagerness to share her considerable knowledge of President Fillmore with people interested in learning more about him.

We arrived in the early afternoon and were quickly included in a small group who were just being invited into the home's front parlor. Yet even here, I noted, President Fillmore was not solely the focus of our first docent's presentation. We were told about the Riley family who had purchased the house in 1830 when the Fillmores moved to Buffalo, and then we learned about Margaret Evans Price, a children's book author, who had moved the home to its present location in 1930, using it as an art studio.

The Fillmore invisibility problem was made even more palpably clear to me when, on display in this modest front parlor, I saw a framed copy of a fundraising letter that had been sent out by the

East Aurora Historical Society in hopes that recipients would contribute donations in support of the refurbishment of the house. This missive included an "actual section of wood from the East Aurora home of Millard Fillmore." Although each piece of wood was barely an inch long and only a half-inch wide, it struck me as bizarre that the Historical Society would find it necessary to give away chips of the floor joists in order to attract donors to contribute to the restoration of the only remaining home of a President of the United States.

The museum had made earnest efforts to track down and acquire a number of artifacts that had once belonged to the family. Millard Fillmore's East Aurora law desk was here in a small side room. In an upstairs bedroom, a 100% silk Tumbling Block pattern quilt made by Abigail was spread out as a coverlet on a bed once owned by the Fillmores. In the back kitchen, a scrub table consisting of two wide wooden planks joined down the middle stood before the kitchen fireplace. "We believe that Mr. Fillmore himself made that table," our docent informed us.

Kathy Frost was our docent in the last room on our tour: the library, an addition made to the house by Margaret Evans Price in 1930. It held the most significant Fillmore artifacts. Here was a pianoforte that had been owned by the Fillmore's daughter, Mary Abigail; here were the traveling trunks of their son, Millard Powers. Kathy also pointed out to us the famous lithograph of Henry Clay addressing the Senate as he presented his Compromise Bill of 1850. "Notice in the upper right," she instructed us, "you'll see Mr. Fillmore presiding over the deliberations in the Senate chamber." I frankly confess that, although I had seen this lithograph reproduced in several history books, I had never noticed Fillmore's presence in the engraving. He was becoming more visible to me each time Kathy spoke.

Then, pointing across the room to a large mahogany bookcase occupying much of the opposite wall, she continued, "Both Abigail Fillmore and the President were avid readers. When they arrived at the White House, Abigail was astonished to find that there was no presidential library there. She requested a budget to establish one and received an annual sum of $1,250 to do so. She bought this bookcase to house the collection she started." We looked at the books crowded into this impressive case.

"Are these the books she purchased?" a member of our group asked. "No," Kathy responded. "As far as I know they are all still in the White House Library that she began. But there are two or three volumes here that the Fillmores owned. You'll see them opened on the shelves with lighting over them." Here Kathy pushed a couple of buttons on an electronic remote, and lights appeared above three open volumes in the case.

Our tour was nearly over, and Kathy invited the group outside to join another docent to go over to the carriage barn where an original Fillmore sleigh was stored. I lingered behind, however, wanting to talk a bit longer to this knowledgeable woman.

"What speaks to you most about this house, Ms. Frost?" I asked her. "What tells you the most about President Fillmore?"

Kathy thought a moment, and then she said, "The fact that he built this house with his own two hands," she answered, smiling. "Look at that wooden beam," she walked over to it and gently moved her fingers across its polished surface. "Smoothed by Mr. Fillmore's own hand. That speaks to me."

I loved the reverence in her voice. "It strikes me," I replied, "that, if the Compromise of 1850 had given the country another thirty years of peace, there would probably be busloads of people coming here each year to celebrate the life and accomplishments of this President who helped to save the Union."

Kathy smiled again and responded, "Perhaps, but we're happy just to have the chance to tell his story to any visitor who comes."

I thanked her for the tour and moved outside to find Carol. We weren't quite finished yet with Millard Fillmore. Our next presidential stop would be a few hours east, the site of his birthplace near Moravia, New York. It would turn out to be a textbook example of how to make a President disappear.

The drive to Moravia, particularly after leaving the interstate, was a study in picturesque rural roadways and breathtaking scenery. Long lakes appeared in the valleys whenever the crooked two lane roads crested a hill, farmland spread out on either side of the highway, and the intensely blue sky was lightly mottled with fluffy clouds that made the day seem like a pastoral idyll. Our immediate goal was the encouragingly named Fillmore Glen State Park to visit a replica of the log cabin where the 13th President had been born in January of 1800.

We finally arrived in Moravia and then followed our GPS system's directions to the south end of town, just beyond which lay the state park. After turning into its entry, we saw a small gatehouse at which we were instructed to stop and pay an admission fee. We did so and received a map of the expansive park grounds.

The location of the cabin was marked on this map, but we took several wrong turns before Carol finally spied it on the far side of a field. "There it is," she said, pointing in its direction. We entered a parking area nearby, but found no identifying markers to urge visitors down any perceptible path leading to the cabin.

The roughhewn structure was almost buried in the deep woods of the hillside that rose behind it, and we could see that no one was near the cabin as we moved across the field toward it. The only visible identification of the site was a simple wooden sign which read "Millard Fillmore   1800-1874,   Thirteenth President of the United States."

Millard Fillmore's Reconstructed Log Cabin near Moravia, NY

The home's interior was as basic and rustic as any imaginable pioneer setting. Here indeed was a "log cabin President," as assuredly as Andrew Jackson or Abraham Lincoln had ever been. It contained only two tables, a few chairs, a cradle, and a sparse assortment of necessary utensils. A door in the front and two side windows gave the inner rooms their only light. A large stone fireplace was centered in the cabin, presumably providing the entire structure with adequate heat in the bitterly cold winters of this Finger Lake section of New York. I was struck with the remarkableness of the fact that a future President could have ever emerged from a setting as inhospitable as this. How could we ever forget or neglect to value such an example of individual drive and persistence? Surely, I thought, there must be a greater recognition of President Fillmore here than this simple isolated cabin. And then I saw a beautiful garden just east of the site with a flag on a silver pole waving gently in the breeze.

"Carol," I called out. "Let's go over and see whether they made a more fitting memorial of the President over there."

This new location certainly was more appreciably well-kept than had been the cabin site. Close to the flagpole we found a lovely bronze plaque which carried the following inscription:

U.S. CIVILIAN CONSERVATION CORPS
FRANKLIN D.ROOSEVELT'S TREE ARMY
We do hereby commemorate CCC Camp No. SP. 33 and the side camp that were located in Fillmore Glen State Park (1934-1938) and those CCC men who protected and enhanced the natural resources and their beauty in the watersheds of the Finger Lakes
Arbor Day 1993 – Cayuga Chapter New York Forest Owners Association

Even here in a state park bearing his name, Millard Fillmore was being trumped by the achievements of another, more famously visible, President from New York. It was a telling preamble to our upcoming final stop of the day.

"Should we try to find the original cabin site before we leave the vicinity?" I asked Carol as we returned to our car.

"Absolutely," Carol responded immediately. "We're not in this area very often, and the guidebook says it's only about five miles away."

I agreed and, as we left the park grounds, I stopped again at the gatehouse to get directions to the site.

"You can't miss it," the park ranger on duty assured me. "Just take the third right turn out of town and head up into the hills. You'll see a picnic pavilion on your left. That's where the Fillmore cabin once stood."

I have come to mistrust the phrase "You can't miss it," and this occasion provided me with another instance of why this is the case. We took a wrong turn and, after traveling several more miles than five, we headed back to Moravia where we recalibrated our route and got it right this time. Sure enough, as we drove up the rather precipitous hillsides, we came to an open meadow on which stood a pavilion with a prominent flagpole topped by a fluttering American flag.

By the roadside a historical marker indicated that "in the adjacent field" Millard Fillmore, 13th President of the United States, had been born in January of 1800.

We pulled up a gravel driveway near the pavilion in which a group of senior citizens were readying a picnic lunch. We certainly didn't want to disturb the group, but we had to take a few photos, so we left the car to get our shots in as unobtrusive a manner as possible. I noticed a beautiful plaque placed near the pavilion, and I walked up to it to see what the local Historical Society had to say about this place. To my surprise I found a very different inscription here than anything I had anticipated:

Millard Fillmore Pavilion
13th US President, 1850-1853
Donated by Nucor Corporation through its Nucor
Steel Auburn, Nucor Building Systems Indiana and
Vulcraft New York divisions, working with the citizens
of Summerhill. Wholly designed and constructed by
Nucor using Nucor steel products containing 70-98%
recycled steel.

I didn't know whether to laugh or simply sigh, but whatever emotional reaction I was experiencing was interrupted by a sweet older lady named Betsy who walked over to me to let me know that her group had reserved the pavilion for the day. I assured her that we were only stopping momentarily and that we were doing research for a book on presidential homes. Betsy was immediately interested.

"But," I couldn't resist observing, "everyone seems to have pretty much forgotten President Fillmore here in Moravia."

"Oh, I don't know," Betsy protested gently. "I believe there's a room in the Historical Society downtown that has some of the Fillmore belongings ... and then ..." her eyes lit up, "we have Millard Fillmore Days."

I was intrigued. "Really?" I questioned her, "What happens then?"

"Oh, it's a big time for arts and craft sales. It was rained out last year, though. That was a shame. But then there's a man who always reenacts history. He gets all dressed up like ..." Betsy paused, trying to remember a name. " ... like," she began again," not Mr. Fillmore, but another politician of that age. I think it was ..." Another long pause. " ... not Seward but ...."

"Henry Clay?" I ventured.

"Yes! Henry Clay! It's a great time for everyone. And, of course, there's the cabin in Fillmore Glen State Park."

I assured Betsy that we had just come from there, and I thanked her for taking the time to speak with me. She wished us well and turned to rejoin her friends as their picnic was just getting underway. Carol and I walked back to our car. We pulled out of the parking lot onto the road and headed east back toward the interstate. It was some time before we spoke.

"Let's just remember Millard Fillmore for a while," I suggested. Carol nodded in agreement. "Now you see him," I thought, "now you ...."

13

Franklin Pierce: "...young for the station..."

14th President Franklin Pierce (1853-1857): The Pierce Homestead in Hillsborough, NH

My father was an opera singing, roughhewn, "over the Rhine," scrubby-Dutch carpenter turned general contractor from Cincinnati, Ohio. In my memory he started out most mornings with a 6 1/2 ounce bottle of Coca-Cola in one hand and a peeled banana in the other. He would consume this unusual breakfast while sitting in his favorite armchair in our living room, thinking through the challenges of the upcoming day. "Putting in my worry time," he called it.

Yet what impressed me most about my dad's abilities as a home builder was the way in which he could speak to the various workmen in his employ. He was master of a number of languages, all of which related directly to the task at hand. On many occasions I have heard him speak fluent Carpentry to the carpenters, perfect Wiring to the electricians, and flawless Pipe Fitting to the plumbers. And, even more remarkable, he was able to speak to each workman in a voice exactly suited to the man he was addressing. One he would finesse with compliments and occasional commiseration. Another he would command in a vocal tone that, to my young ears, seemed like thinly veiled brutality. The wonder of it all was the end result. His workmen invariably built homes with a degree of excellence that made my father one of the city's most respected and sought after home builders. By the end of his career, he had established such a reputation that architects gave him commissions without even asking him to submit bids. "If you want the job done right," they would say, "get Karl Beim-Esche."

Once, as a young adult, I asked him about his method of speaking to the various journeymen he had hired. "How do you know how to talk to each of them?" I asked, adding, "I might have been critical of the one you soothed, and I probably would have been gentle to the one you yelled at. What's the secret of knowing exactly what words and what inflections to use that will get the results you're after?"

Dad looked thoughtful for a moment. Then he answered me with a single word.

"Experience," he said.

As a people we Americans love youth. We love products that are "new" and "improved." We name our cities New York, New Castle, and New Haven. If we think of the Old World at all, we give our states such names as New Hampshire, New Jersey, and New Mexico.

Politically, our souls are stirred by the promise of a "New Deal" or a "New Frontier." But sometimes the eager acceptance of whatever is *new* can carry with it a dangerous tendency to discount whatever has proven itself to be most wise. Youth can indeed mean freshness, idealism, and vigor. Yet it can also mean inexperience, ill-advised certainty, and miscalculation. In 19th century American history, it meant Franklin Pierce.

Even his first biographer, his collegiate (and ultimately lifelong) friend, Nathaniel Hawthorne, observed the extraordinary rapidity with which Franklin Pierce had advanced in the world of politics. In his campaign biography of Pierce, Hawthorne observed, "He was elected a member of Congress in 1833, being young for the station, as he has always been for every public station that he has filled" (366).

Indeed, Franklin Pierce's rise to prominence had started early when, in 1820, at age 15, he entered Bowdoin College in Maine. Graduating four years later, in 1824, Pierce went on to study law, passing the New Hampshire bar in 1827 at the relatively callow age of 23.

After less than two full years of practicing law, he was elected to the New Hampshire state legislature. At 24 years old, he was easily its youngest member, and yet he cut a very impressive figure in that legislative forum. Three re-elections later (each term lasting one year), he was voted Speaker of the legislature. In 1833 he ran and was elected to the national House of Representatives; he was 29 years old when he took this first step onto the national stage. Between sessions of Congress, Pierce returned to New Hampshire, married the daughter of a former president of Bowdoin College, and, in the following year, was re-elected to Congress for a second term. In 1837, before this term in the House had ended, the state legislature of New Hampshire voted to send Pierce to the United States Senate where, once again, now in his 33rd year, he had the distinction of being the youngest member in that body of august legislators, being surrounded by such giants as Daniel Webster, Henry Clay, and John Calhoun. Political ascendency had come upon Franklin Pierce with impressive speed.

Yet in spite of this series of precocious advancements, in some ways Franklin Pierce may still have felt himself lagging behind his most important influence and example: his own father, Benjamin Pierce.

Benjamin, while lacking the education he had provided for his son, had the sort of background that made him a very hard act to follow. At 17, while plowing his uncle's farmland, he had learned of the first shots of the Revolution. Immediately he had left the plow in the field, borrowed his uncle's gun, and had gone off to join Washington's army, where he served with distinction until the end of the war. He had returned home with the rank of Brigade Major.

After moving to New Hampshire, Benjamin had been instrumental in forming the Hillsborough County militia, and by 1805 had been made a Brigadier General of the militia of the entire state. He also served in the New Hampshire state legislature from 1789-1802 and was a delegate to the state's Constitutional Convention in 1791. He was a member of the Governor's Advisory Council from 1803 to 1809 and again in 1814, and was twice elected Sheriff of Hillsborough County. In 1827, the year when his son Franklin was just beginning his law practice, Benjamin Pierce was himself elected to the post of Governor of New Hampshire. He died in 1839, at the venerable age of 81.

The story of his son Franklin, the future President, begins in 1804, the year of his birth in a log cabin, the original site of which lies in the bed of a lake near the town of Hillsborough. Only a month after Franklin's birth, Benjamin and his growing family moved into the house he had built with his own hands, now known as the Homestead, a combination inn, meeting place, and family residence. The house still stands near the old Post Road in Hillsborough, and it was here that Carol and I began our tour of the locales associated with the life of our 14th President.

We arrived early in the morning and made our way to the side entrance of this impressively large clapboard home. We were met by a gentleman named Alan who introduced us to our docent for the morning, Annie. We paid our admission, and Annie led us into the back of the house through its kitchen area. She reminded us of the dual nature of the home, its public function as well as its private use. She also emphasized the importance of Benjamin's example to his young son Franklin who, she noted, had grown up surrounded by history in which his own father had played a vital role.

It was soon clear to us that it was Benjamin Pierce, rather than Franklin, who was going to be the focus of our tour, and, since it was he who had built the house after all, that seemed quite understandable. Carol and I had noticed that the back of this home, unlike the front, was painted red, so we asked Annie about that rather distinctive feature. She laughed and noted that we would also see that red paint in several of the rooms in the interior of the house. ("It was the least expensive paint available to Benjamin who was always mindful of economy," she explained.) After a short stop in the family dining area, Annie moved our small group into the public part of the house, the front parlor which had served as an inn.

"This room was very significant to the Pierce family. Benjamin's inn provided a source of income, but it also was the setting of many political discussions. The future President learned his political lessons and acquired his political beliefs, *here*." Annie gestured with a full swing of her hand.

Nathaniel Hawthorne, in his campaign biography, substantiated Annie's conclusions when he described a special celebration that had been held at the Homestead on December 26, 1825, Benjamin's 67th birthday:

> *...General Benjamin Pierce prepared a festival for his comrades in arms, the survivors of the Revolution, eighteen of whom, all inhabitants of Hillsborough, assembled at his house. The ages of these veterans ranged from fifty-nine up to the patriarchal venerableness of nearly ninety. They spent the day in festivity, in calling up reminiscences of the great men whom they had known, and the great deeds which they had helped to do, and in reviving the old sentiments of the era of 'seventy-six.' At nightfall, after a manly and pathetic farewell from their host, they separated—'prepared,' as the old general expressed it, 'at the first tap of the shrouded drum, to move and join their*

> *beloved Washington, and the rest of their comrades, who*
> *fought and bled at their sides.' (Hawthorne 361)*

Immediately following this description of Benjamin's "festival," a gathering that had occurred in the very room where we were all standing, Hawthorne draws a key conclusion, a summation with which Annie would have fully agreed:

> *A scene like this must have been profitable for a young*
> *man to witness, as being likely to give him a stronger*
> *sense than most of us can attain of the value of that*
> *Union which these old heroes had risked so much to con-*
> *solidate—of that common country which they had sac-*
> *rificed everything to create; and patriotism must have*
> *been communicated from their hearts to his, with some-*
> *what of the warmth and freshness of a newborn senti-*
> *ment. No youth was ever more fortunate than Franklin*
> *Pierce, through the whole of his early life, in this most de-*
> *sirable species of moral education. (Hawthorne 361-362)*

Well, perhaps. But the power of such a heritage can also be a considerable weight on a young man, particularly on a young man so quickly elevated to positions of authority and national consequence.

Annie then led us across the front hall to her "favorite room," the Ladies' parlor which featured a fresco-like wallpaper that had cost Benjamin the then considerable sum of $170. Even here, however, Annie was quick to point out a place where the wallpaper strips didn't quite match. "Benjamin saw no purpose in buying more wallpaper than was absolutely necessary," she observed.

Passing once more into the front hall, Annie led us upstairs to show us the ballroom, a single room that ran the entire length of the front of the house. Located directly above both the inn and the Ladies' parlor, this very large space, Annie explained, was frequently used as sleeping quarters for overnight visitors to the inn. Then she added, "Of course, dances were held here, too, as Benjamin

Pierce's home was widely known as a perfect venue for social gatherings."

Next, Annie took us back into the "family" side of the second floor where she showed us the children's bedrooms. In Franklin's room there was a campaign poster from 1852, the year of his presidential run. It was yet another reminder of Benjamin's presence in Franklin's life. In large black and white letters, the poster read "The Father and the Son: The One fought to make, The other labors to PRESERVE the Union."

We descended a narrow winding staircase back to the kitchen area and thanked Annie for our tour. A few minutes later we were on the road to Concord. "What would a young man like Franklin Pierce feel that he owed to his heritage?" I found myself asking. From his earliest moments he had been made aware of the impressive achievements of his father. Furthermore he himself had attained positions of elevated status years before he had earned the kind of success that would have logically led to such eminence. Rubbing elbows with some of the legislative giants of his day, had Franklin felt fully qualified to regard such men as colleagues, as peers, as equals? (Even in the Mexican War, because of the political offices he had held, Pierce had been promoted to the rank of Brigadier General before he had ever heard a shot fired in anger.)

I found myself remembering his inaugural speech, given at a time of mourning for his eleven year old son Benjamin who had died tragically in a train accident two months earlier. Had any American President ever spoken words so poignant as these at the very moment of taking office?

> *My countrymen: It is a relief to feel that no heart but my own can know the personal regret and bitter sorrow over which I have been borne to a position so suitable for others rather than desirable for myself.... You have summoned me in my weakness; you must sustain me by your strength.*

His immediate listeners in 1853 had assumed that the new President—at 48, the youngest man who had ever held the office—was referring to his recent personal tragedy. I wondered, however, whether, in addition, he might also have been mindful of his Vice President, William R. King, who was terminally ill and who would die within the month. Surely Franklin Pierce was already missing the welcome guidance of this man, a seasoned legislator, whose more than twenty-five years in the Senate and expertise in foreign relations would have been a distinct asset to the young President. Then again, Pierce may have simply been expressing a genuine feeling of self-doubt, an admission that might logically and honestly have occurred to anyone so "young for the station." Would the Pierce Manse in Concord hold any insight into this question? We would soon find out.

This presidential home, The Pierce Manse, is maintained by "The Pierce Brigade," an organization "dedicated to preserving the legacy of President Pierce." It had been the home of Franklin and Jane Pierce after Franklin's departure from the Senate in 1842 until his return from the War with Mexico in 1848. Carol

The Pierce Manse in Concord, New Hampshire

and I paid our admission, and our docent, a pleasant man named Tom, led us into the home's kitchen—again we were entering what would have been the rear of the house—and then through another door into the formal dining area.

Everything on display was immaculately kept, from the polished wood of the breakfront to the crockery arrayed on the dining room table. The fireplace with its brass andirons and a flawless mirror over the mantelpiece completed the lovely picture of this room, but there was nothing here which provided me with any meaningful insight into Franklin Pierce the man.

Tom then invited us into the parlor, the front room of the house. It, too, had an air of carefully preserved and maintained orderliness. However it also held an artifact that caught my eye immediately.

It was a small desk positioned between the two front windows of the parlor. It had a red leather inset writing surface, and its legs were carved wood that formed a Gothic arch on either side. A piece of delicately lathed wood served as a footrest and stabilized the legs. Tom saw my interest and was happy to comment on this artifact. "That," he began, "was the desk that President Pierce used in the White House."

Franklin Pierce's White House Desk

"Really?" I responded. "It's so small!" Its surface was slightly less than three feet wide, and its depth even shorter, perhaps just over a foot and a half. A brass lamp which occupied its left corner and a book laid flat on its surface, together with a framed picture on a tilted display stand, took up a considerable portion of its remaining area.

"Yes," Tom insisted, "President Pierce particularly enjoyed that desk, and it is one of the gems of our collection here. Of course, the Pierces did not live here during or after their White House years, but since this is the location dedicated to preserving and presenting his memory, we are delighted to have it."

Moving upstairs, Tom showed us the Pierces' bedroom and the other bedrooms on this floor. Pathos was a dominant feature here. Although they had lost their first child in infancy, it had been their second son, four year old Frank Robert, who had died of typhus in this house. Yet here the main focus was on Jane's disconsolate mourning for their third son, Benjamin. His picture and a pair of his baby boots placed lovingly on a bedroom fireplace mantle spoke eloquently of the tragic melancholy that had characterized so much of Jane's life after January of 1853. I thought of how lonely Franklin must have felt as both his one surviving child and his wife, one through a tragic accident and one through an impenetrable depression, had left him at the very moment he most needed their support and approbation.

And then I remembered the desk in the parlor. "It's the desk of a student," I found myself thinking, "not the desk of a tested leader." And going back to scrutinize it more thoroughly, several of Pierce's presidential decisions came into a clearer focus in my mind.

Throughout his entire life, Franklin Pierce had found himself influenced and molded by the character of older, more experienced men. His father had "fought to make ... the Union," so, as President, Franklin would accept any concession to insure its preservation. His father had been a delegate to the convention which had added New Hampshire's vote to the tally of states ratifying the Constitution, so, as President, Franklin would insist that that precious document must be protected and adhered to without question, even in its toleration of human slavery, an institution that Franklin personally believed was a moral and social evil. As President, Pierce had also been powerfully influenced by expert politicians like Stephen A. Douglas. It had been Douglas, for instance, who had backed Pierce's proposed Gadsden Purchase in exchange for a presidential endorsement of the Kansas-Nebraska Act of 1854. Both of these pieces of legislation had produced unintended consequences that had served to divide rather than to unite the nation. Northern states had seen the purchase of land in southern Arizona and New Mexico as pandering to the desires of the slave states. The Kansas-Nebraska act had initiated a wave of violence in the disputed territories that threatened to bring the nation to the brink of civil war.

But Franklin Pierce had not come to the Presidency with the knowledge and perspective that might have helped him foresee such tragic developments. He was, as he had always been, and as his friend Nathaniel Hawthorne readily admitted, "young for the station" to which he had been elected. He was still young, still sitting at a young man's desk, when he was given charge of the Ship of State. Young and alone.

After his four years as President, Pierce was disappointed not to be nominated by his party for a second term. He traveled to Europe with his wife, hoping that a change of climate might relieve her melancholy and her physical illnesses, but any improvement in Jane's condition was only temporary. After more than two years abroad, they returned to the United States to live out the remainder of their lives as clouds of impending war gathered and then violently broke out. Jane died in 1863. Franklin would follow her six years later.

There is no question that Franklin Pierce was a good man, a loyal son, and a loving husband and father. He was also a staunch believer in and defender of the Constitution of the United States. Yet his greatest legacy as a President may well be a cautionary tale. How does one know whom to trust? How does one decide when to negotiate and when to stand resolute? How can one come to anticipate results that were never intended to take place? Answering such questions accurately involves skills that can define the success or failure of any Chief Executive. While many factors are surely requisite to arrive at insightful solutions to such questions, it is probably important not to discount that single word answer my father gave to me so many years ago: "Experience."

14

James Buchanan: The Fruits of Compromise

15th President James Buchanan (1857-1861): Wheatland in Lancaster, PA

In Ken Burns's groundbreaking documentary on the Civil War, historian/novelist Shelby Foote makes a key speculation regarding the nature of American governance. He states, "Americans like to think of themselves as uncompromising. Our true genius is for compromise. Our whole government is founded on it."

In a startlingly similar vein, James Buchanan, once he had returned to his beautiful estate in Lancaster, Pennsylvania, after his tumultuous years as the nation's Chief Executive, wrote a memoir, *Mr. Buchanan's Administration on the Eve of the Rebellion*, a rather strident defense of his Presidency.

Its introduction sounds the central thesis of the entire work: "Both before and after he [Buchanan] became President he was an earnest advocate of compromise between the parties to save the Union, but Congress disregarded his recommendations" (Buchanan v).

One would think, then, that Shelby Foote would regard James Buchanan as a heroic American President, rooted in and self-consciously aware of the spirit of compromise on which the United States' "whole government is founded." However, this is not the case. In his classic three volume study of the Civil War, Foote joins the general throng of historians in his negative assessment of James Buchanan's response to the secession crisis that faced the nation: "James Buchanan, badly confused, was doing nothing in [his] last weeks in office. Having stated in his December message to Congress that while a state had no lawful right to secede, neither had the federal government any right to prevent it, privately he was saying that he was the last President of the United States" (Foote 18).

It hardly needs mentioning that, as recently as 2011, Buchanan has been ranked a dismal 42nd out of the first 43 U.S. Presidents in terms of his effectiveness as a leader. Although, to the very end of his life, James Buchanan believed that he had been a good President—and that, he further asserted, over time, this fact would come to be generally understood by succeeding generations—this view of his years in office has yet to be adopted by any major historian.

As Carol and I found ourselves negotiating the highways west of Philadelphia in southeastern Pennsylvania, quite frankly this visit to Buchanan's presidential home in Lancaster almost felt like an errand of mercy. (Oh well, my thought process concluded, we *were* visiting Philadelphia anyway, and Buchanan *had been* a President, and we have dedicated ourselves to the project of seeing as many presidential homes as possible, so why not spend a morning checking him off the list?) What we were to find in Lancaster, however, was genuinely surprising.

For starters, the town appeared to be quite proud of their native son. Signage leading us to "Wheatland" was frequent and prominently displayed. Then the estate itself, with its expansive lawn and almost regal pastoral setting, was meticulously kept up under the watchful eye and guidance of The James Buchanan Foundation for the Preservation of Wheatland. And, most unexpected to us, there was a significant crowd of visitors here on the day we had come.

The first tour had just begun, and we had to wait for the second, while even more tourists arrived to comprise a third! This was quite a showing for such a universally maligned President.

But Wheatland itself offered at least one obvious explanation for its popularity. As I circumnavigated the exterior of the house and positioned myself at various points on its flawless carpet of lawn, the sheer loveliness of the landscape was impossible to miss. The architectural splendor of the home's Federal design, together with the stately oaks environing it, worked together to establish a locale that thoroughly illustrated the hopes President Buchanan had articulated when he had described this location as having "... the comforts and tranquility of home as contrasted with the troubles, perplexities, and difficulties of public life." No American President had ever been more conversant with "the troubles, perplexities, and difficulties of public life" than had the beleaguered James Buchanan. He had returned here after his term as President with a sense of profound relief. Wheatland, as several guidebooks suggest, exemplified admirably the comfortable world of a successful 19th century country gentleman.

On the day of our visit, docents, all accoutered in period garb, guided visitors from the long back porch of the home into its central entry hall which gives onto a sumptuously adorned dining room, an elegant parlor, and President Buchanan's library and study areas, all resplendent with furnishings original to the years of his residency.

Upstairs, we were conducted through several bedrooms, including the President's, and we were urged especially to note his paneled bathroom with its deep, zinc-lined tub, considered a luxury in its day. More eloquent to me, however, was a modest nook on the upper floor which included a small desk, two benches, and a reading light that

James Buchanan's Nook at Wheatfield in Lancaster, Pennsylvania

had clearly been used as a private writing space. This intimate area had the real coziness of a home, unadorned for visitors. I could easily imagine ex-President Buchanan crafting sections of his aforementioned memoirs in this secluded and protected setting, or his niece, Harriet Lane, sitting here, gazing out onto the beautiful grounds as she wrote her correspondence.

All this wealth and patrician splendor, however, did not seem to explain fully why Buchanan, a lifelong bachelor, would have needed such an estate. To understand this, it is important to learn more of his family biography.

James Buchanan was the firstborn son of an Irish immigrant who, through hard work and an eye for business, had become a successful landowner. Ultimately the future President would have seven other siblings and, as a result of his active and lucrative legal practice, would become the most prosperous member of the family. By the time he retired from his position as Secretary of State in the Polk administration in 1848, he had twenty-two nieces and nephews and thirteen grandnieces and grandnephews. Of these he was guardian to seven who had been orphaned.

Wheatland, then, was not only the result of a successful legal and political career. In fact, the estate had been purchased with the express purpose of accommodating his ever growing gaggle of relatives. As such, the house stood as a testament to the generosity and care James Buchanan felt toward those who depended on him for their well-being. And, as President, he had felt equally responsible for the well-being of his country. The key to assuring its peace and prosperity, he believed, was compromise.

Throughout his legal and political life, James Buchanan had learned the value of compromise. As a lawyer, and most especially, as a foreign minister to both Russia and Great Britain, he had distinguished himself as a man particularly adept at striking a balance between contending parties that would logically lead to a legal or political solution acceptable to each. As Secretary of State, Buchanan had essentially brokered the Oregon compromise that President Polk had finally accepted in lieu of his famous mantra of "Fifty-Four Forty or Fight." On a less successful note, Buchanan had worked tirelessly to avoid an open war with Mexico by trying to settle the territorial disputes between that nation and the United States. He had failed in this, he believed, not because of any lack of effort on his own part but because of the hawkish mentality of the President under whom he was serving.

As I walked through the tranquil beauty of the grounds of Wheatland, it was easy to imagine how this place could have come to stand in President Buchanan's mind as an antidote to the "troubles, perplexities, and difficulties of public life," particularly as those "troubles, perplexities, and difficulties" were due, in large part, he felt, to various parties' unwillingness to learn the redemptive power of compromise.

Nowhere is this thought more clearly stated than in the pages of his memoir. The President observes therein that the abolitionist movement, with its uncompromising insistence that "it was sinful to live in a political confederacy which tolerated slavery in any of the States composing it," had actually, and ironically, impeded the "natural process of emancipation" already present in many areas of the South. Furthermore, because of the virulence of abolitionist attacks against slaveholding southerners, among the people of the South "there sprung up a party as fanatical in advocating slavery as were the abolitionists of the North in denouncing it" (Buchanan 11, 14).

In each case, of course, the tragedy, as the ex-President saw it, was the failure of both parties to reach the sort of compromise that would leave each side willing to live peaceably with the other. That no such compromise had been achieved, he concluded, was the great tragedy of the 19th century—a tragedy which he had foreseen and which he had labored heroically to prevent.

Wheatland must have illustrated to him the fruits of a life dedicated to finding workable middle ground between contending parties, fruits that would lead naturally to peace, generosity, and affluence. The devastated landscape of the defeated South, by contrast, graphically illustrated the horrors of adversaries who preferred destruction to compromise. If nothing else, the stark difference of the two landscapes, the aging ex-President was sure, would ultimately redeem his reputation as a politician who had done everything he could do to avert this national disaster.

Only it hasn't played out that way. Why not?

One answer, my answer, is that, despite my admiration for Shelby Foote as a writer and historian—and that admiration runs very deep—his speculations regarding America and compromise do not tell the whole story.

"Americans like to think of themselves as uncompromising," he states, and then he hurries on to argue that, in fact, the American genius is for compromise, not adamancy. Yet many of our country's most important moments of history tend to contradict his contention.

The men who gathered in Philadelphia for the First and, later, the Second Continental Congress, just a few miles East of Lancaster, had indeed begun as compromisers. They had been English subjects trying to placate a sovereign. What ultimately made them Americans, however, was the realization that compromise would render them forever subject to powers over which they had no control. With Thomas Paine's rousing call to attend "the birthday of a new world," these early Americans founded a new nation on their refusal to compromise.

"But what about all the compromises made in the very Constitution of the United States?" I can hear a voice ask. "Surely there would have been no country to argue about had differing interests not been willing to compromise." And, while this is most certainly a valid observation, it is equally valid to note that many of the most famous compromises of American history (e.g. the 3/5ths compromise, the Missouri Compromise, etc.) only postponed rather than actually solved the problems they were trying to correct.

In fact much of the subsequent history of the United States has been concerned with Americans having to come to understand and to embrace the fact that a refusal to compromise can be the great protector of personal liberties. From such famous words as "Millions for defense, sir, but not one cent for tribute" to "Nuts" to "Mr. Gorbachev, tear down this wall," Americans have had to learn to identify themselves as stalwart defenders of, not compromisers regarding, whatever they value most highly. Their stand against tyranny wherever it has existed has become the essential, defining ingredient of the American character.

Our government is not based on compromise, as Foote suggests, nor is our national genius a mastery of the ability to compromise. And neither, it is important to note, is the best of American statesmanship mere jingoistic bullheadedness. Our *genius* lies in our unshakeable faith in the potential of all men. But our *government* is based on intelligent distrust. The checks and balances written into the Constitution of the United States bear witness not so much to the importance of compromise as to the unwillingness of Americans to let any branch of government, legislative, executive, or judicial, have unchecked authority over the American people. To misunderstand these truths is an error which citizens of this country find it hard to forgive.

Slavery was a tyranny, a tyranny that was eating away at the very foundation of the American experiment in the liberty of all mankind. President Buchanan saw slavery as a social issue calling for a compromise position. Americans, North and South, disagreed both with his position and, finally, with him. He never understood why he was so vilified. He retired to the beauty of Wheatland, convinced that he had been correct.

But he had been wrong.

15

Abraham Lincoln: Lenses

16th President Abraham Lincoln (1861-1865): Home in Springfield, IL

I had almost decided not to go. Even though the scheduled speaker was Joseph Ellis whose books, Founding Brothers and *Passionate Sage* had been instrumental in my understanding of and appreciation for the Revolutionary period of American history, I had just finished a long day of teaching, and I was looking forward to a pleasant evening at home. But while I was still debating about whether or not I should attend the lecture, all at once my phone rang. It was a friend urging me to accompany him to the talk. We set a time to meet, and, a couple of hours later, I was finding a seat in a crowded library venue. It was a decision I have never regretted.

Ellis's introductory remarks would be a revelation to me. They would have a profound impact on my way of thinking about history. And they would provide me with a fascinating perspective on the legacy of Abraham Lincoln, our most celebrated and perhaps least fully understood President.

Dr. Ellis began his talk by noting that, in his research, he had located a county (as I recall it was somewhere in rural Pennsylvania) the current population of which matched precisely the population of the thirteen American colonies at the time of the Revolution. He followed this observation by posing a question to us all.

If that county, he wondered, were today confronted with the same political situation of our original thirteen colonies, did we think that we would see modern versions of such luminaries as George Washington or John Adams, Thomas Jefferson or Alexander Hamilton coming to the fore to face the crisis?

Everyone in the audience knew exactly where Dr. Ellis was going with this. How incredibly, perhaps even providentially, fortunate our nation had been that the very men who would prove themselves to be the political giants of the late 18th century *had* been alive in America at precisely that moment of our country's history when we had needed them the most. I looked around the room and saw many of us wistfully shaking our heads. "No," we all seemed to be saying, such a constellation of political talent and determination could have occurred only once and certainly not today. "No," not with our current crop of fractious politicians rather than inspired statesmen. How grateful we all should be that our Revolution had occured exactly when it had.

But then Dr. Ellis gave us all a wry smile, and, answering his own question, he stated simply, "Yes." An audible murmur ran through the audience. What was he suggesting? After letting his answer hang in the air for a moment, he went on to explain that he had come to the conclusion that, more often than not, it was history itself that had created some of our greatest leaders. In fact, he noted, history and historic moments or opportunities had often lifted men to heights of achievement that would have been impossible without the emergencies that had been forced upon them. These men had become inspired leaders as a direct result of these challenges, and sometimes in ways that even they themselves would never have imagined possible. It had happened in the colonies in 1775, he concluded, and it might well have happened in modern day Pennsylvania.

This, of course, was simply a thought-provoking speculation, but for me, it provided a perspective through which to begin to understand Abraham Lincoln's rise to greatness as a result of the defining historical event of his life: the Civil War of 1861-1865. For it is both safe and quite accurate to state that no other American President's life, either before or after Abraham Lincoln, has been so thoroughly associated with a war. Almost everything said or written about Lincoln appears in the context of that devastating era of our nation's history. Predictably, then, one's feelings about this President tend to depend upon the lens through which he or she views that war.

If one sees the Civil War as a close brush with the dismantling of our nation, Lincoln emerges as "The Preserver of the Union." If one sees the war through the lens of the Southern "Lost Cause," Lincoln becomes the perpetrator of the bloodiest loss of American lives in the nearly two hundred and fifty years of our history. Through the lens of seeing the Civil War as a struggle to purge the United States of the curse of slavery, Lincoln emerges as "The Great Emancipator." And these are only a few of the most widely held perspectives one finds in the vast amount of information and opinion readily available to anyone interested in learning more about our 16th President.

All this creates an interesting problem for the numerous presidential home sites open to the public for the purpose of sharing—and occasionally recreating—the life story of Abraham Lincoln. Just which point of view about our most famous President will be presented?

Carol and I have visited six of them now, from backwater rural Kentucky to the urbanized streets of Washington, D.C., from Pigeon Creek, Indiana, near the Ohio River to New Salem, Illinois, on the Sangamon. And of course, on several occasions we have traveled to Springfield, Illinois, to see the Lincoln home there. Each of these "Lincoln sites" is well worth visiting, yet, for me at least, Abraham Lincoln remains frustratingly, sometimes tantalizingly, elusive in most of them. Why?

Perhaps because, sometime in the midst of that unspeakably ghastly Civil War, Abraham Lincoln began to disappear, to irreversibly vanish, and in his place, both during the final years of that war and, most especially, after his assassination, arose a resurrected figure bearing the Lincoln name who would become one of the greatest of all American heroes.

What light would his homes cast on this phenomenon? Which Lincoln, the man or the legend, would they present? Carol and I would spend several years traveling to these places in our attempt to find out.

Abraham Lincoln's Birthplace National Historic Site in Hodgenville, KY

To begin at the beginning of Lincoln sites, we drove down a number of two lane roads to arrive at the Abraham Lincoln Birthplace National Historical Site near the small town of Hodgenville, Kentucky. This National Park Service location includes an impressive monument with a rather massive looking Doric temple structure at the top of an expansive stone stairway comprised of fifty-six steps, one for each year of the President's life. This monument was built on the spot where, in January 1809, Thomas and Nancy Hanks Lincoln's cabin stood at the time of their son Abraham's birth. At the foot of the stairway is located a small cave in which an underground spring still sends fresh water to the surface. This marks the center of the Lincoln family's land, the so-called "Sinking Spring Farm."

Inside the impressively grand temple can be found a log cabin which, at the time of the dedication of this monument in 1911, was thought by some to be the original cabin in which the President had been born. Today the cabin is identified by the National Park Service as "representative" of the log cabin that had been built on this location by the Lincoln family, a symbol of

Abraham Lincoln's Reconstructed Birthplace Log Cabin in Hodgenville, KY

the modest origin of the boy who would grow up to become one of our greatest Presidents. But, somewhat reminiscent of George Washington's "Memorial House" at Pope's Creek, even this humble cabin has been altered to reflect his enhanced historical stature.

The original dimensions of the cabin would have been about 16'x18', a ratio typical of log cabins from this era. The cabin within the monument has been reduced to 12'x17'. The original structure's height, however, would have been about 12'. The symbolic "representative" cabin measures nearly 15' in height. These are very subtle changes, yet they create an artifact that looms above visitors, confined as they are by the interior of the monument's relatively tight walking space. Already, even at the place of his birth, Abraham Lincoln was beginning to appear larger than life.

Thus the Lincoln birthplace site has the feel of being orchestrated. We approach the memorial with veneration as we mount its long stone stairway, and we enter quietly and reverently to walk around the cabin inside. But where is any account of what Lincoln himself later identified as the single sentence that would describe his early life: "The short and simple annals of the poor" (Donald 19)? There appears to be more grandeur than poverty here. At least as regards the monument.

Outside is a different matter. The overall location is still wonderfully remote. Birdsong rather than traffic noise predominates, and thick forested land surrounds the site, giving the visitor a sense of solitude and peace which must also have greeted the boy born in this place. Yet, not surprisingly, Lincoln himself had no memory of his infancy spent at Sinking Spring Farm. By the time he was one and a half years old his family had moved ten miles northeast from here. Lincoln's earliest boyhood recollections would come from this second location at a place named Knob Creek, our next stop at this National Park Historic site.

The road to Knob Creek was impressively undulating and quickly wound down into valleys lying amidst tree-covered, mound-like hills (or "knobs") through which the highway ran northeastward in a serpentine fashion. Before long we arrived at a parking area on our left,

Abraham Lincoln's Boyhood Log Cabin at Knob Creek, Kentucky

near a split rail fence just beyond which stood another log cabin. This structure was identified as not original, but rather as a latter-day copy of the Lincoln homestead. Its dimensions, however, were the correct 16'x18' and 12' tall, and it had been constructed on the very spot where the Lincoln cabin had been placed. Knob Creek itself was not immediately visible, but the steep angle of the hills surrounding the flat farmland on which the Lincolns had planted their crops left no doubt that rainwater and spring water would certainly have flowed down to the base of these slopes, creating the creek that had given this place its name.

As far as land cultivation was concerned, this Knob Creek property was ideal. There had been no dense forest to clear in order to ready the ground for planting, yet the "knob" hills surrounding the seven acre field provided all the timber any settler in the region could ever have needed. Rain water would have soaked evenly into the flat land, percolating down to nourish the root systems of whatever had been planted, and the road to markets ran near to the front door of the cabin that the Lincolns had built here. Young Abraham remembered working in this "big field" adjoining his family's cabin, and he had thoroughly enjoyed the nearby streams where he had fished and played. Why, then, had the family moved away?

Here, once again, the question of lenses arises. Those attempting to view Lincoln's life as a long and steady progression towards assuming the legendary role of "The Great Emancipator" tend to focus their attention on Thomas Lincoln's abhorrence of slavery. It was the recent admission of the Indiana territory as

The Lincoln's Field at Knob Creek, Kentucky

a free state, they insist, that had prompted him to leave his beautiful farmland in Kentucky. Seen through this lens, Thomas Lincoln's motive had been to remove himself and his family from any place, no matter how well suited to cultivation, that permitted slave labor. Yet Abraham Lincoln himself would acknowledge in later years that, although his father was no lover of slavery, their move had been made "... chiefly on account of the difficulty in land titles in Ky [sic]" (Donald 23-24). Even so important a figure in Kentucky history as Daniel Boone had also migrated westward out of Kentucky because of the legal difficulties he had encountered in trying to retain clear title to his land.

Knob Creek, not unlike the birthplace at Sinking Springs, emerges as a beautiful setting for a still rather undistinguished life. Where is the Abraham Lincoln of our national monument in Washington, D.C.? Not yet visible here in Kentucky. Perhaps such matters would become clearer after we crossed the Ohio river and traveled approximately 120 miles to the northwest toward our next stop.

"Welcome to Indiana" the sign reads after one has passed over the Ohio River at Louisville, turning onto I-64 heading west. And then, for the first time I had ever noticed it—though I had traveled through this state more times than I could easily recall—at the bottom of the sign were emblazoned the words "Boyhood Home of Abraham Lincoln." Although it is Illinois that identifies itself as "The Land of Lincoln," clearly Indiana wanted to stake its claim as well.

The Pigeon Creek site would be the final "wilderness" locale associated with Abraham Lincoln, and it would also provide a most effective window through which to view and understand the frontier life of the early years of the 19th century.

One enters the Lincoln Boyhood National Memorial through winding roads and a densely forested landscape. Upon reaching the Visitor's Center parking lot, guests follow a wide pavement walkway toward a semi-circular stone building on the walls of which are mounted impressive concrete panels containing bas-relief sculptures depicting the various eras of President Lincoln's life.

Inside this park entrance structure is a small museum and an auditorium that plays a film chronicling key events of the years the Lincoln family spent here, including most significantly the death of Abraham's mother and the remarriage of his father. The boy had been seven years old when he and his family had arrived, and he would be twenty-one before he left—a formative period of life by any standard.

The real heart of this Boyhood National Memorial site, however, is its elaborate recreation of the Lincoln cabin and farm. The actual site of the cabin is marked by a foundation stone outline, but the recreated farm nearby, complete with outbuildings, cultivated fields, grazing

Abraham Lincoln's Boyhood Log Cabin in Pigeon Creek, Indiana

livestock, and costumed interpreters going about the daily chores of pioneer life, provides the most interesting information for visiting tourists.

The Pigeon Creek settlement, though still a remote setting on the edge of the western wilderness at the time the Lincolns had arrived, was nowhere near as lonely as had been the earlier family locales. Between 180 and 200 people were carving out a life here, hunting, fishing, clearing the land, and cultivating crops. Thomas Lincoln himself had purchased two eighty acre plots of ground. Compared to many other settlers of the time, we learned, the Lincolns were prospering. Their farm would come to include a smoke house, a hen house, a barn, a corn crib, and a carpenter shop, as well as their cabin, all of which have been faithfully reproduced here.

"Thomas Lincoln's tools," a reenactor at the carpenter's shop informed us, "were the wonder of the district." Chickens pecked at feed sprinkled on the ground near the hen house, sheep and cattle grazed in the grassy fields around these outbuildings. We even saw a Ferdinand-like bull resting in the shade of a nearby maple tree. The whole setting painted the clearest picture I had ever seen of the daily rounds of frontier life.

Of course there were still dangers to be faced. Although the native Indian populations had largely moved west by the time Pigeon Creek was being settled, it was deemed wise to place the settlers' living quarters over a hundred yards away from the natural well spring that provided the community water. "You wouldn't have wanted to put your home too close to that spring," another reenactor answered a tourist who had questioned the settlement's distance from this water source. "If you had, you and your family would most likely have run into the bears, panthers, and wolves that also drank there and still roamed these woods in significant numbers."

In the end, however, it was disease, not danger nor dissatisfaction, that had caused the Pigeon Creek settlement to fail. Cows grazing on wild foliage produced tainted milk for the farmers, and many, including Abraham's mother, died here as a result. (Her grave can be visited on a hill which lies between the Visitor's Center and the reconstructed farm.) Thomas Lincoln would relocate his family to Illinois, always in search of better land and a healthier life. By the time Abraham had reached young adulthood, he was ready to move on independently.

And here, yet another lens through which to view his life comes into play: the lens of personal ambition. No one who ever knew Lincoln well ever doubted his highly developed desire both to improve and to distinguish himself. Lincoln's admirers cast this character trait in the light of his yearning to serve and, finally, to preserve his nation. His detractors argue that this insistence on achieving personal prominence would result in highly questionable political maneuvering. Yet despite such a dichotomy of opinions, it is clear that although both his birthplace and childhood homes illustrate the roughhewn character of his beginnings and the rigors of frontier life, it is his next two settings that bear witness to this lens of personal ambition.

In this new period of his life, Lincoln determined to better himself, and he would achieve a success far greater than anything his father could have imagined. This determination would lead Lincoln to literature and then to the rhetoric of debate. It would lead him to his first experiences as a candidate and into the practice of the law. Ultimately it would lead him to the Presidency. First, however, it led him to New Salem, Illinois, the next stop in our travels.

Lincoln's New Salem State Historic Site announces itself as the backdrop for a defining period in Abraham Lincoln's life. The pamphlet visitors receive upon entering the park explains, quite accurately, the reasoning behind this claim:

Recreation of New Salem, Illinois

> *The six years Lincoln spent at New Salem formed a turning point in his career. From the gangling young man who came to the village in 1831 with no definite objectives, he became a man of purpose as he embarked upon a career of law and statesmanship.*

While one might quibble with the word "gangling" here, the gist of this description rings undeniably true. Certainly nothing in Lincoln's earlier background would suggest the development that occurred during his years at New Salem. And what makes this even more remarkable is the fact that he had never intended to settle here.

"Lincoln came here by accident," a thoughtful and articulate New Salem site interpreter named David informed me as I toured this locale. David went on to explain to me that Lincoln had been piloting a raft down the Sangamon en route to the Illinois River and, thence, to the Mississippi on his way to New Orleans when the craft had gotten stuck on the mill dam near the New Salem grist mill. While

Lincoln labored to free the raft and continue on his way, his employer, Denton Offutt, disembarked and wandered up the steep hill to see the village of New Salem.

What he saw convinced Offutt that money was to be made in this new center of frontier mercantilism, and soon thereafter he planned to build a store here and have his employee, young Abraham Lincoln, take charge of it. When, after his trip to New Orleans, Lincoln returned to New Salem, he found that the promised store was not yet under construction, but he liked the town and, for the first time in his life, was free to make his own decisions about his residency. He chose to stay.

But it would not be Offutt's store that would hold the most importance to Lincoln. It would be the community of New Salem itself. This place was unlike anything he had ever experienced. It was, certainly in comparison to Sinking Springs or Knob Creek, an actual frontier town, a center of trade for the surrounding area. Nearly twice as large as Pigeon Creek had been, it was a community that included a variety of tradesmen in addition to farming families. Here Lincoln would be able to borrow books from Jack Kelso, a hunter who lived in a dogtrot home and whose personal library of twenty-eight volumes was the largest in New Salem. And here in the evenings Lincoln would join men around the fireplace of the town cooper, Henry Onstat, to swap stories and debate the issues of the day. It would be from New Salem that Lincoln would volunteer to serve in the Black Hawk Indian War and, as a result, would win his first electoral victory as other men from the town chose him to be their captain. And it would be here at New Salem that Lincoln would become locally famous for his abilities as a story-teller, a voracious book reader, a scrupulously honest businessman, and an ambitious self-promoter.

Economically, however, New Salem was a disaster for Lincoln. When he finally left the town to begin practicing law in nearby Springfield, his entire worldly possessions fit into two bags he could easily carry, and he was several thousand dollars in debt. But Lincoln had set his course, and he would pursue it tirelessly in Springfield. If New Salem had been the Alpha, the beginning, of

Lincoln's personal ambition, Washington, D.C. would constitute its Omega, its end. Lincoln had come to Springfield as a newly minted lawyer, eager to establish a successful practice. He would leave as the newly elected 16th President of the United States.

But the Presidency was a long way off, more than twenty years in the future. Lincoln's immediate objectives in Springfield were making a living, honing his talents as a speaker and legal advocate, paying down his financial obligations, and making a name for himself. The Lincoln Home National Historic Site, run by the National Park Service, proudly displays evidence of Lincoln's success in achieving all of these goals.

Lincoln's home in Springfield, "the only house the Lincolns ever owned," the National Park guides remind visitors, occupies land just east of the business center of town. It is surrounded by several other 19th century houses to give visitors a better sense of the neighborhood into which Abraham and Mary Todd had moved in 1844 with their firstborn son, Robert.

Our docent at the site was a pleasant and spirited young woman named Kelly who led our tour group of about twenty people up the five stone and four wooden steps into the home's entry hall and then into the front parlor. She proudly announced that the house contained fifty-five pieces of original Lincoln furnishings and possessions, and she also explained how the Lincolns had enlarged and expanded the residence as their family had grown in both number and affluence. Three of the four Lincoln children had been born here, Kelly informed us. Moreover, during his residency, Lincoln had retired all of the debt he had incurred in his business ventures in New Salem. He was now making a salary in his legal practice that was nearly five times what would have been earned by the average citizen.

In short, the Lincoln house in Springfield stands as a testament to the fact that the backwoods boy from rural Kentucky had "made it." From the front parlor's floral patterned carpet and tastefully understated wallpaper to its finely worked wooden chairs with upholstered seat cushions together with matching display shelves of bric-a-brac, from the white china tea service in the dining room to the children's stereoscope in the family sitting room, this home illustrated the success possible for a 19th century self-made man.

This is not to call this Springfield home sumptuous, however. The house would pale by comparison to James Madison's Montpelier or Andrew Jackson's Hermitage. It would even seem unassuming beside John Adams's final home at Peace field. But such eastern splendor was not yet to be often found in a midwestern town so recently established as Springfield, Illinois. Nevertheless, when contrasted to the quality of life enjoyed by those with whom he had dwelt thus far, Abraham Lincoln would have been seen as extremely, even enviably, well-to-do.

Kelly led our tour group up the fourteen stairs (the same number as Lincoln's shoe size, she told us) to the second floor. Our first stop was the front room and office. Here, as well as in the immediately adjoining bedroom, the Lincolns' affluence was on full display. Elaborate, even rather garrish, paisley designed wallpaper decorated the interior of both rooms. Beautiful dressers were placed in each room, and a Franklin stove provided both chambers with ample heat. In the north corner of the front room Kelly pointed out Lincoln's law desk atop of which stood a shelving unit containing a variety of papers stored in its pigeon-hole compartments. These suggested to onlookers Lincoln's considerable case load. Law books laid akimbo on top of the shelf also gave the unit the feel of a genuine work space. It was symbolic of the dedication and tireless labors Lincoln had expended in order to give his growing family the affluence they enjoyed.

After a brief look into the boys' bedrooms, Kelly led us back downstairs to the kitchen which boasted Mary's pride and joy: a cast iron stove so elaborate that she had wanted to bring it with her to the White House. Lincoln had convinced his wife that she probably would not be doing much cooking for the family in Washington, D.C., and so it had remained in Springfield.

With that last stop in the kitchen, a single room as large as some of the log cabins Lincoln had lived in as a child, our tour was over. As I stood back out on the corner of Eighth and Jackson streets, gazing at the house, I felt quite palpably the distance Lincoln had come from his childhood days in Kentucky to this comfortable dwelling in the state capitol of Illinois. Abraham Lincoln had prospered. But this house showed no particular evidence of the legendary Lincoln, no evidence of what he would later identify as "that gnawing" desire for political prominence that can lead a man to seek the Presidency (Goodwin 575). All of the homes we had visited thus far were clear waymarks of an American success story illustrating the possibility of upward social and economic mobility. But none of them appeared to presage the rise of a hero of legendary greatness. Why not?

Because they all lacked the key element that Joseph Ellis had identified in his opening remarks that night in his lecture: a defining moment of history. That moment, for Lincoln, would be the great and tragic American Civil War. It was hurtling toward him, even on the eve of his improbable election to the Presidency. Its relentless approach was gathering momentum in the final lame duck months of the Buchanan administration. One by one, beginning with South Carolina, the states that would come to comprise the Confederate States of America were seceding from the Union. By early 1861, en route to his inauguration, Lincoln would have to pass through Baltimore, Maryland, in a special train and in the dead of night to avoid the imminent danger of assassination.

Beside the White House itself, there is only one more Lincoln residence available for visitors interested in following the arc of Abraham Lincoln's life: the Lincoln Cottage at the Soldiers' Home, located on high ground about three miles north of the Capitol building in Washington, D.C. It would be our most revealing stop.

As one first approaches this "Cottage," the word seems distinctly out of place. The home is a large Gothic revival mansion, an admirable choice for a presidential retreat which, from June to November in 1862-1864, is exactly what it was for the Lincoln family.

On its expansive back porch, the President could and did play with his son, Tad, as they enjoyed the fresher, cooler air of the heights overlooking Washington. The capitol dome is still visible from certain spots of the extensive lawn that spreads southward from the home. But, most importantly, it was here at the Lincoln Cottage that, for the first and only time, a Lincoln home clearly reflected the legacy of our 16th President.

The Lincoln Cottage at the Soldiers' Home in Washington, DC

This legacy, like the man himself, is complex. Evaluating it still depends to a great extent on the lens through which one is looking. But it is based on three undeniable facts all of which relate closely to this home and what transpired here. The facts are these: 1) By the end of 1865, largely as a result of Lincoln's insistence and prodding of legislators, the 13th Amendment to the Constitution abolished slavery in the United States; 2) By the end of 1865, approximately 625,000 Americans were dead who had been alive five years earlier; and 3) By the end of 1865, the territory previously identified as The United States of America was still intact and still so identified.

These three indisputable facts are both interrelated and inextricably linked to the Lincoln Cottage through their association with the war, this war that would ultimately define—and create the legend of—Abraham Lincoln. His moment of history had arrived. Here at the Lincoln Cottage, he would decide what to do with it.

History had presented the two previous Presidents with a polarized Congress that represented an increasingly divided nation. Both men's response to this crisis had been to claim their belief in and unswerving allegiance to the Constitution of the United States, a document that included an acknowledgment of the existence of "unpaid servitude" and also protected the rights of slave owners. These Presidents had insisted that they were Chief Executives of the entire country, not merely of the regions which held their own beliefs. Earlier in his political career, Lincoln had frequently ex-pressed a very similar point of view in his public pronouncements, but now he took a different tack, a tack available to him because of the armed conflict with which history had presented him.

As he and his family moved into the spacious Lincoln Cottage in the early summer of 1862, the war was going badly for the Union. McClellan's Army of the Potomac had been pushed back from Rich-mond, and Pope's Army of Virginia had been defeated at the Second Battle of Manassas. From the front door of the Cottage, Lincoln could see new graves being added to the National Cemetery on the grounds nearby. In the evenings he often walked through the graveyard, the acreage of which was quickly becoming full of dead Union soldiers.

Nothing was more important than winning this war, he came to realize as he watched the graves multiplying, sometimes more than fifty in a week. But to do so, he would have to be willing to oppose sections of the very Constitution he had earlier sworn "to protect and defend." While living at the Cottage, he would finally decide to act on the inescapable conclusion that a nation "conceived in Lib-erty" could not also be allowed to continue to condone or protect the moral evil of human slavery.

Visitors to the Cottage see a largely unfurnished interior. When the Lincolns resided here at four month intervals, they had brought their furniture with them. The tall ceilings and panoramic views still impart a feeling of calm and quiet beauty that must have been soothing to the personal heartaches and national calamities that haunted both the Lincolns and the country at large. In the Cottage's front parlor, just to the right of the entrance, in a room whose win-dows looked out toward the cemetery, Lincoln drafted the doc-ument that would change the very nature of the Civil War: the Emancipation Proclamation. As soon as the war became a moral, rather than a Constitutional, altercation, a war pitting slave holders against warriors fighting for human liberty, the tide quickly and in-exorably turned in favor of the North. From the Cottage Lincoln saw both the horrible toll of the conflict and its higher moral pur-pose. Lincoln's stand for the right, rather than for the law as set forth in the Constitution, created his legend as "The Great Emancipator."

But not without a horrendous cost. There was hardly any family, North or South, unscathed by the carnage of the Civil War. Well over half a million dead left a scar on the national landscape that would take decades to forgive, and perhaps never to forget. Add to this the example of a leader who had placed his personal sense of moral right over the Constitutional law of the land, and there remained—and continues to remain—the uneasy possibility of subsequent Presidents reaching similar, and perhaps much more questionable, conclusions.

For Lincoln did not "preserve the Union," as at least one of the lenses of history insists that he did. He *was* instrumental in creating a new and different Union, but the country that emerged after the Civil War was not the country that had existed prior to it. The land claimed by the United States was the same, but this new Union was largely a result of conquest, the victorious North over a defeated and devastated South. Years would pass, and the old states would be readmitted to this new Union, but its very existence had been determined largely by military might. The rights of individual states would never again be permitted to mount any lasting challenge to the social and political policies of the national government.

The Abraham Lincoln of the Lincoln Cottage metamorphoses into the legendary Lincoln so venerated today, the President who chose the moral right over all else. And, of course, Lincoln *was* right in the highest sense of that word. Slavery and democracy are, and had always been, antithetical notions. The fact that the toleration of slavery and slave ownership had been necessary in order to insure the nation's original founding was an ironic and terrible mistake that had to be rectified. Doing so created, in Lincoln's words, "a new birth of freedom" and a distinctly new nation along with it.

Abraham Lincoln had risen beyond poverty, beyond his meager education, beyond his successful career as a frontier lawyer. His moment of history had provided him with the opportunity and the occasion to undo the ill-fated compromises of the Founders of his country. With the abolition of slavery, Lincoln had been able to create an even "more perfect union" than the one into which he had been born. Doing so transformed the man into a legend.

But it remains important to see beyond the lens of legend and not to forget to acknowledge the price of the terrible war that defined Lincoln's place in history: a gruesome tally of casualties, a challenge to and, on occasion, disregard of the Constitution of the United States and its Bill of Rights, a potentially dangerous precedent for all future Chief Executives. Lincoln's moral victory constituted a major turning point in the history of the United States. Yet it is the amalgamation of that victory with its cost that provides the most important, the clearest, and the most honestly complex lens through which to fully understand the meaning of the life and the legacy of Abraham Lincoln.

16

Andrew Johnson: "Grounded"

17th President Andrew Johnson (1865-1869): Homestead in Greeneville, TN

Burke loved us. He loved us the way a mother loves the teacher who sees great untapped potential in her child who has always been labeled "difficult" and "unfocused." He loved us the way I used to love the student who entered senior English class with bright eyes and asked, "Will we be reading Shakespeare this year? He's my favorite." Yes, dear reader, there are students who do that--and genuinely--who love the bard and relish reading his works. And, yes, there are teachers who can look past youthful willfulness and attitude to see the promise in an under challenged child. And yes, National Park rangers can deeply appreciate visitors who have taken the time to know something about the subject of their site prior to pulling into the parking lot. Burke loved us.

We had arrived here about three o'clock in the afternoon and had found the Visitor's Center to be completely empty with the exception of Burke, the ranger on duty. I approached him enthusiastically and informed him about our book on presidential homes. I then mentioned that I believed President Johnson was one of the most underrated Chief Executives in the history of the United States. Carol quickly chimed in, noting that she found Johnson's rise from illiteracy to political prominence a truly inspirational story of the possibilities of any American willing to make a determined effort to get ahead in life. Burke smiled broadly as he nodded in agreement. "Finally," you could almost hear him thinking, "some folks who really want to appreciate President Johnson."

Then aloud he said, "And you know, the family made it here to Greeneville walking next to a cart being pulled by a blind pony. Even though young Andrew had learned the tailoring craft by this time, the family was truly starting off with nothing." For the next thirty minutes or so, Burke held us rapt with stories of President Johnson's life, and our follow-up questions indicated to him both our interest in and our preparedness for our visit.

A tip to travelers: this stop at Greeneville, Tennessee, illustrated to me the value in accumulating as much knowledge as possible about a President prior to seeing his home. Carol and I had spent the day driving south from Strasburg, Virginia, just west of Washington, D.C., and as we did so, Carol had read aloud for several hours various materials we had collected about President Johnson before our trip. Hearing all this information not only prepared us for seeing the Andrew Johnson sites in Greeneville, but it also made us familiar with names and moments connected with Johnsonian history about which we could ask more intelligent questions of the National Park rangers than we otherwise might have done. Years of teaching has proven to me that nothing is more gratifying to someone knowledgeable about a topic than a probing question posed by a willing learner.

It helps, too, of course, if the subject is interesting, and Andrew Johnson's life is an almost unbelievable story of one man's ascendancy despite overwhelming odds. In his case, all too often, the odds had won, and yet he remained unalterably faithful to the United States and, most significantly, to the Constitution. The fact that his final request was that he be interred, draped in an American flag with a copy of the Constitution laid beneath his head, was completely consistent with the way in which he had lived his life.

Today, if Andrew Johnson is remembered at all, it is usually in the following three ways: 1) he was a drunkard who came to his vice presidential inauguration inebriated; 2) he was a racist who was absolutely certain "...that blacks were inferior to whites 'in point of intellect...' " and, as a result, he had devoted himself to "...keeping the South a 'white man's country' for several more generations" (Trefousse, *Best of My Ability* 126, 130); and 3) he was the first President to be impeached.

What we are seldom told are some other significant historical facts: 1) While southern states were leaving the Union in 1860 and 1861, Andrew Johnson was the only senator from the South to retain his seat in the United States Congress and to openly reject, on Constitutional grounds, the southern states' right to secede; 2) Soon thereafter, Johnson was proclaimed by no less a source than *The New York Times* to be "the greatest man of the age" for his courageous stand on this issue; 3) At President Lincoln's request in 1862, and despite great personal danger to himself and to his family, Johnson had withdrawn from the Senate and returned to war-torn Tennessee to serve as its military governor, even though much of the state, including his own home in Greeneville, was still being held by Confederate forces; 4) In an effort to reinforce his dedication to the Union, Republican President Lincoln had chosen Andrew Johnson as his vice presidential running mate in 1864, even though Johnson had always identified himself as a Jacksonian Democrat; this was the only occasion in United States history where two men of opposing political parties had run together on the same ticket; 5) Andrew Johnson was the only ex-President ever to be elected and to serve as a United States Senator, subsequent to his years as Chief Executive.

Clearly these two lists of historical facts present two very different perspectives concerning Andrew Johnson. How would his museum and home sites here in Greeneville help us understand such radically different points of view?

After our initial conversation about the President, I asked Burke to identify the quality that he most admired in Andrew Johnson. He answered without a moment's hesitation: "President Johnson never forgot where he had come from, who he really was. Some people, particularly politicians," Burke continued, "have a tendency to act as if their past never happened. Once they achieve prominence, they seem to disavow their roots. Andrew Johnson never did that. When political opponents would mock him as 'the mechanic president,' for instance, poking fun at his blue-collar background as a tailor, President Johnson would turn their comments back on them, announcing his pride in his simple working class roots. He would insist that his humble beginnings gave him an understanding of the common man, the citizens whom he had come to Washington to serve." Burke paused thoughtfully before continuing: "He was the most thoroughly grounded politician I have ever studied."

Then Burke followed up with two key observations: "When you go over to the Homestead, don't miss the stream in the back yard of that property. That, so the story goes, was the place where the Johnsons had first camped upon their arrival here in Greeneville. In later years the President could stand on his back porch and be quickly reminded of his first moments here. That was just like him. And don't miss," he added, "the horseshoe paperweight on the desk in his office. As a tailor he had used it to weigh down his fabric when he was cutting out patterns, and as an elected official he had taken it with him to Washington as a constant reminder of his working class origins."

One of the remarkable attractions of the Visitor's Center Museum graphically illustrates those origins. It is the actual tailor shop in which Johnson had begun his professional life here in Greeneville. He had purchased this simple structure in 1830 for $51.00, but had not been able to buy the land on which it was then standing. As a result he had had the building moved to its present site, and it was at this location that he had established himself in town as a journeyman tailor. The room in the museum where the tailor shop stands today was carefully constructed around it, so that the shop remains on the very spot it was located when young Andrew Johnson worked here.

It is easy for visitors to the museum to look inside the shop. Doing so speaks volumes about this enterprising young man. Because he had been apprenticed so early in life, Johnson had not been able to enjoy much formal schooling. Instead, he would hire people to come in and read aloud while he sat cross-legged on the large cutting table to work with fabric. In this way he had been able both to keep up with the political events of the day and to familiarize himself with some of the literary works which his busy life would not have given him time to read. His wife, Eliza, a girl he had seen when he had first come to Greeneville and whom he had married when he was 18 and she 16, helped him to learn to write and spell. And he also had quickly realized that he had a gift for oratory as well as for tailoring.

Burke led us to a glass case in another room of the museum. "Don't miss this display," he enjoined us. "This was his copy of his favorite book, *The American Speaker*. It was a collection of famous speeches, and it inspired him to speak out for himself. This book changed his life."

Indeed it had. The tailor shop became a center for debate and disputation. Here Andrew Johnson would learn how to speak his mind about the issues facing his nation and to do so in a way that made others listen to and agree with him. It was the launching pad for a political career that, after humble local beginnings, would lead him to the governorship of his state, to the United States Congress, and even to the White House.

So wherein lies the key to an understanding of this man, this thoroughly "grounded" politician from eastern Tennessee? Among all the pieces of literature he had heard read to him as he had earned a living for himself and for his family, the most important had been the Constitution of the United States and the Bill of Rights. These documents had come to form the very core of his thinking.

To illustrate this, one need only review his comments in the United States Senate in December of 1860, when the senators from South Carolina were leaving that body to follow their state into rebellion. On that occasion Johnson had proclaimed loudly, "I am opposed to secession. I think that this battle ought to be fought not outside, but inside of the Union, and upon the battlements of the Constitution itself." He continued by stating that he was unwilling "to walk outside of the Union which had been the result of a Constitution made by patriots ...." He concluded that the government established by such luminaries as Washington, Adams, Jefferson, and Madison should be "good enough for us."

This was the speech that had drawn praise from *The New York Times* , and it made Andrew Johnson an overnight hero throughout the northern states while it branded him a traitor in much of the south. It also was the beginning of the contradictory opinions regarding Johnson so clearly evidenced in the two lists of historical facts mentioned earlier.

Each of these historical facts is literally true, but, as is always the case, the facts have contexts that contain vital information pointing to more complex and sometimes larger truths than are immediately apparent.

Take, for instance, the charge of drunkenness. It is a fact that Johnson came to his inauguration as Vice President in a somewhat wobbly condition. But the cause had been medicinal not celebratory. Johnson had reluctantly returned from his duties as military governor of Tennessee at Lincoln's urging. By the time he had arrived in Washington, the Vice President-elect had become quite unwell and feverish. To combat his illness, he had asked a friend for a drink of whiskey prior to the inauguration, and its effect on him had been disastrous. Had he kept still, people might not have noticed his state, but he decided to speak at length. His remarks rambled and were clearly the product of his inebriation. Johnson's subsequent mortification led him to stay incommunicado for several weeks. Abraham Lincoln himself, however, had the last–and best–final assessment of his new Vice President: "Andy ain't a drunkard." Enough said.

The charge of racism, however, is more difficult to challenge. On what non-racist grounds, for instance, could a President veto both the Freedmen's Bureau Bill and the Civil Rights Act, the latter of which would ultimately be enacted in 1868 as a result of the 14th Amendment to the Constitution? Johnson's answer to this question is both clear and, to a modern reader, rather confusing. When speaking to a crowd of admirers, he assured them, "Honest conviction is my courage. The Constitution is my guide." How could this be?

The very fact that before the Civil Rights Act could become law a constitutional amendment had been necessary indicates that Andrew Johnson knew the law as well as anyone in Washington. He was particularly familiar with the first ten amendments to the Constitution, Madison's Bill of Rights, the tenth article of which stated "The powers not delegated to the United States by the Constitution … are reserved to the States …." Since there was no Constitutional provision for making freed slaves citizens, any act of Congress that arbitrarily did so would, in his eyes, be unconstitutional because such a law would infringe upon the rights of the individual states to determine how they would handle this matter. Hence, the presidential veto.

But any fair assessment of President Johnson's racial views must honestly admit his prejudiced opinions regarding the newly freed slave population. In 1865, he would write a letter to Benjamin B. French, the commissioner of public buildings in Washington, D.C. which put the matter beyond question: "Everyone would and must admit that the white race was superior to the black, and while we ought to do our best to bring them … up to our present level, that, in doing so, we should, at the same time raise our own intellectual status so that the relative position of the two races would be the same" (Trefousse, *Andrew Johnson*, 236). The fact that many other whites in America shared his views does not alter the clear prejudice such words reveal. Yet, Johnson could argue, a similar sentiment had already been voiced in the very Constitution he had sworn to protect and defend when the signatories of that document had agreed to count a slave as only "three-fifths" of a person when determining any state's total number of inhabitants. (It would take three Constitutional amendments—the 13th, 14th, and 15th—and more than a century of civil strife to finally approach racial equality throughout the United States.)

Regarding President Johnson's impeachment, again the historical fact needs the larger context of history. The radical Republicans in Congress were outraged at Johnson's plans for the readmission of former Confederate states to the Union, and they wanted to limit the power of the Presidency in any way they could. By enacting the Tenure of Office Act of 1867, they had attempted to make it impossible for the President to dismiss a member of his cabinet without congressional approval. Johnson went ahead and fired Edwin Stanton anyway. Stanton, a Lincoln appointee, had been funneling privileged information to Johnson's political enemies. Now the Republicans thought they had a way to dispose of their unwanted President. Andrew Johnson was impeached in the House of Representatives on the grounds of his disregard of the Tenure of Office Act. In the subsequent trial held in the Senate, he avoided removal from office by the narrowest of margins.

Although it took over fifty years to clear up this abuse of congressional power, in the 1926 case of Myers v. United States, the Supreme Court included in its majority opinion an acknowledgement that "the Tenure of Office Act of 1867, insofar as it attempted to prevent the President from removing executive officers who had been appointed by him by and with the advice and consent of the Senate, was invalid." Somewhere Andrew Johnson must have been smiling.

Our last activity here in Greeneville was a visit to the Johnson Homestead, the house where the Johnsons had lived starting in 1851, the house Eliza and the children had fled in 1862 when Andrew had been sent to Nashville to become the military governor of the state, and the house to which the family had returned after Johnson's presidential years. It was a large but unassuming brick structure located directly on one of the main roads leading into the center of town. Here we were to meet another wonderful National Park guide, a gentleman named Daniel. Burke had called ahead to notify him that we were coming ("You will enjoy these two," I had heard him assure his colleague), and Daniel welcomed us from the back porch of the home as we left our car and neared the building.

Daniel had his own stories to tell about Andrew Johnson. He began by asking us to imagine Johnson's feelings upon first entering the United States House of Representatives as an elected member of that august body and learning that his desk adjoined the desk assigned to former President, now Representative from Massachusetts, John Quincy Adams.

As he then led us into the front hall of the house, I was struck by the pragmatic utility of this home. No elegant furnishings graced the area where guests would have come in directly from the roadway—just a simple hall with a door on either side and a straight stairway leading to the second floor.

Daniel opened the right hand door, announcing as he did, "This room was President Johnson's bedroom and study." A double bed had been placed against the inner wall of this room, while opposite it, on the street side wall was a breakfront and a small wooden desk, piled high with books, papers, and a single reading lamp. Almost immediately

Andrew Johnson's Horseshoe Paperweight

upon entering, I remembered Burke's instruction: "Look for the horseshoe on President Johnson's desk." There it was, readily visible. It was a wonderful reminder of that "grounded" quality that Burke had so admired. This was no elegant horseshoe memento presented to an important public figure. It was a simple and obviously used object that was now being employed as an effective paperweight. But it also connected its user to the life of the "mechanics" of his country, one of whom he had most certainly and proudly been. I was happy to be close enough to the desk to be able to get a clear picture of this telling artifact, and we then continued our tour of the house.

There wasn't a great deal more to see. Opposite President Johnson's room on the first floor was a parlor where he could meet with guests. It was not decorated in any notable way and, like everything else here, had clearly been arranged in the most utilitarian manner possible.

Upstairs we were shown some recently discovered graffiti that had been left by Confederate soldiers as they had ravaged and damaged the home at the end of the war. Daniel also led us into the Johnsons' sole guest room and then into Mrs. Johnson's second floor bedchamber where she had lived as an invalid for many years. "Her illness had separated them," Daniel quietly commented, responding to our question about why Johnson had chosen to sleep in his office on the first floor.

The final portion of our tour of the home was a series of rooms off the ell which extended perpendicularly from the original house. These were children's rooms, a formal dining area, and a downstairs kitchen, all connected by a covered porch walkway.

Andrew Johnson's Creek in Greeneville, Tennessee

As we thanked Daniel for his thoughtful guidance, he reminded us to take a stroll behind the house to see the stream, still preserved on the property, where the Johnsons had first camped out upon their arrival in Greeneville. We walked down from the Homestead about a hundred yards or so, and there, surrounded by some split rail fencing, lay a pool of clear water that the stream had made. Was the story true? It was impossible to determine, but obviously the family had wanted this spring on their land, and it remained here nearly a century later as a reminder of the Johnson family's inauspicious arrival.

Andrew Johnson had been an unexpected President. He had assumed power at one of the most difficult periods of the history of the United States. And he had followed a leader who is still universally regarded as one of the greatest of American Presidents. Johnson had fully shared Lincoln's beliefs about reconstructing the union, yet he also seemed unable to appreciate the depth of the pain the Civil War had inflicted on the northern states. Even more significantly, he had not comprehended that the larger meaning of emancipation was not simply that slavery had been abolished, but that all people were now to be seen and treated as equals.

At the end of his life, he was once again elected to serve in the Senate, continuing his legacy of service. Still, as Burke had told us right after our arrival, he had never forgotten his roots, his humble origins.

This quality of being so resolutely "grounded" in the reality of his beginnings must have made the challenges he had had to face—his battles with Congress, his impeachment and trial—all the more bearable. He had known many hardships throughout his life. But this "grounded" quality must also have made his many successes—ten years' service in the United States House of Representatives, four years as Governor of Tennessee, five years as a Senator from the state of Tennessee, two years as the military governor of Tennessee, six months as Vice President, three and a half years as President of the United States, and his second election to the Senate seven years after his Presidency—all the more remarkable in his eyes. He was—and is—a man well worth remembering.

Perhaps his best epitaph was written by a columnist of the Cincinnati *Commercial* who was covering the story of Johnson's unprecedented re-election to the United States Senate, subsequent to his Presidency: "With Andrew Johnson in the Senate, we can dismiss all fears for the safety of the Constitution" (Trefousse, *Andrew Johnson* 372). This had been his goal all along.

17

Ulysses S. Grant: "...a dream remembered"

18th President Ulysses S. Grant (1869-1877): Whitehaven in St. Louis, MO

Almost everyone, it seems, wants him. Kent State historian Philip Weeks, in his 2003 collection of articles entitled *Buckeye Presidents*, proudly announces Grant as "...the first Ohio-born president ..." which, of course, is quite true. Yet, Weeks also feels compelled to add later in the same sentence, "...few people actually thought of him as a native of the state" (49).

Illinois, too, lays claim to this hero of the Civil War. Galena, Illinois, proudly boasts the Victorian brick home presented in 1865 to

Grant by the grateful citizens of Galena on the occasion of his triumphal return to the city he had left five years earlier.

Then, there is New York. Not to be outdone by Ohio and Illinois, the New York state park system, together with the Friends of Grant cottage, lovingly preserve the Mount McGregor retreat near Sarasota Springs where Grant spent his final days feverishly laboring over his *Personal Memoirs* just prior to his death. And, of course, New York's most prestigious claim to Grant is evidenced in his magnificent tomb in New York City's Riverdale Park, certainly a crown jewel location to memorialize the great man.

How, then, does it come about that the Ulysses S. Grant National Historic Site, administered by the National Park Service, is to be found in Missouri, near St. Louis?

This question may only be fully answered by addressing another query. Despite all the various claimants to Grant's legacy, what, if anything, was it Grant's desire to be claimed by? Or more simply, what did Grant long for, what did he desire above all else?

The life and military career of Ulysses S. Grant may provide one of the greatest ironies of American history, an irony most clearly on display at the plantation house of White Haven in Missouri. Not that this site is without its literal connection to Grant's life. As was the case in Ohio, Illinois, and New York,

Ulysses S. Grant's Hardscrabble in St. Louis, Missouri

Grant lived for several years on the land of what is now known as the Ulysses S. Grant National Historical Site. It was here at White Haven that he first met and fell deeply in love with Julia Dent, the sister of one of his army friends. It was here that he returned in 1854 to live and farm after first leaving military service. It was here that he built the one still standing structure that evidences his actual handiwork, an oversized log cabin he nicknamed "Hardscrabble" which is currently located on land owned by the St. Louis Busch family as part of their "Grant's Farm" tourist attraction just west of the National Park site. But none of these facts, on the surface, would appear to give Missouri a more legitimate claim to Grant than any other of the would-be contestants for this honor.

And here the irony begins.

Surely no one would appreciate as much as Grant himself these states' determined rush to claim him as their own—this man who, during his lifetime, was so often both lauded and reviled. His victory at Ft. Donaldson may have made him a national hero ("Unconditional Surrender Grant"), but the first day of fighting at Shiloh led to widespread accusations suggesting his ineptness as a strategist and inadequacy as a commander. Such seismic shifts in popular opinion were to dog Grant throughout his military and political life.

For a historian, the challenge of plotting the nation's vacillating opinions about and support of Grant becomes almost exclusively a matter of timing. After Cold Harbor, he's a heartless brute, an insensitive waster of human life. After Appomattox, he's the nation's greatest general since Washington. When he accepts the Republican party's nomination for President and states as his campaign motto, "Let us have peace," he is the needed unifier, the one man who can bring "an end to sectional and partisan bickering and racial friction so that the reunited nation could move forward" (Simpson 68). After the Credit Mobilier and Whiskey Ring scandals, Grant becomes the disingenuous bumpkin, subject to being duped by unscrupulous con men out to use him to further their own political influence and to line their own pockets.

And where, in all this dissonance, lies the truth?

The record of Ulysses S. Grant, like the varied opinions stated above, appears to be contradictory. As the poet Shelley observed of the west wind in his great "Ode to the West Wind," Ulysses Grant, like that wind, was both "destroyer and preserver." This is the central irony of his life and career, and this is what is on permanent display here at White Haven.

After the National Park's introductory film about the life of Grant, both the screen and the blackout wall behind it rise to reveal a view of the plantation house of White Haven toward which visitors are then invited to walk. The guide moves slowly up a path toward the house, peppering his repartee with interesting questions, such as

"What does it mean to be an American?" and "What, if any, are the necessary limits of personal freedom?" Such queries proceed from the uneasy truth that this home, this Ulysses S. Grant National Park Historic Site, had once been owned and run by Colonial Frederick Dent, Grant's father-in-law, a Southern sympathizer and a slave owner.

The house is painted a lush light green which, on a summer day, makes it blend into the surrounding trees and grass like a bucolic dream. Standing on the front piazza, the porch where Grant had sat with Julia during their courting days, it is hard not to want to drift off into the quiet beauty that pervades the site.

Inside the house, however, there is a striking change. The rooms are completely empty, with the slight exception of some video monitors and electronic picture frames that reenact moments of the history of the house or show a variety of vintage photographs of the various people, including Grant, who lived here. One moves from room to room, each still somewhat permeated by the hypnotic green ambiance of the home's exterior color, but one finds no tables, no chairs, rugs, or wall hangings. Occasionally there is visible a stone fireplace that suggests the age of the structure, but overall, the home is strangely soulless, an empty shell without an inhabiting spirit.

This lack of furnishings is explained by the park ranger as being the result of a fire that had destroyed the Grants' stored belongings, belongings which they had planned to move back into White Haven after having had it remodeled in 1875. The park ranger goes on to state that, rather than decorating the rooms by guesswork, using period pieces to substitute for the Grants' lost furniture, the decision had been made to leave the home empty. However, the ranger assures visitors, White Haven had definitely been the spot where the Grants had wished to return after their presidential years. And, as if to thoroughly prove the point, we were reminded that Grant had held onto the property almost until his death in the year 1885, even though neither he nor Julia ever returned to live here.

"Why not?" is the question that hangs in the air. No one here at the site forwards an explanation. Surely there must have been some more substantial reason than the loss of a set of family furniture. In fact, the answer to this question may point to the central truth, and the central irony, of Grant's life.

How could Grant ever have come back to this place to live? He had spent his heart and soul and had risked his life continuously for four bitter years, devastating the White Haven world and all that it represented. He and his armies and commanders (most famously William Tecumseh Sherman) had leveled and plundered the plantation culture wherever and whenever they had found it. He had put to the sword the slave-dependent economy of the South. And rightfully so.

But, in a strange and apparently self-contradictory way, Grant was not completely immune to the beauty, even to the charm, of the South he had destroyed. It was here in the plantation setting of White Haven where he had found the great and only love of his life. It was here that his first two children had been born. Yet the nation he had preserved could no longer include a White Haven. One wonders whether Grant ever consciously realized the full meaning of his victory.

At the very opening of the 1939 classic film, *Gone with the Wind*, a movie that swept the Academy Awards of its year and remains one of the most beloved of all American films, there is a scene depicting slaves working the plantation of Tara, the central setting of the story to come. Over this image scrolls a stated sentiment most germane to Grant and his relation to White Haven:

There was a land of Cavaliers and Cotton Fields called the old South ...
Here in this pretty world Gallantry took its last bow ...
Here was the last ever to be seen of Knights and their Ladies Fair,
of Master and of Slave ...
Look for it only in books for it is no more than a dream

remembered.
A Civilization gone with the wind ...

In a very real way, Ulysses S. Grant was, even more than his Commander-in-Chief, Abraham Lincoln, the savior of the United States of America. It was his tenacity and fierce determination that had held together the Union army which, on several prior occasions, had crumbled beneath the combined burden of daring Confederate gamesmanship and overly cautious Union strategies. Grant had changed all that. He was determined to win, determined that the nation he loved would not be broken in two in order to justify the inhumane and inhuman practice of slavery.

But the country that emerged from the smoke of the Civil War would be a very different nation from the one that had plunged into the conflict in 1861. This newborn United States would quickly become a land of industry and invention crisscrossed with railroads, its skies blackened with coal smoke, its cities overflowing with ever larger waves of immigrant workers all eager to take part in an American dream that was constantly changing even as they reached out to grasp it. It would be the age of Carnegie and Rockefeller, of Morgan and Harriman.

Yet, even in the mind and heart of the great general, there may have lingered an image of the "dream remembered" of a "pretty world" "called the old South" where "Gallantry [had taken] its last bow." Grant had seen this gallantry firsthand, but whether or not it had made any meaningful impression on him at the time remains unrecorded. It had occurred on that April day in 1865 when Robert E. Lee, dressed impeccably in his best gray uniform, had surrendered his ravaged army to a man "dressed for the field, with boots and breeches mud bespattered" (Freeman 489). This was more than a meeting of two opposing generals. It was a fleeting intersection of two worlds, of the past and of the future, of a kind of America that had been and of a new America that would be.

It was this new America that Grant had ushered into existence. As its President he would often find this newborn nation hard to manage and virtually impossible to oversee adequately in all its innumerable aspects. But it was an America in which there would be no more slavery in its literal sense, and it would be an America that, in the century to come, would stand as a bulwark against tyranny wherever it sprung up in the world.

Only without White Haven. That world was as empty as this site stands today. There was a gentle melancholy in that fact for Grant. He held onto the property until the year before his death, perhaps for no better reason than the many happy personal memories it brought to his mind. Perhaps on some level, he longed to return there, however momentarily. Perhaps he deeply desired one last enjoyment of that "pretty world" of intoxicating verdure.

But there was no going back. Not ever.

Ulysses S. Grant's Home in Galena, Illinois: The Gift of a Grateful Nation

Ulysses S. Grant's Home in Galena, Illinois

Galena is a town I hadn't expected. Nestled in the top northwest corner of the state of Illinois, it had seemed almost inaccessible to the casual traveler. On several occasions prior to the spring of 2010, Carol and I had planned a visit here, only later to conclude that the place was too remote, too "off the beaten path," to be able to be included in our travel plans. But surely, I thought, if we ever **do** get to visit such a backwater location, it would be quaint and peaceful.

By the time Carol and I finally made it here, however, we found an astonishing array of boutiques, restaurants, and shops clustered along what remains of the once busy Galena River. Even more importantly, we were treated to a visit of another home of Ulysses S. Grant.

The house itself, like its famous occupant, was unassuming, direct, and unpretentious. One enters a small front hall that leads almost immediately to what our docent described as "General Grant's favorite room"–the library. It is a small chamber not measuring more than 12 x 15 feet in which were to be seen two large bookcases, a central table with two or three chairs, and a cigar holder, left from the time of Grant's residence. It was a serviceable room, but it paled by comparison to the libraries of Grant's immediate successors, Rutherford Hayes and James Garfield. Certainly it was a room full of volumes indicating an active and engaged mind–but in no way was it a scholar's study.

Across the hall from this first room was a larger, lighter front parlor, the home's most formal area, filled with horsehair rockers and mementos from the Grants' world travels in the years immediately following his Presidency.

Then there was the dining room, another large space with a multi-leaved table which displayed samples of the Grants' presidential china.

And, aside from the modest kitchen in the back of the house, nothing more was to be found on the first floor.

The upstairs rooms were reached by a precipitously steep spiral stairway which ended in a small hallway that gave onto five small bedrooms. The site curators had associated each room with one of the Grants' four children, though only the youngest two of them had actually ever lived here. President Grant and Julia's bedroom was the largest, yet even it could not have been more than fifteen feet square. Their bed boasted a beautifully carved dark wooden headboard, but the linens were plain, the room heated by only a freestanding black coal stove (they were ubiquitous throughout the home).

In sum, the Galena house, like the General and President to whom it had been given by the town's grateful citizens, was unprepossessingly plain, bland, ordinary.

It is amusing to read accounts—and there are many of them, dating all the way back to firsthand reminiscences of his friends and early acquaintances—that identify Grant as somehow "mysterious." It is arguable that no less mysterious man ever led an army or occupied the White House. The only truly mysterious element of Ulysses S. Grant is the fact that so many others found him to be mysterious. What accounts for this? Perhaps the lamentable fact that straightforwardness is so frustrating to scholarly and/or ambitious minds.

President Grant **was** straightforward—a straightforward failure and a straightforward success. The house in Galena was a perfect reflection of his character. It is exactly what it appears to be: an adequate dwelling for a family of five—no more, no less.

Ulysses S. Grant's Childhood Home in Georgetown, Ohio and Birth Home in Point Pleasant, Ohio: Lys

Ulysses S. Grant's Boyhood Home in Georgetown, Ohio

As far as Nancy Purdy was concerned, the matter was settled. There was no debate. Ulysses S. Grant was America's greatest general. He was one of our most important Presidents. He was, first and last, an Ohioan. And Georgetown was his home. "He lived here in the house you're standing in front of longer than anywhere else in his entire life," she informed us on the pleasant April morning when she met Carol and me to guide us through the local sites associated with our 18th President.

In our travels throughout the United States visiting presidential homes and sites, we have come to appreciate especially the efforts of the men and women who have devoted themselves to the presentation and preservation of the lives of the men who have served our country as its Chief Executive. Each President deserves such thoughtful caretakers of his legacy. Ulysses S. Grant can rest easy in this regard. Nancy Purdy is standing watch.

I knew from the moment I heard her voice on the telephone that Carol and I would love getting to meet her. Nancy and her husband live in the Bailey House, a residence that had been purchased by the Purdy family in 1871 and which currently doubles as Georgetown's only bed and breakfast establishment. Located just half a block up the street from the Grant site, it allows Nancy to move with remarkable ease between her dual roles as Grant site docent and interpreter and inn proprietor.

"The Bailey family," she informed me in our first telephone conversation, "played an important part in Grant's life. Their son Bart was a childhood friend of 'Lys, though he was a year or two older."

" 'Lys?" I interrupted her momentarily.

"Oh, that was Ulysses' nickname as a boy. Everybody knew him as 'Lys because he preferred his middle name to his given first name, Hiram. But that's another story. Anyway, Bart Bailey, the son of a local doctor, had been awarded a spot in West Point, but he wasn't able to pass his examinations that would have permitted him to stay. Mrs. Bailey confided to Mrs. Grant that her son had been expelled, and Mrs. Grant told her husband. He contacted his Senator and had him convince the local Representative, a man named Thomas Hamer, that 'Lys should get the open spot. So in 1839 young Ulysses Grant went off to West Point." There was a long pause on the telephone. Then Nancy added, "Can you imagine how the history of our country might have been changed if Ulysses had never gone to West Point? We may well owe the Union to Bart Bailey who opened up a space that allowed the man who would become our greatest general to acquire the knowledge he needed to lead his armies to victory!"

At that moment, I knew that Carol and I were going to travel to Georgetown, Ohio, to visit the sites there connected with Grant and to meet Nancy Purdy. She had stories I had never heard.

As we wound through small and curvy country roads into Georgetown, our GPS indicated that we were nearing our destination. "You have arrived," it finally informed us, but after parking our car, I saw no house that looked like the photographs I had seen of this site. I had thought that the Grant house was a two-story structure painted bright white. Nothing here corresponded to that image. Nevertheless, before we had had much of a chance to look around further, a pleasant woman walked up to us and introduced herself as Nancy Purdy.

"Welcome to Ulysses S. Grant's hometown," she began cheerfully.

We exchanged introductions, and then I asked her, "Is this," pointing to the large house before which we had parked, "the Grant Boyhood Home?"

"It certainly is," she answered smiling.

"All the pictures I've seen of it showed it painted white," I commented.

"It *was* ," she answered quickly, and it seemed to me that she was pleased that I had been aware of this. "The Ohio Historical Society has just spent a great deal of money, over a million dollars, restoring the home, and I'm very grateful. The Grants *did* paint their brick home white. The paint sealed the bricks and prevented them from being subject to the elements. But the researchers were sure that the home wouldn't have been painted, so they removed it as part of their restoration work."

"Over there," Nancy continued, pointing across the street in front of the home, "was the tannery where Ulysses' father Jesse Grant worked. You probably know that Ulysses *despised* the tannery. But," she continued, "you must also know that he *loved* working with horses. He wasn't a lazy boy. He just hated the bloody work of the tannery."

Nancy fully appreciated the irony of the fact that the greatest general of the Union forces during the Civil War had detested "the bloody work" of his father, but, as it was the fact, she proceeded with our tour without hesitation.

She gave us a detailed history of the house: how it had been built in 1823 and its attached kitchen constructed in 1825, how Jesse Grant had added its enlarged front section in 1828, and how the home had been sold by the Grants in 1845. Finally in 1979, after decades of relative neglect, the home had been purchased and saved by John and Judy Ruthman who turned it into a museum the following year. Nancy finished this part of her narrative as we approached the rear door of the home. Before we entered, she looked at me.

"You're interested in what these places teach you about the Presidents who lived in them, I believe."

I nodded in agreement.

"Then look at that stone. Don't forget it. I'll tell you its story after we've seen the house."

The stone to which she had called my attention was a rather massive piece of flat creek stone over eight feet long by four feet wide and perhaps eight or nine inches thick. A plaque had been placed in the upper middle of its length, but I hadn't the time to read it before Nancy invited us inside.

Massive Flat Creek Stone

As we moved from room to room, Nancy would point out wooden chairs that had been crafted by Jesse Grant and domestic implements that would have been used by his wife, Hannah. She also commented on various decisions made during the recent restoration of the site. But most of all, as I had hoped, Nancy was full of stories. Stories, not about the Ulysses S. Grant of the Civil War, but stories of 'Lys's youth in Georgetown.

We heard about his remarkable way with horses and how, at the age of five, 'Lys had astonished the townsfolk by standing barefoot atop a horse as he galloped through town. We learned that by the time he was seven years old 'Lys had begun to haul freight and passengers to make money for the family. "It was his way out of the tannery," Nancy reminded us. She even shared with us her belief that the young 'Lys and his childhood friend, Dan Ammen, may have been surreptitiously involved in activities with the Underground Railroad. "Jesse was an ardent abolitionist," she said, "so 'Lys's sympathies had always been on the side of escaping slaves." "In fact," she added, "it was Jesse's abolitionist beliefs that had led him to construct a brick home in the first place. Arsonists burned frame houses. They couldn't do much to brick."

Of course there was no way to test the veracity of many of these tales, though Grant himself alluded to some of them in his memoirs. But they were wonderful stories, and young Ulysses Grant emerged from them in my eyes as a living, breathing boy rather than the stolid, determined soldier of the history books. Nancy hadn't forgotten the stone, however. As we exited the house, she brought us before it once again.

"When 'Lys was twelve or thirteen years old," she began, "a Dr. Buckner of Georgetown had had this rock carved out at the nearby White Oak Creek. It was to have been set as the front stone step of a house he had recently built for himself. When the time came to move the stone, however, the five men sent to do the job couldn't budge it. They returned to Dr. Buckner and explained to him that the stone was too heavy to be transported safely to the desired site."

Nancy looked at us before she continued. "Now you'll learn something important about Ulysses Grant," she began. "Young 'Lys heard about Dr. Buckner's difficulty, and he assured him that he could move the stone himself and set it in place. 'Would the doctor pay him to do so?' he had asked. 'Of course,' Dr. Buckner had responded." Nancy stopped again. "Can you figure out if or how he succeeded?"

It was an interesting question. The stone was massive. Surely it weighed at least a ton. Frankly, it appeared to be an impossible task, and Nancy was happy to finish her story.

" 'Lys took a team of horses and a wagon down to White Oak Creek. Finding the stone, he dug a trench on either side of its length. Each trench was deeper on one end, and he gently backed the wagon wheels into the trench ruts on either side. Then he dug holes beneath the stone through which he pulled chains and attached them to the axles of his wagon. Once this was done, he mounted the wagon very slowly and then deliberately urged the team up out of the creek bed. As the wagon wheels moved toward the shallower part of the trenches 'Lys had dug, the chained stone came along with the wagon, hanging beneath it. 'Lys carefully drove the team to Dr. Buckner's house site, cut new trenches where the stone was to be set, backed his wagon and its load into those trenches, and placed the stone by removing the chains. It remained there until 1907," Nancy concluded almost reverently.

This story was local lore, of course, but there must have been some general credence given to it, for when the old Buckner house was being demolished, the stone had been saved and moved to a nearby cemetery. Then when the recent restoration of the Grant home was under way, Nancy had urged the Historical Society to bring it to the home site. "And here it sits," she reported triumphantly. "Now you tell me," she added, "was there ever a problem that Ulysses Grant couldn't solve?" She paused. "Even bringing an end to slavery?"

With these questions still ringing in our ears, Nancy took us to see the old one room schoolhouse where Grant had received his rudimentary education at the hands of an architect turned teacher, J. D. White. Carol and I wanted to treat Nancy to a lunch in Georgetown, and, after our quick tour of the schoolhouse, she graciously accepted our invitation. We drove into town and paused in our walk to the restaurant to see the newly finished statue of General Grant just off the town square. Lunch was filled with more stories. About the statue. About the general.

I was so glad we hadn't missed the opportunity to meet this wonderful lady.

Later that day, Carol and I drove south to Point Pleasant where stood the Grant Birthplace, a tiny rental home where the future President had been born in April of 1822 and where he had spent the first year of his life. The docent at the site was an articulate young man named Greg who showed us through the 19'x15½' interior that constituted the home's entire living space.

Grant's Birthplace in Point Pleasant, Ohio

This single room was bedchamber, nursery, kitchen, and parlor all in one. The cradle on the floor beside the double bed was said to be like the cradle that had rocked the young Ulysses, and the rifle suspended over the mantelpiece was similar to the gun Jesse Grant would have hung there. Just beneath the foot of the bed was displayed a more reliably original item: a box across the top of which Jesse Grant had spelled out his initials, "J R G," in brass tacks. And tucked into one corner of this all-purpose room was another piece of furniture that had actually belonged to the Grant family: a substantial china cabinet.

Just outside the front windows of the home the Ohio River flowed by quietly, marking the boundary line between Ohio and Kentucky, between the free states and slave territory. And now Greg's enthusiasm began to show clearly as he spoke to us about the subject that was most dear to his heart: abolition. He reminded us that Jesse Grant had apprenticed as a tanner with Owen Brown, father of the famous abolitionist. Greg had several interesting Underground Railroad stories in his repartee, and we enjoyed hearing them. However when I shared Nancy Purdy's belief that 'Lys Grant himself might have been involved in helping escaped slaves find their way to freedom, Greg was a bit skeptical.

"There's no documented evidence of that," he commented. "It might be true. Certainly we know that his father was involved in the abolition movement, but absent any tangible proof, it's hard to say." I decided not to pursue the topic any further.

There wasn't much more to see here, so in less than an hour we were ready to depart. Carol, however, had stopped to look intently at a plaque hanging on the wall of the entrance room to the site. She called me over to see it.

"There's another remarkable caretaker of Grant's memory here in Ohio," she spoke softly. "Look at this."

I moved over to the plaque and read its inscription: "To Loretta Fuhrman in recognition of 25 years of service to the U.S. Grant Birthplace. April 27, 1991."

"This was awarded 23 years ago, and Greg told us that Loretta still serves here as a volunteer. That's 48 years of devotion!" Carol exclaimed. "Pretty impressive!"

Indeed it was. And as we drove west toward Cincinnati on the road running beside the river, my thought returned to that other faithful caretaker of Ulysses Grant's memory, the woman with whom we had spent our morning: Nancy Purdy. I kept recalling her final questions to us as we had stood looking down at that massive piece of rock and its apparent immobility: "Was there ever a problem that Ulysses Grant couldn't solve? Even bringing an end to slavery?" I realized that this flat creek stone had been much more than an occasion for telling a memorable anecdote, much more even than a seemingly impossible problem for a young teenaged boy to solve. It stood as a testament to the character of Grant himself, the leader, the future President. It was hard evidence of his determination, of his imagination, and of his ability to do whatever it took to get a job done. This was why Nancy had insisted that we end our house tour there. She had wanted us to understand fully that 'Lys Grant had been no ordinary child, no ordinary young man. He was greater than that. In fact, he had been most aptly named. He was a "Ulysses" indeed.

18

Rutherford B. Hayes: The Foundation of Prosperity

19th President Rutherford B. Hayes (1877-1881): Spiegel Grove in Fremont, OH

A stately forest, a sawed off tree limb with an unexploded artillery shell embedded in it, and a lithograph of Ralph Waldo Emerson. These images have come to add meaning to my understanding of

Rutherford B. Hayes, and I had known nothing about any of them prior to visiting Spiegel Grove in Fremont, Ohio. They each indicate, yet again, the importance of seeing the places where our Presidents have lived and the value of pausing to reflect on the environments they took the time to create.

The overall effect of spending a morning at Spiegel Grove was to explode the cliché riddled name of Rutherford B. Hayes and put in its place a compelling image of a man whose reputation, as his contemporary, Mark Twain, predicted, "...would steadily rise into higher and higher prominence ... until at last it would stand out against the horizon of history in its true proportions" (Hoogenboom 112).

The images of both Rutherford and Lucy Hayes, perhaps more than any other President and First Lady before or since, have become so clouded with clever epithets that one might be tempted to wonder whether or not taking the time to visit their home in Fremont, Ohio, would be worth the effort. Aren't the cynical quips all that one need say? (I have consciously decided here not to repeat such misleading witticisms, as doing so would tend merely to reinforce them rather than to debunk their veracity.)

For many, Hayes's election was an egregious miscarriage of political justice and his wife's abstemious nature merely an occasion for bemused contempt. Yet the home at Spiegel Grove attests, quite oppositely, to an honest and open dignity that more than belies any such facile characterizations of its owners.

In fact, upon arriving at Spiegel Grove, one's first impression is that of entering an arboretum. Specimen trees spread luxuriant foliage throughout the grounds, and only gradually does the home itself become visible as the road winds closer to the Presidential Library and Museum, placed in close proximity to the house.

In the days after our visit, I have come to appreciate the metaphoric nature of the entrance to this site, for a similar effect has happened to my thinking about Hayes as a result of seeing this house: a man almost wholly obscured has gradually become clearer the nearer I have approached his dwelling place.

The Presidential Library, Carol and I learned soon after we entered to buy our admission tickets, was the first such institution ever opened to the public (and it included an impressive letter gallery featuring many handwritten as well as typed notes from later Presidents inquiring about various details regarding the establishment of their own libraries).

The Museum had on display a variety of Hayes artifacts, ranging from his early years to his post-presidential period, including a wonderful dollhouse (a Christmas present for their beloved daughter, Fanny, given to her while the Hayes family was living in the White House), an elegant American Indian armchair made entirely of elk horns, and the horse drawn carriage that Hayes had employed during his Presidency.

Tucked away in an opposite corner of the museum, however, was another sort of remembrance: a grim souvenir of significant meaning to anyone wanting to understand one of the seminal shaping influences in the life of this President.

The Sawed Off Tree Limb and the Unexploded Shell

At first, I didn't know what to make of it. A section of a tree, perhaps three feet tall, was standing on its end in a corner of the museum. Midway in its length a circular disc of metal was buried in the wood. I took a moment to read a nearby plaque before I realized what I was seeing. It turns out that it was a regular practice of soldiers in the Civil War to bring home with them pieces of trees with bullets or bullet holes from the battles in which they had fought. Hayes's memento, the card informed me, was unusual in that the limb contained an unexploded artillery shell (though, visitors were assured, it had been defused prior to its placement in the museum). It was a striking and indelible reminder that much of Hayes's outlook on life had been forged on the battlefields of the Civil War. Hayes's war experiences, perhaps more than any other events in his life, had shaped both his values and his character.

Depending on which books one reads, Hayes had been wounded either four or five times during the conflict (they all agree that he had had four horses shot out from under him). This fact adds a meaningful dimension to any understanding of his greatest presidential desire: the restoration of harmony within the Union, with a full agreement on the equal rights of all its citizens. These were rights for which Hayes had fought with tireless devotion (even deferring his opportunity to serve in the U.S. House of Representatives until the termination of the war). No one desired peace and equality before the law more than did Rutherford B. Hayes.

But this war memento was also a reminder of dilemmas which still lay before him. Right from the start of his administration, Hayes had faced the unexploded shell of continuing racism and a defiantly dissatisfied Reconstructed South. Even the results of his contested presidential election had threatened to plunge the divided nation into violent dissent.

Hayes, in an effort to pacify his opponents, had vowed from the outset to be a one-term President. This promise, rather than being a mistaken gesture of weakness, as some historians have seen it, was actually typical of Hayes's insistence on living up to his word. He had campaigned on a platform of civil service reform, and, by insuring that political patronage would have no meaning to him, as he would serve only a single term as President, he was announcing the seriousness of his intent to bring about the changes he had outlined. Indeed his entire Presidency was based on the notion of defusing unexploded shells of racism, of bitter sectionalism, even of fractures within his own political party. His simple motto, articulated in his inaugural address, stated, "He serves his party best who serves the country best." Hayes was that rare politician who genuinely believed his own rhetoric.

Spiegel Grove fully reflects the direct simplicity and honest humility of the man. When moving from one room to the next, a visitor is constantly reminded, not simply of Hayes, but of his descendents, many of whom lived here and distinguished themselves in service to their country. This house is no memorial to a single leader, but rather to a large and extended family, including Rutherford, who had worked without stint to insure the continuance of the American way of life.

The Emerson Lithograph

Yet the high-minded goals that had motivated Hayes were not to be achieved during his Presidency. He was forced to confront the undeniable fact that the newly elected Southern Democrats would not conduct themselves in the honorable ways he had hoped would bring about the end of discrimination. This realization must have heavily reinforced the burden of his office.

As we stood in his beautiful study with its skylight and spacious writing desk, our docent pointed out to us a large collection of pictures adorning the one wall not covered with bookshelves.

"These are all pictures of men with whom Mr. Hayes fought in the war. They were his closest friends," we were told. Yet I couldn't help noticing, right in the center of the large group of mostly military portraits, the gentle, smiling face of the Transcendentalist poet and philosopher, Ralph Waldo Emerson. Well-known Hayes historian Ari Hoogenboom, writing of the post-presidential epoch of Hayes's life, had noted that "he [Hayes] found comfort in the writings of Ralph Waldo Emerson" (113), and here was a clear corroboration of the President's esteem for this famous figure of American letters.

And why not? After all, it was Emerson who had written, "I am constrained every moment to acknowledge a higher origin for events than the will I call mine" ("The Over-Soul" in *Essays: First Series* 252). Certainly such assurance of a divine plan for life articulated a gold standard antidote to the fallacious greenback morality President Hayes had faced from his racist opposition. And even more importantly, it was Emerson who would sound the call for what came to be, in his later years, Hayes's most persistent and cherished cause: universal education. In his essay on "The American Scholar," Emerson had written,

> The one thing in the world, of value, is the active soul. This every man is entitled to; ... not the privilege of here

and there a favorite, but the sound estate of every man.
(Nature, Addresses, and Lectures 91)

No wonder Hayes had placed Emerson's portrait so prominently on his study wall. Emerson, as much as any of the military men whose pictures were displayed around him, had sounded a trumpet call of liberty that resonated deeply in the heart and soul of the maligned President who dreamed of a universal education for "every man."

The Stately Forest

As one sits on the wide and open porch of Spiegel Grove, a porch where, in some of my favorite photographs of Rutherford and Lucy Hayes, the family seemed supremely happy, the aspect is of an almost endless number of beautiful, individually placed, and fully matured trees. They, more even than any room of the house, have come to typify for me the legacy of Rutherford B. Hayes.

Trees don't grow overnight. They need to be planted and tended, watered and pruned. They may even take more than a human lifetime to fulfill their full promise, to reach their final height. But, with the right cultivation the result can be magnificent, and it is arboreal magnificence that surrounds one here.

As a general, Hayes had witnessed the destruction and heartache occasioned by bitter civil strife. As a President, he had learned the hard lesson that the difficulties and divisions of the nation would not be resolved quickly. The solution to all such problems, he came to believe, was education. Education would provide the foundation for the prosperity he so wished for his nation. He was willing to stake everything on it. Hayes spent the final years of his life residing here at Spiegel Grove, speaking in favor of and personally contributing to, educational programs—particularly those instituted to benefit African-American youth. As Ari Hoogenboom observes, "He [Hayes] had faith that progress in race relations would come not from military occupation but over time in small increments through education that would result in the enforcement of the laws by civil tribunals" (108).

Standing on the spacious porch, looking at the expanse of forest beyond the fringe of mowed lawn, one sees the breathtaking results that can take place "over time in small increments." Hayes did not live long enough to see the multiracial society for which he fought. Even universal education would have to weather many judicial storms before it could take root and thrive throughout America. But, more today than ever before, it has taken root, and the trees of Spiegel Grove stand as silent sentinels planted by a man who believed in the power of inevitable growth leading to ultimate victory. It would be a victory that, as Mark Twain had prophesied, would "stand out against the horizon of history in its true proportions."

19

James A. Garfield: "...love's labor..."

20th President James Garfield (1881): Lawnfield in Mentor, OH

James A. Garfield's home in Mentor, Ohio, just east of Cleveland, stands as an interesting metaphor of the man. The house, like President Garfield, began humbly as a farm to which he had wanted to bring his growing family in order to have his sons learn from the land the lessons it had to teach. Yet the real beauty of the home, its element of glory, didn't emerge until after Garfield's death when his widow, his beloved "Crete," added a magnificent second half to the house, in large part for the express purpose of keeping the memory of her husband preserved for future generations.

This memory, Garfield's heritage, however, has proved somewhat problematic, and this may account for the fact that, of the four United States Presidents who have been assassinated, Garfield has remained the least remembered, the least admired, even the least known.

It is tempting, in trying to assess the career of James Garfield, to compare him to his immediate predecessor, Rutherford B. Hayes. There are several reasons to want to do so. Aside from both hailing from northern Ohio, both men had grown up without fathers, Hayes's father dying before his son's birth and Garfield's father dying when his son was only two years old. Both Hayes and Garfield had served in the Civil War; both had been elected to the U. S. House of Representatives during the war; both had been allies of the Radical Republicans in their policies regarding Reconstruction; and neither had actively attempted to win the Republican nomination as the party's presidential candidate in the year he was elected to that high office.

Yet, except in their common struggle to overcome the disadvantages of growing up essentially fatherless, Garfield almost invariably suffers by this comparison. Hayes had fought throughout the war and was heroically wounded several times. Garfield saw action only twice, and his only "victory," an engagement known as The Battle of Middle Creek, was subsequently seen as a fortunate circumstance of facing an opponent as callow as he. Hayes, although elected to the House of Representatives during the war, refused to be seated in the chamber until the end of the conflict, regarding the cause of fighting for the Union a higher calling than being a legislator. Garfield, when elected, resigned his commission in the Army and came to Washington to serve as the youngest member of the House of Representatives. Hayes's reputation in Congress after the war was that of a quiet legislator who consistently backed voting rights for freed slaves. Garfield, similar to Hayes, espoused repeatedly the importance of insuring voting rights for freed blacks, but his voice was heard so frequently and at such length that even his friends and allies advised him to avoid "speaking too many times during his first term" for fear that the other members of Congress would "begin to think he was 'too fond of talking' " (Shaw 128). Hayes had retired to Ohio after two terms in the House of Representatives to become Governor of the state, thus fitting himself for the challenges of the office of Chief Executive. Garfield became a Washington insider, serving eight terms in Congress, even moving his home to Mentor, Ohio, in order to retain a seat in the legislature because his old district had been gerrymandered in favor of the Democrats.

So what **was** Garfield's unique appeal? Wherein had he achieved a positive distinction, separating him from other politicians of his age? In two key areas: his intellect and his articulateness.

James Garfield was a brilliant man with an agile mind. He was an intellectual who loved weighing the numerous sides of any argument. Extremely well read, he had learned to love the give and take of Socratic dialectic at Williams College, and he enjoyed reflecting on both philosophical and political matters. This quality made him very effective in the House of Representatives, as he was always willing to understand the many sides of any issue under consideration. The same quality, however, would make it more difficult for him to lead, as he would always have a tendency to hesitate when considering the alternatives of any decision.

Garfield's second great asset was his eloquence. In spite of his overly developed rhetorical zeal as a freshman legislator, Garfield ultimately earned high praise for his ability to present his ideas in a memorable fashion. One reporter wrote, "Mr. Garfield is one of the few Republican statesmen of the day who is a real orator and whose speeches one cannot easily sketch before he delivers them—that is, he is not a party hack and has personal opinions and utters them" (Shaw 129).

Even in placing the name of his political ally, John Sherman, before the Republican National Convention as a candidate for President in 1880, Garfield's speech had been so compellingly delivered that when, as he was concluding his remarks, he asked rhetorically, "What do we want?" at least one convention participant answered spontaneously, "We want Garfield!"

No one appreciated his intellectual brilliance and linguistic acumen more than his wife, Lucretia. In many ways and on several key occasions, it was to be her devotion that would be most successful in encouraging his attempts to achieve the greatness of which she was sure he was preeminently capable.

Such distinction, however, was not to be. Despite his promise, despite his oratorical flair, Garfield's Presidency was to be little more than a footnote in American history. He lacked the tenacity of Grant and the experience of Hayes. He remained an intellectual idealist, eager to consider the many aspects of any problem, but hesitant to come down emphatically on any one side. It was a characteristic that made him some powerful enemies. In the end, even a deranged one.

Charles J. Guiteau, a mentally disturbed man who had recently been denied a diplomatic post, had misinterpreted Garfield's typically equivocal statements regarding sweeping civil service reform. Believing that the President's position was now in adamant opposition to the spoils system, Guiteau had shot the President. Although Garfield clung to life for nearly three months, he finally succumbed to his wounds, dying less than a year after taking office.

Garfield had not been President long enough to have created a clear administrative agenda, and, given his temperament, it is debatable whether or not he ever would have done so. If there were ever to be any permanent appreciation of his character and promise, it fell to Lucretia to create it. It was a task to which she would dedicate the remaining years of her life.

The home at Lawnfield, then, is much more a monument to Lucretia's devotion to the memory of her husband than it is a reflection of Garfield himself (unless one sees in the restored, oversized, 75' tall pump-house windmill that visitors pass on the way to the site's parking lot a tangible reminder of the quixotic idealism of the scholar/President).

The interior of the original farmhouse is dark and overly full of heavy Victorian furnishings. The heart of the home, however, is not to be found here, but rather in the addition Lucretia constructed in the years following her husband's death.

Lucretia Garfield's Addition to Home at Mentor, Ohio

A large stairway ascends to a second floor, leading upward from the back of what would have been the rear wall of the original farmhouse. This wide staircase turns midway, then continues up to the large doorway of what our docent described as "the very first presidential library." Carol and I had recently been told that President Hayes's Library had been the first such collection, and our docent was quick to explain.

"Hayes had the first public library of his memorabilia and presidential papers. The Garfield library was private, open only to those who applied to Lucretia for permission to see or examine President Garfield's papers. She was the first person ever to create such a collection, and, as such, she set the standard for all succeeding presidential libraries."

The room into which we entered was expansive, especially compared to any of the rooms we had seen in the original section of the house. And, even more impressively, it was open and bright. The long, irregularly angled library walls were resplendent with shelf after shelf of books. Garfield, they revealed, was interested in everything, from history to metaphysics, from philosophy to rhetoric. The rugs, the chairs, the spacious feel of the interior made me want to wander through this treasure trove of literature and thought. It was a scholar's heaven, a heaven that Garfield himself had not lived long enough to enjoy.

"And look here," our docent urged us, pointing toward the end of the room. "This is the vault Lucretia had installed in which to hold all of the President's correspondence and papers."

"It looks like a bank vault," Carol noted aloud.

"That's exactly right," our docent responded. "Lucretia was so concerned that none of her husband's writings be lost that she instructed the builders constructing this addition to include a lockable room so sturdy that, were the entire home to burn to the ground, its contents would survive the flames. So they placed this solid steel bank vault here, right off the library, and this is where Lucretia kept all of the President's important papers. The family finally donated them to the National Archives in 1964, but, prior to that, they were all deposited here. Would you like to step into the vault to see it?"

Somewhat hesitantly, we agreed, but I wondered if all the papers were gone, what was the point?

"All we keep in here now," the docent continued, "is the funeral wreath sent to the Garfields by Queen Victoria. Lucretia thought it was so beautiful, she never wanted to lose it, so, after the funeral, she had the wreath sent to a wax sealer who painstakingly removed each flower, preserved it with a coating of thin, clear wax, and then remounted it in its original position. You can see it still looks fresh today."

And, amazingly enough, it did. The wreath was placed on one of the upper shelves of the vault and was encased in a large box with a clear glass lid. The black background of the box's interior made the wax-protected flowers look all the more vivid as we gazed at this unusual memento of an earlier age.

Proceeding back downstairs, we were led into a room at the rear of the addition that had been turned into a small museum which charted the various periods of Garfield's life, and then we left through the back door to head down to the National Park Office through which we had entered the home site.

Lucretia really loved him, I found myself thinking. Surely no one knew him better than she, and undoubtedly, no one had been able to appreciate his mind, his character, even his fallible humanity to a greater extent than had this woman. She probably even had poignantly understood that, unless someone guarded his legacy, he well could have been forgotten in the passage of years. Lucretia's superb addition to the simple farmhouse home bears clear evidence of her determination that this would never happen. She outlived him by 37 years, but one comment she made in 1916, two years before her death at the age of 86, speaks so eloquently of her love that it deserves recording here. Referring to the rather stern, stoic, bearded face of her husband that looks out from various photographs taken of him throughout his life, she observed,

> ...none of his pictures suggest at all the way his face lit up in conversation.... [In fact he always] turned an attentive gaze and ready ear, and offered a hearty handgrasp, with a kindly charm of manner that stands out in everything written or said about him, as distinguishing him from all other men. (Shaw 138)

One senses here at Lawnfield that Lucretia never lost sight of that "attentive gaze." It became her life's work, her love's labor, to enshrine it in the home that continues to bear his name. Her devotion is his most enduring monument.

20

Chester A. Arthur: "I do, I will."

21st President Chester A. Arthur (1881-1885): Birthplace in Fairfield, VT

No one ever expected that Chester Alan Arthur would become President of the United States. James Garfield, the Republican presidential nominee in 1880, was only fifty years old (two years younger than Arthur) and was in excellent health. In fact, it was something of an irony that Chester Arthur had been placed on the

Republican ticket at all. He was a "Stalwart," an advocate of traditional party politics and the "spoils system" practice of rewarding partisan supporters with jobs. This, together with his well-known connections to Roscoe Conkling, a longtime Senator and leader of the New York State Republican party machine, made Arthur the kind of political insider that supporters of Garfield were interested in holding in greater check.

Two years earlier President Hayes had removed Arthur from his lucrative position as Collector of Customs for the Port of New York because of concerns relating to his management of the customhouse and the plethora of workers there whose only qualification for employment had been their political loyalty to the city office holders who had hired them.

So what explains his 1880 nomination for the Vice Presidency? Politics pure and simple. The Republicans' greatest political desire—as still holds true for all political parties—was to win the presidential election. It was widely believed (and rightly so) that they would be unable to do so without winning New York's electoral votes. Putting a Conkling man on the ticket, it was hoped, would mollify the Republicans who were opposed to Garfield's perceived commitment to reformist policies. With Arthur on the ticket, conventional wisdom concluded, the Republicans had a much better chance to carry New York.

And so they did. The Garfield-Arthur pairing scraped by with a razor thin victory in the national popular vote (only a shade more than 2000 votes out of over nine million cast), but they enjoyed a more comfortable 214-155 margin of victory in the Electoral College. So far, everything was proceeding according to plan. Even those who had questioned placing Arthur on the ticket could hardly be disappointed with the outcome of the election. The editor of the reformist magazine *The Nation* was willing to concede that, "There is no place in which his [Chester Arthur's] powers of mischief will be so small as in the Vice Presidency (Weisberger 154).

And then came the afternoon of July 2, 1881.

In the Baltimore and Ohio train station in Washington, D.C., a deranged man with a pistol fatally wounded President Garfield, afterwards shouting to the startled crowd, "I am a Stalwart; Arthur is now President of the United States." On September 19, 1881, after two months of occasional improvements followed by distressing turns for the worse, the President finally died as a result of his wound, and a shaken Chester Arthur was given the Oath of Office in the front parlor of his downtown Manhattan home. He had become the 21st President.

The nation was stunned. This was the second assassination of a United States President in a sixteen year period. And what kind of Chief Executive would a man make who had been removed from a high administrative position under suspicion of dishonest management? Now Chester Arthur held the highest office in the land.

Three weeks earlier, Chester Arthur had received an unusual letter, written by a woman he had never met. Her name was Julia Sand, and most of what is known about her comes from the twenty-three letters she wrote the President between 1881 and 1883. Her first missive sounded a prescient tone:

> The hours of Garfield's life are numbered—before this meets your eye you may be President. The people are bowed in grief; but—do you realize it?—not so much because he is dying, as because you are his successor. What president [sic] ever entered office under circumstances so sad? ... Your kindest opponents say, 'Arthur will try to do right'—adding gloomily—'He won't succeed though; making a man President cannot change him.' ... But making a man President can change him! Great emergencies awaken generous traits which have lain dormant half a life. If there is a spark of true nobility in you, now is the occasion to let it shine. ...The great tidal wave of sorrow which has rolled over the country has swept you loose from your old moorings & set you on a mountaintop alone. ... what shall posterity say? It is for you to choose ....

Who was this extraordinary correspondent? We know that she was the daughter of a German immigrant and that she was born in 1850. We also know that she never married and, at the time of her decision to write the new President, she was living on East 74th Street in New York City. She was painfully shy—except as a writer—and was frequently bedridden.

The extent of Julia Sand's influence on Chester Arthur is, of course, conjectural, but what is beyond dispute is the marked turn-about of disposition and political beliefs that characterized his administration. Stating that "For the vice-presidency I was indebted to Mr. Conkling, but for the presidency of the United States my debt is to the Almighty," Chester Arthur became the kind of Chief Executive that no one would have anticipated.

First, he refused to grant desirable government posts to candidates recommended by Roscoe Conkling. Next, and even more impressively, he became an outspoken advocate of Civil Service reform, overseeing numerous investigations of alleged corruption in government. Most notable of all, he signed into law the Pendleton Act of 1883, the first important legislation establishing non-partisan Civil Service examinations to be given to applicants seeking government appointed jobs. He also vetoed a "Rivers and Harbors Bill" because of its inclusion of excessive "pork barrel" projects unnecessary to the original intent of the legislation. Something very significant had happened to Chester Arthur.

One thing more we know about Julia Sand. She knew her Shakespeare. In a letter she wrote to President Arthur a month into his administration, when the kinds of changes noted above were already becoming evident in his decision-making, she observed, "What a splendid Henry V you are making!" And later in the same message she spelled out her meaning more clearly: "I do not like to think of men as blocks of marble, things that ... cannot be made to expand. I prefer to think of them as things with infinite powers of growth."

Her opening allusion here was to Shakespeare's character of Prince Hal in *Henry IV, Part One*. Hal, the prince who would later become Henry V, one of England's greatest leaders, had, as a young man, earned a widely known—and well deserved—reputation as a roisterer and ne'er-do-well. His chief companion in Shakespeare's

play chronicling his youthful exploits is a marvelous comic character named Falstaff. At one point Falstaff pretends to be the King and
lavishes much praise upon himself. Hal objects to this and playful-
ly suggests that, in fact, Falstaff is nothing more than "... a devil ...
in the likeness of an old fat man." Falstaff protests this characterization, reminding the Prince that to banish Falstaff and his merry
tomfoolery would be to "banish all the world."

Hal has a strangely serious, brief response. "I do, I will."
(II.iv.446-481)

Julia Sand had seen clearly that the President–of whom she
wrote: "As yet I have not met anybody who believes in you as I
do,"–was becoming a man of stature and principle. It is worth noting that Arthur kept all of the letters she sent him.

By the time the election of 1884 was approaching, it was clear to
Arthur that his party would never nominate him for a term of his
own. His reform efforts had outraged the Stalwarts in the Republican party, and the moderate wing of the party still mistrusted the
Conkling-man they had known before his rise to power. Yet after he
departed from office, reporter Melville E. Stone recalled a comment
written by no less an astute observer of politics than the venerable
Mark Twain:

> I am but one in the 55,000,000; still in the opinion of
> this one-fifty-five- millionth of the country's population,
> it would be hard indeed to better President Arthur's ad-
> ministration. But don't decide till you hear from the rest.
> (Stone 147)

The inevitable humor of the last sentence aside, this is meaningful praise from "America's Voice."

So what might Chester Arthur's homes reveal about him? The
building that was his longtime residence both before and after his
term of office still stands at 123 Lexington Avenue in downtown
Manhattan. Wedged into a block of five-story brownstones, its
façade no longer suggests the affluence and prominence this address would have conveyed at the turn of the twentieth century. A

small plaque identifies the location, but the building now houses an Indian grocery store and deli on its first two floors. The upper three stories have been remodeled into urban apartment units.

The one Arthur presidential home available for visiting is his birthplace site in Fairfield, Vermont. And it was toward this rather remote setting that Carol and I were journeying in the summer of 2013.

We crossed from New York into Vermont via ferryboat over Lake Champlain just above Plattsburgh and sped northward on the interstate. There was plenty of time to talk as we traveled.

"Why do you think Arthur underwent such a change after becoming President?" Carol asked me as we neared St. Albans and our first major turn onto increasingly narrow rural roads.

Remembering his political history, I ventured a couple of answers.

"Well," I began, "when the assassin identified himself as a Stalwart who was enthusiastic about having Arthur become President, it surely placed a lot of pressure on him. If Arthur had remained a machine politician, there could have been people wondering whether or not he had helped to engineer the assassination."

"True," Carol responded, "but Arthur's devastation when he learned of the assassination attempt, his exemplary behavior in the months immediately following the shooting, and his grief when President Garfield died—his servant found him weeping like a child with his head in his hands—makes me think he clearly had nothing to do with the attack on Garfield."

"I agree," I continued, "so maybe Arthur's turnabout was an astute assessment of the times. Arthur had always been a successful reader of the political landscape in which he found himself. After Garfield's death, popular opinion had swung decidedly in the direction of reform. Maybe Arthur was just riding the wave, as he had done many times before in his rise to prominence."

Carol listened quietly without comment. Then, in a rather soft voice, she said, "I think that perhaps he didn't change at all. I think he simply allowed himself to become what he had actually always been."

We were traveling a two-lane road now, with impressive ascents and descents as well as numerous twists and turns. The smell of cow dung fertilizer penetrated our still closed car windows, and large—occasionally gigantic—granite boulders shouldered their way up through the earth in the rough and hilly farmland.

"There it is!" Carol called out, and I looked up the ascending grade to see the bright yellow side of a small house set near to the road before us. In just a minute or two, we were turning into an empty parking lot across from the site. We had arrived.

Although the house itself was a replica of the diminutive manse where the Arthurs were living at the time of Chester's birth, a stone marker standing in close proximity to the site indicated that this was indeed a meaningful stop. It read as follows: "On this spot stood the cottage where was born Chester A. Arthur the twenty-first President of the United States. Erected by the State of Vermont." This was the place where Chester Arthur spent his earliest years.

And what a setting it is. The cottage occupies a piece of level ground about two thirds of the way up a steep hillside and is a faithful replica of the manse where the Arthur family lived at the time of their occupancy. It overlooks a valley of small farms with verdant mountains in the distance. The only sounds Carol and I heard on this

Chester Arthur's Birthplace Marker, Fairfield, Vermont

late afternoon were an occasional truck downshifting in order to climb the steep grade of the hill and, after the truck had passed, birdsong. Gnats also abounded here and buzzed around our eyes and ears.

The cottage itself was no larger than a log cabin. Its clapboard siding made it seem less primitive, but its first floor contained only two rooms and a brick fireplace in the center of the structure which would have provided necessary heat to each. The chimney passed straight through the center of the peak of the home. Sleeping quarters would have been located in the attic.

Standing back at our car and looking across the road at this simple—and rather lonely—place, I was struck by the sense of pervasive peace I felt here. Tranquility. The beauty of a bird's melody. An occasional tinkle of a cowbell from a small herd grazing nearby. The distance between this country manse and the hurly-burly of downtown Manhattan seemed unimaginably immense.

As we left the the cottage, we drove back down the hill and turned north. In a moment or two we pulled up to a rise on which had stood the small brick church where Arthur's father had been a minister. Here again, there was a quiet that sank deeply into our eyes and ears. Around the church site spread the forested hills and farms from which William Arthur's rural congregation would come each Sunday to be spiritually guided (and occasionally chided) by him.

Driving the country roads back toward the interstate, both Carol and I felt extremely glad to have visited this place. We were reminded of Arthur's early legal cases involving the abolitionist causes that had been so important to his preacher father. And the injunction of Julia Sand seemed very akin to our thinking: "Great emergencies awaken generous traits which have lain dormant half a life." But Carol's insight also resonated in my thought. Perhaps what had happened to Chester Arthur was much more of a return of character than the "growth" that Julia Sand had urged upon the new President. That lonely "mountaintop" to which the "great tidal wave of sorrow" had lifted Arthur may have been simply his remembrance of the mountaintop of his birth, a return to the roots that had nurtured him from the very beginning.

We couldn't know for sure, of course, but it seemed very possible that, at the moment of his ascension to the office of President, Chester Arthur may have found himself reminded of the simple goodness and clarity of his earliest years. His administration certainly indicated his willingness to stick to what was right, to honor his debt "to the Almighty" that his father had imbued in him from his earliest moments, rather than to continue a course of political expediency.

When he became President, Arthur had a clear decision set before him. Would he continue to act as a Stalwart party machine politico and advocate of the spoils system? Almost everyone expected that such would be the case. Instead, he looked at the long road of ascending power he had traveled, often through means that he himself had identified as highly questionable, and then he had decided to reverse course. Would he really have the courage to turn his back on the morally compromising political process that had brought him so high? His answer, like Hal's, was simple and direct: "I do, I will."

21

Grover Cleveland: "...all that a president ought to be."

22nd and 24th President Grover Cleveland (1885-1889, 1893-1897): Birthplace in Caldwell, NJ

The Civil War had been rough on Democrats. Starting with the controversial election of Abraham Lincoln in 1860, Republicans had identified themselves as the party of national union and of freedom for previously enslaved Americans. The Democrats had been the

party of compromise regarding slavery and of equivocation regarding the continuation of the war. After the Northern victory in
1865 and the subsequent readmission of the Southern states to the
Union, the only region of the country that had remained stoutly
Democratic was comprised of those very ex-Confederate enclaves
that had voted for the last Democratic President: the now widely
discredited James Buchanan.

Following Lincoln's first election, Republicans would hold the
White House in what Mark Twain later described as "a constitu-
tional monarchy with the Republican party sitting on the throne"
(Twain 2). The sole exception to this political dominance would be
Grover Cleveland.

His two non-sequential terms in the White House ran from 1885
to 1889 and from 1893 to 1897. But, as Mark Twain would also observe, "Mr. Cleveland's couple of brief interruptions do not count;
they were accidents and temporary, they made no permanent in-
road upon Republican supremacy" (Twain 2-3).

What explains this extraordinary political landscape? Why, in a
span of over forty years, was Cleveland the only Democrat to be
elected President? How had he managed to buck the Republican
tide, even temporarily? And where could I look for answers to such
questions?

In the first book I ever purchased regarding presidential residences, Irvin Haas's *Historic Homes of the American Presidents*, 2nd
edition, 1991, a volume that included chapters on the American
Presidents from Washington to the first George Bush, the name of
Grover Cleveland was not even mentioned. All the other late 19th
century Presidents were there. Each one, from Ulysses Grant to
William McKinley, had historic homes, some even with presidential
libraries to memorialize their years in the White House. But Cleveland was nowhere to be found. Why was it that Cleveland was so
ignored, perhaps even forgotten, among his presidential peers?

As I continued to collect volumes on presidential homes and as
the internet began to host a plethora of websites on the subject, I
finally became aware of the existence of two houses related to the
life of Grover Cleveland: his post-presidential residence in Prince-

ton, New Jersey and his birthplace house, located in Caldwell, New Jersey. The Princeton home was owned privately, but the birth house, I discovered, was open to the public.

Although I became immediately interested in the possibility of a visit there, it was initially difficult for me to discover much substantial information about who or what organization it was that was overseeing its operation. Also, the site's hours were very limited. While planning our trip, I learned that the venue closed each day for an hour around lunchtime to accommodate the needs of its sparse staff. Just what would Carol and I encounter there? In the summer of 2010, we traveled to Caldwell to find out. (Current visitors to this site's web page are informed that this locale has been open to the public since 1913. Why it was not mentioned in earlier presidential homes books remains a mystery to me. The location is listed as one of several historic sites operated by the state of New Jersey, though tourists are still urged to "call ahead" to insure that the house will be open at the time one expects to arrive.)

Carol and I had been visiting relatives on Long Island, and after a pleasant midmorning drive into New Jersey, we pulled into the side parking lot of the Grover Cleveland birthplace in Caldwell. A cheerful young woman was sitting on the front porch, awaiting our arrival (we had telephoned prior to our visit to insure that someone would be there to meet us), and she happily led us into the front hall.

The house had never been owned by the Cleveland family, she informed us, but had been the manse dwelling provided by the nearby First Presbyterian Church where Cleveland's father, Richard, had held the position of pastor. The Clevelands had lived here for the first four years of young Grover's life before they had moved to western New York, the result of Richard having received a call to the pastorate of the Presbyterian Church in Fayetteville.

Only the first floor of this house was accessible to the public, but there had been obvious efforts expended to collect furnishings appropriate to the period in which the Cleveland family had lived here, including a crib which purported to be original. But there was not much revelatory material on hand to explain either the source of the remarkable political success of Grover Cleveland in later life nor the contemporary neglect his reputation has undergone. In all, we enjoyed a very pleasant tour of a modest country manse, but the only piece of information that truly resonated with me was the family's physical proximity to their church.

These people took their religion very seriously, and this, I have come to suspect, is actually the key to the Cleveland mystery.

Our next stop would be in Princeton, New Jersey, some fifty miles southwest through lovely countryside on minor and sometimes two lane highways. While Carol and I drive for the next hour or so, let's consider some history.

By 1884, most Americans were sick of being reminded of the Civil War. While they still revered the men who had fought to preserve the Union (every President since Andrew Johnson had been involved in fighting the war), the age had a new set of heroes and a new collection of villains, occasionally men identified as both by those who knew or were influenced by them: John D. Rockefeller, Andrew Carnegie, J.P. Morgan. " 'Captains of Industry' or 'Robber Barons?' " my good friend, Jim Evans, a longtime teaching colleague, used to ask his class of United States History students, and this was a query that many Americans were asking themselves in the industrially explosive period that Mark Twain would characterize as "The Gilded Age."

This was a time of great wealth being made, great technological improvements becoming visible everywhere throughout the nation, and great masses of people settling in urban environments, taxing the limits of those cities' abilities to provide healthy and safe living conditions for the workers moving there. With all this came great corruption. City "bosses," ensconced in such centers of power as Tammany Hall in New York City, bought and sold political and judicial influence with a brazen abandon that is hard to believe in the 21st century. Wealthy businessmen often resorted to cutthroat tactics to eliminate competition and swell their already burgeoning coffers to previously unimaginable heights.

Then in the early years of the 20th century, there appeared a group of politicians, both Republicans and Democrats, who would identify themselves as "progressives." And just before the period of their political ascendancy, Grover Cleveland, a Democrat, had been elected President of the United States.

In some key ways, Cleveland was a breed of "progressive" before the name had achieved its widespread popularity. Even a casual perusal of his history reveals the fact that young Grover Cleveland early established himself as a man of noteworthy character. As Erie County Sheriff, as Mayor of Buffalo, and as Governor of New York, Cleveland was simultaneously a zealous advocate of fairness and honest business dealings and a formidable foe of corruption, regardless of the political party of those subjected to his meticulous investigations. While his unusually non-partisan reviews made occasional enemies of those for whom the "spoils system" had become a way of life, they also earned him plentiful praise from Republicans and Democrats alike who were looking for a political alternative to the status quo of kickbacks and back room horse-trading.

When the presidential campaign of 1884 approached, the Democrats felt they had finally found a candidate who might successfully challenge a Republican opponent. And here, the stars were aligned in Cleveland's favor.

One of his weaknesses as a candidate was the fact that, due to his need to provide for his family after his father's early death, Cleveland had hired a substitute to serve for him in the Civil War. While this had been a completely legal practice, it stood in stark contrast to the pedigree of the post-war Presidents who had served before him. It turned out, however, that the Republican candidate of 1884, James G. Blaine, had also hired a substitute to stand in his place during the war. The military issue, then, was a wash.

More serious, however, was the accusation that Cleveland had fathered an illegitimate child. Here, Cleveland's handling of this situation was both dignified and masterful. Instructing his political friends, "Whatever you do, tell the truth," he admitted to having had a relationship with the child's mother years earlier and also that he had continued to provide for the child until such time as it could be adopted.

While recent historians have raised the possibility that the child's actual father may have been Cleveland's married law partner, Cleveland never attempted to shift the blame from himself nor tried to hide his support of the illegitimate child. His forthright response to such a potentially devastating revelation convinced voters of his reliable candor, even when such openness might reveal his human frailties. Cleveland was elected President with a narrow margin of just over 20,000 popular votes out of over 9 million cast.

And now the problems would arise. The very straightforward candor that had made him such a desirable candidate would work against Cleveland's partisan support once he had been elected. On the issues of labor unions and Civil War veterans' claims, for instance, the new President worked tirelessly to benefit only those who, after his careful and personal review, most deserved aid. The result was often a wave of disappointment and disapproval. How could workers, heartened by the President's signing of a bill legalizing national trade unions, understand his later decision to send in soldiers to break the Pullman strike? How could Civil War survivors accept the condition of having to defend their claims for financial benefits before a man who had never served a day in uniform?

Add to all this the most serious economic downturn in the history of the United States up to that time, and the Cleveland administration appeared to many to be little more than a hodgepodge of occasionally contradictory policies. Perhaps, too, these events explain that unique characteristic of his Presidency: that, although narrowly winning the popular vote in his bid for re-election in 1888, he had lost in the electoral college, only to prevail and earn a second term four years later, in 1892. He appears to have been the kind of President about whom it was hard to make up one's mind. I felt that I was getting closer to an answer regarding the neglect surrounding Cleveland's presidential legacy. If one isn't sure about the worthiness of the man to be remembered, why go to the trouble of safeguarding his memory? Even the Americans who had voted for him seemed at best indecisive.

Such indecision was not a problem for Cleveland himself, however, and this renders him rare among American Presidents. In 1908, years after his two non-consecutive presidential terms when he was now residing in his beautiful home in Princeton, New Jersey, he turned to his wife, Frances, and spoke his last words: "I have tried so hard to do right."

Even at this final moment, Cleveland had been painfully candid. His words hadn't trumpeted his virtues or political achievements; they identified only his honest efforts. His home in Princeton, New Jersey, would help to illustrate and confirm this verdict.

Grover Cleveland's Final Home in Princeton, New Jersey

President Cleveland's home to which he and his family retired after his Presidency is privately owned and is not open for tours. Its address was available, however, and Carol and I found the street with no real difficulty. I quietly and, I hope, unobtrusively, walked partway down the driveway to take a few pictures of the locale.Their meaning would not occur to me until several days later when Carol reviewed the pictures of the two sites we had visited on this day. Their correlation would provide an insight into our 22nd and 24th President for which I had been looking all along and would add a very meaningful coda to our trip through New Jersey.

"Clark," Carol exclaimed as she examined the photos I had taken. "Look at these houses. They're separated by over fifty miles and by many years, but they are astonishingly the same!" It was as if blinders had been lifted from my eyes. Yes, very different homes, the later one much more elegant, yet all the similarities were shockingly clear: the central pediment, the black shutters on the windows with the simple Greek columned porch, the addition on the right, even the color scheme.

What a perfect parallel to the life of this President. Even the styles of his homes, from birth to death, remained consistent, just as he, throughout his life, had tried to maintain the early religious principles of fairness and goodness that he had learned as a child.

Doing so had not assured him of popularity, but neither had it gone completely unnoticed. On the day following his death, his renowned contemporary, Mark Twain, commented on the profound worth of Grover Cleveland's life: "A great man is lost to the country: a great man and great citizen, the greatest citizen we had .... I speak of Grover Cleveland. He was a very great president, a man who not only properly appreciated the dignity of his high office but added to its dignity.... Mr. Cleveland was all that a president ought to be ...." (Twain 347).

Even the honest, earnest Grover Cleveland could not have desired a more appreciative eulogy. He had "tried ... to do right" from beginning to end.

22

Benjamin Harrison: "I Pledge Allegiance..."

23rd President Benjamin Harrison (1889-1893): Home in Indianapolis, IN

One of the unalloyed delights of visiting the homes of the men who have served as President of the United States is the opportunity to hear a docent's recounting of the best qualities and achievements that had characterized the lives and administrations of each of these remarkable personalities. In some cases, this would appear to be all too easy a task. George Washington's role as General and "Father of his Country" makes his importance to the history of our nation an obvious given. Franklin Roosevelt's astonishing four consecutive electoral victories, together with his role as national inspirer of hope during both the Great Depression and the Second World War, also attest to his indisputable historical significance.

But what about those Chief Executives whose lives seem, frankly, less meritorious, even less worthy of remembrance, than the "giants" just mentioned? For them, visits to their homes can provide a most instructive window into a political and social time frame that history books often miss. And this was certainly the case in our visit in late April 2011 to Indianapolis and the home of Benjamin Harrison.

To get a quick sense of just how badly misunderstood a President can be, let me briefly cite one rather heartless assessment of Harrison's Presidency that typifies much of the current historical consensus about our 23rd President:

> *Although he entered the White House hoping to burnish the heroic glory once associated with his grandfather's name, Harrison instead (and ironically) proceeded much as his grandfather might have done (had he lived), doing the bidding of party leaders and trying to stay out of trouble. Sadly, Benjamin Harrison might well be remembered more fondly today had his administration also ended prematurely. (Clinton 172)*

In point of fact, one need not conduct extensive research into the life and Presidency of Benjamin Harrison to call into question much of the above quotation. Harrison had been, after all, the young Indianapolis lawyer who, when introduced to a large crowd at a political rally as "William Henry Harrison's grandson," had quickly responded, "I want it understood that I am the grandson of nobody. I believe that every man should stand on his own merits" (Geib 141). And he had also been the man who, as President, refused to appoint to his cabinet the nominees of various Republican state political bosses—a refusal that, according to some historians, may have been the single most influential factor in his failure to win a second term in office.

But beside all this, what might a visit to his residence reveal that could disentangle such a cacophony of opinion regarding the worth and character of Benjamin Harrison? This was what both Carol and I hoped to learn as we stood on the prominent front porch of the Harrison home in downtown Indianapolis on a drizzly and rather unseasonably cool April morning.

At exactly ten o'clock, the opening hour, we pressed the front door bell and almost immediately were invited into a rather dark entry hall by a very cheerful older man named Jim.

"Welcome to the Benjamin Harrison home," he began quickly. "My name is Jim, and I will be your docent this morning. My tour of the home takes an hour and a half." Here followed a long pause. "Longer if you have questions," he nodded, tellingly.

"By the time you leave today," he added, "I hope you will know and appreciate much more about President Harrison." I could recognize immediately that we were in for some serious information, and Jim, after taking our admission fees, launched into his presentation.

It was quickly apparent that our docent was an ardent advocate for Benjamin Harrison. As both Carol and I **did** ask questions and, in doing so, evidenced to his satisfaction that, prior to our visit, we had done our homework regarding General Harrison and his ancestors, Jim warmed to us quite quickly.

Despite Jim's infectious enthusiasm, however, the home itself seemed atmospherically heavy. Both the formal front parlor and the succeeding family room area were dimly lit and featured heavily stained wood paneling. These rooms were made even more somber by the fact that shutters had closed off most of what outside light there was on this cloudy, misty day. It was hard not to associate this setting's characteristics with the various historical descriptions of President Harrison as "stern" and "aloof."

Our first glimpse of a more lighthearted mood came as Jim approached what looked like a large music box in the family room.

"This is a 'Reginaphone,' " he remarked. "Remember the Harrisons had no television, no radio. This was their entertainment." He placed a metallic arm on a rotating metal disc, and the result was nearly magical.

The room filled with a lush, sonorous melody that lasted the better part of five minutes.

"It's lovely," Carol whispered to me as we stood and listened, and I concurred. Clearly the Harrisons had enjoyed music and had appreciated the latest technology. It added a touch of gracious beauty to the otherwise stern dignity of their home.

The next room was the study, and it held another surprise for me as I wandered over to the President's oversized bookcase. I had expected to find the collection of law books and case studies that were immediately the focus of my attention (Harrison being the only ex-President to have resumed his law practice after leaving the White House). But in addition to the numerous legal studies housed here, there were also very prominently displayed copies of Sir Walter Scott's Waverley novels and a generous collection of Charles Dickens's works.

"Dickens was important to Mr. Harrison," Jim noted, observing my interest in these volumes. He continued, "Some people feel that Dickens's portrayals of the poor had a direct impact on President Harrison's wishes to help the underprivileged and the disenfranchised."

This was an aspect of the serious and austere President that I had not anticipated. And another insight was awaiting both Carol and me just across the hall.

It is probably worthwhile noting here that presidential dining rooms most always tend to bore me. This is largely because they are invariably laid out in very similar ways: the banquet table fully extended and sporting complete sets of presidential dishware worthy of a state dinner. My point here is that one seldom gets much of a glimpse into the inner life of a President among such compilations of crockery. But here I was in for another surprise. Caroline Harrison, it turns out, had been an artist of some considerable merit.

Her watercolors were on display throughout the room, and, even more impressively, Caroline had actually designed the Harrison presidential china—a stunning blue and gold motif of grain stalks, reminiscent of Indiana farmland. I was charmed by these decorative and functional pieces of art. Just as I had felt in the family room across the hall, the Harrisons clearly had loved and valued beauty.

Jim now led us back into the hall and invited us to ascend a wide spiral staircase that appeared to float upward with no visible means of support—yet another rather elegant touch in this otherwise staid and formal interior.

The second floor hall leading to the family bedrooms boasted a 12-foot ceiling. Mary Harrison, the President's daughter, had one of the front rooms. The other bedchamber was that of the President and his wife, Caroline. (Incidentally, I was impressed by the manner in which Jim, our docent, was perfectly willing to tell the story of Harrison's second, rather controversial, marriage to his wife's niece, subsequent to the death of Caroline. He recounted the facts with neither titillating detail nor apology. Jim was never chary of the truth, but he was also disinterested in perpetuating gossip.)

Finally, Jim escorted us up to the third floor, the ballroom, which now contained numerous chronologically arranged collections of artifacts chronicling various events in the President's life. And it was here that I was to find the key to the puzzle for which I had been looking.

One glance around this room crammed full of memorabilia from almost every epoch of Harrison's personal life and political career left me with a clear understanding that the great and defining chapter of Benjamin Harrison's life had had very little to do with law, with politics, or even with his personal relationships. That great and defining chapter had been written in 1864 and 1865 in the bloody and blood red soil of northern Georgia.

The Civil War had been the turning point of Harrison's life. His experiences during that conflict would come to color all his later political biases, and they would also define his most cherished goals as the nation's Chief Executive.

He had been neither a passionate nor a knee jerk recruit. When the war began in 1861, Harrison had chosen not to volunteer, due largely to his financial obligations and the delicate health of his wife. Only after a direct appeal by Oliver Morton, the Governor of the state of Indiana, had Harrison agreed to raise an Indiana regiment of soldiers for the Union cause. But once committed, he had become as dedicated a soldier as his grandfather could ever have wished.

The history of Harrison's leadership as part of Sherman's march to Atlanta has been documented in many places more thoroughly than I care to tell it here, but the overall result of his war experiences explains much about both his personal style and his politics in the years following the war.

Suddenly the calm and stoic grandeur of this beautiful home spoke clearly of a man who had been tested and "had not been found wanting." The somber but elegant furnishings, the unostentatious but still formal atmosphere of the first floor rooms, all bore perfect testimony to the character of a soldier who had had no taste for glory but for whom shirking had nonetheless been an impossibility. This was a man who loved beauty but who was also unafraid to confront horror.

And then, as I walked from exhibit to exhibit in the third floor ballroom of this grand mansion, I found a small plaque that identified the most lasting legacy of the Harrison Presidency, a legacy of which I had been previously unaware.

In 1892, a Bostonian named Ralph Bellamy (cousin of the more famous Edward Bellamy whose 1888 utopian novel, *Looking Backward*, had caused such a stir) had written a first version of what would become known as the "Pledge of Allegiance":

> *I pledge allegiance to my flag and the Republic for which it stands; one nation indivisible, with Liberty and Justice for all.*

Harrison had loved it, going so far as to issue a presidential proclamation that this pledge should be spoken at every flag presentation ceremony held on Columbus Day celebrations throughout the nation. An original version of Bellamy's words encased here in a simple black frame was tucked modestly away in a corner, surrounded by campaign banners and other political paraphernalia.

It struck me as providing the key insight, the Alpha and Omega, into President Benjamin Harrison's character. He had been a lawyer, a politician, a senator, even the President. But what that terrible Civil War had taught him most compellingly was that he was first and foremost an American who had taken advantage of the natural gifts he had been given at his birth, who had proven his mettle in the crucible of war, and who had dedicated his life to making the Union "indivisible." Everything else paled by comparison.

True, he had been a conservative Republican, a believer in the substantiality of the gold standard, and a supporter of tariff protection for emerging American industries. He had also, contrariwise, been deeply concerned about monopolistic trusts and the corrupting influence of political patronage. But beyond all these issues, he had played a part in resolving the greatest crisis in his country's young history. He had been able to proudly march in the Grand Review of the triumphant Union army in 1865, and he would become in later years one of the most loyal and ardent participants in Veterans' Reunions.

Harrison was a man for whom the American flag was much more than a colorful ensign. He would have been delighted that the flag was on prominent, permanent display outside his home—as it is, now. For him it was more than a token. It spoke of everything for which his life had come to stand as a symbol. His parting words when leaving the White House ring especially true here on North Delaware Street in Indianapolis:

> *I did try to make the administration thoroughly American and hope that something was done to develop an increased love of the flag at home and an increased respect for it abroad. (Clotworthy 178)*

As every school child in America repeats the great Pledge of Allegiance which was first spoken as a result of President Harrison's 1892 Proclamation, his hope for an "increased love" and an "increased respect" seems very much a living legacy to us all. This Indianapolis home had told its story of success, fortitude, and respect, just as Jim had hoped it would.

23

William McKinley: "Remember the Ladies"

25th President William McKinley (1897-1901): Saxton McKinley House in Canton, OH

There is a mild irony and a calculated brilliance surrounding the Saxton-McKinley House located in downtown Canton, Ohio. This building, which, our docent informed us, had only narrowly escaped demolition after it had undergone numerous—and occasionally rather colorful—incarnations over the years, had never actually been a permanent home for the McKinleys. It had been Ida Saxton's family residence, and she and William had occupied the house only while their own home was under construction further up Market Street. That dwelling, the setting for McKinley's famous "front porch campaign," no longer exists.

The Saxton-McKinley House is also somewhat ironic in the fact that while it has become the centerpiece of the recently established First Ladies National Historic Site, Ida Saxton McKinley herself was one of the least imposing women ever to have served as First Lady of the United States.

The site choice is brilliant, however, because of its placement in Canton. Any red-blooded American man knows that the real draw of Canton, Ohio, is the Pro Football Hall of Fame, a mecca for sports enthusiasts and lovers of NFL memorabilia. Placing the First Ladies National Historic Site in downtown Canton heightens immeasurably the overall appeal of this vacation destination. Let the football fanatics head over to the Hall of Fame game. Those less interested in tales of the pigskin can learn more about the First Ladies.

Of course, neither option explained my presence here in Canton. Although I love football, I'm not a statistics guy. And my primary interest in this site was learning more about President McKinley, not the First Ladies.

All this, perhaps, explains the mild surprise Carol and I heard over the phone as we called the number of the First Ladies museum to get a parking admission code for our visit on a rainy morning in June.

"You want to come **today**?"

"Yes, we're really looking forward to seeing the museum and house!"

"How many of you did you say are coming?"

"Two."

"Okay." She gave us a code number, followed by a long pause. "Well, then ... fine. We'll see you soon."

We made our way into downtown Canton, and I dropped Carol off in front of the First Ladies Museum, so she wouldn't have to walk in the rain for the block or so from our assigned lot. After parking the van, I skirted the puddles as I made my way back to the door of the museum and bolted up the several stairs leading to the entrance hall.

Once inside, I found that Carol had already purchased our tickets, and we were free to wander around the museum area until our docent arrived.

The large museum interior had once been a bank building. Arrayed around the room's circumference were a series of glass cases containing items related to or produced by an impressive number of First Ladies.

There was a great collection of still photos depicting Nancy Davis Reagan's movie performances and Betty Ford's dance career. Other items of interest included ceramic paintings by Lucy Webb Hayes and several beautiful oil landscapes from the collection of Ellen Axson Wilson. There was even a novel penned by Frances Folsom Cleveland opened for viewing. Although I hadn't known what to expect from this small museum, I found my appreciation of the talents and achievements of our First Ladies deepening and expanding with each new display.

There was also a small collection of dresses and other fashion accouterments that had been worn by the First Ladies, together with several settings of presidential china, but those items were of more interest to Carol than to me.

By the time we had completed our circuit of the museum cases, our docent had arrived. She then gave us some interesting information about the formation and goals of the museum and instructed us to go down to the Saxton-McKinley House to continue our tour. Happily, the rain had stopped, and we could proceed without opening our umbrellas.

We were to enter the house from the rear side door, and we were welcomed into the front hall by a cheerful and enthusiastic docent. After a brief history of the house, we crowded into an elevator (obviously an addition from a later era), and proceeded to the third floor on which there was a complete collection of photographs and reproductions of paintings picturing each of the First Ladies. Several of the more recent First Ladies had corresponded with the museum at the time of its formation, and their letters were also on display.

One more stop, this time to look briefly into the tiny study President McKinley had used during his and Ida's short stay here, and our tour was finished.

Overall, there hadn't been much insight into President McKinley in this locale (though the layout of the house, with its expansive front porch and hallway leading to the rear exit was structurally very similar to the house from which he had conducted his 1896 campaign). Nor was there any mention here of the assassination that had cut his second term so short. But as this was the only original McKinley home still standing, I was glad we had come to see it.

Happily, we weren't completely finished with McKinley in Canton, however. The desk clerk at our motel had urged me, learning of Carol's and my interest in things presidential, not to miss the McKinley Memorial and Presidential Library. After our tour of the Saxton-McKinley House, we decided to extend our visit to see these attractions. It was an excellent recommendation.

The McKinley Memorial is located in a beautiful park setting just outside of Canton, and it is an impressive structure. Over a hundred marble stairs lead visitors up to the domed memorial where William, Ida, and their two daughters' graves are located. Carol chose not to accompany me on the climb, but I must say, the view from the top was

William McKinley Memorial in Canton, Ohio

magnificent. Descending the stairs carefully, I then made my way to the nearby doors of the William McKinley Presidential Library and Museum.

Even this building, however, was a shared venue. The ground floor contained a science museum, while half the upper level included an interesting but irrelevant, presidentially speaking, reconstruction of a turn of the century town (somewhat reminiscent of a similar display in Chicago's Museum of Science and Industry).

Finally, centrally located on the second floor was a room devoted solely to President McKinley. A large area filled with authentic furnishings once owned by the McKinleys recreated a portion of his oval office. There were also several additional arrangements of furniture that depicted other of his living spaces. Glass cases contained marvelous mementos: a variety of his campaign items, together with objects related to key political and foreign policy issues with which McKinley had had to deal during his one full term in office. A display I found particularly interesting was dedicated to the Spanish-American war and included a photograph of Admiral Dewey, the hero of Manilla Bay. There was also a blue glass candy bowl cast in the shape of the USS Maine and a bell made from recovered metal from that same significant sunken vessel. This was history, and I would not have wanted to miss a chance to see and appreciate these telling artifacts.

William McKinley Artifacts

Still, it seemed that President McKinley had been rather passed over by Canton. His Market Street home had been torn down, his presidential library had obviously not been sufficiently frequented by visitors to merit its own designated location. In Canton, it appeared, football had won. (The standing of the First Ladies National Historic Site was yet to be determined.)

Right in front of the Presidential Library Museum, however, was a portrait statue of President McKinley with a plaque that spoke as eloquently in his favor as any memorial I have even seen. The sculpture itself was simple. It was a life-sized bronze bust of the President that looked more happy and contented than the stern and stiff official photographs that usually appear in his biographies. The bust, including the suggestion of a double-breasted jacket, rested on three steps, all placed atop a square cut black granite column.

After leaving the museum subsequent to our brief visit, I strode past this statue and walked toward the parking lot, finally noticing that Carol had stopped following me. She gestured that I should return to the place where she was standing, and, wondering what it was that she had seen, I came quickly over to her.

"Look at this," she said quietly.

The inscription was dark against the background of the polished

William McKinley Portrait Bust

stone, but I removed my glasses to note what had been embossed onto the plaque at the bottom of the column shaft. As usual, Carol had been right. It was important for me to see this memorial.

William McKinley Plaque

WILLIAM McKINLEY
25th PRESIDENT
OF THE UNITED STATES
BORN 1848 * DIED 1901
HE WAS AN OBEDIENT AND AFFECTIONATE
SON, PATRIOTIC AND FAITHFUL AS A
SOLDIER, HONEST AND UPRIGHT AS A

CITIZEN, TENDER AND DEVOTED AS A
HUSBAND, AND TRUTHFUL, GENEROUS,
UNSELFISH, MORAL, AND CLEAN IN
EVERY RELATION OF LIFE.
ERECTED BY
THE EMPLOYEES OF
THE PHILADELPHIA POST OFFICE

"How many Presidents could have all that said about them?" Carol whispered, as we read the plaque together. I nodded immediately and thought to myself, "How many **men** could have all that said about them?"

In Canton, Ohio, there had been significant and important efforts made, in the words of that great First Lady, Abigail Adams, to "remember the ladies." I was also grateful that, close by his impressive final resting place memorial, the employees of the Philadelphia Post Office had chosen to remember the best of President McKinley. His remarkable example of devotion to his family and service to his nation richly deserve this honor.

"The Advance Agent of Prosperity"

I have never fully understood the prevailing indifference surrounding the Presidency of William McKinley. Unlike most of our "forgotten Presidents" (e.g. Millard Fillmore or Chester Arthur), McKinley was legitimately elected, rather than being an "accidental" President. He was re-elected to a second term by a comfortable margin of both popular and electoral votes. Add to this the fact that, like Abraham Lincoln, McKinley was assassinated by a man

McKinley Campaign Poster

bent on disrupting—even destroying—the American form of government, and it would stand to reason that William Mckinley would
loom large in the history of his country. It even can be argued that
his administration marked the beginning of an "American Century" in which the United States would come to play a crucial role in
the social, political, and economic history of the world. So why—and
how—has he remained so "forgotten"?

In Canton, Ohio, the answers I had found revolved largely around
the National Football League Hall of Fame as well as the newly
minted First Ladies National Historic Site. True, the impressive
McKinley tomb *was* there, and, nearby it, the William McKinley
Presidential Library and Museum. The primary function of that
building, however, seemed to be to house Canton's Science Center
and Planetarium. The site's presentation of materials related to
President McKinley was comprised of a handsome, though somewhat limited, display of artifacts located in one area of its second
floor. I had not noticed in Canton any other marked evidence of a
community-wide acknowledgement of the historic importance of
their most famous former resident.

In the spring of 2014, Carol and I headed to Niles, Ohio, the birthplace of our 25th President, in hopes of finding a locale that was a
bit more successful in giving him his due respect. My research had
informed me that a replica of the McKinley birthplace home had
been constructed in Niles in 2003 and also that the city contained
an architecturally impressive memorial library and museum created to honor his leadership. We called ahead and were assured that
we could tour these sites. Finally, I couldn't help hoping, we might
find a community fully appreciative of the legacy of William McKinley.

The road into Niles from the interstate wove through countryside
that could only be fairly described as "extremely distressed." Rundown homes, boarded up storefronts, and a general air of disrepair
and abandonment seemed the prevailing tone of the landscape.
More than once Carol asked me, "Are we sure we're going in the
right direction?" as we continued northward on the route our GPS
had indicated. Finally we crossed a bridge into a city center that

looked more promising. Seconds later, right on the main street of town, the rebuilt McKinley birth home stood gleaming brightly in the morning sunshine.

"Well, this is better," Carol observed, and a block further on, the view was better still. In fact, it was positively arresting. To our immediate left the expansive white marble façade of the William McKinley National Memorial spread out before us. It looked for all the world as if it belonged on the Mall in Washington, D.C., yet here it was in the heart of downtown Niles. "Marvelous," I thought to myself, "we're going to see a city that reveres its presidential pedigree."

As we pulled into the parking lot at the back of the Memorial, it was hard to stop marveling at the scope and grandeur of the site. Leaving the car, we moved into the open atrium of the Memorial which was dominated by a striking twelve-foot tall sculpture of President McKinley. Arranged around it in the semi-circular pavilion of Doric columns were portrait busts of other key political and economic figures of the late nineteenth century. Teddy Roosevelt, Marcus Hanna, Andrew Carnegie, and Henry Clay Frick, together with other notables of the era, constituted a ring of honor within this central space. Although I was thoroughly enjoying each of these sculptures, I was also beginning to wonder where and how we would make our connection with our docent when a pleasant looking man strode up to us and extended his hand.

McKinley Memorial in Niles, Ohio

"You must be Clark and Carol. Welcome to Niles. I'm here to show you around the home this morning."

Statue of William McKinley

I was still reveling in the sculptures surrounding us, and so, after our brief introductions, I couldn't help commenting on the stately splendor of this setting. "It's a magnificent monument," I commented. Our guide was visibly pleased and quickly offered us a brief history of the construction of the Memorial. Joseph G. Butler, a schoolmate of McKinley's, had spearheaded a movement to build a fitting place in Niles to honor the memory of his longtime friend. In 1910, after receiving congressional approval to solicit funds, Butler had worked for five years to raise money for the project. A competition had been held to submit plans, and the contract was ultimately awarded to the prestigious New York firm of McKim, Meade and White. The culmination of their efforts had occurred in 1917 when former President William Howard Taft had officiated at the dedication of the Memorial. "This place must really be the pride and joy of Niles," I observed.

"Used to be," he noted, sighing slightly. "Over there," he pointed to the south side of the building, "is our public library. The other side here," again he pointed, "isn't used much anymore. There's an auditorium—but the acoustics aren't so good. There's also a display of McKinley artifacts. But nobody these days seems to want to learn much about President McKinley, so it stays locked up unless I open it for someone who wants to take a look."

"You keep the museum locked up?" I asked somewhat incredulously.

"Yes. There have been significant cutbacks in the museum's budget. And anyway, these days only a handful of people come to visit.

I'll open it for you later if you like. Now let's go down to the birth-place house. I know you both are interested in presidential homes. Its history is quite unusual."

Our guide then proceeded to lead us onto a side street from which we could approach the rear of the reconstructed McKinley birthplace house and research center.

He let us in by a back door and offered us seats around a table on which he had prepared a notebook full of photographs of the McKinley birth house taken at various moments of its colorful history.

For the next half hour or so we were regaled with the story of the McKinley birth house: how the family had lived there from the late 1830s until 1852, how in the 1870s the house had been transformed into a general store, and, most amazingly, how, in the late 1890s after McKinley had been elected President, the house had been purchased and split in two by a would-be impresario who displayed, and charged admission to, the half in which the President had been born. Its final history had begun in 1910 when another enterprising exhibitor, Lulu Mackey, bought both halves of the home and reunited them on acreage she owned that became known as McKinley Heights. Over the years the number of visitors had sadly declined, and in 1937 the house had burned down.

All this brought to my mind the recurring question I had been asking myself: "Why do *you* feel that President McKinley has been so generally forgotten?" I asked.

He answered quickly, "Oh, that's easy. Theodore Roosevelt. He was so dynamic, so engaging. By comparison President McKinley must have struck everyone as an old stuffed shirt. Once you knew Teddy Roosevelt, ... well anybody would have suffered by comparison."

I had heard this explanation before, but I wasn't completely convinced. Without a doubt, Teddy Roosevelt had come on like a force of nature, but I wondered what else, if anything, might account for the neglect of his assassinated predecessor. Before I could continue this line of thought, we were invited to go upstairs to see a treasure.

After a brief elevator ride up to the second floor, we were led into a meeting room with a high ceiling and a long table with chairs set up around it. On the room's largest wall hung a gigantic framed poster of William McKinley, a relic from the presidential campaign of 1896 that measured every bit of ten feet tall.

"Who gets to see this incredible poster?" I asked. "It's an amazing piece of history!"

"We hold our meetings in here, so everybody who comes to those meetings sees it. Actually though," he added, "I try to sit with my back to it so that I don't have to have President McKinley staring down at

William McKinley Birthplace in Niles, Ohio

me." He laughed. I noted that below the pictured countenance of McKinley was emblazoned his campaign slogan: "The Advance Agent of Prosperity." And with this, our guide led us through a doorway into the second floor of the 2003 reconstructed house at the front of the building where we had been conversing.

Each room was decorated with furnishings that, although not original McKinley pieces, were completely consistent with the first half of the 19th century. I was very impressed with the obvious care that had been taken to recreate this world.

"School groups must love to come here," I suggested. "This is a very helpful window into a time that the kids could only imagine."

"School groups don't come here anymore," he commented regretfully. "There have been so many state-wide cuts to education funding that no school around here has the money for taking field trips. Even our library staff has been drastically reduced—we lost 30% of our operating budget this year."

"Who comes here then?" I asked.

"Just people like you," he answered. "Only a couple of hundred a year. I open up the place for them just like I did for you."

After our circuit of the birthplace home's rooms, we exited again out the back door of the research center and walked quietly toward the Memorial site.

"If you want, I'll open up the museum for you," our guide offered.

"Yes, we'd like that," I answered him, and we proceeded past the library and sculpture area toward the large north doors of the locked museum.

He turned the key in one of these doors and invited us inside. We entered the building and quickly found ourselves in a very large auditorium area, ringed with a cantilevered balcony that constituted the building's second floor. It was up there, we were informed, that the McKinley materials were located. "Yet again," I thought, "President McKinley has been relegated to the second floor of a building bearing his name."

We climbed a broad staircase leading up to this museum and found there a variety of display cases and artifacts dating from McKinley's era. As I stood before the ornately carved wooden chair in which the President had sat during cabinet meetings, I couldn't help feeling that such treasures deserved a wider audience than they were currently receiving. And then came the flag.

Laid out flat in a horizontal display case was a uniquely fabricated battle flag that had been presented to President McKinley by one of the battalions that had served in the Spanish-American war in Cuba. And suddenly it hit me. Of course. This is another reason why this President has been so neglected. He has been the victim of one of our nation's most unique maladies, a disorder I have come to call "Victor's Remorse." As General Patton observed in his most famous speech to his soldiers in World War II, "Americans love to win." But we also frequently seem terribly ashamed of having won. Our wars with the Indians, with Mexico, with the Spanish, even with the Japanese, all have given rise to neap tides of national guilt, of self-criticism, second-guessing, and self-deprecating soul searching. Such feelings have tended to tarnish the memory of every political figure associated with these victories: Andrew Jackson, James Polk, Harry Truman, and particularly William McKinley. History books frequently label the McKinley administration as the era of "American Imperialism," and his annexation of Hawaii plus the acquisition of the spoils of the Spanish-American war (Cuba, Puerto Rico, Guam, and the Philippines) are sometimes cited as shameful moments of American expansionism. But are such criticisms deserved?

In a glass case on this second floor, a four page handwritten letter was on display, dated October 1883, and addressed to a constituent named J. P. White. Then a Congressman, William McKinley had written this letter, apparently in response to criticisms that had been leveled at him. Although the exact nature of the dispute that had prompted the letter was not identified, a logical guess might be that, as a member of the influential House Ways and Means Committee, McKinley had been attacked for his support of increased tariff protection for American industries. Regardless of the specific reasons for writing it, this letter addresses quite eloquently issues that the future President would continue to value most highly. He identifies his position with admirable clarity:

> *No man who knows me would believe me capable of advising that working men should be deprived of labor and wages for political or for other reasons. My whole public life has been devoted to the advocacy of a system which gave men employment and kept the shop running.*

This was William McKinley in a nutshell. And it suggested exactly what he had meant thirteen years later when running for the Presidency as "The Advance Agent of Prosperity."

We tend to forget the economic circumstances leading up to our so-called "Imperial" period of expansionism. The United States had become one of the most industrially productive nations in the world, but this fact had led to an unforeseen economic crisis. Our industries' capacity to produce items for consumption had outstripped the ability of our population to buy them all. As supply continued to exceed demand, the result could have been a significant slowing down of industrial expansion together with massive layoffs of American workers.

How could such a bleak scenario be avoided? How could a President insure that our economy would continue to be an engine of growth that "... gave men employment and kept the shop running"?

For many of the best minds, the answer was both clear and simple: gain more access to foreign markets, particularly those of the Asian nations.

Alfred Thayer Mahan's extraordinarily significant study, *The Influence of Sea Power upon History*, was published in 1890. Its central thesis, historian Scott Miller explains, was a clarion call to action: "As an industrializing power the United States would eventually have to seek new markets and sources of raw materials. It followed ... that the country must do everything possible to protect its sea lanes, build a strong navy, and acquire territory" (53).

Yet it had never been President McKinley's intent to "acquire territory" in the conventional sense of imperialistic expansionism. He eschewed the notion of conquest for the purpose of adding new states to the union. In neither the case of Cuba nor of the Philippines was America's intent to acquire territory that would ultimately become part of the United States. The goal set for each of these nations was self-government and independence.

But in order to help our own country remain economically prosperous, we needed to open trade routes for our products, and these strategically located territories had to remain friendly to the United States and, particularly in Asia, had to guarantee American shipping reliable bases and secure ports where both navy and cargo vessels could reprovision themselves and from which they could have access to the Asian markets.

History has shown that securing these guarantees proved much more difficult than anyone had anticipated. Insurgent groups in both Cuba and the Philippines who had been fighting the Spanish for years now turned their ire on their American "liberators." The result had been a prolonged period of continued misunderstanding and bloodshed.

Yet both as a Congressman and, later, as President, William McKinley had dedicated his "whole public life" not to the notion of expanding the territorial boundaries of the United States, but rather to the capitalist system which had resulted in dependable jobs and greater profits for both ordinary citizens and the captains of industry. His desire to be "The Advance Agent of Prosperity" had motivated nearly all of his legislative and executive decisions. By tending to disregard his intentions and the causes lying behind those intentions, I believe that many historians may have arrived at a mistaken conclusion regarding what has come to be called the "Age of American Imperialism."

At the end of our tour, our friendly guide locked the doors to the museum, and we shook hands and thanked him for shepherded us around. Slightly sighing, he commented, "Kids today just don't seem to care about old Presidents anymore." I thought about Mount Vernon and its many thousands of annual visitors, and Monticello, and the Hermitage in Nashville, but I decided not to mention them. Instead, we thanked him and wished him well.

As Carol and I drove out of Niles and passed once again through the rather forlorn landscape of Northeastern Ohio, it was impossible not to feel the irony of this impoverished region's disinterest in the life of the man who had worked so hard and faithfully to be "The Advance Agent of Prosperity" for all Americans.

The lunch hour had almost passed by the time we reached the highway, so Carol and I decided to stop at an Arby's located close to the entrance onto the interstate.

"Where do the people who live around here work?" we asked a store manager who had come up to our table with an order of fresh French fries.

"It's been pretty rough," she answered. "Lots of businesses have moved away. But," she continued with a broad smile, "they're building a new casino right next door." She pointed just up the hill from her location. "That should bring in lots of business."

We finished lunch, and as we made our way back to our car, I looked up at the newly cleared land. "A casino?" I asked myself. "Will *gambling* really solve the problems facing this community?" By contrast, President McKinley's efforts to insure a different and much more reliable means of national prosperity seemed all the more remarkable, all the more worthy of being remembered.

We had come. We had seen. But, as we exited back onto the interstate heading south, it appeared to me that, despite the worthy efforts of the people who were trying to honor and preserve the legacy of one of our least remembered Presidents, in the Niles of 2014, only public disinterest and budgetary cutbacks had conquered.

24

Theodore Roosevelt: "Do you remember the fun of him?"

26th President Theodore Roosevelt (1901-1909): Sagamore Hill in Oyster Bay, NY

Samuel Clemens hated him. At least as a President. Writing under his famous pen name, Mark Twain, his final assessment of Theodore Roosevelt was both caustic and direct: "Roosevelt is far and away the worst President we have ever had ...," and then he added with venomous irony, "...and also the most admired and the most satisfactory. The nation's admiration of him and pride in him and worship of him is far wider, far warmer, and far more general than it has ever before lavished upon a president ..." (Twain 34). Twain's explanation of the incongruity of this amalgamation of vitriol and tongue-in-cheek praise is a wonderful example of his withering satire in its fullest glory:

> Mr. Roosevelt is the most formidable disaster that has befallen the country since the Civil War—but the vast mass of the nation loves him, is frantically fond of him, even idolizes him. This is the simple truth. It sounds like a libel upon the intelligence of the human race, but it isn't; there isn't any way to libel the intelligence of the human race. (Twain 18)

What had led our most famous humorist to unleash such a diatribe? What enormities, personal or political, had President Roosevelt committed to merit such a rebuke?

Twain's autobiographical notes provide answers to these questions, but in doing so, he also reveals a painful truth that was taught to me by my maternal grandmother. "Clark," she once said to me on the occasion of my losing my temper in her rather august presence, "when you find a fault in someone that makes you furious, remember that you are only seeing in that other person one of your own leading characteristics. 'That thou seest, that thou beest.' " I have never fully forgiven my grandmother for imparting that bit of wisdom to me. But I have never forgotten it either.

So what were Twain's chief objections to President Roosevelt? Boiled down a bit, they can be summed up as five basic faults:

1. He was childish.
2. He had an unreasonable hatred of rivals.
3. He was egotistical and was always calling attention to himself.
4. He was impulsive.
5. He lacked presidential dignity.

Citing numerous instances of the President's behavior to illustrate his concerns, Twain lampooned Roosevelt's youthfulness ("he is still only fourteen years old after having lived half a century");

scolded his having taken time to give a magazine interview eviscer-
ating the findings of a naturalist with whom he disagreed; derided
his ego ("hasn't he tacitly claimed some dozens of times that he is
the only person in America who knows how to speak the truth?");
criticized his vacillating motives in foreign policy regarding Cuba
and the Philippines; and lamented his crude demeanor ("He repre-
sents what the American gentleman ought not to be") (Twain 12, 20,
33).

Not that such criticisms were completely unfounded, nor was
Mark Twain the only person leveling them. Even Roosevelt's own
daughter, Alice, once famously remarked of her father, "He wants
to be the bride at every wedding, the corpse at every funeral, and
the baby at every christening" (Wead 107). What is unusual is that
Twain elaborated his discontent so stridently. He had often been
critical of people in power, but much more frequently he had come
to the defense of the Presidents he had known, from the beleaguered Ulysses Grant to the universally disparaged Chester Arthur.
For some reason, however, he treated Theodore Roosevelt very dif-
ferently.

Yet to anyone who knows much about Samuel Clemens's (AKA
Mark Twain's) life, his accusations seem more than slightly hyp-
ocritical. Roosevelt, childish? This from Twain whose wife, Livy,
though ten years his junior, gave him the nickname of "Youth" to
identify his unrepentantly boyish nature? Roosevelt, peevish and
petty about rivals? This from Twain, a man whose envy of other
novelists (most notably James Fenimore Cooper) led him to ridicule
and demean their "literary offenses"? Roosevelt, a chronic
attention-getter? This from Twain, a man who, after the death of
his wife, insisted on wearing white suits even in the winter for
the purpose of being immediately noticed by passers-by? Roosevelt
impulsive? This from Twain, a man whose restless urges had impelled him to travel incessantly throughout both his country and
the world in constant search of new experiences? Roosevelt undig-
nified? This from Twain, a man whose very language in *Huckleberry Finn* had been identified as "rough, coarse, and inelegant ...
more suited to the slums than to intelligent, respectable people"

(*The Boston Evening Transcript*, 17 March 1885)? What was going on here?

An answer that would have warmed the cockles of my grandmother's heart is aptly forwarded by Donald Tiffany Bliss in his politically perceptive book *Mark Twain's Tale of Today*:

> *Clemens and Roosevelt had much in common. As young men they had ventured out west and experienced frontier freedom from which they drew strength and confidence throughout their lives. They shared an insatiable intellectual curiosity; a love of reading, writing, travel, and nature; gregarious and loquacious personalities; a penchant for publicity; and a desire to fill center stage. Perhaps they were too much alike and recognized in each other their own flaws as masters of hyperbole. (388)*

Perhaps the nation's "admiration ... and pride ... and worship" of the President that Twain had so savagely mocked was doubly painful to a man who had yearned for those same accolades from the American people, but whose life had dealt him such devastating tragedies and reversals of fortune that any hope of the adulation and reverence now enjoyed by President Roosevelt seemed like a cruel and distant dream.

Yet the time would come when Mark Twain *would* join Theodore Roosevelt in enjoying the national preeminence that they each desired. Both would be beloved, revered, and, most importantly, remembered. And for essentially the same reasons, though in each man's respective field of endeavor. Ironically, these reasons relate closely to the very qualities Mark Twain had both criticized in the President and had himself possessed: youthful vigor, fierce competitiveness, confident self-esteem, inspired flexibility, and refreshing and natural candor. When visiting the presidential homes of Theodore Roosevelt, it is this list of qualities which are important to bear in mind. They are nascent in his rebuilt birth home in downtown Manhattan, but they are full-blown realities in his beloved Sagamore Hill.

The history of the four-story brownstone home where, in October of 1858, the future President had been born, provides clear confirmation of the frantic fondness and even idolatry with which some Americans venerated him. After living at this address for thirteen years, the Roosevelt family had moved in 1872, just as this part of the city was beginning to lose its residential ambiance. The Roosevelts finally sold the house in 1896, and "... the building was transformed into commercial property with the first three floors expanded with additions that resembled large bay windows" (Picone 100).

By this time, of course, Theodore had begun to distinguish himself politically, first in the New York State legislature, next on the U.S. Civil Service Commission in Washington, D.C., and then as president of the New York Police Commission. And he was just beginning his ascent to power. As Assistant Secretary of the Navy, war hero in the Spanish American War, Vice President and, from 1900 to 1908, President of the United States, Theodore Roosevelt established himself as a most formidable presence in national politics.

In 1916, the 20th Street reconfigured building that had been the President's birthplace was torn down and a midtown two-story café was constructed on the site. After the President's death in 1919, just three years after the demolition of the home, supporters purchased the property, razed the café, and replaced it with an exact replica of the earlier brownstone. Surviving members of the Roosevelt family contributed some of its original furnishings as well as other artifacts, and, in 1923, the site was officially opened for visitors interested in seeing the place (or the facsimile thereof) where their beloved "TR" had been born. Mark Twain had died in 1910, and so was spared the indignity of a comment.

When Carol and I visited the site with relatives who lived in the New York area, we enjoyed our tour and relatively brief circuit of the rooms on display. It was a dark day with on and off showers, and my feelings about the setting were perfectly articulated by Theodore Roosevelt himself as, in later years, he had recalled this home:

> *It was furnished in the canonical taste of New York, a pe-*
> *riod in which men of substance liked to have their homes*
> *reflect the dignity and solidarity of their traditions and*
> *their lives. The black haircloth furniture in the dining*
> *room scratched the bare legs of the children as they sat*
> *on it. The middle room was a library, with tables, chairs,*
> *and bookcases of gloomy respectability. (Haas 110)*

While "gloomy" is perhaps too harsh a word for the interiors we were encountering, even on a rather somber day, "respectability" fits them to a tee. We saw rooms set in perfect order, as if important company were coming, with very little evidence of the lives lived here.

One exception was the porch at the back of the third floor. Of course, when the Roosevelt family had lived here this area had looked out on a lovely backyard. Now the view from the porch is limited to the brick facades of nearby buildings. Yet this was the location where the young "Teedie" had spent hours in the gymnasium his father had provided for him, building up his physical stamina to match his already tireless mental energy.

His buoyant character, youthful exuberance, and impetuous self-promotion would ultimately demand a more expansive setting, a home he would personally design and commission to be built. It, more than any other place, presents Theodore Roosevelt writ large in architectural form: Sagamore Hill in Oyster Bay, Long Island.

But Sagamore Hill is more than a home. It is the hub of a world unto itself. Part hunting lodge, part trophy room, part barracks, it is, and was always intended to be, a center of activity for the ever-expanding Roosevelt family. There is a feeling here of endless adventure and limitless expeditions possible on its spacious grounds and wide fields and forested areas. President Roosevelt loved riding his horses, gallivanting with his children, hiking and camping, swimming and boating—all the strenuous and wonderful outdoor activities that he had come to love and that had been denied him in his growing up years. He was determined that his own children would experience the beauty of nature and the rigors of outdoor activity. Stories abound that picture the President, even when meeting with political operatives or visiting dignitaries, racing off to play with his children at the magical hour of four in the afternoon.

One approaches the house up a long road that winds past a windmill and several outbuildings which functioned as stables, barns, and storehouses. Finally the road curves up to the main house with an overhanging entryway, and this is the door through which one enters.

Right from the start, visitors become aware of the two separate faces of Sagamore Hill. Theodore's is the most dominant. The Library, which also served as the President's office, is located on the immediate right of the entryway hall. A desk, complete with a telephone—still a very modern invention in TR's time—sits within the space created by a large bay window on the south side of the room where it receives ample light. On the opposite wall are bookcases filled with volumes that reflect the wide range of interests of this naturalist/explorer/adventurer President. On the walls above the bookcases hang an oil portrait of his father and lithographs of such Americans as Ulysses Grant, John Marshall, and George Washington whose lives had inspired Theodore from his youth. And most notably around the room are a variety of animal skins (sometimes with heads still attached) on the floor or draped over chairs. TR never wanted his exploits as a big game hunter and as a man's man to take a back seat to any of his other responsibilities or interests. The animal skins served the same purpose as Mark Twain's ubiquitous white suits: they were surefire attention getters.

The second face of Sagamore Hill is to be found directly across the hall from TR's library and office. It was Edith Roosevelt's parlor and drawing room area. It possesses a markedly different atmosphere than that of the rest of the house. Walls painted a light blue with gently contrasting darker blue cornices and curtains create an interior that seems completely infused with illumination. The effect is heightened by large windows on the south and west walls together with brightly patterned blue and white oriental rugs and similarly hued upholstered furnishings arranged in an ample half circle be-

fore a fireplace with a mantle painted the blue of the walls. One author describes the overall effect of the room as "genteel," and there
is no better word with which to describe this space (Howard 111).

Even here, however, the spirit of Theodore intrudes like a child
who wants to insure that he is not being overlooked. A large snow
white polar bear rug (with snarling head) is spread out on the hardwood floor just behind a delicately upholstered settee, while another animal skin is draped across the blue and white oriental rug in
front of the fireplace at the center of the conversational grouping
of armchairs and couches.

As one leaves the room, crossing by more animal skins on the
floor, and moves back into the hallway area, any sense of lightness
or delicacy fades quickly. We are once again in the President's
world of dark wood paneling and accumulated trophies.

The two remaining rooms off this passageway are the dining
room and the home's most memorable interior: the storied North
Room of 1905.

The dining room is a spacious but unpretentious area with a central table and what could pass as six wooden camp chairs gathered
around it. Bright red curtains and an inset sideboard give the room
a sense of radiant warmth. Still, one is always reminded of the President's hunting exploits as both a large moose head and mountain
goat head look down from the walls. Here the President, the First
Lady, and their children, as well as visitors to the home, gathered
for meals and experienced the democracy of Roosevelt family dining. Around this table, children as well as adults were invited, even
expected, to converse, to share their insights, and to ask questions
of each other. At least one of the Roosevelt children would later
comment that the best education he ever received had been given
to him at this table.

Proceeding back into the home's central hallway and moving to
the right, one arrives at the North Room. TR's famous addition to
Sagamore Hill served as an expansive space (30' by 40') in which
to receive and entertain his guests. But it was more than that. The
North Room is designed and decorated to impress, to intimidate

anyone invited into it. It serves as a uniquely American version of Versailles.

It has been said that the French kings enjoyed making visitors to Versailles wait, sometimes for hours, in the various rooms named after planetary gods. Their intent had been to overwhelm those entering the palace with the wealth, power, and grandeur of the monarch they had come to see. In like style, the North Room of Sagamore Hill bears witness to the dauntless courage and innumerable triumphs of the man whose trophies adorn its interior. Two giant tusks guard the entry to this room, after which one descends a few steps into a large central space. The polished wood ceiling soars overhead to about 20 feet high. Two enormous buffalo heads loom over each side of an oversized fireplace. On the opposite wall, two mature male deer heads are also on display. There are bookcases in the window nooks and a wide variety of porcelain vases from around the world are placed throughout the interior. And, of course, animal skins are present in abundance. The entire room speaks of wide-ranging experience, successful safaris, and energetic study.

This was the setting where TR liked to entertain guests, leaving them both overawed with, and humbled by, the achievements of their host. It is the crown jewel of Sagamore Hill.

Upstairs the rooms are less interesting. Off the hall running the length of the building are simple bedrooms—including the room on the second floor where the President died in his sleep in 1919—and a nursery. Up another flight are more bedrooms, his daughter Alice's room among them, and a third floor office called the "Gun Room" where the President kept his arsenal of firearms and where he would retreat to write. All these upper floor rooms were places to sleep and wash up, but clearly at Sagamore Hill the point, as is usually the case in hunting lodges, was to be outside as much as possible. Outdoors, one could find endless summer days of happy adventures; outdoors, one could study nature up close; outdoors, one could head off in many directions and follow only the impulses of one's heart and interests. Best of all, outdoors, one could simply be oneself, free from protocol or decorum. Like Teddy Roosevelt. Like Mark Twain.

Standing on the wide porch at Sagamore Hill, looking out on the field of long grass where, years earlier, hundreds of people had gathered to hear the President speak from this very spot, it struck me that what we most remember and revere about TR is something very different from his politics. Yes, he was a reformer, a soldier, a broker of peace, a conservator of the natural world. But most of all, he was a boy, a boy of endless energy and enthusiasm. A boy who could accomplish more tasks in a day than most of us would attempt in a month. He dreamed big and lived big, and no one who ever met him was unaware of the volcanic energy that coursed through him.

Noted historian David Herbert Donald, who once guided a group of tourists to Roosevelt's gravesite, ended his remarks that day by recalling a little known incident that had occurred only a few days after the President's death. A New York City Police Captain who had been made responsible for overseeing the arrangements of the ex-President's funeral had approached Corinne Roosevelt Robinson, Theodore's sister, in the church and, with tears in his eyes, had said to her, "Do you remember the fun of him, Mrs. Robinson? It was not only that he was a great man, but, oh, there was such fun in being led by him" (Renehan, Jr. 223).

It *is* the "fun of him" that we remember best. And here, once more, the parallel with Mark Twain, TR's famous contemporary volcano of energy and drive, strikes a vibrant chord. For it is also in "the fun of *him*" that Twain's readers most delight. They do not often think much about his serious and darkly forbidding tracts on the news of his day, topics ranging from imperialism to lynchings. They certainly almost never consider his nearly rapturous admiration for Joan of Arc nor his insistence that Francis Bacon was the actual author of the plays of William Shakespeare. But they *do* revel in the exploits and adventures of Tom Sawyer, Becky Thatcher, and Huckleberry Finn, in the truancies necessitated by summer days and the nearness of the river, in the pranks, in the hairbreadth escapes. They recall the days of youthful exuberance and the nearly infinite latitude of childlike imagination.

We acknowledge and respect both the political achievements of Theodore Roosevelt and the literary expertise of Mark Twain. But we *love* "the fun" of these two "boys."

In the months after Twain's death, his longtime friend and fellow writer, William Dean Howells, wrote a memoir in which he identified the grandeur of his friend's accomplishments. Howells wrote, "Clemens was sole, incomparable, the Lincoln of our literature" (101). In a similarly admiring vein, I have concluded that, for me at least, Theodore Roosevelt was the Mark Twain of our Presidents. Probably both of them would recoil from such a pronouncement. I can almost see them challenging each other to a boyish tussle in an effort to prove the comparison untrue. It would be just like Teddy, just like Sam.

25

William Howard Taft: His Home, My Home

27th President William Howard Taft (1909-1913):
Childhood Home in Cincinnati, OH

Of all the chapters in this book, I feared that this one might be the most difficult to write. The reason is both simple and, perhaps, cloyingly sentimental. But since it is also the truth, I feel a need to mention it before proceeding.

Cincinnati is the town where I grew up, and it has come to hold a plethora of conflicting memories for me. When Carol and I decided to drive there from St. Louis in the summer of 2004, I chose to head southeast on I-64 from St. Louis to Louisville, and then turn north on I-71 up to Cincinnati. I knew that the alternative northern route was somewhat shorter (I-75 to Indianapolis, then down I-74 to Cincinnati), and I had driven that route many times over the years. But not now, not this time.

My feelings were due to the fact that, in the winter of 1984, my parents had set out from their home in Cincinnati to have a lovely visit with their St. Louis family, Carol, our infant daughter, Katie, and me. The road between Cincinnati and Indianapolis, however, had become icy, and my mom, in attempting to avoid a collision with another car, had hit a median at full speed. Although both she and my dad had been airlifted to an Indianapolis hospital, and I had arrived only hours later, in a matter of days, my mother had passed on.

I simply didn't want to drive that stretch of highway again. Would I have recognized the place where the accident had occurred, and would I have been tempted to try to imagine my mom's final happy moments just prior to the icy collision that had changed everything in her—and her family's—life? I didn't want to know the answers to such questions.

Two years after the crash, my dad, who had survived the accident but not the loss of my mother, had also passed on. As a result, the road to Cincinnati, indeed the entire city itself, had come to stand for me as a sort of vivid memory of innocent youth and a happy adolescence, followed by a painful, irretrievable loss. What would it be like to see my childhood hometown again? What would my more mature perspective understand that my youthful eyes had missed?

All this coursed through my mind as the miles melted away between St. Louis and Louisville and then between Louisville and Cincinnati. My research into the Presidents and their homes was leading me back to this city of my past. What would I find there? Would I recognize anything? After all, it had been nearly twenty years since I had last seen Cincinnati. Then, finally, we crested the Kentucky hill that overlooked the winding Ohio River, and "The Queen City of the Midwest" came into view.

Cincinnati lay fully visible on the far side of the Ohio River, just beyond Newport, Kentucky, and the upcoming interstate highway bridge. The city looked remarkably similar to how I remembered it.

The Carew Tower still dominated the skyline, and, although there were newer high-rises, office buildings, and even two stadiums clustered near the river, the pyramidal Fifth Third bank tower next to the Carew made the overall look of the city hearteningly familiar. We crossed the bridge and veered right along the Ohio shore in search of our stop: The William Howard Taft National Historic Site. I knew it was located somewhere in the general downtown area, but in all my years of living here, I had never visited it. This trip to Cincinnati would be both personally significant and historically energizing. It was one of my earliest sorties into a deeper appreciation of the backgrounds and seminal influences in the lives of our Presidents. And it turned out to be an early chapter in what has become one of the most engaging intellectual pursuits of my life.

Who cares about William Howard Taft? Certainly as a boy I had not. True, the Taft name was well-known throughout southwestern Ohio (there was the Taft Museum downtown where I had given my first trembling piano recital; the Taft Broadcasting Company, our local NBC affiliate; and numerous political Tafts), but at that time, I had never thought much about the fact that a President had come from Cincinnati.

In fact, had I known anything about Taft, it probably would have been the comical, trivial kind of information ("Who was the fattest US President? William Howard Taft at 350 pounds!"). With two years of high school American history under my belt, I might have been able to identify the fact that William Howard Taft had been Teddy Roosevelt's handpicked successor for the Presidency in 1908 and that some of Taft's decisions as President had so infuriated TR that he had chosen to run against his former friend in 1912. Also that, by doing so and thereby splitting the Republican vote, Roosevelt had assured the election of his progressive rival, the Democratic candidate, Woodrow Wilson.

This historical information must have seemed relatively unimportant to me during the years I lived here as a boy. Clearly it had not furnished me with enough reasons to encourage me to decide to visit Taft's home. Yet, as I have so frequently learned in my subsequent travels, such decisions or, in this case, non-decisions, can deprive us of many meaningful insights. My stop here today would ultimately teach me much that I had not known about William Howard Taft.

That he was a large man is, of course, indisputable, as was the fact that Taft had been TR's first choice for the Republican nomination for President in 1908. But Taft had never been an inept Chief Executive. Our visit would both confirm and illustrate the considerable worth, rather than the mere girth, of this often misunderstood and invariably underrated President.

We exited the highway, wound our way up the crowded and surprisingly steep Cincinnati hillsides through a somewhat depressed cityscape, and finally came within sight of the Taft home, a prominent yellow brick structure crowning what, in an earlier age, must have been an airy and scenic overlook of the city of Cincinnati to the west.

Now surrounded by buildings of later and lesser-quality construction, the Taft residence retained a kind of dowager dignity, almost as if it were gathering up its presidential skirts to keep from contact with a steadily encroaching urban world.

I parked our van in front of a well-marked but rather conspicuously empty lot in front of the Visitor's Center, and we proceeded into the nearby Taft Education Museum area. A pleasant, somewhat bemused, guide welcomed us and informed us that a house tour would begin shortly.

As I wandered around the small museum, I noted that, even here, William Howard Taft appeared to be something of a second fiddle. On this day the most impressive display, rather than a chronicle of the achievements of Taft's presidential administration, was an odd—but undeniably unique—collection of crocheted reproductions of several presidential homes. The Taft Home was included among the other model houses, but it was so extremely modest and plain, particularly when contrasted to the much more splendid recreations of Mount Vernon, Monticello, and The Hermitage that its inclusion appeared almost a nod of sympathy to viewers like us who had at their immediate disposal only the nearby Taft dwelling to tour. We weren't learning too much more than comical trivia yet.

Happily, this was about to change. We exited the museum and walked up toward the front of the house. By this time, other cars had nearly filled the small lot, and, before long, Carol and I found ourselves waiting with an interested group of tourists, all looking forward to getting a glimpse into the life of our 27th President. The house's central door opened, and we were invited into its generously large but still completely unassuming front hall.

Our tour began toward the back of the house where we quietly filed past the room where Taft had been born. Our entire group was then reconvened in the front study. Here, we were informed, the young William Howard Taft and his half-brothers, Charles and Peter, had done their homework religiously after school each day before being allowed to go outdoors. The rather sepulchral tone of the heavy and dark room felt antithetical to the image of growing boys who (the guide continued) had loved playing baseball after they had finished their schoolwork. (William Howard Taft, I remembered, would be the President to establish the custom of the Chief Executive throwing out the first pitch of the baseball season.)

The gem of the tour, however, was still to come.

Crossing back through the front hall, the guide led us into the large parlor with a southern exposure. Sunshine poured into the room from windows that ran the whole length of the house.

"This room," she intoned, "was the formal parlor. Usually it would not be a place where children would have been permitted to roam." She glanced around the room for any children who might be impressed by such information. Finding none, she continued her account of an amazing moment that had occurred right here in the bright and welcoming space in which we were standing.

She spoke of a day when the young William Howard Taft had been five or six years old. The Civil War was still raging, and the Union needed vital funds to support the provisioning of its armies. Ulysses S. Grant and James Garfield, both then serving as officers in the Union army, had visited Judge Alfonso Taft at his home in order to work up a bond to raise money for the war effort.

"In this room," our guide concluded, "on that day there were three men who would later become Presidents of the United States: Ulysses S. Grant, James Garfield, and, hiding under the table but listening with an intensity that would keep this moment forever fresh in his memory, William Howard Taft."

I have never been able to verify the truth of this story, but it was a lot more interesting than the merely comic trivia so often associated with President Taft. It is probably also worth noting that there are a few solid reasons to credit the possibility of this account's veracity, as Alfonso Taft *was* a well-known and influential man in Cincinnati, and both Grant and Garfield were themselves longtime Ohioans.

As we moved to the upstairs area of the home, we found a large variety of museum displays and exhibits that had been placed throughout the second floor rooms, all focusing on Taft's achievements in public office. These were much more illuminating than had been the Visitor's Center's offerings.

Before serving as President, an attractive poster board presentation explained, Taft had been a superb Governor of the Philippines, proving his abilities as a capable administrator. In another section of this second floor area, I was to learn that it had been Taft, not Roosevelt, who had overseen the completion of the Panama Canal.

In addition, Taft's presidential administration had achieved some noteworthy legislation (including a constitutional amendment permitting the first graduated income tax, another reason some might choose to want to forget him). But what, above all, emerged with clarity as I moved from one display to another was an impression that Taft had been an extremely honest, intelligent man, a coalition builder instead of a dynamic generalissimo.

Following Teddy Roosevelt, such a personage surely would have tended to be undervalued by a nation drunk with the personal charm of their recent Chief Executive. Yet Taft's record on trust busting was even more far-reaching than had been Roosevelt's. And, more impressive still, was the fact that Taft would go on to be the only ex-President ever to serve as Chief Justice of the Supreme Court, his most distinctive contribution to that office being a clear reverence for and thoughtful interpretation of the U.S. Constitution.

There was much to be said for Taft—certainly more than the size of his bathtub or Teddy Roosevelt's famous retort when he learned that Taft had visited various locales in the Philippines on horseback

("I pity the horse"). Once again I was reminded that anyone who has ever assumed the power and responsibility of being President of the United States deserves a close and sympathetic look before being dismissed as a joke or a cipher. William Howard Taft was neither. He was a man who loved the law and who was willing to serve his country when called upon to do so. His grave is located, interestingly enough, in Arlington cemetery, one of only two Presidents laid to rest there.

This trip to Cincinnati, then, had been both informative and therapeutic for me. The city still felt like my childhood home, and the fact that it was also the childhood home of William Howard Taft had given it a newfound worth in my eyes that had eased both my fears and my sense of personal loss. In my case, the great American novelist Thomas Wolfe had been wrong: I **could** "go home again."

26

Woodrow Wilson: "...a dream life."

28th President Woodrow Wilson (1913-1921): Birthhome in Staunton, VA

When describing his richly imaginative boyhood days, a mature Woodrow Wilson would write, "I led a dream life" (Brands, Woodrow Wilson 3). It's a deceptively simple description. Like the man himself, this statement contains the possibility of at least two distinct yet contrasting interpretations. The phrase "a dream life," on one hand, can be seen to signify a perfect life, a life which has become a realized ideal. Conversely, "a dream life" can also refer to an existence rendered somehow unreal, a life of unfulfilled hopes and desires. In the case of the life and accomplishments of Woodrow Wilson, neither meaning is wholly true. Or wholly false.

The two exterior aspects of the birth house in Staunton, Virginia, provide a surprisingly apt example of the duality referred to above, a duality that will become increasingly evident in the life of Woodrow Wilson.

From the street, the eastern façade of this modest home set in a small town just west of the Blue Ridge is basic and unpresuming. It is an unpretentious, appropriately humble rental manse, perfect for a young Presbyterian churchman just beginning in life. A plain brick structure, the home's only apparent decorative element is a simple covered porch over the door of the entryway. And here in December of 1856, Thomas Woodrow Wilson was born.

Rear of Woodrow Wilson's Birthhome in Staunton, Virginia

The western side of the manse, however, carries with it an astonishingly different ambiance. As seen from the adjoining garden, the rear of the building appears to be a grand mansion with four stately snow-white Doric columns supporting a projecting pediment with double balconies. The house crowns its hillside with the splendid aura of a Southern plantation. The two sides of this earliest home in the life of Woodrow Wilson mirror the dual nature of this man who managed to be simultaneously both a straightforward, honest, religiously devout public servant who did his best to redirect and benefit every institution over which he was put in charge, and at the same time a self-righteous moralizer whose adamant refusal to accept any opinion but his own would lead to heartbreaking failures to achieve his most cherished goals.

These two apparently contrary personality traits were linked by a single quality that was arguably Wilson's greatest asset: his visionary idealism. Yet, on several key occasions, the two sides of his dual nature worked against each other. Both were, however uncomfortably, aspects of the same man, as both eastern and western facades of the Staunton home are, however improbably, sides of the same house.

Much has been written about Wilson's unusual ascent to the nation's highest elected position. He was the first—and still the only—President to hold an earned Ph.D. He was the first ex-college president to become Commander-in-Chief. He was highly unusual in having run for only one political office prior to winning the Presidency. And he was probably the first President to openly believe himself to be appointed by God to lead the nation—and the world—into a secular and terrestrial heaven on earth of prosperity and peace.

His detractors, of course, point to a different set of characteristics, also based on historical facts. Wilson, although claiming to be dedicated to a restoration of social justice, was racially prejudiced, advocating segregation as a means of maintaining civil order; Wilson, although claiming to be opposed to military activism, became, according to historian Walter LaFeber, "the greatest military interventionist in U.S. History" (Chace 199), sending troops to restore order in Nicaragua, Haiti, the Dominican Republic, and Mexico during his first term alone; Wilson, although backing the women's suffrage movement, had also commented, while teaching at Bryn Mawr, that "Lecturing to young women of the present generation on the history and principles of politics is about as appropriate and profitable as would be lecturing to stonemasons on the evolution of fashion in dress" (Axtell 123). The list of such contradictory stands goes on and on. And yet the historical verdict delivered on the Presidency of Woodrow Wilson is almost without exception extremely positive. Why?

As one of my favorite characters in the political drama *West Wing* put it, "They'll like us when we win." Wilson, even in some of his darkest hours, has emerged in the historical record as a winner. Under his leadership, Princeton became a more scholastically challenging institution of higher learning, the state of New Jersey enacted many progressive reforms, and the Allied Forces, with the aid of the United States military, prevailed in the Great War. But the explanation for Wilson's continued high stature in the pantheon of American Presidents is more complex than just a tally of achievements, however noteworthy. Understanding the nature of his victories, and even the pathos of some of his greatest defeats, is essential to explain his ongoing reputation as one of our greatest Presidents. And his house in downtown Washington, D.C. would provide helpful clues to reaching such an understanding.

Woodrow Wilson owned only one home in his entire life, the house on "S" Street, to which he retired after his second term as President. He had desired to run for a then unprecedented third term, but by 1920, even his most ardent admirers realized that his physical condition would not permit an active campaign, much less a dynamic administration.

On a bright April day in 2012, Carol and I disembarked the Washington metro at Dupont Circle, negotiated our way to Massachusetts Avenue, then walked several blocks north toward 24th Street. Our morning stroll took us past one foreign embassy after another, and I found myself remembering Wilson's famous quote from the beginning of his term as President: "It would be an irony of fate if my administration had to deal chiefly with foreign affairs" (Chace 196). Even **after** his Presidency, I noted silently, Wilson had been unable to separate himself from the world problems he had had to face throughout his years as America's Chief Executive. After about fifteen minutes, we reached 24th Street, and then turned onto "S." The house was on our immediate right, and it would reveal much about the complex allure of our 28th President.

Woodrow Wilson's Final Home in Washington, DC

The house looked immediately imposing and grand, yet not completely unfamiliar. Like the Staunton manse where Wilson had been born, the façade was red brick with a projecting porch providing a cover over its front entrance. Here, however, the similarities ended. The weight and girth of the Washington home's architecture communicated an undeniable "gravitas." Its four stories with the three decorative Roman arches defining the second floor windows almost belied the structure's function as a private dwelling. This house was, without question, a mansion, and its inhabitants, persons of consequence. When Carol and I were informed during our tour that the home contained a total of twenty-eight rooms, it came as no surprise to either of us.

We walked up to the front door and rang the doorbell. Moments later, we were greeted by the woman who would be our docent for the house tour. After a cordial welcome, she indicated that we should take a seat in a small room on the first floor that had once been a secretary's office. Here we were to watch a short video presentation on the life and achievements of President Wilson, aptly entitled "Woodrow Wilson: American Idealist." It was a brief summary of the President's successes, ranging from his stewardship of Princeton University to his presidential years of progressive legislation, including the establishment of the Federal Reserve. Then the film moved into Wilson's wartime challenges. While including an account of his ultimately unsuccessful efforts to pass the combined Versailles Treaty/League of Nations legislation through the U.S. Senate, the emphasis was clearly on his stalwart, even life sacrificing, efforts to do so. As the final credits rolled, it was impossible not to feel that we were being invited into the home of a 20th century hero.

By this time, we had been joined by several other visitors, and we all gathered in the front hall. Our docent began with preliminary remarks describing Edith Wilson's careful screening of visitors to the house, a precaution she had taken due to the President's weakened condition at the time of his residence here. Then we all were invited upstairs to our first stop: the grand parlor on the second floor at the front of the house.

This was a sumptuously ornate room, filled with tokens of appreciation and gratitude from a variety of friends and leaders around the globe. On the left as we entered, there hung an enormous antique tapestry that covered the entire wall. Elsewhere throughout the room were placed sculptures, paintings, and various other objects d'arte that had been presented to the Wilsons during their European travels. Of particular note to me was a beautiful oil painting reproduction of one of Michelangelo's Sistine Chapel figures, a gift to the President from the Vatican in acknowledgement of his being the first sitting American Chief Executive to pay a state visit there.

"This is the room," our docent informed us, "where you would have been taken to see President Wilson, had Edith determined your visit to have been of sufficient importance." Then she added, "You wouldn't have stayed long, whatever your business."

There was something quite regal, almost Versailles-like, about such protocol. Of course, the President's ill health had dictated most of Mrs. Wilson's vigilance. Still the feeling here was anything but Jeffersonian casual.

Our tour's next stop was President Wilson's private library, always a treat for a bibliophile like me.

This large room was paneled in darkly stained wood with an entire wall dedicated to floor to ceiling bookcases. "Wilson's actual collection of books was donated to the Library of Congress," our docent observed, "but the volumes you see are all titles he would have owned."

Just in front of this bookcase was a large desk and, on the opposite side of the room, close to the windows, were reading chairs and tables filled with books and bric-a-brac. For the next several minutes, our docent spoke about Wilson's fascination with scientific advances, noting particularly his love of the new communication medium of motion pictures.

"The silent movie star Douglas Fairbanks, Sr., presented President Wilson with a movie projector, and the Wilsons loved pulling down the screen there ..." (she pointed to the ceiling just above the bookcase wall where a retractable screen was visible) "... to watch the latest films right in this room." Turning, she gestured toward the next room as she continued to speak: "As you enter the solarium you will see the microphone which President Wilson used to broadcast the first presidential speech on the recently invented medium of radio."

The group filed out, but I couldn't pull myself away from the library just yet. As I gazed around the room, I had to admit that this certainly was a scholar's enclave, a perfect setting for a university president. But something was not completely right. The library was dark, too dark, I thought, for prolonged study. Even the electric lamp placed on the desk gave out only a feeble glow that lent the room a subtle air of melancholy. It suggested to me a distinct parallel to Wilson's term as president of Princeton.

He had taken over the helm of his alma mater with one overarching aim: to strengthen the rigor and scholastic reputation of the institution. Under his stewardship Princeton moved close to the national forefront of recognized academic excellence, a preeminence which it retains to this day. Yet, it must also be noted that Wilson had found it impossibly difficult to transform as thoroughly as he had wished the institution he loved so dearly. Despite his best efforts, the fraternal eating clubs, which he believed worked against the seriousness of the scholarly community, were retained as a result of alumni insistence that they be allowed to continue. Similarly, Wilson's dream of a graduate school located at the very center of the university was dashed by a wealthy donor who insisted on placing it on the periphery of the grounds, safely distant from undergraduate disturbances. These lost fights had been deep disappointments to Wilson, and they turned his career path forever away from academia. His tenure as university president, then, like the somber atmosphere of his library/study in his Washington home, provided a prototypical example of the dual nature of Wilsonian success: his impressive achievement had been tainted with defeat. It would not be the last of such simultaneously glorious yet still disappointing victories.

My eyes now rested on the Rembski portrait. It would turn out to contain the central revelation of my visit. Carol had mentioned this painting when she had first circumnavigated the room, whispering to me that it disturbed her that an American President's portrait would feature a map of Europe as a backdrop, rather than the United States. I hadn't taken much notice of the painting at the time—I was more interested in the contents of the bookcase—but now I stood before the portrait and gave it my full attention.

A somewhat tired, but nonetheless handsome and determined President Wilson sits at an angle, looking directly out toward the viewer. There is a book on the table at which he sits, and he is holding a pencil as if ready to write or draw. Behind him, as Carol had noticed, was displayed an oversized map of Europe. It appears to be incorrect. The countries are not configured as we know them to be. But the map in this painting is, in fact, a visualization of Wilson's ideal Europe, a Europe that had never come to pass.

The portrait, commissioned by Edith Wilson's brothers as a gift for their sister, nearly twenty years after the President's passing, is the perfect metaphor for Woodrow Wilson. Like the Staunton house, the painting has two distinct sides. In the foreground is Wilson himself, cool, detached, staunchly committed to his mission of bringing lasting peace to a war-ravaged continent. In the background is his dream world, a world of permanently established nations with equitably drawn and unchanging borders, maintained by a League of Nations, itself unsullied by the pollution of self-interest or any thought of territorial gain. French president Georges Clemenceau had curtly quipped, "He [Wilson] thinks he is another Jesus Christ come upon the earth to reform men" (Chace 202). Yet standing here in the quiet room, I couldn't help but think that perhaps, just perhaps, that is **exactly** how Woodrow Wilson had seen himself, only without the venomous and sacrilegious sarcasm.

His plan was an impossible dream, of course. The United States Senate, though extremely desirous of ending a war that had engulfed much of the world, could never ratify a peace treaty that would have effectively placed the might of the U.S. military into the hands of an international League of Nations. Neither the Constitution, they argued, nor the American people, would ever permit it.

Wilson died three years later, having led his nation to victory in a war that had never officially ended. His effort to bring about the "dream world" of permanent international peace was in ruins. But magnificent ruins.

Our docent invited our tour group to ascend another flight of curved stairs up to the Wilsons' bedchambers. On a landing just outside these rooms, there was a Wilson-era typewriter, together with copies of hand-typed notes he was so fond of making for himself. Finally, we descended to the kitchen to end our tour.

But the Rembski portrait would not leave my thought. Wilson had been a visionary, a religious man, dedicated to establishing a lasting "peace on earth." As such, he has rightfully taken a place in the ranks of the world's greatest leaders. Yet he was also convinced that it was his vision and his vision alone that could bring about such a peace. The words of his introduction to the text of his Fourteen Points make his point unequivocally clear, even in their use of the imperial "we": "The programme of the world's peace ... is our programme, the only possible programme, as we see it."

I found myself pondering the subtle line which separates a courageous stand for principle from an obstinate insistence on one's own viewpoint. When should visionary idealism defer to a worldly but achievable reality? At the end of the day, it is the street side view that usually prevails, even if the dream is vividly painted, expertly framed, and reverently displayed. The character of President Wilson was defined by the constant battle between the two meanings of his "dream life." And both are on display in the homes where he lived.

27

Warren G. Harding: "Normalcy" on Display

29th President Warren G. Harding (1921-1923): Home in Marion, OH

At first glance, the home of Warren G. Harding in Marion, Ohio, looks, dare one say it, "normal." It's an unpretentious two-story clapboard structure, painted a deep forest green, whose only luxurious feature appears to be an elegant Ionic columned porch that runs the length of the front of the house and culminates in a sweeping circular curved sitting area that wraps around the right corner of the front of the residence. Here, in 1920, lived a man who would win the Presidency by a larger margin of victory than any President since James Monroe's uncontested second term, a hundred years earlier. Harding's campaign had been based on the promise to return the nation to a state of "normalcy" after the political activism of the progressive Presidents before him, and this message had been wildly successful with the electorate.

Yet, by 1924, this President who had died while still in office would be so universally vilified that his Vice President and successor, Calvin Coolidge, would refuse to attend a ceremony dedicating the Harding funeral monument in hopes of distancing himself from the disgraces of the preceding administration.

What had happened? And what could this simple frame structure do to clarify, to demystify, this remarkable reversal of national public opinion regarding Warren G. Harding?

After we had pulled our car into the site's parking lot and paid a small admission fee, Carol and I made our way to the tour's starting point. Our tour guide greeted us by inviting us to join the other assembled visitors already seated in the spacious circular porch area. There were still several empty chairs, and the cool shade and pleasant breezes wafting through the late afternoon made the prospect most appealing. It was quite easy, as we took our seats, to imagine a casual group of interested people assembling here to speak to the editor of *The Marion Star* as he might have held forth on the political issues of the day: women's suffrage, prohibition, the advisability or inadvisability of the United States' participation in the proposed League of Nations, all were key issues facing the nation in the early years of the twentieth century. And it was also from this porch, our docent reminded us, that Harding had waged his successful presidential campaign.

Taking a page from Presidents past (most notably James Garfield and William McKinley), Harding had chosen not to crisscross the country in a frantic attempt to garner votes. He had preferred, rather, to honor the tried and true practice, perhaps even the "normal" practice, of extending front porch homespun politics onto a national scale. As one historian put it, "In Harding, rural and small town America enjoyed one more chance to represent the nation" (Sosnowski 261). Of course, the proponents of intellectual "gravitas" believe that only disasters can result from such hayseed representation, and the Presidency of Harding would appear to bear striking proof of their contentions. The house itself, however, would tell a substantially different, much more complex, story to those of us about to venture inside.

We all moved into the front hall of the home where our tour guide/docent, an amiable and vivacious local high school teacher, positioned us around the raised landing at the foot of the stairway leading to the second floor.

"Right here," he began, "on July 8, 1891, Warren G. Harding married Florence De Wolfe. It was his first and her second marriage." Of the importance of Florence to Warren's political aspirations, I will defer to the plethora of historians who have a variety of—sometimes rather outrageous—theories regarding their relationship. What the house told **me** was that choosing such a spot for a wedding bore none of the trappings of the wealth and privilege of which the Hardings are so often accused. The hall was modestly sized; our group of about twelve visitors nearly filled it.

The entire house was to be comparable in scale. As we ascended to the second floor, I was struck by a panoramic photograph of the front of the home, surrounded by what appeared to be several hundred people listening to Harding give a speech from the front porch where we had been sitting only moments before. I questioned the guide about crowd control.

"They must have had to close down the street for a crowd like that," I commented (the road into town passed directly in front of the house).

"They did do that. Regularly," he added. "By the time of the election nearly 600,000 people had come to Marion to see and hear Mr. Harding speak from that porch."

It was a number that was almost impossible to believe. But the photograph was firsthand proof of the sorts of crowds that must have become commonplace in Marion during the campaign season of 1920.

Upstairs we were conducted past several rooms, but we often had to wait in the hall while others of our group viewed the complete interiors of any one of them. They were too small to accommodate twelve people at any one time. We saw the bedchamber set aside for the visits of Florence's son from her first marriage, a son being raised not by Florence and Warren but by Florence's father. In the master bedroom, a visitor commented on the twin beds, and this led our docent into a tale of the Harding's' marital difficulties.

Here, once again, we were to confront what anyone interested in learning more about President Harding almost invariably encounters: scandals. Yet it is more than slightly interesting that the veracity of one of the most damning of his accusers has come to be seriously questioned by recent historians researching the ex-President's life. Nan Britton's volatile book, *The President's Daughter*, proclaimed itself to be an intimate account of her affair with Harding during his senatorial years. Since the book was published after Harding's untimely death, he had no chance to refute personally the charges made against him. However, according to an August 12, 2015, *New York Times* article, the most recent DNA investigations have made a convincing case that Harding *was* the father of Nan Britton's daughter, Elizabeth. These kinds of accusations are hard to dismiss. Even our cheerful docent was full of juicy gossip about the moral compromises for political ends made by both Florence and Warren Harding.

"The twin beds speak for themselves," he concluded.

Well, maybe. Of course, Harding was no angel. We all enjoyed seeing his copy of a small, wallet sized, leather bound "book" bearing the innocuous title, *The Four Swallows*, itself actually a cleverly disguised flask containing four vials of alcohol, an officially prohibited beverage at the time. And there was also no question of his determined interest in Republican politics and party loyalty. But neither was there anywhere in the house any ostentatious display of wealth, of privilege, or of the fruits of corrupt political gain. The docent opened the drawers of the President's dresser to show us ...

starched collars, undershirts, socks. Hardly the spoils of a political robber-baron.

Back downstairs, we moved into Harding's study. His small, but respectable, library featured a few unpretentious bookcases placed around the edges of the cozy room. In one corner stood a rather impressive looking period phonograph.

"Would you like to hear President Harding?" our docent asked. Everyone quickly assured him that we would love to do so.

"I don't do this often, because the record is rare, but here is a recording of a speech President Harding made right here on the front porch."

Our guide placed the antiquated needle delicately on the quickly revolving disc, and, through the scratches and pops of the old record, came a pleasant, actually rather soothing voice promising prosperity and justice for all Americans. Nothing flashy. No pyrotechnics. Normal, I'd say.

Our last stop was the kitchen. It boasted an oversized cast-iron oven, electric lighting (courtesy, we were told, of Harding's friend Thomas Edison), and a large early refrigerator. All of these items would have been state of the art possessions in 1920, but none were significantly beyond the financial means of a successful newspaper publisher and editor of the time, which, of course, Harding had been before and even during his political career.

I remained with the docent in the kitchen as most of the visitors exited the home, and I couldn't resist asking him a question or two.

"Why is it that all we usually hear about Harding is Teapot Dome and Nan Britton? I even read one Harding biography that completely omitted mention of the Washington Naval Conference, the first international gathering to meaningfully discuss worldwide disarmament."

"And why," **he** added, "do we never hear of his achievements in balancing the national budget and simultaneously lowering taxes?"

"Because he was a Republican," another one of the hangers-back remarked laconically. Everyone laughed at that, and we all left the house together. But in the week since my visit, that quip has lingered in my thoughts.

In many ways, Harding may have been our first truly "modern" Republican President. Like George W. Bush, like Ronald Reagan, Harding had had no pretensions, no intellectual pedigree prior to his election as President. He was a down-to-earth man with many of the foibles, perhaps too many, that characterize ordinary men, but his achievements were greater than the modest background from which he had come.

He had worked to bring Americans together, subsequent to the bitter wrangling that was the result of Wilson's insistence on linking the Versailles Treaty to his vaunted League of Nations. Harding had argued strongly for America's membership in the World Court. He had created the Office of Budget which would begin much needed oversight of government spending (even though it would reveal malfeasance in members of his own administration). He had nominated former President William Howard Taft to the Supreme Court, a man who would become widely regarded as one of the most effective Chief Justices in the history of that distinguished body.

Standing outside the house at 380 Mount Vernon Avenue, looking at its plain façade, all these seemed like rather considerable achievements. And driving five minutes to his classically beautiful memorial where Harding and Florence rest beneath the graceful branches of a Japanese willow tree, it is hard to disagree with the conclusions of Professor Thomas Sosnowski:

Harding Memorial in Marion, Ohio

The president who appeared much beloved in his lifetime for his folksiness and political homilies became much maligned within months of his death. The harmonizer never had an opportunity to bring out the facts about his presidency and to write his memoirs. As a result, it took four years in his tomb and memorial to await a proper pres-

idential solemnity and dedication. At the turn of the following century, it is unfortunate that the worst is still believed, except in Marion where 'their' citizen is honored and respected. (273)

It was as if I could hear the voice of his home speaking to me, and to all of us, telling us what it had been trying to say all along:

This was the home of Warren G. Harding. He was an editor, a politician, a Senator, a President. He had both excellent and faulty judgment. He achieved much and little. But look around. Whatever his strengths or his shortcomings, this place attests to one clear truth: he never lost sight of who and what he was and where he came from. And that says something worth honoring and respecting about him.

I couldn't agree more.

28

Calvin Coolidge: Keeping Store

30th President Calvin Coolidge (1923-1929): General Store/Birthplace/Summer White House in Plymouth Notch, VT

In the winter of 1981, newly elected President and First Lady, Ronald and Nancy Reagan, were settling into and redecorating the White House. President Reagan chose to place on the wall of his Cabinet Room the portrait of President Calvin Coolidge. In the years following his Presidency when he was writing his autobiography, President Reagan explained this decision:

> *I'd always thought of Coolidge as one of our most under-rated presidents. He wasn't a man with flamboyant looks or style, but he got things done in a quiet way. He came into office after World War I facing a mountain of war debt, but instead of raising taxes, he cut the tax rate and government revenues increased, permitting him to elim-inate the wartime debt and proving that the principle ... about lower tax rates meaning greater tax revenues still worked in the modern world.* (244)

It was a fitting tribute to our 30th President, surely one of our most misunderstood and genuinely self-effacing public servants in the history of the United States.

I am often asked by people who know about our travels to the various presidential homes Carol and I have visited, "Which of them is your favorite?" It is a difficult question to answer, as each has provided us with fascinating insights into the lives of the President(s) who lived in these places. But for those who pursue their query past an expression of general interest, I urge them, if they truly want to see firsthand the background and the soul of an American President, not to miss a chance to visit Plymouth Notch, Vermont. This site is more than a home. It is a way of life, a way of life that prepared an American who had never thought of himself as a great man to become an admired and respected President of the United States.

Yet misunderstood nonetheless. Why? Because he was a President so unlike most historians' usual definition of that word that they not only frequently fail to appreciate his achievements, but also, on some occasions, miss him altogether. Robert Cowley, an authority on the decade of the 20's, sums up the standard assessment of Coolidge's Presidency:

Historians have not treated Calvin Coolidge kindly. The thirtieth president has been portrayed as a man who practically slept through his five and a half years in the White House. His failure to rein in stock market speculation has been blamed for the Crash of 1929 and the Great Depression that followed. Frederick Lewis Allen has called Coolidge 'one of the most negative characters ever to attain to high office,' and it's hard to identify him with a lasting piece of legislation. In an often-quoted 1962 ranking of the presidents, his name appears near the bottom—as his contemporary H. L. Mencken put it, 'among the vacuums.' (212)

This criticism deserves some careful scrutiny. While it suggests what many modern historians expect to see in a Chief Executive (i.e. alertness, pro-activity, positivity, and legislative achievements), it completely fails to grasp Calvin Coolidge's bedrock assumptions about what it is that a President should—and should not—be.

Here is a brief look at President Coolidge's account of a "normal" day in his White House:

It was my custom to be out of bed about six-thirty .... It was my intention to take a short walk before breakfast .... Soon after eight found me dictating in the White House library in preparation for some public utterance. This would go on for more than an hour, after which I began to receive callers at the office.... Each one came to me with a different problem requiring my decision, which was usually made at once .... The afternoon was reserved for attention to the immense number of documents which pass over the desk of the President... Before dinner another walk was in order...We gathered at the dinner table at seven o'clock and within three-quarters of an hour work would be resumed with my stenographer to continue until about ten o'clock. (202-204)

Surely, any reasonable reader of the above account would have to conclude that President Coolidge had not "slept through his five and a half years in the White House," unless, of course, those two aforementioned "walks" could be attributed to somnambulism.

In response to Frederick Lewis Allen's accusation of Coolidge's negativism, I will once again permit the President to speak for himself:

> *The words of the President have an enormous weight and ought not to be used indiscriminately. It would be exceedingly easy to set the country all by the ears and foment hatreds and jealousies, which, by destroying faith and confidence, would help nobody and harm everybody. The end would be the destruction of all progress....The only way I know to drive out evil from the country is by the constructive method of filling it with good. The country is better off tranquilly considering its blessings and merits, and earnestly striving to secure more of them, than it would be in nursing hostile bitterness about its deficiencies and faults. (186)*

Here once again Coolidge shows his critics to be on the wrong side of the truth. He was clearly a leader desirous of affirming the great "blessings and merits" of the country, not choosing to belabor or ruminate over whatever faults remained to be corrected. His desire to help the country progress by "filling it with good" was as far from negativity as light is from darkness. How is it, then, that these historians are so obviously missing Calvin Coolidge's presidential character? I believe it is because they fail to grasp his definition of leadership.

To start off, it is a definition almost totally without ego. Has any President ever described the post in more self-effacing terms than Calvin Coolidge did in his *Autobiography*?:

> *The presidential office takes a heavy toll of those who occupy it .... While we should not refuse to spend and be*

spent in the service to our country, it is hazardous to at-
tempt what we feel is beyond our strength to accomplish.
(239)

While such an admission of the daunting challenges of the Presidency might strike a reader as a none too veiled confession of
Coolidge's feelings of personal inadequacy, he himself never saw it
that way. Upon learning of his ascent to the office of Chief Executive, he writes, "...when the events of August, 1923 [i.e. President
Harding's death], bestowed upon me the presidential office, I felt
at once that power had been given me to administer it" (173). What
he meant by his newfound "power ... to administer it," however, was
radically different from what most modern historians would expect from a President. In the *Autobiography* Coolidge's explains this
"power" at some length:

> *While I felt qualified to serve, I was also well aware*
> *that there were many others who were better qualified. It*
> *would be my province to get the benefit of their opinions*
> *and advice.... In the discharge of the duties of the office*
> *[the Presidency] there is one rule of action more impor-*
> *tant than all others. It consists in never doing anything*
> *that someone else can do for you.... Like some other rules,*
> *this one has an important corollary.... They must be en-*
> *trusted to some one who is competent.* (173, 198)

In other words, President Coolidge realized from the outset that
the myriad duties of a President far exceeded the abilities of any
one man to fulfill them adequately. He would need to depend on
"competent" government officials to work out "the problems that
arise under their jurisdiction" (198). The "Presidency," he concluded,
"placed at the apex of our system of government ... is a place of last
resort to which all questions are brought that others have not been
able to answer" (198).

This managerial mode of executive leadership is a far cry from
the "Bully Pulpit," initiative-driven, highly partisan models of so

many other Presidents. But Coolidge was also a student of history. For inspiration, he looked very consciously back to Thomas Jefferson, and yet his perspective was that of a refreshingly candid and distinctively non-idolatrous New England Yankee:

> *In spite of all his greatness, any one who had as many ideas as Jefferson was bound to find that some of them would not work. But this does not detract from the wisdom of his faith in the people and his constant insistence that they be left to manage their own affairs. His opposition to bureaucracy will bear careful analysis, and the country could stand a great deal more of its application. The trouble is that we talk about Jefferson but do not follow him. In his theory that the people should manage their government, and not be managed by it, he was everlastingly right. (215)*

"Independence forever!" had been the last public pronouncement of John Adams in the final days of his life. Coolidge's approving coda to that earlier proclamation is that the people should be left free to manage their own affairs without interference from their government. But where did this particular brand of leadership come from? Where could one see the roots of Coolidge's unique blend of governance, this combination of the President's need for dependable and competent assistance together with a fierce respect for and insistence upon each individual citizen's self-reliance? The answer to this question is on daily display in a small Vermont farming town rooted in rocky soil and nestled between tree-covered hills, a town named Plymouth Notch.

On the day we visited, Carol and I drove south from Burlington, and as we left the interstate to skirt the Green Mountain National Forest, the road turned and twisted, rising and falling through scenic vistas and quaint villages.

"Pretty out of the way spot," we both agreed, and we were glad to have the help of our handy GPS system to lead us to the Calvin Coolidge Homestead State Historic Site. The weather on this mid-

July day was perfect, a clear sunny sky occasionally punctuated with a few cumulus clouds. Then suddenly on our left was a sign identifying the driveway to our destination. In a few moments we pulled into a spacious parking lot, left our car, and followed a clearly marked path through a manicured lawn and up to the doors of the site's Visitor's Center.

"Welcome," a pleasant volunteer greeted us as we entered. "We're so glad you came to visit us today." We paid our admission and were directed to a door where, we were informed, we should follow the path up to the village where a tour group was just beginning to assemble. "Your guide will lead you through the town. You'll see everybody gathering right in front of the general store," the volunteer called after us.

We exited the Visitor's Center and followed the pathway. There, spread out before us, was an entire farming village, complete with a general store with an attached house in back. A large barn on our immediate right looked out on the road leading up the hill through the village. There was a church on the left side of the road, while on the right stood a white house with bay windows and a front porch with several rocking chairs. Beyond it, a bit further up the road, stood an impressively large white building with three or four cars pulled into a small parking lot beside it. This place was more than a Presidential home site. It was a fastidiously preserved Vermont farming community.

Just as we had been told, visitors were beginning to gather in the road outside the stairs leading up to the General Store. Carol and I joined the group, and soon a guide appeared and invited us to mount the steps and proceed inside.

Walking through the front door of this establishment was like walking through an enchanted portal into the past. The store was fully stocked. Floor to ceiling shelves on either side of the salesroom contained all of the kinds of merchandise a remote farming community would need. Everything here, from housewares to pairs of boots, from bolts of cloth to hard candy protected by glass display cases, appeared only to be waiting for the arrival of working men, women, and wide-eyed children begging for sweets to create a Norman Rockwell canvas come to life. In the center of the store was a freestanding Franklin stove that, in more inclement weather, would have provided a dry warmth throughout the entire interior.

At the back of this salesroom was a narrow passageway leading to the house attached to the rear of the store, the house where, on July 4, 1872, Calvin Coolidge had been born.

After our guide had introduced us to this store setting, the place where the young Calvin Coolidge had seen his father make his living, as well as to the entire grounds of the Calvin Coolidge State Historic Site, she led us back out the front door and down the stairs. As she did this, she reminded our group that upstairs, over the store's salesroom, was a large second story space that had been used for dances and social gatherings in the village. "You might like to stop up there later in your visit," she added with a slight twinkle in her eye, and she gestured toward a steep stairway.

Our immediate goal, however, was located just around the corner. It was the house adjacent to the back of the General Store where we had begun our tour.

This home was a weathered brown clapboard structure with two small upper floor windows, one lower floor window, and a side door that had been the chief entryway. Wildflowers grew on either side of the steps leading up to the house, and our group had to enter single file as we made our way into the

Calvin Coolidge's Birthplace in Plymouth, Vermont

small parlor that was our first and only stop.

The room was an unadorned, simple space. A wooden rocking chair, a spinning wheel, and a Windsor bench were its chief furnishings. Floor planks showed signs of wear and attested to the unpretentious social standing of the Coolidge family at the time of their residence here. Right off the parlor was a bedroom just large enough to accommodate a double bed with a homemade quilt and a side table holding an oil lamp. In that room, our docent confirmed, our 30th President had been born.

Immediately next to this bedroom was the narrow passageway that led directly into the sales room of the General Store. I looked down its length toward the Franklin stove. It was impossible to question the convenience of the layout. Work and home were practically under the same roof.

Calvin Coolidge's Boyhood Home in Plymouth, Vermont

Our docent explained how, four years later in 1876, after the birth of the Coolidge's second child, the family had bought the white house across the road. "It was there," she added, "that Calvin and his sister Abbie would grow up. It was there where Calvin would learn some of his earliest and most important life lessons. It was to this home that he always would return from boarding school, from college, and from professional life. And it was also there, on the night of August 3, 1923," she looked around at our very attentive group, "that Calvin Coolidge would take the presidential oath administered to him by the town's notary public, his own father." We needed no additional invitation to follow her back out through the parlor door and across the road toward this most historically significant home.

And, for the Coolidges, economically significant as well. The Coolidge Homestead, as it is now known, provided quite visible evidence that John Coolidge's enterprising labors in running the General Store, together with his tireless efforts in working his farmland, had paid meaningful dividends. The family, while not wealthy in any cosmopolitan sense, was prospering.

The Homestead was considerably larger than the Birth House and provided plenty of room for the expanding Coolidge family. As was typical of John Coolidge, he had set about at once to make improvements to his newly purchased property. He added a barn as well as the front porch piazza to the home and in later years would oversee the additional touch of bay windows in the sitting room. This was the home where young Calvin would come to experience and, in later years to remember fondly, the rigors of farm life. Here, too, was a room rich in what he would later term "sacred memories" of his beloved sister Abbie who passed away in 1890 and of his "mother, who sat and reclined there during her long invalid years..." (178).

It was this front sitting room which most captured my imagination as our group was shepherded through the first floor of the Homestead. The plain square table in the center of the room, the family Bible, and the kerosene oil lamp—everything was arranged exactly as it had been on that August night in 1923. This remarkable preservation had been enabled by Coolidge's surviving son, John, and his wife, Florence. In 1956 they had ceded the home to the Vermont Board of Historic Sites, together with all the sitting room furnishings that had been present on that unique inauguration night. Because of their generosity I was experiencing another one of those special moments that sometimes occur when visiting a beautifully curated presidential home: the feeling of being in the very presence of history.

There were other rooms in the Homestead, of course, including a kitchen and pantry, as well as the room where John Coolidge had been roused from sleep with the news of his son's ascendency to the highest office in the land. President Coolidge's bedroom had also been recreated downstairs to permit visitors to see it. But the sitting room, that special bay windowed area where, for the first and only time in the history of the United States, a father had administered the presidential oath to his son was the crowning moment of my tour.

Our guide then led us out a back door into the pleasant air of the open fields and tree covered hills behind the house. We were free, she told us, to walk around the rest of the site on our own.

The large white building further up the road on the right, we learned, was the Plymouth Cheese factory and outlet, one of the original founders of which had been John Coolidge. Even today it continues to produce and sell this famous Vermont export.

I was attracted, however, to a brown weathered structure immediately across the street from the Homestead: the blacksmith shop. Inside on its walls hung dozens of work tools: saws of every shape and size, vices, pliers, and other implements with which I was wholly unfamiliar. The floor of the shop was cluttered with workhorses, planking, and wooden wheel hubs. Calvin Coolidge had loved this place. Here he had learned from, as well as assisted, the "large-framed powerful man with a black beard" that his father had hired to do the smithing (11). In one corner, protected beneath a bright blue blanket, was a carriage frame said to have been fashioned by John Coolidge himself. Plymouth Notch was a community of individuals who assumed responsibility for meeting their own needs. Everyone pitched in, and everyone worked. It felt very much like the system of governance President Calvin Coolidge would champion years hence.

Next to the blacksmith shop was the Union Christian Church where the family had worshipped and John Coolidge had served as a deacon. The interior of this church is simple and beautiful: varnished wooden walls and unadorned pews overhung by a chandelier with white frosted lamps. The pew where the Coolidge family had sat when attending services was indicated by the placement of an American flag. Most moving here, however, were the words of Calvin Coolidge etched into white stone on the wall in the small foyer of the church. It was a text he had spoken in Bennington, Vermont, on September 21, 1928, the last full year of his Presidency. For a man often referred to as "Silent Cal," it is uncharacteristically eloquent:

Vermont is a state I love. I could not look upon the peaks of Ascutney, Killington, Mansfield and Equinox without being moved in a way that no other scene could move me. It was here that I first saw the light of day; here I received my bride; here my dead lie pillowed on the loving breast of our eternal hills. I love Vermont because of her hills and valleys, her scenery and invigorating climate, but most of all, because of her indomitable people. They are a race of pioneers who have almost beggared themselves to serve others. If the spirit of liberty should vanish in other parts of the union, and support of our institutions should languish, it could all be replenished from the generous store held by the people of this brave little state of Vermont.

If there ever were to be written a gospel of President Calvin Coolidge, the sentiments expressed here would be central to its message. He begins with a declaration of love for his native state, together with a full appreciation of the personal history that had engendered this love. Then Coolidge identifies the key qualities in life which he finds most admirable, most valuable: indomitable spirit, dedication to service, a deep love of liberty, support of the government, selfless generosity, and courage. All of these qualities were essential in making life in Plymouth Notch fulfilling and prosperous. No wonder he valued them so highly. They were qualities that he would carry with him for the rest of his life, all the way to Washington, D.C.

Before Carol and I left Plymouth Notch, we remembered the advice of our docent not to miss the second floor of the General Store. We returned there, mounted once again the steps at the front of the store, and then ascended the rather cramped staircase on the left of the storefront porch. The day was getting warm, and it became quickly obvious that there would be no air conditioning upstairs. When we arrived on the second floor landing, we saw a small television monitor playing a video. Had this really been worth the climb?

Indeed it had been. The video was silent film footage of President Coolidge on vacation here at his home in Vermont. He had allowed himself to be filmed in overalls, pitching hay and going about some of the farm chores that had been his responsibility in his earlier years. Most remarkable, however, was the fact that nothing in Plymouth Notch had changed. The flickering newsreel from nearly ninety years ago showed an exact image of the village we had just visited. It was Brigadoon come to life.

The large room directly above the General Store had an interesting history. Although on the day we visited it was not set up to serve any particular purpose, a sign in the room explained how this expansive space had functioned in a variety of ways, from being used as a basic storage area to serving as a gathering place for social activities and Grange meetings. Most notably in 1924 President Coolidge had transformed this area into a Summer White House from which he could conduct necessary government business during his vacation here. His decision to work in this space was completely fitting. From his earliest years, Coolidge had concluded that his great desire in life had not been farming, despite the valuable lessons that working the land had taught him. "My own wish," he wrote in his *Autobiography*, "was to keep store, as my father had done" (19). In many key ways, even as President of the United States, he was doing precisely that.

But what exactly does the phrase "keep store" mean? To Calvin Coolidge, the answer was characteristically simple and direct:

> *Wealth comes from industry and from the hard experience of human toil. To dissipate it in waste and extravagance is disloyalty to humanity. When I became President, it was perfectly apparent that the key by which the way could be opened to national progress was constructive economy. Only by the use of that policy could the high rates of taxation, which were retarding our development and prosperity, be diminished, and the enormous burden of our public debt be reduced. (184)*

These are the sentiments of a storekeeper. Be industrious, work hard, avoid unnecessary expenses, pay off debt, and, by doing all this, set the stage for prosperity.

The results of such keeping store, by the end of the Coolidge administration in early March of 1929, appeared to justify completely the "constructive economy" that had been his watchword:

> *This policy has encouraged enterprise, made possible the highest rate of wages which has ever existed, returned large profits, brought to the homes of the people the greatest economic benefits they ever enjoyed, and given to the country as a whole an unexampled era of prosperity. (184)*

"But," I hear a chorus of historians cry, "what about the upcoming Depression? What did Coolidge do to try to avert the economic devastation that was just around the corner from the rosy outlook, quoted above?" In fact, one can say, "He did as much as possible."

Although modern historians disagree sharply over whether or not the drastic downturn of the nation's economy in the 1930's was inevitable, almost everyone agrees that the Great Depression was caused by three distinct factors: (1) the economic inability of our European allies to repay their war debts and the resistance of Germany to pay the crushing reparations demanded of them following the World War of 1914-1918; (2) the agricultural crisis that arose in the post-war years, first as a result of overproduction in the United States, and second as the consequence of a devastating drought, the famed "Dust Bowl"; and (3) the rampant speculation in stocks by investors whose financial resources were significantly less than the debts they were incurring.

Both Presidents Harding and Coolidge had been well aware that a European default on either its loan repayments or its reparation debts could be economically devastating to the economy of the United States. As a result, each Administration had worked to reduce dramatically the balance owed by both England and France. In addition, Charles G. Dawes in 1924 and, later, Owen D. Young in

1928 had headed commissions that forwarded plans to lower German reparation payments to levels that that nation could pay. Without the second and third crises identified above, the economic depression might never have occurred, or, if it had, it might have been much less severe and long lasting.

But those second two crises *had* come about. However, blaming President Coolidge for either of them seems both unrealistic and unfair. The model he exemplified in his own life certainly should have discouraged farmers from overproduction. The war had heightened worldwide demand for American agricultural products, and many American farmers, hoping to cash in on this bonanza, had taken out ill-advised loans to expand their croplands exponentially. But it would only stand to reason that, after the war was over, the demand would go down, and the excess crops would depress prices. Equally clear is the fact that no President could have anticipated the Dust Bowl. It was the combination of all these factors that had created a perfect storm of adversity.

Regarding the frenzy of financial speculation in the Stock Market, Coolidge believed that individuals had the right to make their own financial decisions, but he also repeatedly counseled citizens that "economy" should characterize any investment. Yet he never subscribed to the idea that it was the government's responsibility to protect people from their own bad choices. This would be a political mantra of later years.

As Carol and I drove away from Plymouth Notch, I felt that I was leaving a unique world of distinct beauty. Was it a world whose time had passed, even when Calvin Coolidge was still serving as President? Or was it a world that still had a worthwhile message for the 21st century? Questions worth pondering, I thought, as we drove quietly onward towards Northampton, Massachusetts.

"Constructive Economy"

Frankly, I wasn't initially sure whether Northampton would be a necessary stop in our travels to sites associated with Calvin Coolidge. Yes, he had moved here after attending college at Amherst. Yes, he had met his future wife, Grace Goodhue, here around the time he was establishing his law practice. And yes, there were two houses in Northampton that had been Coolidge residences. But both homes, my research had informed me, were privately owned and unavailable for tours. The remaining attraction here in Northampton, Massachusetts, was the Calvin Coolidge Presidential Library and Museum, but even its pedigree appeared odd. It was simply a room located within a public library, and furthermore, the museum's hours were quite restricted. Our time in Plymouth Notch had been so meaningful, what could such inaccessible and limited locales add to the picture we were already forming in our minds?

In a word? Confirmation. All the above reservations we had about Northampton prior to our visit proved to be accurate. Nevertheless, this place offered a rare opportunity for anyone attempting to assess a President's character: the chance to match his rhetoric with his life. In the case of President Coolidge, we would find the match to be exact.

Calvin Coolidge's Duplex in Northhampton, Massachusetts

Our first stop was the home at 21 Massasoit Avenue. This pleasantly situated residential street was quite easy to find. The houses on either side of the road were two-story dwellings maintained in varying degrees of thoroughness by the middle-class families who lived in them. A few of the residents clearly prided themselves on their gardens, but no house on the block aspired to any degree of prominence over the others. The Coolidge home on the right side of the road did not differ materially from any of the other residences on the street. No flagpole was present in the front yard. No historic marker had been placed on the curb. The only evidence of its particular significance was a very modest plaque placed on the wall next to the front door indicating that Calvin Coolidge had lived here from 1906 to 1930 and that, as a result, the site had been included in the National Register of Historic Places.

What *was* somewhat surprising was that this home was a duplex, a two family residence with a shared wall and identical front porches on opposite ends of the building. In itself, of course, there was nothing remarkable about this arrangement. It made perfect sense for a young lawyer and his wife to begin their life together in such a place. They could live here and start to raise a family both comfortably and economically.

But the Coolidges had continued to live at their 21 Massasoit Avenue address even after Calvin was elected Governor of Massachusetts. They maintained this home during the nearly six years they spent living in the White House. When they finally returned to Northampton in 1929, the Coolidges fully intended to spend their retirement years living in this house peacefully and frugally as ordinary citizens. But it hadn't worked out that way. The incessant traffic of people driving down this street in hopes of catching a glimpse of the ex-President and First Lady became interminable. It was no longer possible for the Coolidges to enjoy even a modicum of privacy here. It was time to relocate.

What an example to set. Cincinnatus had nothing on Calvin Coolidge. In his *Autobiography* President Coolidge wrote, "We draw our Presidents from the people. It is a wholesome thing for them to return to the people. I came from them. I wish to be one of them again" (242). This house bears unassailable witness to the sincerity of that desire.

But Calvin Coolidge had always been an extremely private man. He had never enjoyed being in crowds, and his last home, The Beeches, would give him the opportunity to stay in the town of Northampton yet still have the solitude in which to think and write that he had always valued.

The Beeches, Calvin Coolidge's Final Home in Northhampton, Massachusetts

Unlike any of his earlier residences, The Beeches is a mansion. Still in private hands, it is located at the end of a long driveway on land that lies immediately adjacent to a middle class neighborhood. It is not possible to get too close to this home, but it is easy to imagine that the panoramic view from its rear windows must include a glorious outlook on the valley and mountains beyond.

Few, I think, would begrudge the President the three years of relative peace and quiet he and his wife spent here from 1930 to 1933. Late in the morning of January 5, 1933, he died suddenly and unexpectedly in his dressing room. He was only 60 years old.

Our last stop was the Coolidge Library and Museum, located inside the public Forbes Library in downtown Northampton. The President himself had contributed many of his papers to the keeping of the library, starting as early as 1920. Once again, it was a perfect example of his belief in and insistence upon "constructive economy." The nation deserved to see, study, and appreciate these documents as well as his collected mementos relating to his life and political career, but why establish an expensive separate institution to curate them? His friend, Forbes librarian Joseph Harrison, had begun collecting materials relating to Mr. Coolidge as soon as he had been nominated for Vice President. Why not simply continue to add to the collection? Over the years President Coolidge and, after his decease, his wife and children had done precisely that. The Forbes Library remains the only public library in the United States that houses and maintains a presidential collection of documents and artifacts.

On the morning that Carol and I visited the library, the Coolidge Museum room was closed. However, after speaking to a librarian at the reference desk and explaining our project to her, she called up an assistant, a pleasant young woman named Annie, who instructed us to proceed upstairs, promising to meet us at the entrance to the museum. We did so, and, upon arriving, we waited by two oversized wooden doors. Annie soon joined us, unlocked these doors, and pushed them open. In just a moment we entered this large room with a high ceiling. It held a treasure trove of Coolidge memorabilia.

On one side of the room was preserved the glass door of the Coolidge and Hemenway law office, where he had practiced for many years. His law desk and several photographs of the office interior were also here. Toward the center of the room were glass cases containing some of the most famous items associated with the Coolidge Presidency. On prominent display was the ceremonial feather headdress Coolidge had been photographed wearing in 1927 on his being adopted by the Sioux tribe as Chief Leading Eagle, their first ever white chief. In another case was a cowboy hat, boots, and chaps with CAL imprinted on each leg. The circumference of the room was crowded with a plethora of mementos and photographic images of various moments of Coolidge's political career. Annie was clearly delighted in our interest in and appreciation of the items on view in this space.

Standing in the center of this room, looking up at the oil portraits of the President and First Lady, I experienced what I had felt in the sitting room of the Homestead in Plymouth Notch: the very presence of this quiet man who so valued modesty and "constructive economy." President Coolidge was no poser; the man you saw was the man he was. His description of the Presidency fits every other aspect of his life: "It was my desire to maintain about the White House as far as possible an attitude of simplicity and not engage in anything that had an air of pretentious display. This was my conception of the great office" (217). This has also come to be *my* conception of this great man.

29

Herbert Hoover: "Mister, we could use a man like Herbert Hoover again."

31st President Herbert Hoover (1929-1933): Birthplace in West Branch, IA

In the introduction to this collection of essays, I made the observation that my trips to presidential homes have invariably carried with them new perspectives on and fresh insights into the lives of the men who have served as Chief Executive of the United States, views that have not always confirmed the published opinions of historians. I also noted, almost without exception, my esteem for each of these Presidents had grown as a result of my firsthand encounters with the locales associated with them. But there are also a few even more extraordinary and rare moments when my understanding of a President has been completely turned on its head—totally altered—as a result of my visit. Such was the case in my travels to West Branch, Iowa, to see the National Historic Site dedicated to memorializing the life and work of Herbert Hoover.

Of all the past Presidents, Hoover would seem one of the easiest to pigeonhole. Assuming the reins of government in early 1929, he presided over the greatest financial catastrophe in the annals of American economics. As one historian put it, "Herbert Hoover was one of the least successful presidents in American history. His failure in the White House was the result of circumstances beyond his control as well as an inflexibility of personality and outlook that undermined his ability to deal with the greatest economic collapse in the country's history" (Dallek 218).

In 1932, while running for re-election, Hoover garnered only 59 electoral votes, losing to Franklin Roosevelt by a staggeringly large margin of over 11 million votes out of about 46 million cast. He was seen as out-of-touch with the needs of the poor and destitute, unsympathetic to the plight of labor, naively solicitous of the wealthy, and impotent to bring about any significant lessening of the despair felt throughout the country. More than anything else, Hoover's intractability and rigid ideology had led a frantic and weary America into a passionate acceptance of Roosevelt's "New Deal" as an antidote to this despair.

The voices of Edith and Archie Bunker, singing the theme song of the popular and long running television series *All in the Family*, had warbled, "Mister, we could use a man like Herbert Hoover again." The creators of the show had intended the line to be understood as comic irony, finding humor in a narrow-minded bigot like Archie Bunker yearning to return to the depression-era administration of this failed President.

Yet in West Branch, Iowa, such a dour assessment seems to have no clear connection to the young man who grew up here. In fact, West Branch seems much more like the ideal hometown setting of Meredith Wilson's *The Music Man* than any sort of training ground for an unsympathetic, inflexible ideologue. And the Herbert Hoover Presidential Library and Museum on this site provides a much more complicated—and, yes, sympathetic—depiction of this interesting man than the image typically communicated in history books.

First of all, there is the house. Hoover's birthplace sits on a corner lot in the center of the National Park site which presents not merely a single structure, but an entire recreation of West Branch at the time of Hoover's young life. There is a wide street with period houses and white picket fences defining a broad, tree-lined avenue. There is a blacksmith shop, a one-room schoolhouse, a Quaker Meetinghouse, all arranged around the two-room dwelling where, on August 10th, 1874, Herbert Clark Hoover had been born.

Two rooms—the parlor measuring about twelve by twelve feet, snuggled up to a side room (with trundle bed) about seven by twelve—comprise the entirety of the structure. The interior is sparsely furnished, though impeccably clean. This is no plush country manse, and I had to wonder what winters here must have been like, even with the fireplace in the shared wall between the rooms.

Hoover's father had run a blacksmith shop right across the road from the house, and Mrs. Hoover had earned extra money as a seamstress. The family privy still stands in the back yard, its crescent-moon symbol no longer carrying meaning to young tourists of the 21st century.

How could any man coming from such a background be unsympathetic to the needs of impoverished people? And, in Hoover's case, the sparseness of his childhood was further emphasized by the untimely deaths of both his father (when Herbert was six years old) and his mother (when he was ten). Hoover was separated from his siblings at the age of eleven, though the families in town had taken steps to provide for all three of the Hoover children, and Herbert had found himself traveling alone by train across the country to Oregon to live with an aunt and uncle he had rarely seen.

Again, such a difficult childhood would seem inconsistent with the image of the President portrayed by later historians. Had he forgotten the difficulties of his upbringing? Had he put behind him these painful reminders of near destitution and hardship that had defined his childhood years?

Clearly not, as it had been Hoover himself, along with the support of his wife, Lou, also an Iowan, who had arranged to purchase the two-room West Branch birth home in 1935. In other words, in the depth of the Depression, following an unceremonious drubbing at the polls in 1932, Hoover had wanted to be sure this humble structure would be preserved and restored so that it would continue to provide, in his own words, "… physical proof of the unbounded opportunity of American life."

"Unbounded opportunity." This phrase, more than any other, characterizes the life of Herbert Hoover. And its implications, on clear display here in West Branch, explain both the early phenomenal success he had achieved in the 20's and the later disappointment, even perhaps disillusionment, he suffered in the 30's.

The Quaker upbringing of Herbert Hoover instilled in him two distinct values that he would continue to espouse throughout his life: a determined work ethic and a spirit of helpfulness, reaching out to aid those in need.

He had seen each value illustrated graphically in his own young life. Both father and mother had labored tirelessly to provide their young family with a decent life and education. After tragedy had struck the Hoovers, members of the community had come together to provide homes for each of the now-orphaned siblings. And they had done so willingly, even happily. The children had been seen, not as added burdens to the families who had taken them in, but rather, in the custom of the Quaker faith, as blessings added to each home. This was especially evident in Herbert's case, as the family who had already included him as a cherished family member was deeply saddened when his Oregon uncle had requested that the boy be sent west (in part, at least, to fill the place left vacant by the death of this same uncle's only son a few months earlier). Herbert Hoover knew the importance of hard work, and he took very seriously the biblical injunction to "love thy neighbor as thyself."

The subsequent events of his life bear striking evidence of both. Historians tend to recount with relish the fact that Hoover became one of the best paid men in America in the ten years after his graduation from Stanford University. Yet the story of how this came to be is truly a Horatio Alger tale come to life.

From loading ore in a Nevada mine for over a year, to rugged mining oversight in Australia and China, the young Hoover had devoted his talents and energies to labors that would have daunted a lesser man. There were impressive displays in the Herbert Hoover Presidential Library and Museum detailing Hoover's adventures and exploits in these far-flung regions. Yet, even more impressively, when, in 1917, his organizational skills had been noted by the government of the United States, Hoover had readily taken on the responsibility of Director General of American Relief Administration, the national program through which food would be provided to over 350 million people in 21 different countries, Europeans devastated by the fighting of World War I. The museum featured a number of messages sent to Hoover in response to his work at this time. A typical example was an elaborately decorated certificate from Hungary:

> We herewith express our profound gratitude to The Honorable HERBERT HOOVER, Honorary Chairman of First Aid for Hungary, who lent his support and directed the work of First Aid for Hungary Inc. in the dark hours of Hungary's fight for freedom. In the name of the unfortunate Hungarian people, we offer to Mr. Herbert Hoover our heartfelt thanks.

Even here in the United States, it turns out, Hoover had been well known for his labors in organizing and running the administration of the nation's postwar relief efforts.

To be "Hooverized" during the World War I years was to be engaged in humane efforts to help the needy worldwide. There were "meatless Mondays" and "wheatless Wednesdays" so that needed food could be saved to send to war-ravaged countries throughout Europe.

By 1928 Herbert Hoover was arguably the most popular American not holding an elective office. When he ran for the Presidency in that year, he won in a landslide.

So how did such a hardworking, able, capable, compassionate man become so maligned only four years later, and why did his talents fail to rescue America? For three key reasons: the two central values identified above and a third, critically important, dominating factor—his lack of personal charm.

As the American economy collapsed in 1929, bringing down with it many of the economies of Europe, Hoover would have seemed to have been the perfect man for such a moment in history. His altruism was legendary, as was his indefatigable work ethic. Yet neither he, nor, frankly, any of the men he entrusted with helping him guide the Ship of State, had any clear sense of the depth and breadth of the economic morass facing both the nation and the world.

In order to successfully avert complete social chaos, more than Hoover's compassionate volunteerism would be needed. And it was here that he must have found himself face to face with some major disappointments regarding the extent of the lack of selflessness displayed by the American captains of industry.

Hoover's Quaker roots would have naturally led him to assume that those with the greatest wealth would readily want to engage in public service. Surely, he may have told himself, they would immediately desire to step forward to provide necessary aid to alleviate the suffering of displaced and/or unemployed workers. Yet the industrial titans of the age made virtually no significant efforts in this direction. Many did little more than attempt to minimize their own financial losses in the economic collapse confronting them.

Similarly, the American labor force no longer seemed to believe in the bedrock ethic of hard work as the primary means of self-advancement. Instead of increased personal resolve at this time of crisis, Hoover saw depressed and hopeless Americans simply hanging their heads in collective despondency when they failed to find the jobs they so desperately needed.

Hoover must have been crestfallen, deeply discouraged, and, what was infinitely worse, it seems clear that he showed it. His demeanor became stiff, even mechanical. He now appeared to the very populace who had swept him into the Presidency only two years earlier to be a man unable, perhaps even unwilling, to deal with the emergency at hand. Hoover's dual personal ethic of charitable giving and hard-nosed resolve were simply no match for the Great Depression. By 1932, the nation turned to Franklin Roosevelt for a "New Deal," an era of government oversight and federal aid. Nothing less, they believed, could break the grip of the crisis facing them.

Hoover was finished politically, but he was always willing to do whatever he could to benefit his fellow man. Although his Presidency had certainly constituted the low watermark of his public life, he would serve several subsequent Presidents, most notably Harry Truman, in organizing aid efforts following the end of the Second World War. He remained vitally interested in politics and, most particularly, in encouraging the development of American character for the remainder of his life.

After touring the Presidential Library and Museum, I found myself walking back to the simple two-room home located at the center of the restored town of Hoover's birth. There were no visitors at the moment, but the National Park guide, a woman named Sarah, was happy to chat with me.

I asked her what it was like to be stationed at such a modest location. She smiled and said, "You'd be surprised at some of the experiences you have in a place like this."

"Could you tell me about such an experience?" I asked.

"Sure," she began. "I had one just about a month ago. A tour group came through, and I was showing them around all the buildings of the site, ending up here at the birth house. The group looked around, and I then pointed them toward the Presidential Library and Museum as a final stop on their tour. One man, an elderly gentleman, hung back from the group, and I asked him whether or not I could help him in any way."

"Yes. Could you show me where is located the Isis statue?"

Here Sarah interrupted her story to ask me if I had noticed this sculpture as I had walked toward the library earlier.

I confirmed that I *had* seen this very odd work of art. It was a most unusual image of the Egyptian goddess of restored life, with its face covered with a veil. At the time I hadn't understood at all its significance in this location, but Sarah quickly continued her story.

"I told the gentleman that the statue was situated directly on the walkway leading to the Presidential Library and Museum. He asked me if I would take him to it, and I was happy to do so, though I wondered what interest this sculpture could

Statue of Egyptian Goddess, Isis, at Hoover Presidential Site

have for him. When we arrived there," Sarah continued, "the man's eyes filled with tears."

"This is good," he had said. Then he had turned to her and explained, "I was one of the children in Belgium who helped collect pennies to put this statue here. Mr. Hoover saved my life, and I traveled to America so I could come to this place and see our statue before I died."

Plaque of Statue of Egyptian Goddess at Hoover Presidential Library in West Branch, Iowa

Sarah's eyes were full of tears. Mine too.

After I had returned to the museum to find Carol, I asked one of the National Park attendants if anyone had ever tried to estimate the number of lives Hoover's humanitarian efforts had saved.

He replied immediately, "Our current estimate is about one billion." I was stunned. "That's got to be more than any other American President," I said.

Nodding meaningfully, the attendant added, "More than all the other Presidents **combined.** "

The creators of Archie Bunker may not have meant it sincerely, but they had gotten it right nonetheless: "Mister, we **could** use a man like Herbert Hoover again."

30

Franklin D. Roosevelt: "Savior," "Caesar"

32nd President Franklin D. Roosevelt (1933-1945): Springwood in Hyde Park, NY

The two words of the title of this chapter come from quotations from people who experienced firsthand the Presidency of Franklin Delano Roosevelt. For me these words stand for much of the complexity I have found in trying to appreciate more fully the meaning and importance of his years as Chief Executive and Commander in Chief of the United States. But these words also appear in distinct contexts, and before proceeding any further, I would like to establish by whom and under what circumstances they were voiced.

Speaking in an interview included in the 1994 PBS *American Experience* video documentary on the life of Franklin D. Roosevelt, British-American journalist Alistair Cooke recounts an unusual experience he had early in 1936, during the last few months of FDR's first term in office. Cooke had noted that "Everywhere there were pictures of Roosevelt." Some of them were not very good likenesses, however, and once, as Cooke was checking into a hotel, he happened to notice a particularly bad example of one. The image in question featured the addition of artificial rouge on the President's cheeks. Cooke joked about the photo, and, immediately, the desk clerk summarily asked him to leave the premises. The experience left the journalist with a vivid understanding of President Roosevelt's status in the minds and hearts of the American people: "For the time being, the entire country decided he was the savior."

At the other end of the arc of Roosevelt's life, I. F. Stone, writing for the journal *The Nation*, tried to put into words the extraordinary scene unfolding before his eyes. He saw the incredible spectacle of thousands of mourners lining the route of the train bearing back to Washington the body of the recently deceased President. He then marveled at the even larger crowds that gathered in the Capitol and the outpouring of sympathy and anguish that Roosevelt's death had occasioned. Describing the scenes he was witnessing, Stone wrote, "The Romans must have felt this way when word came that Caesar Augustus had died" (Stone 310).

"Savior." "Caesar." These two epithets, I believe capture the essence of one of our most consequential of Presidents.

It may well be that only those people who were alive in the 1930s can fully appreciate why Americans living in that moment of history were so eager to find a savior. The challenges of this decade were overwhelming: the nation's unexpected financial despair in the wake of a celebratory period of unimaginable affluence; an unremitting dearth of jobs, of rain, of hope at a time when the United States had just fought the "war to end all wars"; a worldwide collapse of financial markets, followed by the rise of tyrannical leaders in both Europe and Asia that threatened to engulf the globe in a second world war. These truly were desperate times. And, as the old adage goes, "desperate times call for desperate measures." What the adage fails to address, however, is the potential cost of such "desperate measures."

Unquestionably, our thirty-second President, Franklin Delano Roosevelt, faced a series of colossal problems. And upon his election to the Presidency in 1932, Roosevelt moved immediately and decisively to address them. The result was a profound change in what had been the traditional relationship between the American people and both their President and their government.

And here several key questions arise. Were the changes President Roosevelt initiated in his famous first 100 days in office courageous and innovative efforts to confront and correct the economic and social problems at hand? Or was he using the dire economic conditions with which the country was faced as an opportunity to redefine and redirect the very nature and purpose of government? Were his various programs changeable, perhaps even temporary, measures enacted to save the nation in a time of both internal and external peril? Or were they meant to create a permanent social and political climate that would be a lasting testament to his view of America's role in the world? Was President Roosevelt simply addressing as directly as possible the thousands of pleas being sent to him each month by ordinary Americans in need (e.g. "Mr. President don't let them take our home away")? Or had President Roosevelt come to the conclusion that this moment of tumultuous history called for a radical redefinition of the very nature of American government and presidential leadership, a redefinition that would forever alter the relationship of the people to the state? And, perhaps equally important, are such questions really either/or propositions? Is it possible that, for some of them at least, the answer is "yes" to each? Such was my thinking as Carol and I began planning our travels to Franklin Roosevelt's homes.

There are two locales in the United States which are associated closely with FDR. The more famous of the two is Springwood, the Roosevelt family estate in Hyde Park, New York, perched on the hills overlooking the Hudson River. The second Roosevelt site is the so-called Little White House, a smaller, private home that President Roosevelt commissioned to be constructed in Warm Springs, Georgia, near the pools of warm water which had alleviated, however momentarily, his physical disability. Would it be reasonable to expect that either of these two homes might provide insights into the questions posed above? Or, like the famous Shoumatoff portrait that was being painted of the President on the last day of his life, would such queries remain "unfinished," their answers unresolved?

On our first visit to Hyde Park, Carol and I had been struck by the enormity of the site's parking lot and the astonishing number of cars, vans, and tour buses that arrived, bringing, the National Park web site estimates, over half a million visitors each year to experience the estate. In July of 2013, we were early visitors to the site, and yet even so our tour group numbered slightly more than thirty people.

Before we departed from the Visitor's Center, however, we were invited to view the introductory film. This, as would be the case for most of the rest of the Hyde Park site, would turn out to be a very clear presentation of Roosevelt as "savior." Aside from presenting the essential facts of FDR's life, what emerged in this biopic was the image of a man fated for greatness. His polio became the vehicle of his empathy for the poor and needy. His sympathies were gargantuan, his wisdom peerless. When, only a few months after winning his fourth presidential election, he suddenly died, we see a montage of powerful images of despondent and weeping Americans who voice such sentiments as, "Now that President Roosevelt has died, who will care for us?" The answers forwarded by the movie are the various departments and programs (e.g. TVA, FDIC, FHA, SEC, and Social Security) that continue to provide assurance and aid to the American people of today. And, the film makes it very clear—and quite accurately so—that we owe them all to Franklin Delano Roosevelt. Through their ongoing influence in our lives, his role as "savior" continues to benefit all Americans.

Our tour guide was an amiable gentleman who walked us over to the site of the estate.

"Welcome to the Franklin Roosevelt home at Hyde Park," he began. "If any of you were hoping to see a mansion today, you came to the right area. The Vanderbilt place is just up the road there," he gestured toward the north. "This home, however, is not a mansion. It is a manor house."

Standing in the summer heat before the palatial structure spreading out horizontally before us, I'm not sure many ordinary Americans would have appreciated the subtle difference our tour guide was calling to our attention. Then it struck me. Saviors probably shouldn't have mansions. It would be unseemly. Let me simply say, however, that this "manor house" is a relatively sumptuous setting, however one chooses to identify it to visitors.

Entering the home, we congregated in the large front hall, surrounded by naval prints, political cartoons, young Franklin's bird collection, and a life-sized statue of FDR as a young man. "What you see on the walls and shelves around you is only a small part of the entire Roosevelt collection," our guide began. "The complete holdings include 2100 naval prints and over 250 birds. Some of the bird collection is currently housed in the Natural History Museum in New York City." Our docent looked around our group and nodded knowingly. "They're that good," he added.

We were then invited to view the rest of the first floor at our own individual pace before we were to reassemble in the front hall and proceed upstairs. There were several worthwhile stops on this floor, including the beautifully decorated Dresden room, indicative of the wealth and refined taste of the Roosevelts. For me, however, the most impressive space of all was the enormous library and living room at the south end of the hall. Magnificent floor to ceiling bookshelves covered one entire wall, and a variety of conversational groupings of chairs and couches were placed throughout the rest of this large area that ran the entire depth of the house. Persian rugs graced the polished hardwood floors, and a full-length portrait of Roosevelt at the time of his election as Governor of New York stood prominently displayed on an easel.

"President Roosevelt hated that painting," our docent assured me, "but his mother loved it, and it *was* her house."

A ramp led down to the level of this room, a reminder of President Roosevelt's disability. Another booth-sized chamber just up the hall was used as a hand pulled elevator in which his wheelchair would fit exactly. Then, using his powerful upper body strength, the President would lift himself via pulleys up to the second floor.

After our circuit of the first floor rooms, our group gathered in the front hall from which we were then led upstairs. Our second floor tour was again largely self-guided. It began with Franklin's boyhood room (which in later years had housed his own children), and then continued with the bedroom where the President had been born. Also on display were the guest quarters used to accommodate visiting dignitaries. All of these chambers were found off the hallway leading down the center of the house.

Most interesting, and telling, to me, however, were the rooms located in the southern wing of the home directly over the living room and library. They quite clearly attested to the famous strain in the tripartite relationship of Franklin, Eleanor, and Franklin's mother, Sara.

The President's bedchamber remains as it looked on the occasion of his final visit to Springwood in March of 1945. By this time, he was living essentially as a single man. The hexagonal bay window area looks out toward the south, and, at the foot of his bed is a divan where Fala, his faithful Scottie, slept, his leash now laid lovingly across the cushion on which he used to lie. On the room's west windowsill, a small sculpture of Fala—or, at least of a Scottie—stands in memory of this most loyal family friend.

The next room down the hall was reserved for Eleanor. She was living almost exclusively at her Val-Kill cottage, but this room was still maintained for her use. It is a spare, sparsely furnished, rectangular chamber with a double window facing south. Unlike the President's room next to it, there is no cross ventilation here. On one side of the windows along the wall, a twin bed. On the other side, a writing desk with a single chair. It feels dark, with only one small lamp near the bed providing any additional illumination.

At the end of the hall is a third bedroom, Sara's chamber. It is a mirror image of the President's room and includes another hexagonal bay window with three southern aspects, an additional window, in her case facing east, for cross ventilation, a dressing table, and a large circular mirror. Mother and son, with Eleanor squeezed rather uncomfortably between them.

Yet the overall effect of Springwood was a powerful affirmation of the President's extraordinary life. Here Franklin Roosevelt had been born the adored child of his mother and an inheritor of wealth and high social status. Yet he had refused to disappear into this realm of affluent privilege. Even when physically handicapped, he had ventured into the world beyond to lead it out of despair and misery, to give it hope, to use, as the introductory film had characterized it, his "champagne ebullience" to raise the spirit of the American people and to encourage them that better days were inevitably on the way. Despite his disability, despite his estrangement from his wife, he had remained resolutely faithful to his stewardship of the nation, whether it was foundering in economic depression or faced with world war. President Roosevelt's tenacious efforts to achieve both social and military victory, even when his own physical condition was deteriorating, more than attested to his well-deserved characterization as a secular "savior."

But what about "Caesar"? Was he also present here at Springwood?

"Don't miss the stables next door," our docent mentioned to me as we were leaving the manor house. "It's the only time you'll ever see Corinthian columns between horse stalls."

We thanked him and proceeded next door to a large building just north of the home. The stable doors were open and, once we entered, sure enough, between each stall were white painted column shafts with Corinthian capitals.

"I don't believe this," I whispered to Carol. "Here's a touch of imperial majesty if ever there was one." Even though the original design was Greek, the Romans had loved the detail and extravagance of the Corinthian architectural order. It communicated exactly the degree of wealth and power the Romans

FDR's stables in at Springwood in Hyde Park, New York

wanted to associate with their empire. They built Corinthian temples everywhere they conquered. Another visitor was wandering through the stables, and she stopped to talk to us.

"President Roosevelt's favorite horse was named Bobby. I've just been down to see his stall. The plaque says that FDR trained him and that Bobby was his favorite because he did everything that he had been taught to do." Carol and I walked the length of the building, noting the various pieces of equestrian equipment still on display in the tack room and looking up once more at the Corinthian columns. "Hail Caesar," I thought to myself.

Our next stop was to be the Presidential Library. And here again we would be confronted with President Roosevelt's dual identity.

"Savior" was on display everywhere in this building. And not without reason. Room after room in the museum chronicled in both print and video clips the stark economic realities that had faced President Roosevelt from the very beginning. But, I found myself wondering, had FDR ever seen *himself* as "savior"? Could this title have simply been conferred upon him by a populace yearning for a hero?

An answer appeared in a glass case containing the typewritten text of President Roosevelt's first inaugural speech. Its wording is justifiably famous, beginning with the sentence "I am certain that my fellow Americans expect that on my induction into the Presidency, I will address them with a candor and a decision which the present situation of our Nation impels." And then moments later comes that most memorable line, "...the only thing we have to fear is fear itself...." It was a thrill to see the actual text that Franklin Roosevelt had held on March 4, 1933, to be able to read the typed words that would begin his journey to reassure and reenergize the American people. But then I noticed an additional sentence, written in pencil at the top of the first page. FDR must have decided to add this new thought to the very beginning of his address. It read, "This is a day of consecration."

However, when the moment had come to speak, he hadn't used the line, even though it was written clearly at the top of his manuscript. "Consecration" is an interesting word. In the Catholic Mass it refers to the moment of transubstantiation, when the wine and bread actually become the body and blood of Jesus Christ. It also has the meaning of holy devotion to a cause. FDR, it appears, *had* seen himself as a "savior." But he hadn't saved anything yet. Perhaps this explains why he decided not to begin his remarks with this reference to "consecration."

Nevertheless elsewhere in the museum, the curators had apparently concluded that the President *had* ultimately achieved a success deserving of the word. In a video presentation on FDR's programs designed to revitalize the economy, Roosevelt's post-war vision is emphasized: that every American citizen should be guaranteed a job, a decent home, and effective health care. The camera then focuses on a picture of a paper dollar bill, an image that features specifically the place where the words "In God We Trust" appear. Immediately over this motto are superimposed the emblems of programs instituted by President Roosevelt to help save Americans in need: the FDIC, TVA, SEC, and Social Security. The film concludes with the President's recorded words: "The federal government has a moral obligation to promote the common good." Spoken like a savior. Or, perhaps, like a Caesar.

Toward the end of our time in this museum, I noted that the National Park brochure which had been handed out to us as we had entered calls attention to the fact that "President Roosevelt donated his home and 33 acres to the American people in 1943...." This, added to the overall impact of the persuasive message this site delivers, reminded me of another man's promises and bequeathals.

In Act III of Shakespeare's *Julius Caesar*, Marc Antony addresses a crowd of Romans who have just learned of the death of Julius Caesar. Antony reads Caesar's will, reminding the people of just what kind of man they have lost:

> *To every Roman citizen he gives,*
> *To every several man, seventy-five drachmas....*
> *Moreover, he hath left you all his walks,*
> *His private arbors, and new-planted orchards,*
> *On this side Tiber; he hath left them you,*

And to your heirs forever: common pleasures,
To walk abroad and recreate yourselves.
Here was a Caesar! When comes such another?
(III. ii. 243-244, 249-25:4)

When was it that Franklin Roosevelt traded his reputation as "savior" for the more dubious title of "Caesar"? A good case can be made for a specific date: Monday, January 20, 1941, the beginning of his unprecedented third term in office.

Roosevelt critics might argue that the change had occurred earlier, specifically after his re-election in 1936, when the President attempted to get executive power to add Justices to the Supreme Court in order to offset the ongoing legal challenges to his New Deal programs. But, to me at least, this frustration with the Court was simply understandable pique in the wake of a landslide electoral victory that had ushered him into his second term. The word "Caesar" is bigger than presidential frustration with the Supreme Court, a frustration that has often been shared by Chief Executives, regardless of their political affiliations.

I believe that Franklin Roosevelt became "Caesar" when he slipped into the assumption that, due to the severe and looming challenges facing both the United States and the world at large, he *alone* was capable of leading his country out of harm's way. The fact that so many Americans had come to agree with him only underscores the point.

More than a decade earlier, in 1929, ex-President Calvin Coolidge published his autobiography. One particular passage in it sounds an important warning: "It is a great advantage to a President, and a major source of safety to the country, for him [anyone serving as President] to know that he is not a great man. When a man begins to feel that he is the only one who can lead in this republic, he is guilty of treason to the spirit of our institutions" (173).

While the word "treason" may feel overly harsh, the gist of President Coolidge's observations is clear: a democratic republic is predicated on the belief that *any* citizen who understands and is dedicated to the nation's founding principles should be seen as capable of leading its government. The "spirit of our institutions" rests on that basic principle. Our first President, George Washington, faced, at the close of his second term, equally foreboding circumstances. France and England were forcibly boarding American ships on the high seas, territorial treaties that had been made at the end of the Revolutionary war and which had been reaffirmed by the recent negotiations of John Jay were still not being honored, and British agents were inciting native American peoples to conduct raids into United States territory. Yet even at this moment of crisis, Washington had resisted the temptation to become an American king. Two terms as President, he concluded, were enough. He chose to step down rather than seek a third term, not so much because he believed that his successor could do a better job than he, but because he understood that not stepping down would set a precedent that would undercut the very ideals on which his nation had been founded.

President Coolidge, later in his autobiography, explains this danger more fully:

> It is difficult for men in high office to avoid the malady of self-delusion. They are always surrounded by worshippers. They are constantly and, for the most part sincerely, assured of their greatness. They live in an artificial atmosphere of adulation and exaltation which sooner or later impairs their judgment. They are in grave danger of becoming careless and arrogant. (241)

In the case of Franklin Roosevelt, were such warnings relevant? I leave it to the scholarship and perspicacity of my readers to arrive at their own conclusions. Suffice it to say that Carol and I found clear evidence of FDR as both "savior" and "Caesar" at Springwood in Hyde Park, New York.

So what about The Little White House in Warm Springs, Georgia? Would there be "savior" implications here? Or vestiges of "Caesar"?

As Carol and I had traveled the winding two lane country roads south of Atlanta in April of 2012, we really had not known what to expect of this location. My first journal entry from that day identifies my initial impression of the site: "Quiet. Silence. A palpable sense of peace. That was the overwhelming feeling that pervades the atmosphere of the home." And, I should add, it is a most beautiful structure without a trace of ostentation.

Our guide at the site was an enthusiastic gentleman named Terry. He loved this place. "Come down here at 7:00 in the morning," he told us knowingly. "It's a whole different world."

FDR's Home in Warm Springs, Georgia

"A different world," I repeated to myself as Terry led us through this modest retreat. "If President Roosevelt had needed anything, it was that—if only for the space of a week or two whenever he could get down here. A different world from his disability, a different world from the seemingly never ending series of crises that plagued the nation throughout his years in office."

The home included the usual Roosevelt touches: pictures and models of sailing ships adorning almost every shelf and wood paneled wall; the President's handcrafted wheelchair standing in a corner of the front hall; numerous volumes lying akimbo in a bookcase placed close to a stone fireplace. The windows in this combination living room, study, and dining area, the one large open space in the house, looked out onto a vista of Georgia pines and undeveloped woodland. Only after a careful scrutiny of the landscape was it possible to spy one or two of the nine security posts ringing the property. A "different world" indeed, a world where the breeze sighed gently in the needles of the graceful pines and melodious bird calls floated through the barely moving air. And it was here in this room in the spring of 1945, while his portrait was being painted, that Franklin Roosevelt had suddenly slumped over.

The President's bedroom was a simple chamber about 12'x14' right off the living room. A desk with a chair, a dresser, and the single bed on which he had died were its only furnishings.

Returning to the front hall, I asked Terry if there was anything particular about the house that he regarded as illuminating, anything special that he felt related to President Roosevelt's personality.

"Yes," he responded immediately. "The wood." Terry saw my look of confusion, so he added immediately, "It's natural, not pretentious. The place isn't overly decorated. It's simple, back to nature. Having all this wood around makes you feel the most comfortable of any material."

Ultimately the most fascinating aspect of the Little White House in Warm Springs was the absence of either "savior" or "Caesar." This locale was a retreat. A haven. A spot where the President didn't need to be a President. "Another world," as Terry had so aptly identified it. But it, like the unfinished portrait on display in a small museum area close by the entrance to the site, left me with more questions than answers.

"So, have you come to like Franklin Roosevelt?" Carol asked me as we drove northward toward New England after our most recent visit to Roosevelt's Springwood estate in Hyde Park.

"What do you mean?" I responded, somewhat guardedly.

"Well, we have both said that we always have come away from our trips to presidential homes *liking* the men who have served our nation as its Chief Executive. And I was wondering about how you were feeling about FDR now. Do you *like* Franklin Roosevelt better since you have visited Hyde Park again, together with the Little White House in Warm Springs?"

I realized that this was a question I had been both asking myself and trying to answer most of the day.

"I respect tremendously the hope he inspired and the uplift in spirit he instilled in the American people. His endless energy and willingness to try new approaches to the problems the country faced were extraordinary. Some of his policies saved many of the most destitute of his fellow citizens. Did some other of his programs leave people feeling dependent—on the President, on the government? Undoubtedly so, but *yes*, I like him—his joy, his courage, his optimism. How did Churchill describe it? 'Meeting

Franklin Roosevelt was like opening your first bottle of champagne?' All this makes it impossible not to like him. Two heartfelt cheers for President Franklin Roosevelt!"

"Two cheers?" Carol responded. "Not three? Where's the third cheer?"

"Not three," I answered quietly. There was a somewhat lengthy pause.

"Why not?" Carol asked.

I was thinking of Shakespeare again. "Do you remember in *Julius Caesar*," I began, "when Marc Antony says, 'Friends, Romans, countrymen, lend me your ears; I come to bury Caesar, not to praise him'? That's why."

Carol's brow furrowed a bit. "I don't understand what you're trying to say. And anyway, didn't Antony go right ahead and praise Julius Caesar to the skies, even after telling the people he wasn't going to do so?"

"Yes, that's right. He wanted to make them feel so despondent over losing their Caesar, so lost without a Caesar to guide them, that they would demand another one. That was his plan, and he hoped that he would be that one. Only it hadn't worked out that way. Antony was killed by another contender for power, Octavius—who later became known as Caesar Augustus. When Octavius took over, it was the end of the Roman Republic. No more rule by an elected Senate. No more annually elected Tribunes. Nothing left but a dictatorial empire."

"Then it probably might have been better if Antony HAD simply 'come to bury Caesar, not to praise him,' " Carol noted.

"Certainly for the Republic it would have been. And that's why I can give only two cheers to Franklin Roosevelt. I cheer for his personal courage and his resolute insistence on happier days to come. I cheer for the spirit and determination with which he galvanized Americans into believing in a better future and in improving their way of life. But I just can't lead a cheer for his assumption that no one but *he* could successfully lead the United States, and I can't cheer for the idea that only government programs could be relied upon to save the nation. After running for a third and then a fourth term, after a Presidency lasting more than twelve years, and even though I *do* like him, I have to withhold my third cheer for FDR. In many ways he may well have been the 'savior' of the United States. There are thousands of Americans, including our most highly regarded documentary filmmaker, Ken Burns, who continue to believe this to be the case. But he was also our first American 'Caesar,' and the full meaning of that epoch in our history remains to be written by wiser men than I."

31

Harry S. Truman: The Myth of the "Retired Farmer"

33rd President Harry S. Truman (1945-1953): Home in Independence, MO

Standing before the grand Victorian-Gothic home on North Delaware Avenue in one of the most fashionable neighborhoods of Independence, Missouri, the story of Harry S Truman almost sounds like a tale from the Arabian Nights. A lowly commoner rises to claim the hand of the princess and become king of all the land. An American myth. And that's how they spin it here at the National Historic Park site honoring our 33rd President. Yet there is another version of the life of Harry Truman that is much more complex and—I would argue—infinitely more compelling than the myth. Interestingly enough, the Truman homes present insights into both. The "mythic" Truman and the aspiring leader live side by side here in Missouri.

To begin at the beginning one must pay a visit to a little town in the southwestern quadrant of the state, a town named Lamar.

Prior to the future President's birth in May of 1884, Lamar's greatest claim to fame had been the fact that fourteen years earlier, on March 8, 1870, a youthful Wyatt Earp had been appointed constable for this tiny farming community and had begun his storied career as a law officer. But neither Wyatt nor Harry would stay long in Lamar.

Harry S Truman's Birth Home in Lamar, Missouri

Harry would have no memories of his infant life here. Nevertheless, the small home the Trumans purchased in 1882, the house where Harry would be born two years later, still stands on a corner lot of a street that now bears his name.

Historians have tended to make much of the modest dimensions of this first Truman homestead, beginning to weave, as suggested earlier, a "Truman myth" of the simple man from the farm country of Missouri who would unexpectedly rise to a position of power and prominence unimagined in his wildest dreams.

The day of our tour of the Lamar birth home in the summer of 2011 was hot and muggy. Our guide was to be a dear elderly lady named Louise who remembered ex-President Truman's return to this place in 1959 on the occasion of its official opening to the public. As she invited us to sign the guestbook located in the small museum/gift shop where one's visit to this site commences, she pointed out another guestbook, kept behind glass.

"Look at it carefully," she instructed us, pointing to the top of the page.

There was Harry Truman's signature on the first line of the yellowing guestbook, written in a clear, forceful, and surprisingly legible hand.

"Now read the whole entry," she said.

There followed the usual request for an address, which he had indicated as the familiar North Delaware Street location in Independence. But after that, there was a space where visitors could record their professions. Here, President Truman had written only two words: "Retired Farmer."

"You see?" Louise added. "Mr. Truman never forgot where he had come from. He never tried to be anything other than the simple man he was and that he *knew* he was." The "Truman myth" was beginning to rise about me.

Louise then led us over to the house and into its small front parlor. It was a cheerful room, full of light provided by a bay window on the south wall. Next she showed us the tiny bedroom off the parlor where Harry had been born, a room "so small there was hardly space for the bed," historian David McCullough would write in his definitive biography of the President (37).

There didn't appear to be much more to see here. Louise drew our attention to a freestanding stove that had provided the only heat for the front two rooms, as well as doubling as a one burner range and a means of heating pieces of iron used as bed warmers on cold nights. Aside from this parlor and tiny side room, the only other space in the first floor of this small dwelling appeared to be the kitchen.

There was a staircase near the kitchen, leading to a second floor, and Louise invited me to go up to see the two upstairs bedrooms, both currently undergoing refurbishment. Then she indicated that we had seen everything there was to see. However I noticed another small room just off the kitchen.

"What was this room for?" I asked Louise, as I looked in to find a single bed and some plain furnishings.

"That was for the hired help," she answered.

Leaving the home by the back door, we saw its nearby well, outhouse, and smokehouse. Then Carol questioned Louise about the pine tree that John Truman had planted at the time of the birth of his first son.

"That's the very one," Louise assured us, pointing to a pine on the southeast section of the small corner lot on which the home stood.

It was thick and bent toward the house, and, upon a closer look, appeared to be losing most of its needles.

"It's an old tree, of course," Louise admitted. "We're trying to save it, but I don't know if we will succeed."

After accompanying our guide back to the museum/shop and looking at some of the Truman postcards and paraphernalia on sale there, Carol and I left Lamar and soon were driving once more, heading this time towards Independence, Missouri, and more information about Harry Truman.

As we traveled northward, I couldn't help thinking of that side room off the kitchen at the Lamar house. Here had been a young couple newly married with only enough money to purchase a very diminutive dwelling in a town over a hundred miles away from any relative, and yet they had wanted an extra room for "the help." It struck me as an indication of an aspiration that the "Truman myth" tended to overlook: a desire for wealth, for power, for an uncommon success in the world—for, what 18th century men would know as "fame." Even at this early moment in their marriage, the young Truman family had wanted to be part of the "hiring" class rather than being hirelings themselves. Understanding such aspirations would become a key to my learning about and more fully appreciating President Truman.

So just what exactly **is** the "Truman myth"? It has three distinct parts, at least as it is presented here in Missouri by the National Park Service:

First, that Harry Truman was a common boy from a rural background who had been denied a college education because of his father's financial reversals and the need to go to work on his grandparents' farm in order to help support his family.

Second, that Harry Truman had never sought the Presidency, and yet, when it had been thrust upon him, he had managed to guide the United States through one of the most treacherous periods of its history.

Third, that after his service as President had ended, Truman had desired only to return home to the simple life from which he had come, spending his last years as an ordinary citizen.

The result of these three basic tenets is that Harry Truman emerges as a kind of iconic superman hidden within every man. His story becomes a tale of the power of common goodness which, because of a quirk in history, was transformed into unexpected greatness. Yet it may be important to remember that while still a boy in high school, Truman had concluded that "...men make history, otherwise there would be no history. History did not make the man..." (McCullough 58). If this is so, then the myth needs to be called into question.

Doing so is not always easy because each part of the "Truman myth" contains some literal truth. Furthermore, Truman himself encouraged elements of this myth during his lifetime. Still, the myth misrepresents, sometimes seriously, both provable facts and the character of this extraordinary man. He deserves a closer look.

At both the birth home in Lamar and, even more aggressively, at the Farmhouse in Grandview, the first part of the "Truman myth" is put forth. Both settings are down to earth, as recognizably familiar as a painting by Norman Rockwell. Yet neither setting proves Harry Truman himself to have been "common," regardless of his background. In fact, the Grandview farm in particular suggests that Harry was a most uncommon lad, both during his stay here as a very young boy and later as a young man learning how to run a farm.

It was here at Grandview that, although he was still a child, his mother had taught her son to read before the age of five. And it was also here that, years later when the young man had come back to help run the farm, he would study Cato's *De Agri Cultura* to glean insights into "planting beans, sowing clover, making compost, curing hams, and the medicinal value of cabbage" (McCullough 77).

Such agrarian musing from a classic Roman philosopher was hardly commonplace reading material for a typical rural lad from the Missouri plains. In fact, by the time he had returned to Grandview as a young man, Harry claimed to have read every one of the 2000 volumes in the nearby public library in Independence.

Which leads to the question of Truman's lack of education. While it is undeniably true that he had been forced—by both finances and his poor eyesight—to forgo a college education, Harry Truman had already educated himself to an extraordinary degree—and for an extraordinary reason. He would later remember that "Reading history, to

Truman/Young Family Farm in Grandview, Missouri

me, was far more than a romantic adventure. It was solid instruction and wise teaching which I somehow felt that I wanted and needed" (McCullough 58).

Why would a "common" boy from a rural background feel such a desire, such a need? Perhaps it was because from the start he had understood that he wasn't really "common" at all.

He had read history voraciously. He had "pored over the pages of *Great Men and Famous Women* and *Plutarch's Lives*" and, time and again, had found himself inspired by the examples he saw illustrated there. (McCullough 463) In his *Autobiography*, he would observe, "I came to the conclusion that every citizen should know something about military, finance or banking, and agriculture. All my heroes or great leaders were somewhat familiar with one or the other, or all three" (Truman 27).

Again, why would a young man with no political aspirations care about what his heroes and the great leaders in history had known? And now the second phase of the "Truman myth" deserves a closer look.

Contrary to the myth's assumptions, Harry Truman had desired political preeminence. Everything in his fledgling career in politics attests to that fact, perhaps most prominently his willingness to use—and be used by—the Kansas City Pendergast machine for his earliest successes as a candidate, initially for county offices, and, finally, for the United States Senate. Then why, furthermore, when serving in the Senate, would he work so earnestly to establish a reputation as a watchdog to prevent government waste and corrupt influence peddling in military expenditures, if not to openly disassociate himself from the very machine that had helped him rise to the position he now held, thus setting the stage for even higher advancement? Truman always had wanted success in the political realm. No one who would ever run against him in any campaign would have doubted it for an instant.

But he also knew—his reading had taught him clearly—that the greatest leaders in American history had always appeared to be disinterested in power, preferring the honest pleasures of a quiet common life to the rough and tumble world of politics. And so he claimed himself to be—until it was time to run again.

Lest all this sounds duplicitous on Truman's part, it is important to remember the responsibilities that would fall to him as he rose to become Chief Executive of the United States after the death of Franklin Roosevelt. He would need all the learning, all the preparation, all the wisdom that he had been quietly accruing throughout his life if he were to lead the nation safely through the military, political, and social turmoil facing the United States during the period of his Presidency. From the decision to drop the first atomic bomb to the rescue of the city of Berlin via airlift, from the implementation of the Marshall plan to the founding of NATO, from the integration of the armed forces to the breaking of strikes that threatened the economic stability of the nation, thankfully, President Truman was much more prepared than either he or the "myth" suggested. His readiness enabled his extraordinarily wise handling of the major issues of his day.

Then, in 1952, began the final act, the phase of his life most conspicuously on display at 219 North Delaware Street in Independence.

This address had been Harry Truman's home from the year of his marriage to Bess in 1919 until his death in 1972, and today, it is the single most eloquent advocate of the third section of the "Truman myth."

Guests are led through the house by National Park Guides who emphasize the simple pleasures of President Truman's post-presidential life. We see the spacious, vine covered screened-in porch where Harry and Bess enjoyed private moments on pleasant summer evenings. Then there is the ordinary family kitchen, complete with homely looking patched vinyl tiles that Harry had nailed down rather than incurring the cost of replacing them. Next, visitors are shown the small study with comfortable chairs for Harry and Bess and a lovely collection of books, reflecting their individual literary tastes. Finally, in the front hall, guests to the home are invited to gaze on the walking stick and the familiar hat of the President, still hanging on the pegs where he last left them in 1972. No pomp here. No circumstance. Just an unpretentious setting for an ordinary citizen.

After a brief recounting of the numerous and notable achievements of the Truman administration, visitors to the site are ushered out the front door of the home. "Just as Mr. Truman would have left," the guide reminds us. The myth is complete.

Yet it may not be the reality. As the President himself had observed, he knew his history "from Egypt to the U.S.A." (Truman 27). Since childhood, he had read of the great Roman general Cincinnatus and, even more importantly for him, of General George Washington. Both men had solidified their legacies, their fame, not through ostentatious celebrations but by humbly returning to their homes following their greatest achievements. Harry Truman had carried these facts in his head and heart all his life. So, in 1959, he would sign the guestbook at his birthplace "Retired Farmer," not "President," "Vice President," or "Senator." And in doing so he would join the ranks of the men in history he most admired and would achieve the distinction for which the Trumans had been reaching all along.

Good for him. His hard work, his devotion to self-improvement, his knowledge of history, his desire for fame—all had served both him and his country well. Much better than the myth of the unprepared but fortunate commoner. All his life Harry Truman had suited himself for greatness. That he ultimately achieved it seems only fitting.

32

Dwight Eisenhower: "...the nation...not myself"

34th President Dwight D. Eisenhower (1953-1961): Farm Home in Gettysburg, PA

In June of 1911, Dwight D. Eisenhower arrived at West Point, New York, one of the new cadets at that prestigious institution. He was, at the age of 21, already older than many of his classmates. His mother, Ida, a devout Christian and an ardent pacifist, had not wanted her son to become a soldier, but she had saved her tears until he had boarded the train to leave his Kansas home. For "Ike," as he had been called since childhood, West Point offered more than training for the army. It was his chance to receive a free college education, an education that the limited financial circumstances of the Eisenhower family of Abilene would never have otherwise permitted him to obtain.

"My impression of that first day," he would come to write late in his life in a popular memoir, "was one of calculated chaos" (4). Yet by the end of that first day, something profound had happened to this young man. His own words describe it best:

> *... when we raised our right hands and repeated the official oath there was no confusion. A feeling came over me that the expression 'The United States of America' would now and henceforth mean something different than it ever had before. From here on it would be the nation I would be serving, not myself.* (4)

At the very moment he had taken this oath Dwight Eisenhower had, in fact, made a commitment that would come to direct his entire life. His efforts, his dedication, and his service would all be devoted to his country before anything or anyone else.

Toward the end of Stephen Ambrose's acclaimed biography of President Dwight D. Eisenhower, Ambrose draws a straightforward conclusion: "He was a man born to command" (571). While it is easy to appreciate the achievements, even the glory, that General Eisenhower enjoyed as a direct consequence of his leadership both as a soldier and as a head of state, it may be more difficult to assess the inevitable cost of such a birthright.

There are three Eisenhower residences currently open to the public. Each is well worth visiting as a window into the life of this important man in American history.

The story begins in a rental home in Denison, Texas, where David Dwight Eisenhower was born in October of 1890. His family had recently reached a low point in its fortunes. David, Sr., Ike's father, had rejected farming as a livelihood and had invested all his money in a store located in Hope, Kansas, a small town near Abilene where the Eisenhower clan had settled in the late 1870's. This enterprise had failed, however, and David had moved to Denison, Texas, where he secured work as an engine wiper, a long hours and low wages job far below his qualifications as a college educated man with an engineering degree. Once he had found acceptable lodging, he had sent for his wife, Ida, and two young sons to join him. Even with the family reunited, however, life in Texas was extremely difficult. Ida was pregnant with a third child, the future President. She had no friends in Denison, no family, and little hope for any economic advancement for her husband.

Yet for a visitor approaching this home today, it is nearly impossible to envision the depressed neighborhood at the edge of town into which the Eisenhowers had moved in 1890. Carefully manicured grassy areas and flowering trees now decorate the landscape. The house itself with its distinctive triple gable facade is beautifully maintained and sits on a

Eisenhower Birthplace in Denison, TX

spacious lot, surrounded by a white fence. The only hint of the less than desirable location of this home are some rails about 20 feet from the front of the house, set there to indicate the proximity of the train tracks at the time of the Eisenhower's residence.

On the day of our visit, a pleasant docent met us in a garden area at the side of the property. After her introductory remarks, she then led us toward the home's front porch to give us a quick tour of the downstairs rooms. The front doorway gave onto a small hall and, immediately upon entering, we were instructed to turn right and move into the Eisenhowers' bedroom. This was the setting where the baby who would someday become President had first seen the light of day. A double bed, placed cater-cornered, facing the doorway, juts into the room and identifies the exact location of the President's birth. The additional furnishings on display here include a rocking chair, a cradle, a chest, a cabinet, and a dressing table.

Back across the entry hall is the other room on the front of the house: the living room or parlor. It, too, features pieces appropriate to the time of the Eisenhowers' occupancy, including a table for two set before a side window, a cast iron stove, a bookcase, and a small desk. Both rooms are orderly and meticulously clean, but one senses that a family of five might have found these surroundings to be rather crowded.

The only other rooms on this floor are a dining room area and a kitchen in the back of the home. A stairway leading to the second floor is located on the far side of the dining room. Our docent informed us that there are two upstairs rooms. One provided sleeping quarters for the two older boys, and the other was reserved for a boarder, James Redmon, whose monthly rent was necessary to help the Eisenhower's meet their various financial obligations.

Dwight had not yet reached the age of two when his paternal grandfather Jacob came down to Denison to see the young family. He had a job offer for his son. A new business, Belle Springs Creamery, was opening in Abilene, and they needed a man with David's talents to help run the operation. Could he be interested in making yet another move? Before Jacob's visit ended, he had convinced the couple to return home to Kansas.

Eisenhower Young Childhood Home in Abilene, KS

Not that it would come across to a casual observer as much of an improvement. The growing family moved into what Ike would later describe as "a little cottage on Second Street" (29). The home still stands, although it is privately owned and is not open to the public. This "little cottage" with its three rooms was less spacious than the Denison house had been, but that fact was more than compensated for by its proximity to a large extended family, including Grandfather Jacob who lived only two blocks away. Then there were also old friends and new economic possibilities for David, Sr. And, most importantly, the place was all theirs, no boarders, and the railroad tracks were at least twice as far from the back of the house than they had been from the front door of their rental in Denison. All in all, Ida saw it as a significant move upward.

Dwight would be eight years old before the family moved again. By that time, he had two more brothers, and the living space in the Second Street location had become impossibly cramped. But just at this moment, an uncle had decided to become an itinerant preacher, and he sold his house to his brother David with the understanding that

Eisenhower Boyhood Home in Abilene, Kansas

the family would take in Grandfather Jacob if and when the necessity arrived. For Dwight's family the new home seemed like a veritable palace. There were two stories with three bedrooms on the second floor. Downstairs, in addition to a spacious front porch, was a parlor with a bay window and another connecting room where they could place a piano as well as an extra bed. There was also a dining room area just off the kitchen toward the back of the house. It must have felt like heaven to this family of seven. Two more sons would be born here, and Dwight would spend the rest of his boyhood years in Abilene, not leaving until his matriculation at West Point.

This is the home that currently sits in the midst of the land comprising the Dwight D. Eisenhower Presidential Library and Museum. Thousands of visitors tour the boyhood home every year. And perhaps because of this steady flow of sightseers, it is difficult to picture in this setting the boy who would become the 34th President. Guides lead groups of people to the house, informing them of the additions made when Jacob came to live with the family in 1900. Inside, the rooms are cordoned off by velvet ropes and onlookers are presented with interiors that resemble a Norman Rockwell painting. There are potted ferns placed in the bay window of the parlor, an oriental area rug, a few upholstered chairs and one comfortable looking armchair in the corner of the room. The adjoining room contains a delicate side table and lamp with a porcelain vase. There is also an upright piano with a beautifully polished finish and, on the opposite wall, a single bed with a pillow Ida decorated by hand. The dining area displays Ida's red and white china and memorials of her children's various accomplishments. Yet it is virtually impossible to imagine this family of a mother and father with seven sons and one grandfather ever living in such fastidious conditions. The place would have been a shambles in minutes with only the very slightest use.

The upstairs rooms are closed off to visitors, though a few pictures are placed on the stairway to indicate the layout of the three "dormitory" bedrooms on the second floor. In about fifteen minutes, the tour is over, and everyone is ushered out the back door onto the grounds of the Museum. I have come to this home twice now, and I always feel a tinge of irony for Ida as I walk out the kitchen door onto the side lawn. About a hundred yards from this home, this center of activity for seven growing boys watched over by their dear, long-suffering, pacifist mother, stands her third son's Museum, an extensive assemblage of war memorabilia, including a vast collection of guns, grenades, and military artifacts gathered together to commemorate his life as a soldier.

Ike often said that his heart's home was Abilene, Kansas. His Presidential Library and Museum *are* impressive facilities with priceless artifacts from his very active life. But for me, Ike the man feels oddly absent here. The distance seems almost immeasurably great that stands between this quiet meticulously curated two story frame house and the man who would become the Supreme Commander of the Allied Expeditionary Forces in World War II, the Supreme Commander of NATO from 1949-1952, and the President of the United States from 1953-1961. The young Dwight David would leave Abilene in 1911 and would never live here again.

Nearly forty years later, in 1950, Dwight and his wife of thirty-four years, Mamie, purchased a farm in Gettysburg, Pennsylvania. Its acreage backed right up to the famous battlefield, and it seemed both a curious and an oddly fitting choice of location. On any number of occasions when she was asked about it, Mamie stated that, considering the nearly annual moves that had characterized her and her husband's entire married life, "We had only one home—our farm" (Clotworthy 261). Still in a very literal sense, this home is not "one," but two distinct residences. And they illustrate quite poignantly both the glory and the reality of being "...born to command."

Why Gettysburg at all? After the carnage and seemingly endless campaigns of the Second World War, from Africa to Sicily, from England to France and onto Germany, why buy his first property so close to yet another storied battlefield? Perhaps for that very reason. What better location could a person choose to establish a place of peace, of rest and productivity, a place, in the language of Scripture, in which to "turn swords into plowshares and spears into pruning hooks"?

It may also be important to remember that Gettysburg had personal meanings for the Eisenhowers. It was in eastern Pennsylvania that the first Eisenhower immigrants had settled in the mid 1700's. It was in Gettysburg that twenty-seven year old Dwight Eisenhower had been put in command of Camp Colt, a training base for the newly formed Tank Corps where ten thousand men and six hundred officers were being readied for battle assignments in Europe in the First World War (Ambrose 33). It was also in Camp Colt that Eisenhower had perfected his unique brand of leadership, a combination of strict discipline and willingness—even eagerness—to hear from the men under his command.

And, of course, Gettysburg was American history, a history in which now Dwight Eisenhower had himself played a significant part. For any of these reasons, as well as because it was still close to the nation's centers of economic and political power, New York and Washington D.C., the Eisenhowers found Gettysburg to be an ideal setting for their retirement years.

One reaches the house through the Gettysburg National Military Park Visitor Center where tickets can be purchased, and specified buses transport visitors to the Eisenhower farm. Upon disembarking the bus, visitors are met by a Park Ranger who gives a brief history of the house and the renovations the Eisenhowers oversaw prior to moving there permanently in 1955. Once a group arrives at the home, a Ranger guides them through the first floor and then allows everyone to continue their tour through the remainder of the house in a self-guided fashion.

To my eye, the interior of the home revealed two very separate personalities, the worlds of two very distinct people. I should have expected this even before entering.

Left Side of Eisenhower Home in Gettysburg, Pennsylvania

As I had been taking a few pictures of the exterior, I had been struck immediately by the dichotomy of its tastes and styles. The larger left side of the house was a brick structure. The exterior of this part of the house contained three visibly separate sections. The far left section with a large bay window was an addition to the original farmhouse and contained an expansive living room that spanned the entire depth of the building. Next was the central section, containing the front door of the home, a large entry hall, a stairway leading to the second floor rooms, display cases of Mrs. Eisenhower's china collections, and a formal dining room. Lastly, the right section was the part of the original farmhouse that it had been possible to save and restore. The exterior brick walls of all three of these sections of the left side were painted a bright white.

The far right side of the home provided a startling contrast. It looked like a cottage made of cut stone with its own separate front door, a steeply pitched roof, and dormer windows on its second floor. Although it butted up against the brick sections of the house, two more dissimilar architectural styles would be hard to imagine.

Right Side of Eisenhower Home in Gettysburg, Pennsylvania

What was the meaning of this? I stepped inside with my group, determined to find out.

Just as the outside of the home had suggested, there were two very separate interiors, as well. The living room, front hall, and dining room downstairs and the master bedroom upstairs were Mamie's creations.

Every surface in the large living room area was cluttered with framed photographs, vases of flowers, and bric-a-brac that had been given to the Eisenhowers over the years. Serving as a trophy room of sorts, this space with its baby grand piano, its elegant pouf sofa, its mother-of-pearl black inlaid coffee table, and its stone fireplace from the Lincoln White House, "reflected their public life," our guide informed us. Ike's assessment of this room, however, was both simple and blunt. *The Eisenhower Home Guide* which guests receive on their tour records that he "considered it too stuffy."

The front hall and formal dining room continued to reflect Mamie's interests and tastes. Display cases of various sizes are visible as soon as one enters the hall. Shelf upon shelf of china and porcelain can be viewed here, all collected by Mamie over the years. The formal dining room's cranberry colored carpet and matching upholstered chairs gathered around an oblong table overhung with an ornate crystal chandelier create an air of sophisticated taste. The polished pieces of the silver service visible throughout the room only add to the ambiance.

Upstairs, the master bedroom was also all Mamie. A large king-sized bed with a pinkish rose coverlet, pinkish rose window curtains, and a pinkish rose hued divan placed before a white marble fireplace give the room its accents of color. A few comfortable armchairs completed the setting, but there were no visible signs of masculinity anywhere in the room. To find evidence of the President, one had to look just down the hall.

The so-called "General's Room" was uniquely Ike. It had been the President's dressing room. After his first heart attack, he had added to this diminutive space (perhaps 8' x 10') a single bed on which to take his doctor mandated afternoon naps. One small end table stands by the bed, together with a chest of drawers and an armchair. The only decoration is a portrait, an Eisenhower original, picturing two of his grandchildren. The room is small and sparse, a marked contrast to what we had seen before.

Moving back downstairs into the section of the house that looks like a stone cottage on its exterior, one encounters more of President Eisenhower.

His den is the most identifiably masculine room in the house. Leather armchairs and hassocks, the ceiling's wooden beams which had been salvaged from the original farmhouse that dated back to the 18th century, one wall with built-in bookcases that reached to the ceiling. No bric-a-brac. No flowers. This room constitutes nearly the entire first floor of this portion of the house. For anyone sitting before the fireplace/bake oven (another element salvaged from the original farm), there was plenty of room for conversation, for reflection, even for an occasional game of bridge. It was Ike's perfect retreat.

Right outside the den was the President's office. About the size of the General's Room on the second floor, there was only enough space for a small desk, a modest bookcase, and a passageway to the front door of the cottage. Yet this was Ike's "temporary White House" when he resided at the farm. It looked for all the world like a mobile office for a general in the field.

But there *was* a room, happily enough, that seemed to fit both Mamie and Ike: the enclosed porch on the back of the house. It was said to be Ike's favorite place, where he and Mamie could watch the news or their favorite television shows while they ate their dinners on trays. This long rectangular area with floor to ceiling windows had ample space for a sofa and armchairs to be gathered into a conversational grouping and was still large enough to hold the President's easel and paints where he could pursue his favorite hobby. Here Ike could be Ike and Mamie could be Mamie, but together. It was a happy meeting place for both of them.

Overall, though, the Eisenhower farm tells the story of two people whose lives had diverged markedly and, in some ways, permanently. Their tastes, their styles, their sense of order and of ornament had been formed during the many years of their separation. Mamie had been a loyal wife and mother and had become First Lady of the United States. Dwight was a soldier whose ultimate allegiance had always been to his nation. Their lives were joined together as clearly as the sections of this house, but their differences, their individual, isolated selves were also indelibly etched into "our one home—our farm." Their great personal achievements had come with a high price for each of them to pay.

"Hey mister! What you doin'?"

I had been so preoccupied with locating the Eisenhower Boyhood home on Second Street that, after I had crossed the railroad tracks which lay between the National Park site and this small neighborhood, I hadn't been thinking about much else than taking a few pictures of the outside of the house. Now I moved my camera away from my eyes and found myself facing a young boy about nine or ten years old. I had noticed him riding his bicycle down the street a few minutes earlier, but I hadn't anticipated his return. He was straddling the front of his bike, both his feet now firmly planted on the pavement. Clearly, this was his territory, and I was a trespasser. He wanted an explanation for my incursion onto his turf.

"I'm taking a few pictures of this house," I said, simply.

"Oh," he replied. Then, swinging his leg over the frame of his bike and standing next to me on the curb, he added, "Why?"

"Because a President lived here once," I answered him. "When he was little. President Eisenhower."

The boy's face clouded over. "President Eisenhower?" he repeated," No, you've got the wrong house. I've been to the President's house with my school. It's over there," he gestured toward the south.

"I know," I replied. "You're right. That house *was* the place where the Eisenhower family lived when Ike was eight years old until he left for college at the age of twenty-one. But when the family moved to Abilene from Texas, while Ike was still a little child, they lived here for about five or six years."

"Oh," the boy replied. He watched me move around the front of the house for several minutes, taking pictures from a variety of angles. Finally, he must have felt that I no longer constituted a threat to his territory. I began to head back to the Eisenhower Presidential Center, and he tagged along.

As I was just about to step over the set of railroad tracks I had crossed earlier and make my way back across the parking lot to the Visitor's Center, he turned his bike around toward his neighborhood.

"When are you going to take a picture of my house?" he called after me.

"When you become President," I answered him.

He seemed to like that response. He waved briefly, stood up on his bike pedals, and speeded off.

I turned and headed across the tracks. "Simple, to the point, no nonsense," I thought as I reviewed our brief conversation. "And all by himself. A lot like Ike."

33

John F. Kennedy: Roseland

35th President John F. Kennedy (1961-1963): Birthplace in Brookline, MA

(This chapter is a compilation of two different visits to the John Fitzgerald Kennedy National Historical Site. At the time of our second visit, Rose Kennedy's narrative was not available for a self-guided tour, and a National Park Ranger led us through the home. The text of her presentation, however, was very similar to Rose's recollec-

tions, and anyone can still hear Mrs. Kennedy's remarks
through a link on the National Park Site's web page.)

By all rights, it probably should have been Joe, Jr. He had always been the golden boy, his father's favorite son. He had been the best student out of all his siblings. He had been the most gifted athlete in the family. In 1941 it had been Joe, Jr. who had been the first Kennedy to enlist in the Armed Forces (as a Navy flier), and it had been Joe, Jr. as a baby who had been lifted up in the arms of his maternal grandfather, Honey Fitz, the first immigrant mayor of Boston, as he proudly announced, "This will be the first Irish Catholic President of the United States."

But it was not to be. In August of 1944, Joe, Jr. was killed in an explosion over the English Channel. Now it was his younger brother, Jack, not Joe, Jr., to whom his father looked with expectancy. Could Jack, often sickly but persistently carefree Jack, actually become the standard-bearer for the Kennedy family's political aspirations?

Interestingly enough, this was a role for which Jack had been preparing himself since childhood. Throughout his boyhood years, Jack had competed with Joe, Jr. about almost everything: academic achievements, wrestling prowess, skill in school sports, even in the ability to debate issues over the family dinner table. And time and time again, Jack had come up short of his more accomplished elder brother. But over the years, Jack had begun to cultivate a quality that the decade of the twenties would call "It," a simultaneously indefinable and undeniable attractiveness that many people found irresistible. By the time the mantle of the Kennedy family's hope for preeminence had passed to Jack, he possessed "It" in spades.

This quality was apparent even to the eyes of an eleven-year-old six grader living in the Mount Washington suburbs of Cincinnati, Ohio. Me.

I have never completely understood just why it was that I became so fascinated by politics, but I know exactly when my interest skyrocketed: the summer of 1960 with the Democratic and Republican conventions leading up to the presidential election of that year.

Before this, like most children my age, I had been relatively oblivious to political matters. I had been born during Harry Truman's administration, but Dwight Eisenhower was the only President I had ever been consciously aware of, and what I knew about him was largely limited to my understanding of the fact that he had been the Supreme Commander of the Allied forces in Europe during World War II. I 'liked Ike" because my parents liked him. But in 1960, the political scene was about to change.

First, and most important, Americans were going to elect a new President. For my parents, the obvious choice was Republican Richard Nixon, the man who had served as Vice President for the preceding eight years. His opposition included a variety of Democratic rivals, including a relatively unknown one term Democratic Senator from Massachusetts, John F. Kennedy. It was Kennedy's possible candidacy that most concerned my folks.

First of all, they informed me, Kennedy was a Catholic (and this sent a quite distinct chill down the spines of my ardently Protestant parents); next, they had heard that his father, Joe, Sr., had been involved in questionable dealings in alcohol during the years of Prohibition; and, lastly, and perhaps most importantly, this young man Kennedy was completely inexperienced at a time when the world itself seemed to be trembling on the brink of nuclear annihilation. Electing such a man would be a catastrophe, they assured me.

I believed them. I had never seen my mom and dad so concerned about an election. Maybe that was why politics had begun to loom so large in my young mind.

I noted the ads, read about each possible candidate, and watched the television coverage of the long speeches delivered at the respective conventions of the opposing political parties. As I did so, I became distinctly aware of Kennedy's appeal. It wasn't his knowledge that was impressive. It was his style.

Jack Kennedy was young. He was handsome. And he was married to a woman who looked like she belonged on the cover of *Glamour* magazine. But none of this, I believed then, was enough to earn him a presidential nomination. His family was wealthy, I knew, but wealthy enough to influence an entire political party? I doubted it.

Yet as I watched the Democratic National Convention of July 1960, I experienced a moment when I became certain that Jack Kennedy *would* win his party's nomination and that, in the ensuing general election, he would be a most formidable opponent for Vice President Nixon. Politics, I was learning, could be compelling drama.

The stage was set by Senate Majority Leader Lyndon Johnson who had recently added his name to the list of Democratic nominees for selection as the party's presidential candidate. He was scheduled to give a talk just prior to Kennedy, and his comments were aimed quite specifically at his young colleague.

Johnson began by reminding his audience of the efforts he had made in the Senate to try to pass a key piece of Civil Rights legislation:

> *For six days and nights we had 24 hour sessions. Six days and nights I had to deliver a quorum of 51 men on a moment's notice to keep the Senate in session to get any bill at all. And I am proud to tell you that on those 50 quorum calls Lyndon Johnson answered every one of them, although some men who would be President on a Civil Rights platform answered none.*

He then went on to explain the reason that he had not entered the presidential race earlier, stating that it had been his "... considered judgment that my people had sent me to the Senate to perform the duties of a United States Senator for which I was paid $22,500 a year ... and I did not think [they] would reward negligence."

This speech evoked thunderous applause, and I knew right then that the Kennedy candidacy had been very effectively torpedoed. Johnson had shown up the young Senator as having been absent for critical quorum calls. Johnson had proved that Kennedy, in stepping away from his legislative duties in order to run for higher office, had shirked his responsibilities as a Senator. In looking for the party's presidential nomination, Jack Kennedy was asking the party to reward his negligence!

The fact that it was Kennedy himself who spoke next made the moment fraught with tension. What could the junior Senator from Massachusetts say, what could he do other than fold up his political tent with shame and withdraw from the race? I was glued to the television as Kennedy began speaking. Surprisingly he didn't appear at all rattled. His parry of Johnson's criticism was astonishingly adroit:

> *Let me just say that I appreciate what Senator Johnson had to say. He made some general references to perhaps the shortcomings of other presidential candidates, but as he was not specific, I assume that he was talking about some of the other candidates and not about me.*

This was no denial, no explanation, no apology. Jack Kennedy had simply acted as if Johnson's criticisms had been directed elsewhere! The audience laughed at the sheer bravado of his response, and Kennedy then turned on his opponent with clever praise:

> *It is true that Senator Johnson made a wonderful record in answering those quorum calls, and I want to commend him for it ... I come to you today full of admiration for Senator Johnson, full of affection for him, strongly in support of him for Majority Leader and confident that, in that position, we're all going to be able to work together.*

And just as quickly as that, the Convention erupted in a chorus of shouts, hoots, laughter, and general approbation for the young Senator who had handled himself so expertly at a moment when a lesser man would have crumbled. It set the scene for the upcoming election, and the result never surprised me after what I had seen that day.

The Kennedy Presidency was the first presidential administration of which I still have vivid memories. My relatives in Miami made our family very aware of the Bay of Pigs fiasco in April of 1961. The ensuing Cuban Missile Crisis in October of the following year was seared into my mind on the day I went to school wondering if the world would end in a nuclear war before I would be able to return home to die with my family. The school intercom reported hourly throughout that day on the position of Russian ships approaching the U.S. warships encircling Cuba, and only when we heard that the Soviet vessels had pulled back could any of us breathe easily again.

And then there was November 22, 1963, in Dallas. Everyone in my generation can tell you where he was when President Kennedy was assassinated. I was in school, now a high school freshman. I was in the library when the intercom broke in to announce the news. Everyone was stunned. A President assassinated? In twentieth century America? It hardly seemed possible.

And I remember the days following the assassination: the wall-to-wall television coverage, the breaking news of Lee Harvey Oswald's capture and subsequent murder at the hands of Jack Ruby, the funeral procession, and John, Jr.'s heartbreaking salute. I saw it all. I remember it all.

Years later, Carol and I visited the one home site associated with President Kennedy that had been opened to the public. This, I thought, would be very different from the other presidential venues we had toured if only because I myself had grown up in the second half of the twentieth century. This, I thought, would be a window into a world with which I was already quite familiar. What would I learn about this young President that I didn't already know? Would I find the origins of his "It" factor?

These were questions that filled my thought as we wound our way through the tangle of streets comprising the Brookline section of Boston. What I hadn't expected, however, was that we would soon be encountering the only presidential home we would ever visit that was devoted nearly exclusively to someone other than the President who had lived there.

After a number of wrong turns and unexpected one way streets in this sprawling Boston suburb, our dependable GPS finally directed us to Beals Street, a tree-lined avenue toward the middle of which stood a forest green two story frame home with a prominent flagpole and American flag in its front yard.

We parked our car and, as we approached the house, signs directed us to the back of the home and down some stone steps to the basement level. Upon opening a door at the foot of these steps, we entered a small store area where we were warmly welcomed by a National Park Ranger who offered us an audio-tour that would guide us through the residence.

"Your docent today will be President Kennedy's mother," the Ranger informed us. "She gave this home to the National Park Service in 1967, and she wanted to be able to share her memories with visitors. You will hear her voice as she leads you from room to room, recounting to you the memories she associated with these places. We hope that you will enjoy your visit."

I was thrilled. How amazing, I thought, that we were to be given a tour of this site by the mother of the future President. Wouldn't it have been wonderful to have had Abigail Adams take us through the Old House at Peace field? Or Nelly Madison as our hostess at Montpelier? Our receivers in hand, we were directed up a staircase to the first floor, and I was sure that this would be an experience never to be forgotten.

Our first stop was the living room. As I listened to the recorded voice of Rose Kennedy pointing out the chair where Joe, Sr. would sit and read the paper and the corner where Joe, Jr. and Jack would play after they had come downstairs after their evening baths, the home seemed to come alive with memories of Kennedy family life. I quickly noted, however, that these remembrances were uniquely and nearly exclusively focused on Rose herself, rather than on her more famous husband and son. She could never look at the chair where she had sat in the evenings without recalling her endless hours of darning the stockings of her growing boys. The living room piano had been given to her as a wedding present. The pictures on the wall were copies of paintings she had studied in Europe. And she fondly recalled the walks she had taken with her husband after the children had gone to bed.

But her only comment that shed any light onto the future President's character was a rather offhanded remark that neither Jack nor Joe, Jr. had cared much for piano lessons, preferring the music they heard on the radio. The room was full of "many happy memories" for Rose, but not much insight into the qualities that had made Jack such a political wunderkind.

Our next stop was located on the second floor. Hopefully, I mused, there would be more illumination there.

After climbing the stairs, the first room to which we were directed was the master bedroom, the room where Jack Kennedy had been born. Once again, Rose's focus as she spoke about the room centered on details which, while undoubtedly meaningful to her, were not relevant to gaining any deeper understanding of either the childhood or the charisma of her son, the future President. Rose Kennedy's topics included an explanation of why the bed near the window had been chosen as the birthing bed, what a tremendous responsibility any parent assumes to influence a child correctly, and how proud she had been when her son had been inaugurated as President on that "cold, cold day." She also noted that the linen bedspreads on display had been a gift from her parents and were embroidered with Irish symbols. She ended this stop by pointing out the six-month pictures of each of the four children who had lived here (Joe, Jr., Jack, Rosemary, and Kathleen), assuring us that, although many people thought that all babies looked alike, she could easily distinguish each of her children. Our next stop, she directed us, was the nursery.

It would not be until we crossed the hall and entered that room that I would finally begin to sense the unspoken agenda at work in this place. Rose Kennedy, it seemed to me, was using the home on Beals Street as a vindication of herself, as a woman, as a mother, and as an influence on her presidential offspring. What I could not understand, however, was why she would feel the need to do so.

After all, in many ways, she was the reigning Queen Mother of America's Royal Family. Living until the venerable age of 104, Rose Kennedy was a matriarchal figure whose progeny included three sons who were political firebrands. By 1992, the year of her death, she was mother, grandmother, or great grandmother to over one hundred direct descendants. Rose Kennedy had been called "the backbone of the family" and, more eloquently, "The 'Courageous' Mother of Camelot." A recent biographer, Barbara Perry, has suggested that, had she been born in a more liberated day, Rose Kennedy might well have become a major political force to be reckoned with in her own right. But there were also some dark clouds in Rose's life.

The most obvious of these dark clouds involved her husband's infidelities. Joe, Sr.'s well-documented extra-marital affairs, some of which began relatively early in the marriage, must have caused his Catholic wife a great deal of grief. The list of anti-depressant drugs she used to help herself maintain her emotional equilibrium is impressive even by today's standards. Then there were the dark clouds of accusations by some of her children regarding her maternal "aloofness," most bitterly uttered by her President son, Jack, who, late in his life, complained that his mother "... was never there when we really needed her... My mother never really held me and hugged me. Never! Never!" (Farris 65). Lastly, there were the dark clouds of the moral laxity of her sons. How could such a devout mother have raised boys who, despite their great political acumen, disported themselves, history has shown, in so reckless a fashion as Jack, Bobby, and Teddy? Seen in this light, the Beals Street residence—and Rose's memories and observations in particular—began to come into a clearer focus.

Walking across the hall into the nursery, I was immediately struck by its dazzling whiteness. The curtains, bedspread, and bassinet were all white. Even the chairs, bookshelf, and door and window frames were painted white. Rose Kennedy's commentary informed us that her children had loved books, particularly Jack who had favored tales of King Arthur. Such remarks were clearly efforts to establish Jack's "Camelot mentality" as having dated from an early age. Furthermore, Mrs. Kennedy assured her listeners, she had made careful efforts to "... select books that were recommended at school or by a children's bookshop." But then she added, "My children, however, were indifferent to these edifying selections," mentioning Jack's love of the story of Billy Whiskers, a goat who was constantly getting into trouble and mischief. For the first time, I caught a glimpse of a Jack Kennedy I could recognize.

The rest of Rose Kennedy's remarks in this room revolved around her children's christening dress (made by Franciscan nuns in East Boston) and their baptisms at the nearby St. Aidan's church. After a brief acknowledgement of Jack's favorite toys and a reference to his bout with scarlet fever in 1920, we were encouraged to visit the other rooms on the second floor.

Of particular note was Mrs. Kennedy's office "boudoir" where she conducted her correspondence and, most importantly, kept a card file with records of each of her children's illnesses, medical history, and important dates. Although she recommended "... this idea to any mother," it was hard not to see in this rather clinical practice a tinge of the aloofness of which Jack had complained.

John F. Kennedy's Childhood Table

Retracing our steps downstairs, we stopped at the family dining room. In addition to a large oval table in the center of the room, it contained a much smaller table for the children, Joe, Jr. and Jack, placed on the front wall before a window. Here, Rose recalled, the boys would sit for their meals. The porringers, napkin rings, and cutlery placed on the table were those used by the two brothers, she informed us, and bore their initials. Jack, later in life, would recall the constant competitive nature of gatherings in this room—oratories were demanded of each child—as one of the activities that he had never enjoyed. Rose's remembrance was of historical discussions and "On Sundays we would talk about the gospel at Mass. If they [the children] didn't pay attention one Sunday, they would the next as they knew they would be questioned."

Our final stop was the kitchen. Here Mrs. Kennedy remembered her family's love of Boston baked beans, but she also decided to add one more maternal remembrance. After taking the children on outings to the nearby grocery store, she recalled, "On the way back we would usually stop for a visit at Saint Aidan's church. I wanted my children to realize that church was for every day and not just for Sunday."

For me there was a quiet melancholy as I exited this house on Beals Street. Although Rose Kennedy assured us in her closing comments that the family had been "very happy here," I couldn't help reflecting on Mrs. Kennedy's efforts to dispel the dark clouds of her family's history through the tinted lens of her memory. After all, she had taken lovely nightly walks with her husband, and she had kept meticulous records of her children's important health information. She had done her best to encourage her children's learning and appreciation of the finer things in life. Most importantly, she had made earnest efforts to teach her children the importance of religion and church. What more could she have done, after all? Certainly, she seemed to be saying, none of her family's shortcomings or dissatisfactions could legitimately be attributed to her.

And so the house on Beals Street tells visitors much more about Rose Kennedy than about anyone else in her remarkable family. The origin of Jack's famous "It," and the extraordinary Kennedy charisma possessed by all of the brothers, these remained unilluminated in this locale. The only other site about which I had any knowledge was the Kennedy compound on Cape Cod, but of course, it is still being used by the numerous Kennedy descendants and is not open for visitors.

"There *is* another Kennedy house nearby," the Park Ranger informed me as I spoke to her after our tour. "It's privately owned, but you can see it from the street. It's at the corner of Abbotsford and Naples roads," and she pointed the way there on a map she was happy to give me. "The Kennedys moved there in 1920, after they left this house. You can see that they were doing very well financially," she added.

I couldn't resist the opportunity to see another presidential home so close by, so we got into our car and, only a minute or two later, I was standing at the intersection of Naples and Abbotsford, trying to get a picture of the house.

Compared to the Beals property, this home was a mansion. A broad stairway led up to a white-columned piazza and porch that extended the length of the front of the house and curled around its left side. Above it, on the left front corner of the house, was a circular tower room with windows on three sides. The steeply pitched roof suggested at least two additional floors of living space, and three dormer windows were visible from the front of the house, defining at least three large rooms.

John F. Kennedy Boyhood Home in Brookline, Massachusetts

"However he's making his money," I found myself thinking almost aloud, "Joe Kennedy, Sr. had certainly come up in the world in the three short years between his purchase of the Beals Street home and this palatial residence." Of course, the Kennedy family was growing exponentially. Ultimately they would come to have nine children, but the difference between Beals Street and this Abbotsford/Naples address suggested a quantum leap in lifestyle as well as the addition of a few more rooms for the children.

Try as I might, however, I couldn't get a satisfactory picture. My close-ups invariably cut off important sections of the home, and my longer shots were obscured by the luxuriant foliage that shaded—as well as concealed—the building behind it. Here in Brookline, any secrets the Kennedys may have had remained a mystery.

With the exception, perhaps, of Rose.

34

Lyndon Baines Johnson: Plateau Live Oak

36th President Lyndon B. Johnson (1963-1969): Boyhood Home in Johnson City, TX

"Could you help me?" I asked a Park Ranger as we walked down the street from the Visitor's Center toward the Lyndon Johnson Boyhood Home in Johnson City, Texas.

"Of course," he replied. "What do you need?"

"I need help in getting my mind around Lyndon Johnson," I confessed, almost ashamed that I had felt the need to say it. "He seems so conflicted, so confusing to me. He appears to be a man wrestling with many demons. There are his tremendous efforts to create his "Great Society." But then there's Vietnam and the lies told to the American people as he led them deeper and deeper into that terrible episode of our history. As a Representative he was an ardent supporter of Franklin Roosevelt, but he had stood firmly with other Blue Dog Democrats in resisting efforts to desegregate the South. As President he declared "War on Poverty," yet he was instrumental in creating a welfare system that sometimes disincentivized, if not actually discouraged, people from finding jobs. There's almost no adjective, positive or negative, that doesn't fit President Johnson to some extent. And frankly, I'm confused."

The Ranger, whose name I now read on his badge was Brian, smiled at me as we walked onward toward the home. "I think you're absolutely right," he began. "President Johnson *was* a bundle of sometimes conflicting emotions and aspirations. But I think I can help you clarify his character a little bit." It was several moments, however, before he continued his thought.

"The secret to President Johnson," he spoke slowly, pausing for emphasis, "... is that he wanted to out-Roosevelt Roosevelt."

Initially this comment did not seem to make much sense. It would be hard to find two more dissimilar characters than Franklin Roosevelt and Lyndon Johnson. Their ancestries, their educations, their economic backgrounds and social standings all stood in stark contrast to each other. Roosevelt had been born in the splendor of Hyde Park, New York. Johnson had grown up in the modest home in Johnson City, Texas, toward which we were currently walking. How would his Texas homes relate to Brian's assessment of our 36th President, I wondered, or would they?

By the time we arrived at the Boyhood Home, about fifteen people had gathered there and were congregated on the front porch. Brian strode right into this waiting group and began his tour.

"Welcome to the LBJ Boyhood Home. Today you will hear about two of the most important influences in President Johnson's life:

his mother, Rebekah, and his father, Sam. They were nearly opposites in many ways, yet both contributed significantly to forming the character of their eldest child, Lyndon.

"Rebekah was a refined, college-educated woman, unusual for that day. She was determined to see that her four children appreciated the value of learning. She tutored them on this very porch. But her special room in the house was the parlor."

We filed into the house and, after a few right turns, were invited into this airy front room. Its long windows, bright patterned wallpaper, and well-upholstered chairs set up around the edges of the room gave it an overall feeling of grace, even delicacy.

"Mrs. Johnson would teach her children in this room. She read them poetry and classic literature and encouraged their idealism. Her eldest son, Lyndon, was a particular favorite, and she urged him especially to distinguish himself in his schoolwork. She had high hopes for her boy, and he never forgot to acknowledge and revere her influence in his life." Brian let us look around the room thoroughly, and then he directed our attention to a print hanging over the mantel.

"This is a picture that Rebekah wanted all her children to know and think about. It's called 'All is Vanity,' and some of you may have seen it before, as it's a pretty famous image. The picture shows a beautiful woman applying her makeup and doing her hair before a large mirror. If you stand back, however, the image becomes a skull. Rebekah wanted the children to understand that sometimes first impressions may misrepresent the larger significance of things." Of course, the other key meaning of this famous "vanitas" print regards the dangers of pride and the destructive results of focusing too closely on one's personal goals and desires. That interpretation was left unspoken, but it would come to have a poignant relevance for the future President.

Brian now moved us into the dining room which connected directly to the front hall. "The other influence, perhaps even more powerful than Rebekah, was Lyndon's father, Sam. The dining room and the front hall, which doubled as Sam's political office, were important training grounds for Lyndon as he grew up."

There was an old tube radio with a large horn speaker on a table on one side of the dining room. Brian pointed this out to the group. "There was no electricity here yet, so Sam had to take the battery out of the car and hook it up in order to power this radio. Here he, and especially his son, Lyndon, would listen to the news of the day. As they listened, Sam would turn to his son after each story and grill him with the same three questions: 'What did you hear?' 'What's the significance of this story?' 'What's the impact of what you heard?' He wanted his son to think about the news, to reflect on its meaning and the possible effect it could have on him."

Pointing down the front hall, Brian called our attention to the wooden telephone box on the wall. "Sam Ealy Johnson, along with the various jobs he held to make ends meet, was almost always involved in state politics. He wanted to be able to stay in touch with other party workers. A populist interested in bettering the lives of ordinary people, Sam thought it would be inconsistent with his philosophy to accept any political contributions from banks, oil companies, or big business. Without their backing, he turned out not to be a very effective or powerful presence in the state legislature."

But, Brian added, Lyndon *did* learn a lot about politics from his father. Rebekah refused to let Sam talk politics or swear in the house, so he would repair to the porch outside the master bedroom to meet with friends and talk–often rather colorfully–about the issues of the day. Young Lyndon, Brian pointed out as he led us into the small master bedroom, had a bedroom right next to his parents, and it was easy for him to sneak into their room and huddle under the open window there–he pointed to the place–to listen to these conversations. Years later, his famous–and occasionally infamous–demeanor, referred to by his friends and foes alike as "The Johnson Treatment," attested to the fact that he had learned much from overhearing these heated discussions.

We saw the kitchen, the back porch, and the outhouse toward the end of the tour. Finally, Brian reminded us that it was from the very front porch where we had first gathered that Lyndon Johnson had announced his intention to run for the U.S. House of Representatives in 1937. And, with this, our tour was ended.

I had one more question to ask Brian. "What is the name of these trees around the house? They're quite striking, even a bit eerie."

"Yes," he responded. "They're called Plateau Live Oaks. They're indigenous to the Central Texas Hill Country. If you're going out to the LBJ Ranch, you'll see many more of them. There's one that's over 500 years old right in the front yard of the Ranch. It's called the 'Cabinet Tree' because President Johnson used to hold cabinet meetings under it when he was staying there."

"They're odd trees," I commented. "They don't seem to have a single straight angle. Their limbs are as gnarled as grotesque fingers twisting impossibly in all directions. I don't see how their wood could ever be cut into serviceable lumber or joists. But," I continued, "their shade *is* heavenly on a hot day like today."

"Indeed it is," Brian answered me with a thoughtful look. "Enjoy your trip to Stonewall. There's a lot worth seeing out there."

I walked back to the Visitor's Center and tried to envision the long road that had stretched from his small front porch in Johnson City all the way to Washington D.C. I recalled that when Lyndon Johnson was still the newly elected Representative from Central Texas, he had been given an opportunity to meet personally with Franklin Roosevelt in 1938. Rather than simply basking in the glory of being photographed with his beloved President, Johnson had used the occasion to convince Roosevelt to waive the population requirement that had kept Johnson's rural district from receiving electricity. The story is told that Roosevelt, immediately after this meeting, noted to one of his staff that he had just met a remarkable young man who might just be President someday.

As Carol and I drove westward from Johnson City, an interview that President Johnson had given to an early biographer, Doris Kearns Goodwin, came to my mind. In it the President had made a telling comment, particularly in light of Brian's perceptive insight about the key to Johnson's character:

> *Some men want power simply to strut around the world and to hear the tune of "Hail to the Chief." Others want it simply to build prestige, to collect antiques, and to buy*

pretty things. Well I wanted power to give things to peo-
ple—all sorts of things to all sorts of people, especially the
poor and the blacks. (Dallek 13)

This statement can be subject to a variety of interpretations, of course. A supporter of President Johnson might argue that "Surely these words prove that President Johnson was a genuine altruist. His motives in seeking political power, far from being self-serving, were chiefly to help the poor and underprivileged."

Even a brief visit to the Lyndon Johnson Presidential Library in Austin tends to confirm such a conclusion. One display there features an extremely long glass case containing pens the President had used to sign bills into law. Several were Civil Rights bills, including the landmark Civil Rights Act of 1964 and Voting Rights Act of 1965. But this was only the beginning. After the landslide election that had made him a President in his own right, Johnson had forwarded his "Great Society" programs, including Medicare and Medicaid and several education bills, among which was the Head Start program for preschool children. Add to all these bills the Food Stamp Act of 1964, the Equal Opportunity Act of 1965, and President Johnson emerges as a man truly eager to use the office and power of the Presidency to "give things to people." If, as Brian had said, the President's great goal *had* been to "out-Roosevelt Roosevelt," the scope and number of bills he had been able to shepherd through Congress provide a most impressive testament both to his efforts and to his success.

"But," an opponent might ask, "is it truly the purpose of a President, or of any government for that matter, simply to 'give things to people'? After all, the people whose lives are affected by these bills are citizens. Isn't this a blatant example of using the office of the President to buy their votes? Aren't many of these programs nothing more than latter-day versions of Tammany Hall—on steroids?"

Both of these perspectives were running through my mind as we finally turned off the highway onto the property of the Johnson Ranch near Stonewall, Texas. What might this setting reveal that would deepen my understanding of this complex leader?

It is hard to find any account of a visitor to this place while the Johnsons were residing here who was not treated—and sometimes even forcibly required—to take a tour of the plentiful acreage that comprises the LBJ Ranch. The National Park Service has chosen to continue this tradition. Rather than pulling directly into a parking lot near the Ranch, guests are first directed to a Visitor's Center where they can view a short film on LBJ and obtain a free driving permit and/or purchase a self-guided driving audio tour of the property. Upon returning to one's car, signage leads traffic out an exit toward the Pedernales River, along which the road runs for over half a mile.

As Carol and I drove along the riverside, we noted the spot where LBJ used to pilot frightened visitors through the water in his amphibious vehicle. Watching the sky reflected in the gently moving current, I found myself reminded of Brian's suggestion that the key to President Johnson was that he was trying to "out-Roosevelt Roosevelt." Although the Pedernales River was no Hudson, and Stonewall, Texas, was no Hyde Park, like Roosevelt, Johnson lived in a family mansion close to a river. Like Roosevelt, Johnson prided himself on his estate and loved touring it whenever the occasion to do so presented itself. Like Roosevelt, it also suddenly occurred to me, Johnson had been provided by history with a war to fight. Vietnam, however, was no World War II. I paused to wonder what our feelings about President Roosevelt might have been had *he*, like President Johnson, been unable to prevail in that global conflict?

All these thoughts were interrupted as signs instructed us to cross the Pedernales on a narrow bridge and then turn left down another road on the opposite side of the river. It was here that the myth making began.

Our first stop was to be at the one-room schoolhouse that the future President had attended for a year at the age of four. Here, one is informed, Lyndon Johnson had begun his lifelong commitment to education, and here he would return to sign his landmark Elementary and Secondary Education Act of 1965 providing federal aid to public schools across the country.

Next we were invited to leave our car to visit the reconstructed birthplace home that had been placed on the exact location of the small dogtrot house where, in 1908, Lyndon Johnson had been born. The original frame house had been torn down in the 1940's, but when serving as President, Johnson had commissioned this facsimile to be constructed on the original site. It was then used as a guest residence for visitors to the Ranch.

View from Lyndon B. Johnson's Birthplace in Stonewall, Texas

Today as one walks from room to room, this home seems almost too perfectly primed to suggest the humble stoicism of Central Texas Hill Country life at the turn of the century. Each room is fully furnished and kept in meticulous order. There is no evidence of the deprivation that the newly married Rebekah Johnson had felt here. Yet the views, particularly from the rear of the house, feel much the same as they must have looked in that day: a small flowering tree, a lawn edged with a split rail fence, and beyond an endless tract of grassland. A lonely life under an endless sky.

Down the road on the left was the Johnson cemetery where both Lyndon and Lady Bird Johnson, as well as numerous other family members, are interred, and then, on the right, the home of the President's grandfather, Sam Ealy Johnson, Sr., still stands, a setting Lyndon always remembered from his childhood years.

The road now turned north and took us into a large section of grazing land as well as around the elongated airstrip the President had put in to enable his Jet Star Boeing 707 (nicknamed Air Force One Half) to land close to the rear of his home. And finally we arrived and parked our car in preparation for our tour of the LBJ Ranch house.

We purchased our tickets to the "Texas White House" in the airplane hangar that included a gift shop as well as exhibits depicting President Johnson's life at the Ranch. The venue was quite crowded on the day we had come, but Park Guides divided us into several manageable tour groups, and, after a short wait, we were directed to follow a Ranger to the house.

Its horizontal expanse immediately reminded me of Roosevelt's Springwood estate in Hyde Park, New York, though the architecture of each home was quite different. There, directly to the left of the front of the house stood the majestic "Cabinet Tree." Its colossal expanse shaded over half of the front yard. Our docent opened a door and guided us into the President's office space. Here any resemblance to Springwood ended abruptly.

Lyndon B. Johnson's Ranch in Stonewall, Texas

Lyndon Johnson was absolutely devoted to the technology of his day. Three television sets were linked together in sequence so that the President could view all three of the national networks (ABC, NBC, and CBS) simultaneously. Telephones were ubiquitous throughout the house (an astonishing total of 72 phones in service!), and the President was able to communicate from any room at any hour to anyone in the world whom he wished to reach. "You can see," our docent informed us, "how the President could spend so much time here, ultimately nearly 25% of his presidential years." We were invited to circle this room that had been the nerve center of the "Texas White House," and then we were escorted into the living areas of the Ranch.

Our first stop in this section of the home was in what the Johnsons had called the "Grand Central Station" room. With four doors leading into this room and a staircase heading up to the six upper floor bedrooms with their six separate baths, this room was always a flurry of activity with numerous comings and goings. Opposite the couch in this room was one of Lady Bird's favorite pieces of furniture: a coffee table fashioned from an ancient piece of wood from England's famed Sherwood Forest. A gift to the Johnsons from Frank Stanton, the president of the CBS network, I couldn't miss the subtle humor of this reminder of Robin Hood, the greatest historical proponent of the "take from the rich and give to the poor" philosophy. It fit to a tee most of President Johnson's domestic policies.

As we entered the living room area, another battery of three linked television sets was visible at the far end of the room, though there also were several different conversational areas arranged throughout the long room that ran much of the breadth of the house. Tucked in a corner was a table set up for the playing of dominoes, "the working man's chess" as the President had frequently called the game. Here, on many an evening, both dominoes and politics would be played and strategized into the wee hours of the morning.

The last two stops of our tour were the bedrooms of President Johnson and Lady Bird. The docent indicated that the President's responsibilities had necessitated these separate rooms as he had not wanted to disturb his wife's sleep with any calls he might need to make during the night. On the other side of his large bed was a massage table that he had used to ease the tensions of office, and a door on the far side of the room led directly to a large outdoor pool where the President had enjoyed recreational swims (though even there he had installed a floating telephone to keep him connected to the world). To me this room seemed an unhappy testament to the personal cost of his Presidency.

Lady Bird, of course, had outlived her husband by 34 years. Her bedroom was also her office, and its bright and gracious décor reflected well her buoyant spirit and her interest in promoting and preserving natural beauty. The tape player on which she recorded her personal memoirs was here, as was a camera Lyndon had given her to take pictures of the flowers she so loved.

We left the house by a back door and were encouraged to enjoy the collection of paving stones signed by various famous visitors to the Ranch during the President's lifetime. I noticed that the Ranger who had conducted the latter part of our house tour was sitting on a bench, looking rather tired. I joined him, and he told me that he was enjoying a brief rest after a long day of activity. I couldn't resist posing my favorite question to him.

"What in the house catches your eye as an insight into President Johnson?"

He smiled at me and said, "I don't know if it's an insight, but it sure shows his humor."

"What is it?" I asked.

"Did you see the dollar bills in the office, that first room you went into in the house?"

"Dollar bills? You mean the dollar bills with President Johnson's face printed on them?"

"Yes. They're on the bookcase just behind the President's desk. They were a gift from John Connally who served briefly as Secretary of the Treasury in the early 1970's. Connally and President Johnson were longtime Texas friends, you know," (I nodded) "and Connally got the Treasury to print up 600 one dollar bills with President Johnson's picture on them where George Washington's portrait usually appears. He presented them as a gift to the ex-President, and President Johnson's response to the gift had been 'I'm only worth a dollar to you?' " We both laughed, but I found it significant that President Johnson had kept this gift that was now on display. "After all," the bills seemed to be saying, "Roosevelt only made it onto a dime."

I thanked the guide, and before we left, I walked once more to the front of the home for a final look at the glorious and ancient plateau live oak "Cabinet Tree" that stretched out and arched itself over the lawn. Thinking back on this day, I realized that the key to President Johnson for which I had been searching had been openly visible to me almost from the moment that Carol and I had arrived in Johnson City.

The trees. The plateau live oaks. The President himself was a human embodiment of the plateau live oak trees that surrounded his birth house, his boyhood home, and his beloved Ranch. Like the oaks, he was an unsightly jumble of angles with nary a straight line out of which to make a serviceable plank. He was a hard-nosed realist with an idealist's dreams. He was a wealthy man who distrusted the wealthy. He was willing to lie in order to try to accomplish what he believed to be right in Vietnam. He practiced unfaithful fidelity and was a peace-loving warmonger. He was gnarled and twisted and rugged. His political decisions, like the limbs of the plateau live oaks, both buried themselves in the earth and reached toward the sky. In many ways he was frightening, bombastic, intimidating. Yet, as his biographer Robert Dallek, has noted, he also had an "...unbounded confidence in social engineering by the federal government ...." . No matter that, as Dallek also observed, "... so much of what he believed in did not work all that well in practice" (Walsh 153). At least he was making an effort to improve the lives of millions of his fellow citizens.

Of course trying to "out-Roosevelt Roosevelt" had been an exercise in futility, and the war in Vietnam had turned out to be a painful object lesson in "vanitas." President Johnson's final words to the nation in his last State of the Union address were uncharacteristically subdued: "... at least it will be said that we tried."

Yet by doing so his Presidency *had* come to meaningfully resemble the administration of his political idol, Franklin Roosevelt, many of whose programs were also ultimately dismantled as they were found to be unconstitutional. Perhaps, after all, it was President Johnson's *pursuit* of justice, of equality, and of government-provided financial assistance for all needy Americans that constituted his greatest legacy.

Many of his programs were unsuccessful in eradicating the problems they had been created to solve. They offered temporary relief rather than a permanent cure. Similarly, the plateau live oaks cannot actually prevent the heat and glare of a blistering summer day in Central Texas. But, one would be worse off without them. Sometimes it is the shade that matters most.

35

Richard M. Nixon: "Not because they wished it..."

37th President Richard M. Nixon (1969-1974): Birthplace in Yorba Linda, CA

"The chapter I'm really looking forward to reading is the one about Nixon."

My son Andy and I were just finishing up one of our long distance telephone conversations, and, before closing, he was offering me some encouragement on my book. I needed some clarification regarding his comment, however.

"Really?" I said, somewhat incredulously. "Why is that?"

"Because he was so popular—one of the most loved of all American Presidents. And then he fell so far—becoming one of the most hated of American Presidents."

"One of the most loved of all American Presidents?" I repeated. "How on earth did you draw that conclusion?"

"Dad, President Nixon carried 49 states in his 1972 re-election bid. And he also had one of the largest margins of victory in popular votes recorded in the twentieth century. How could he not have been universally loved?"

Suddenly one of the dilemmas of history felt terribly real to me. My son had read the statistics, and he had drawn reasonable conclusions from them, as those interested in history invariably try to do. But the years of President Nixon's political career were also years I had lived through, and I felt like I had some insights regarding that time period that were not reflected in the impressive numbers my son was citing.

It was true that I had hoped that Richard Nixon would be elected President in 1960. And twelve years later, in 1972, when he *had* already been President for four years, I had cast my first-ever vote in hopes of re-electing him. But I had never loved him. Love hadn't even entered my mind as I had made my decision regarding which candidate I would support. Why not? Because elections in the 1960's and 1970's weren't usually about loving the candidate for whom one was voting. The elections were mostly about fear: fear of war, fear of nuclear disaster, and, most of all, fear of the spread of Communism.

I was a babe in arms in 1950 when Alger Hiss had been convicted of perjury amidst claims that he had been operating for years as a spy for the Soviets, and I was still too young in 1953 to recall the Rosenbergs' trial and execution for their role in forwarding classified documents to the Russians which had aided in the Communists' development of an atom bomb. But I remember vividly being a young boy sitting in the back seat of the family sedan when, over the car radio, a newscaster announced that the Soviet Union had successfully launched Sputnik, the first man-made orbiting satellite. And I remember the concern in my father's voice as he had turned to my mother and had spoken quietly, "We must never let this happen again." Exactly what it was that had happened was unclear to my eight-year-old mind. Were we at war? Could Russian missiles now fall on us from the sky? But whatever the meaning of the broadcast and my father's words, I understood instinctively that my world had just become a more dangerous place, and that fact would come to significantly color the growing up years of my entire generation.

What we were looking for, then, from our leaders was less related to how loveable they made themselves out to be and more connected with how secure they made us feel both about our nation's safety and about our own personal chances for survival. In order to understand the political appeal of Richard Nixon, I believe it is important to understand such truths. Yet at first, the depiction of President Nixon's life here at his Presidential Library and Museum struck me as more idealized than grounded in the grim realities of the Cold War.

The stated purpose of the Richard Nixon Library and Birthplace Foundation was articulated clearly on the brochure handed to each visitor entering the site: "The mission of the Richard Nixon Library and Birthplace Foundation is to honor the leadership of Richard Nixon and to perpetuate his legacy at the Presidential Library that bears his name in Yorba Linda, California." Somehow I had hoped for a more candid and thorough assessment of President Nixon's character than was reflected by this mission statement. I guess I felt that, as someone who had once voted for him, I deserved it.

Carol's and my first stop was at the Nixon birthplace house, located close by the Museum and Library. This modest home had been built from a kit by Frank and Hannah Nixon in 1912. And it was here, in January of the following year, that Richard Nixon had been born.

As we entered the house, we found ourselves standing in its front parlor. On our immediate left, in front of a bay window, was a circular dining table beyond which was a small bedroom, quite visible from the front door. The remainder of the parlor area contained an assortment of chairs and tables which created a conversational grouping. On the far wall next to a modest china cupboard stood an upright piano. Our docent, a woman named Dee Dee, called our attention to various items in the room.

"This dining table was where young Richard learned to debate issues with his father," she began. "It wasn't originally placed here near the window. When the Nixons lived here it stood on the wall next to the china cupboard, and the piano was placed on the inside wall next to the bedroom. Mr. Nixon suggested the table's current placement before the bay window to create more walking space for visitors touring the house."

Next, Dee Dee pointed out the piano, as well as a violin and clarinet which stood nearby it. She informed us that the future President had learned to play all these instruments as a boy. "Mr. Nixon was an excellent musician," she noted. "He probably could have succeeded in making a name for himself in music had he chosen to do so."

Dee Dee then pointed out several copies of *National Geographic* placed on a coffee table near the parlor chairs. "This was President Nixon's favorite magazine as a young man," she informed us. "On one occasion," she continued, "he had found an article in the *Geographic* that had particularly interested him. He had put his hand down on a page that included a map of China and, turning to his family, had said, 'Someday, I will go there!' " Dee Dee paused a moment for effect before continuing. "And, as we all know, he made good on that childhood promise!"

Although she had now turned to lead us toward the back of the house, I didn't want to leave this room without asking about the small bedroom, just beyond the dining room table. I questioned Dee Dee as to whether this was, indeed, the room where the President had been born. "Yes," she answered. "That was Frank and Hannah's bedroom and President Nixon was born right there," she gestured, "on that very bed. Even the coverlet is original."

Our group then passed the fireplace over which hung an oil painting—also original to the house, we were assured—picturing Pilgrim couple John and Priscilla Alden making their way through a lonely and snow-covered forest landscape. "The Nixons were Quakers you know," Dee Dee reminded us, "and the family had always been inspired by stories depicting the struggles of the early Pilgrim settlers."

Our last stop in the house was the kitchen and pantry, the latter of which included a small washtub where President Nixon and his brothers had been bathed. A narrow stairway led upstairs to the single room that all the children had shared until the family had moved to Whittier, California, when Richard was eight. Then Dee Dee opened the back door for us, and our tour of the house was finished.

But what exactly was it that we had just seen? I felt somewhat dissatisfied by the experience, without knowing precisely why. Something was missing here. There was a piece of the puzzle, a critical piece, which I felt myself close to finding, but it was still eluding me. What was it? I thought about the parlor, the copies of *National Geographic*, the musical instruments placed around the room. And that painting of the Pilgrim couple walking into a snow-covered forest. What was it that I was missing?

Carol's and my next stop at this location was the Nixon Library and Museum. I have now visited all of these presidential museums, and I have found them to be, in varying degrees, paeans of praise to the Presidents whose lives they chronicle. As a result, I wasn't surprised by the grandiose polished stone interior of the entrance area and its well-appointed gift shop, nor by the impressive scale of the auditorium to which we were directed where the introductory film on the life of President Nixon was just beginning. I wasn't surprised by the image of the President forwarded by the movie: an accomplished diplomat treading the difficult waters of world conflict (i.e. Vietnam) and social upheavals at home (e.g. Kent State). I wasn't surprised at the emphasis on President Nixon's foreign policy successes (i.e. China and SALT). I wasn't even all that surprised that Watergate was, at best, a footnote in this presentation. But I wondered, as the film ended and we were invited into the museum proper, whether or not I would actually find anything here that would yield a meaningful insight into Nixon the man.

Just before we entered the display areas of the museum, we saw a glass case containing a cornucopia of campaign buttons from numerous earlier presidential elections. Beside this exhibit was a box mounted on the wall with a telephone receiver on either side. Visitors were informed that by pushing a button they could hear Franklin Roosevelt's first "fireside chat." I pushed it, listened, and enjoyed hearing President Roosevelt insisting that I should put my money back in the now federally insured banking system. But why was it here? How was Franklin Roosevelt's radio message related to the story of Richard M. Nixon?

We now moved into the areas dedicated to educating visitors as to President Nixon's growing up years, including frequent reminders of his indefatigable work ethic in pursuing his studies and still helping with the family grocery business. We learned of his academic successes at nearby Whittier College, and we were also reminded that he had landed a scholarship at Harvard, but his family had lacked the resources to pay for his transportation and living expenses there.

The exhibits then traced his rise in politics and his fervent anti-Communist efforts in pursuing the Alger Hiss case. His election to the United States House of Representatives, his later election to the Senate, finally his nomination as the Republican Vice Presidential candidate in 1952—all were presented, illustrating his meteoric rise to national political prominence. A television set was featured in one display where viewers could watch his famous "Checkers" speech in its entirety. The floor around the television was covered with letters and telegrams in support of his continued candidacy as Dwight Eisenhower's running mate in 1952.

Of course there was also an area devoted to his famous television debate with John F. Kennedy in 1960, as well as an acknowledgement of his failed effort to become the Governor of California two years later. But then we moved into 1968 and the years of the Nixon Presidency.

The end of the war in Vietnam, the Apollo mission to put the first men on the moon, the historic visits to China and Russia, even a reconstruction of President Nixon's favorite room in the White House, the Lincoln sitting room, complete with the President's favorite brown cloth chair with its matching hassock—all were presented and described with care. But one room in particular stopped me in my tracks.

The official title of the room, as Supervisory Museum Curator Olivia Anastasiadis later informed me, is "The Head of State Gift Gallery that Includes Figures of World Leaders." This section of the museum had been designed with the express intent of showcasing the area of President Nixon's greatest success as a world leader: foreign policy. After all, it had been Nixon who, as Vice President, had toured the globe, traveling sometimes into very hostile environments, in order to promote goodwill and to confirm the support of the United States both in helping countries resist the spread of Communism and in establishing economic, social, and political freedom throughout the world. Of course, during his years as Chief Executive, President Nixon had opened relations with China and had signed the first nuclear arms treaty with the Soviet Union.

Yet, for me, this room's collection of gifts and explanatory displays chronicling these achievements were less affecting than the life-size bronze figures gathered together here. The sculpted likenesses depicted ten world leaders with whom President Nixon had had significant dealings. But what a group they were! Included were a few figures

Bronze Statues of World Leaders at the Nixon Presidential Library

one might have expected: Winston Churchill, the Prime Minister of Great Britain, and Charles De Gaulle, longtime President of the French Republic. There was also logic in the inclusion of Konrad Adenauer, the Chancellor of post-World War II West Germany, and

Shigeru Yoshida, the Prime Minister of Japan in 1946-47 and 1948-1954. Representing the Middle East were Golda Meir of Israel and Anwar el-Sadat of Egypt. But then, in this museum dedicated to the ardent anti-Communist Richard Nixon, were standing—or sitting—four bronze likenesses of implacable Communist leaders: Nikita ("We will bury you!") Khrushchev and Leonid Brezhnev of the Soviet Union and Mao ("Cultural Revolution") Zedong and Zhou En-lai of the People's Republic of China. Written in bronze letters on the white wall behind all these figures was the following quotation: "They are leaders who have made a difference. Not because they wished it, but because they willed it. R.N."

Here finally was the key to the man for which I had been searching, and I could almost feel a cold chill pass through me as the potential meaning of that interesting quotation resonated in my mind. Each of these leaders had, unquestionably, "made a difference," but that phrase alone was not necessarily comforting. What mattered most was the kind of "difference" they had made.

All of these leaders (and now even the museum's inclusion of Franklin Roosevelt's fireside chat started to make sense to me) shared one defining quality: unquenchable will. And will, of course, when used for the purpose of good, can be a will to survive, a will to resist oppression, to found a nation, to restore a shattered country to wellness, to negotiate peace. On the other hand, when employed for unscrupulous ends, will can become a will to subjugate, a will to imprison, a will to terrorize, to kill, even to ignore the very principles and ideals one had dedicated one's life to defend. President Nixon's words to David Frost, presented on videotape in the section of the museum dealing with Watergate, seem apropos:

> *I let down my friends. I let down the country. I let down our system of government, dreams of all those young people that ought to get into government but who think it's all too corrupt and the rest...and I have to carry that burden with me the rest of my life.*

Here in this very room filled with statues of world leaders, a space President Nixon had designed himself to be part of his permanent legacy, he had created, however inadvertently, a setting that illustrated fully the double-sided nature of willpower, its ability to destroy as well as to inspire. The painting of John and Priscilla Alden hanging over the fireplace of the birthplace home came back to my thought. This quality of willpower, the determination that the Nixon family had so admired in the early Pilgrim settlers, could also be perverted into the sort of willful determination that had led Mao Zedong to launch a "Cultural Revolution" which had cost the lives of more than 1.5 million people. The indomitable will that had inspired Winston Churchill to assure war-weary Britons that "This was their finest hour" could also be misdirected into tempting a President to resort to illegal means to gain an upper hand over his political foes.

Will, of course, is a passion, a powerful emotion. It is a compelling desire that, when in the ascendant, can reject even the most convincing intellectual arguments arrayed against it. Will is, in short, a complete and often unthinking triumph of the heart over the head. Again, from David Frost's interview, the words of President Nixon as he discussed his numerous errors of judgment:

> *The worst ones [were] mistakes of the heart rather than the head. The man in that top job has got to have a heart. But his head must always rule his heart.*

This is, perhaps, some of the best advice any world leader could give or receive regarding the topic of willpower. How tragically ironic, then, that President Nixon himself had failed to heed his own counsel just when he had most needed it.

36

Gerald Ford: "Junior"

38th President Gerald Ford (1974-1977): Boyhood Home in Grand Rapids, MI

One of the main theses of each chapter of this book is that the homes of Presidents can cast meaningful light on the nature and the character of the men who lived in them. Sometimes, however-er, there are no homes to visit–they have either been destroyed or demolished, or the residences have remained in private hands.

In these cases, it's difficult to do more than peer through the lens of history at the exterior of any such dwelling that survives. And this brings us to a consideration of our 38th President, Gerald Ford. Neither his boyhood home in Grand Rapids, Michigan, (pictured above) nor his residence in Alexandria, Virginia, is open to the public. Yet, in a strange way, this inability to look into the world of Gerald Ford fits his legacy to a tee.

As does his enormous presidential museum in downtown Grand Rapids, a venue that struck me as very oddly representative of the nature of his Presidency. Ford was a man who had never been elected by the American people to either the position of Vice President or President of the United States. He had never risen to the position of

Gerald R. Ford Presidential Museum in Grand Rapids, Michigan

Speaker of the House of Representatives, the prize he had most desired in his twenty-five years in Congress. Yet from 1974 to 1976 he would serve as the nation's Chief Executive. How all this occurred, of course, has been endlessly analyzed and examined. Yet even here at his gargantuan museum, Gerald Ford seems not to be the central focus of this spectacular location. Even here he feels strangely tangential to the history on display. It is a phenomenon that was repeated throughout much of his life.

In the first of what would turn out to be many such coincidences, Gerald Ford hadn't been born with that name. On July 14, 1913, in Omaha, Nebraska, he had entered the world as Leslie Lynch King, Jr., named after his biological father. Yet even the birth of a son couldn't keep the King family together, and before young Leslie was six months old, his mother, Dorothy, had taken her son and moved back to Grand Rapids where she had supportive family. Three years after her divorce from King, Dorothy would meet a much worthier man, Gerald Rudolf Ford, and would marry him, giving her young son both a father, and, over a series of years, three siblings.

What's intriguing, beyond the traumas one might expect from the future President's unsettled early family life, is the fact that once his mother had remarried, he immediately began calling himself Gerald Ford. Upon reaching the years of his young adulthood, he had decided to make his assumed name official and permanent. In honor of the man whom he regarded as his true father, he legally changed his name to Gerald Rudolph Ford, Jr. For the second time in his life, then, and this time by his own choice, Ford found himself once again to be a "junior." It would become an eerie motif throughout his life to come.

Ultimately Gerald Ford made politics his career, and after he had served for several terms as a Congressman, he articulated for himself his dream job: Speaker of the United States House of Representatives. In order for this to happen, of course, two events would need to take place: he would have to be seen as a worthy leader, and the Republicans would have to win a majority of Representatives in the House. In 1965, after fifteen years of loyal service to the Republican party, Ford **was** elected Minority Leader of the House of Representatives.

And then came the election of 1968. Because of his position of importance in the House, various Republican leaders urged their nominee, Richard Nixon, to choose Ford as a running mate. Accordingly, Nixon met with Ford and offered him the job. On this occasion, however, Ford declined the position of second best. He felt he could better serve the President and his party in the House, and he hoped that a Republican victory in the presidential race might also lead to a Republican takeover of the House of Representatives. If this occurred, he reasoned, it might elevate him to the coveted position of Speaker. But it was not to be. Although Nixon won the Presidency, Democrats retained their majority in the House. Gerald Ford would remain the Minority Leader, still a kind of "junior," a significant figure on the political landscape to be sure, but just short of the prize he had so wanted to attain.

The rest, as they say, is history. Though re-elected in a landslide in 1972, President Nixon would see his second term become an unqualified disaster. His Vice President, Spiro Agnew, would resign his post amidst charges of financial malfeasance. The President himself would begin to be increasingly mired in a scandal that would come to rock the nation to its political and spiritual core. At this point of crisis, President Nixon turned once again to Ford, a man of unquestionable party loyalty with a reputation for ethical uprightness. Would he be willing to step into the post Agnew had abdicated? This time Gerald Ford could not decline the offer, and on December 6, 1973, he became the nation's first, non-elected Vice President.

This "first" would simply be the preamble, of course, to more stunning events in the next few months. By early August of 1974, Nixon had become so vilified as a result of the Watergate affair that he decided to resign the Presidency in order to avoid an impeachment hearing in the House of Representatives and a possible Senate vote on removing him from office. The unprecedented upshot of this decision was the historic event of August 9, 1974. In the wake of Nixon's departure from office, Gerald Ford became the only man to ascend to the position of the nation's Chief Executive without a single vote being cast for him to be either President OR Vice President of the United States.

As I walked through his vast Presidential Museum in Grand Rapids, I encountered many artifacts of these tumultuous times: the actual tools used by the Watergate burglars, the Agnew and Nixon resignation letters, even reminders of the Bicentennial celebrations that swept across the nation in 1976. But not much Gerald Ford.

His administration had been a frustration from the start. He had lost much goodwill when he made the controversial decision to grant his predecessor in office a presidential pardon, thus protecting ex-President Nixon from any further legal prosecution stemming from the Watergate affair. Although history has tended to confirm that the pardon had not been a condition of his having been selected as Vice President, there were still many who believed that justice had been subverted. Yet, for President Ford, the combined demands of finally ending a war–Vietnam–that he hadn't started and attempting to manage an inflationary yet stagnant economy that had begun to spiral downward before he had taken office were the most significant challenges facing his administration. In April of 1975, the President announced the official ending of the Vietnam War, yet he found it difficult to enact any effective legislative programs to help alleviate the nation's daunting economic woes. He had been labeled by some the "accidental President," and Ford found himself in a political climate very different from that of his Congressional career. Consensus building and compromise had vanished in favor of increasingly strident partisanship.

As I moved from room to room in the Ford Presidential Museum, I was particularly struck by a handwritten note on display, sent to Ford by a woman named Sara Jane Moore after she had spent the first seven months of a life sentence in jail for attempting to assassinate him. In this penciled missive, she identified herself as a woman who abhorred violence and that she had had to completely disassociate his personal life with the office he held in order to decide to shoot him, in hopes of making her political point. She added that although she was glad she hadn't killed him, she still was sorry her assassination attempt hadn't been successful in bringing about the political changes she desired. Somehow, even his would-be assassin had been aiming at the office of the President, not at him. Gerald Ford the man had been only inadvertently her target.

Although Ford captured his party's nomination for the Presidency in 1976, the country was pretty well sick of a Republican White House. Only the fact that the Democrats had nominated a relatively unknown Georgia peanut farmer and governor, Jimmy Carter, made the election as close as it was. But nobody was much surprised when the final votes were tallied. Once again, Gerald Ford had fallen just short of achieving his desired goal.

So I stand here at 649 Union SE Street in Grand Rapids, looking up at this very ordinary middle class home. Aside from a prominent flag flying in the front yard and an identifying marker placed near the sidewalk close to the house, there would be no occasion to think that anyone very exceptional had ever lived here.

Gerald Ford was a good man, measured by any reasonable standard. Even Jimmy Carter, in his inaugural address in 1977, began his remarks by praising Ford's character: "I want to thank my predecessor for all he has done to heal our land." But Gerald Ford was also a man who seemed almost doomed, even fated, never to achieve the full extent of the greatness to which he aspired. Historically, he has remained, to some degree, just as he had once chosen to identify himself: "Junior."

37

Jimmy Carter: The Sweater President

39th President Jimmy Carter (1977-1981): Boyhood Farm in Plains, GA

"I am going to vote for that man!" my mother announced in early fall, 1976.

I was stunned. This was **my** mother, the staunchest Republican I knew, along with my father, at least. This was the woman who had encouraged her sixth grade son—me—to present himself as a virtual Nixon/Lodge campaign button display throughout the hotly contested presidential election of 1960 and who, four years later, had preached to me the gospel of Barry Goldwater. I couldn't remember a Democratic presidential candidate for whom she had cast a ballot since Harry Truman. And in 1976 she was going to **vote** for a virtually unknown peanut farmer from Southwest Georgia! Why? And why, even more significantly, would forty million other Americans agree with her and send this man named "Jimmy" to the White House as our thirty-ninth President?

Of course, he had already had considerable help in the form of Richard Nixon. To a nation weary of months of attention to and media coverage of the Watergate scandal and the subsequent congressional hearings, and to a nation made even more cynical by Gerald Ford's executive pardon of his predecessor from any criminal malfeasance he might have committed, Jimmy Carter seemed like a breath of greatly needed fresh air. He was, in his own words, an "outsider" to Washington, a Washington which, at least by the late summer of 1976, seemed terribly corrupt on the inside. This smiling, confident man from Georgia who assured Americans that, although he might make mistakes as their President, he would never lie about them—this man was a solution for which many Americans were searching: an honest office seeker with no ties to the corruption that had so embarrassed our nation. He would be, his campaign promotional material trumpeted, a candidate to be proud of, "A leader, for a change."

Retrospect, some say, is always twenty-twenty. Thirty years after his four-year Presidency, it seems easy to see where the Carter administration went awry. The new President came to Washington with clear agendas that he pursued regardless of what members of Congress—even those of his own party—advised. He surrounded himself with trusted advisors from Georgia, but, in doing so, elevated them to a national stage on which some were almost completely unprepared to function. His vision of America's global responsibilities had a shining moment with his successful mediation of an historic peace agreement between Egypt and Israel, the Camp David Accords, but later foreign policy moves, from his decision to relinquish U.S. control of the Panama Canal, to his call for American athletes to withdraw from the 1980 Moscow Olympics, to, most seriously, his inability to engineer the release of 52 American hostages held for well over a year by the newly emerged fundamentalist Muslim regime in Iran, left many Americans feeling that our country was becoming perceived as a chronically weak and largely ineffectual player on the world stage. No one seriously doubted President Carter's goodness; his absolute integrity had been proven throughout his life. But for many Americans it had begun to become painfully clear that our new President had much to learn about leading—and encouraging—the nation over which he was in charge.

In my mind, though, President Jimmy Carter quickly had become the Sweater President. This image had begun just two weeks after his inauguration when, before a gently burning fire in the White House fireplace which, I'm sure, he hoped would remind many Americans of Franklin Roosevelt's earlier fireside chats, the newly elected President addressed the nation regarding what came to be known as the energy crisis. For the first time in my life, I saw America's Chief Executive wearing a cardigan sweater as he tried to set a tone that would characterize his administration. He succeeded in this, but not in the way he had intended.

Like Roosevelt before him, President Carter wanted to forge a human, genuine relationship with the American people, but unlike Roosevelt, he came off as rather austere, even chiding. The United States alone of the western nations lacked a comprehensive energy policy, he began. The energy shortage, he intoned, would be permanent and would demand what he hoped would be only "modest" sacrifices from every American citizen (one of which we later learned would be heating our offices and homes to no more than 65 degrees during the winter daylight hours and "considerably lower" at night). In short, the smiling, confident, honest leader who had just won a national election was now the purveyor of bad news: America was wasteful, was unprepared, and was perched on the edge of a crisis that would never really go away. Only great care, systemic conservation, and government policy could save us from ourselves. Hardly Roosevelt's calm assurance that good times were just around the corner.

For Jimmy Carter, the challenges facing the nation were "permanent" and potentially dire. Whether he was right or wrong in his assessments, of course, no one could know definitively, but there was our new President, sitting in an obviously chilly White House, wearing a yellow cardigan sweater and urging sacrifice and conservation. Nothing would ever be quite the same.

No wonder that, four years later, so many Americans would respond to the quite different message coming from another Washington outsider, Republican Ronald Reagan. His vision of an America that still had its greatest days before it cheered and energized the country that President Carter had diagnosed as suffering from a "crisis of confidence." The election of 1980 was a disaster for President Carter. He carried only six of the fifty states, losing re-election by over 7 million votes.

And then came his astonishing resurrection. Not in a political sense—that arena would be forever closed to the outgoing President—but in what turned out to be a much more meaningful sense: as an ongoing example of service and beneficence.

Jimmy Carter, after his unceremonious drubbing at the polls in 1980, became what at least one historian has called "The Finest Former President." When I heard him speak at Principia College in Elsah, Illinois, in 1999, he indicated that his role as ex-President was the favorite of his life. And what an active role it had been. From running the Carter Center for "Advancing Human Rights and Alleviating Suffering" to both supporting and involving himself personally in Habitat for Humanity building projects, to serving as an election official in a variety of international contexts, Jimmy Carter's global endeavors had earned him a well-deserved Nobel Peace prize by 2002, more than twenty years after the end of his difficult term of office.

But I hadn't missed him as a President. I had never felt more politically discouraged in my life than during those cardigan sweater fireside chats when I was once again being chastised because of American greed and wastefulness by a President calling for confidence at the same time that he was announcing a permanent crisis.

I didn't understand this man, though I respected unreservedly the good he had accomplished following his presidential years.

And then Carol and I visited Plains. His boyhood home there would explain much about President Carter.

Plains, Georgia, (population just over 600) is, to put it mildly, off the beaten path. On the day that Carol and I decided to visit, we left behind the comforts and amenities of I-75 at Tifton and began an overland trek on ever increasingly smaller roadways for over an hour. Rural Georgia was quite beautiful, filled with rolling hills and areas forested with pine woods alternating with lush farmland, but by the time we were negotiating the two lane state route 19, I wondered if we might have taken the wrong road and were becoming hopelessly lost in the Georgian hinterlands. Then, suddenly, we had arrived in a town so small that, traveling at forty miles an hour, one could pass entirely through its length in the space of a good yawn. We had found Plains.

The signs indicated that the Carter National Historic Site was just ahead on the right, and a minute later we were pulling into the spacious parking lot of an impressive looking brick building with white columns, a building that had once served as the Plains middle and high school and that was now a National Historic Site honoring the lives and achievements of Jimmy and Rosalyn Carter. We were greeted at the front door by a charming and hospitable man named Russell who was eager to show us around and answer any questions we might have about the site and about the history of the Carter family.

He led us to the schoolroom where the future President had been inspired by one of his favorite teachers, Miss Julia Coleman, and then we were ushered into various other rooms which included a variety of displays recounting the early lives of the Carters. It was a pleasant enough introduction to our visit, but our chief interest was in the

Jimmy Carter National Historic Site, Plains, Georgia

Carter Boyhood Farm to which Russell was happy to give us directions. After spending about a half an hour in the museum, we were once again driving past the tiny town of Plains into the countryside for about two or three miles.

En route on our right we drove by the still security-guarded Carter Compound—the current residence of the ex-President and First Lady—and then turned left onto a small country road that led to the Jimmy Carter Boyhood Farm. There were no other cars in the parking lot when we pulled in, but Russell had assured us that we would soon be joined by another park guide as we came up to the house.

The day was sultry, hot with high humidity, but the walk toward the farmhouse was shady and, before long, we were standing before a tilted plaque with an audio button which we promptly pushed. Jimmy Carter's mellifluous voice suddenly emanated from a nearby speaker, as the ex-President explained to us the modest house toward which we were walking, just thirty or forty feet away.

How wonderful, I thought, to be directed around this site by the President himself, even though in audio form. His tales of a recalcitrant mule and of daily chores brought to life a world almost unimaginable to a 21st century visitor. Here was a President from my lifetime, an ex-President who currently lived only about five minutes away from the low-slung farmhouse before which I was standing, and yet he could remember the old wooden outhouse close to the pathway leading to the home. He could remember vividly the first time running water and then electricity had come to the farm, and how it had changed his life. I found myself in awe that a young boy from such an obscure background could ever have ascended to the highest office in the land. It truly was the American dream writ large directly before my eyes.

The park guide had come up behind us. "You'll wear your arm out, ma'am, before you get rid of all those gnats," he gently quipped.

He was right. The summer air seemed filled with tiny gnats, all eagerly awaiting our perspiring limbs. The future President had lived here from the age of four until he had gone off to college. Had he swatted at gnats just as futilely during all his growing up years?

What must it have been like for a boy of fourteen or fifteen, one of whose frequent chores was to draw water from a well and carry two 2 ½ gallon jugs to thirsty field hands?

As we entered the house, it was clear that we had stepped into a world of simple industry, with, as the ex-President would fondly recall, neither want nor luxuries. Jimmy's room was first on the left as one walked through the rear screen door. It contained a single bed, a dresser, and a small bookcase. One picture, a reproduction of Gainsborough's "Blue Boy," hung on the white wall over the bed. That was all there was to be seen here.

The rest of the farmhouse was similarly spare. There was a kitchen, a small dining room, and a front parlor that, after the advent of electricity to the home, would boast the presence of a small radio. The sisters' bedroom was in the front, and the parents' bedroom—with its desirable fireplace—was located between the children's rooms. The front and back doors of the farm were connected by a single straight hallway, presumably to permit breezes to pass directly through the center of the house. And, to keep things interesting, a train track passed only about twenty feet from the front porch of the farmhouse, creating the audible sensation of imminent doom to any visitors unaware of its proximity.

This was where President Jimmy Carter had grown up, working on the farm, reading in every spare moment he could find, dreaming perhaps of a future when he could have a chance to make a mark in the world. And now it all made sense to me.

Everything about the farm spoke of austere but decent comfort. The shower head may have been a bucket with holes punched in its bottom, but it had finally been moved inside, and the water supply was pumped to it by a windmill rather than needing to be carried there by hand, so what was there to complain about? This was a family who, from the depth of the Depression, had learned the value of hard work and the simple pleasures of conservation and careful use of resources. There was no place here for waste, no space for selfishness. Jimmy Carter had learned his lessons from earth's most expert teacher: experience. How could such a man from such a background ever have anticipated the seismic effect of a simple request to turn down the thermostat for the general welfare? He had been making such sacrifices for the greater good all his life.

I couldn't help thinking of Hoover. In many ways, Jimmy Carter may well have been my generation's Herbert Hoover. Like Hoover, Carter had come from the simplest beginnings and had been early imbued with basic Christian values. Like Hoover, Carter had challenged himself to become educated and had, later in life, single-handedly engineered his own personal success—in his case, making the family farm significantly more profitable than it had ever been. And, still like Hoover, when elevated to national office, Carter had found himself unable to appear personally warm and encouraging. His message, like Hoover's, had been for America and Americans to make sacrifices, undergirded with unrelenting hard work. It was a message on which both men had built their lives, but it was also not an inspiring message. Both men would be turned out of office after a single term by candidates who understood better than they the need to encourage rather than to criticize their fellow citizens. And lastly, both Hoover and Carter would continue to work charitably and ably in their post-Presidential years, adhering faithfully to the credos of their roots.

I don't believe I had ever been more grateful to have visited a presidential home site than I felt here in Plains. I had gotten a glimpse of the greatness of President Carter that I had never appreciated before. He was more to me now than the Sweater President who had so discouraged me.

His life, presented so simply and honestly in this place, conveyed to me two essential messages: first, that every American child coming from any setting and background actually does have the opportunity to become a great force for good—that even the Presidency is a real possibility for anyone willing to work tirelessly to achieve it—and second, that the most effective leaders need to learn the importance of affirmative, rather than negative, stewardship. Food for thought, lessons to live by.

38

Ronald Reagan: "We win. They lose."

40th President Ronald Reagan (1981-1989): Boyhood Home in Dixon, IL

In the 19th century, it had been log cabins. If a candidate for the Presidency could claim he had been born in a log cabin, it automatically established him as down to earth, trustworthy, and unpretentious: highly desirable qualities for a man looking to guide the Ship of State of the largest democratic republic on the globe.

Of course, in those early days there really had been men who had come from such humble beginnings, Andrew Jackson being notably the first. Others (and here William Henry Harrison comes immediately to mind) had to stretch the definition of "log cabin," sometimes to unconscionable lengths, in order to make their resumes seem more homespun than they were in actuality.

By the early 20th century, the log cabin birthplace had become a thing of the past—no one could reasonably make that claim any more—but the need to appear humble and outside the privileged class had become, if anything, even more appealing to voters with the passage of time. Obviously, being wealthy was not an absolute liability (both Theodore and Franklin D. Roosevelt, for instance, had come from affluent backgrounds). But the allure, perhaps even the myth, of the simple man who could understand the needs and dreams of average Americans and who, through hard work and a devotion to service, had risen to the prominence of being chosen as a candidate for the Presidency had lost none of its political potency.

Ronald Reagan, then, was hardly the first politician to tout the relative modesty of his origins, but, in many ways, among the 20th century Presidents, he was one of the most effective in making good the claim. And his success in doing so was attributable to one salient fact: it was undeniably true.

Today when driving into Tampico, Illinois, it feels distinctly as if one has been transported into the past. The wide main street with its meager cluster of brick stores on either side appears very much like it must have looked before the roads had ever been paved. The only missing elements are horses tied up to tethering posts and an occasional watering trough. And it was here, on a snowy February day in 1911, that Ronald Reagan had been born in a small but tidy bedroom of an upstairs apartment.

Ronald Reagan's Birthplace in Tampico, Illinois

It is interesting to note that neither of the Ronald Reagan home sites currently open for public viewing had ever been actually owned by the Reagan family. They both were rental units. And that, perhaps, is the 20th century version of the log cabin.

On the day in April of 2011 when Carol and I visited Tampico, there was still a noticeable chill in the air as we entered the storefront announcing itself as "The Ronald Reagan Birthplace Museum." Inside was an unassuming collection of mementos, both chronicling and celebrating various moments of President Reagan's life, ranging from Illinois to Hollywood to Washington, D.C. The kind lady who ran the museum let us look around for a bit and then was happy to close up shop in order to take us up a steep flight of stairs to the flat on the second floor of the building.

As we stepped into the apartment, it was immediately evident that this had been an adequately comfortable home. The entryway door gave onto a dining area beyond which lay a pleasant living room and the small bedroom where Reagan had been born. Through another door off the dining area was the parents' bedroom which, although it lacked any outside windows, was adequately lit by a skylight. Behind the dining area were the kitchen and a narrow porch. Nothing was very elaborate here, but this certainly was no hovel. The only elements which spoke clearly of the lower middle class were windows that originally had looked out onto a side street and now merely connected this apartment to others in the row lining Main Street. The Reagans had been pinched financially, but they had also lived in a decent apartment when Ronald was born. They would remain here only a few months before Jack Reagan's work would send them off to another town in northern Illinois. In fact, in all, the Reagans had settled in Tampico on three separate occasions at three separate locations, but always as renters and never for very long.

The locale that Ronald Reagan would remember most fondly as the setting of his childhood, and the place that he would always regard as his "home town," lay about thirty miles northeast of Tampico: Dixon, Illinois, the next stop on our brief tour of Reagan home sites.

After Tampico, Dixon must have felt like an urban heaven to the young Reagan family. The city spreads above and below the Rock

River and, at certain times of year, considers itself "The Petunia Capitol of the World." Here Ronald Reagan would live from the age of about nine until he would head off further south to Eureka College in central Illinois. In Dixon he would learn to love sports, and he would establish a record for saving lives at the local swimming area on the Rock River (a record that still stands today). At the local high school he would become interested in the theater, a decision that would lead him to Hollywood, to the governorship of California, and, finally, to the White House. Most importantly, it was here in Dixon that Reagan would acquire the basic moral vision that would guide him for the rest of his life. Much of the man he would become is still there to be seen and inferred from the Ronald Reagan Boyhood Home at 816 South Hennepin Avenue.

Our tour guide was a gentleman named Bill, and a more appropriate docent for this home could scarcely be imagined. Bill clearly loved President Reagan. He was full of Reagan stories and was particularly ready to share tales regarding the historic 1983 visit to Dixon that President and First Lady Nancy Reagan had made which had officially opened this location to the public.

In many aspects, the home seemed both a continuation of the humble adequacy we had seen in Tampico and a conscious step up in prosperity, indicated by the fact that this rental was a house with a front and side yard rather than an apartment. Bill met us on the front porch and ushered our tour group into the entry hall. A wooden staircase on the right led to the second floor. To our left was the living room with its famous fireplace hearth, including the loose brick tile beneath which Reagan and his elder brother, Neil, had hidden pennies.

"There are the four pennies Mr. Reagan placed under that brick tile during his visit here in 1983," Bill pointed out. And sure enough, propped on the very top level of the mantelpiece of the fireplace was a simple frame containing four ordinary looking pennies. "We have to keep picking up the pennies that tourists continue to place beneath that tile," he added, with a smile.

The rest of the first floor, the utilitarian family room, with its squared off, unadorned vinyl chairs and couch, together with the only slightly more formal dining area, its largest boast being a bay window before which the dining table had been centered, all spoke of a home that had been comfortable without a trace of luxury. "Simple heartland values," Bill concluded.

This sort of feeling continued upstairs. Indeed the most elegant—and the word here is strained in its usage—room was the front bedroom which Reagan's mother, Nelle, used as her sewing room (she took in sewing to make extra money for the family) and in which she would invite recently released prisoners from a local jail to spend a night or two until they found work and lodging elsewhere in Dixon.

Of the three remaining rooms upstairs, the one that spoke most lucidly to me was the bedroom that Ronald (called "Dutch") and his brother, Neil (nicknamed "Moon"), had shared in their growing up years. The double bed with its quilted coverlet claimed the majority of the floor space of this back bedroom which had two windows on

Framed Photo of Reagan's 1983 Visit to Dixon, Illinois

two sides of the house. There was just enough additional space for a single dresser pushed up against another wall and barely enough room to get around the bed so that the boys would not have had to crawl over each other when retiring for the night. The wall behind the bed was decorated with high school and college banners. A basketball labeled "Dutch" and a football labeled "Moon" rested on the floor close to the door. On a wall in the hall just outside this room was a bright color photograph that Bill eagerly pointed out.

"When President and Mrs. Reagan visited in 1983, together with the President's brother, Neil, they all sat right here on the bed you're seeing. Do you notice that the President's arm is stretched out toward the footboard? That's because the bed slats hadn't been put in yet, and the weight of all three people might have been enough to break the mattress. We certainly didn't want to see the President and First Lady fall over backward, so Mr. Reagan steadied himself while the picture was being taken!" Somehow this photo of "Dutch" and "Moon" sitting atop the very bed we were looking at made the entire home feel indelibly real. This had been their family home, and the brothers had returned to see it preserved in their honor.

Throughout the house one felt that there was no pretense, no gratuitous expense, yet neither was there any evidence of glaring want. Reagan would remark in later years that, although his family would have been considered poor, neither he nor his brother had ever regarded themselves as such. In his autobiography, President Reagan remembered his father's straightforward credo: "...individuals determine their own destiny; that is, it's largely their own ambition and hard work that determine their fate in life" (Reagan 22).

Of course, such talk in the late twentieth century struck many in Washington as the grossest kind of simplification of the difficult and complex problems of post-Vietnam America. In fact, Reagan's election in the fall of 1980 was greeted with a nearly unanimous gasp by Washington insiders who regarded themselves as an intellectual elite. (One poster at the Democratic national convention that year read, as I recall, "At least elect a good actor for President—Vote for Woody Allen.")

The last room on our tour was in the downstairs kitchen area where Bill offered to field any questions that remained about the Dixon house and President Reagan. Several members of our group posed a variety of questions, after which I forwarded one final query: "What's your favorite Reagan quote?"

Bill looked thoughtful for a moment. "You know," he began, "there are so many. That was one of President Reagan's great gifts. He could joke with the greatest and most powerful leaders in the world yet still make ordinary citizens feel valued and respected. You know the biggies: 'Mr. Gorbachev, tear down this wall!', 'I hope all of you are Republicans' (this to doctors who were operating on him subsequent to the assassination attempt)." Then Bill took a long pause. "I guess my favorite, though," he continued, "was the answer he gave to a political reporter who, during the presidential campaign of 1980, asked then candidate Reagan to outline his strategy regarding foreign policy and the Cold War that had dominated U.S./Soviet relations for thirty years."

Bill smiled. "Mr. Reagan looked intently at his questioner, then repeated, 'My strategy? We win. They lose.' I guess that's my personal favorite quote of President Reagan," Bill concluded.

Here was the same kind of direct simplicity that Carol and I had been witnessing all morning, from the humble flat at Tampico to this modest rental home on the South side of Dixon. And, I vividly recall, it was also just the sort of direct simplicity that had infuriated President Reagan's political opponents. Their demeaning assessments of candidate Reagan had been invariably the same: "How could he be so naïve?" "How uninformed he is, how dangerously ignorant! Does our would-be President comprehend the delicate nuances necessary for successful foreign policy negotiations?" Most of the country's intelligentsia had verged on hysterical despondency when, after his landslide election victory, then President-elect Reagan had taken the oath of office in January of 1981.

Yet Carol's and my last stop in Dixon provided a most interesting coda to our visit—and left something of an answer to the hysteria. About a block or two from the bridge over the Rock River there is a small park by a large church—a park with no trees that can't measure too much more than about fifty feet square. In its center is a large, rather flamboyantly spray painted section of the Berlin wall, and behind it, a modest bronze plaque remembering President Reagan's famous speech at the Brandenburg Gate.

Perhaps, just perhaps, the heartland background of our 40th President with his 20th century log cabin pedigree was the essential factor in bringing about a global stability that had eluded Presidents from Truman through Carter. For President Reagan, the answer had been as direct and basic as the football he had so loved to play: "We win. They lose." Here at Tampico and Dixon, Illinois, it feels like all Americans could—and should—claim victory.

39

Reagan Postscript: "...the other lady in my life..."

Ronald Reagan's "Rancho del Cielo" near Santa Barbara, California

The Reagan Ranch near Santa Barbara, California

Nancy Reagan had her doubts. The one lane Refugio Road that Bill and Betty Wilson had been driving up into the Santa Ynez Mountains had narrowed and then twisted and hairpin curved its way past precipitous drops, rocky creek beds, and gnarled oak forests choked with scrub brush. Finally, always mindful of his wife's comfort, the Governor asked his friend, "Bill, is this going to end at some point?" (Barletta 38) Only a few moments later, it did.

Before them was an enormous expanse of grassland spreading out toward tree topped hills. Distant mountains, clusters of oaks, grazing land as far as the eye could see--endless possibilities for horseback riding, for physical labor, for feeling truly free, unrestricted from the concerns and requirements of political or social expectations. For Ronald Reagan, it was love at first sight.

The ranch itself, at that time called "Tip Top Ranch" because of its remote mountaintop location, was almost beside the point. Its adobe walls were over a century old and needed repair. The lower half of its L-shaped screened-in porch had been covered with plain corrugated aluminum siding. Yet for Ronald Reagan, the man who had confided to his friends his desire to purchase a ranch in the mountains, this was exactly the spot he had been looking for. Almost immediately he purchased the property and rechristened it "Rancho del Cielo," "The Ranch in the Sky."

In September of 2014, Carol and I, seated in an all-terrain Chevy Suburban van, were being driven up that same rugged road, accompanied by Nancy Bourcier, a remarkable and generous friend who had made this visit possible. Our driver was Marilyn Fisher, the curator of both the Rancho del Cielo and the Reagan Ranch Center in Santa Barbara, California. The day would turn out to be a never-to-be-forgotten glimpse into the very heart of our 40th President.

If Carol ever writes her own account of the experience of traveling up this road, I'm sure it will read like a white-knuckle close brush with death. For me, however, Marilyn's confident knowledge of the route and the increasingly spectacular vistas that revealed themselves as we made our ascent into the mountains was more thrilling than frightening. Then finally we crested a small hill and, below and beyond us, lay the Rancho del Cielo and its vast grassland meadow where horses were visible, grazing casually in the late morning sun.

We all disembarked and walked toward the ranch house on a long curving drive that passed through heavy wooden telephone pole fencing and a large gate at the top of which hung a wooden sign with faded lettering that identified the entrance to the Rancho del Cielo. Flies buzzed around us persistently, always happy to land whenever we stopped to take in the quiet grandeur of this beautiful setting. As we neared the house, Marilyn turned to us and called our attention to what would be the first of many features of the ranch that evidenced the handiwork of the President.

"The covered patio area in front of the entryway was added by the Reagans," she began. "The stone and concrete patio floor was a project the President took on himself. He also enjoyed cutting and fitting together the telephone pole wooden fences you see around the house. The President loved working here. When he wasn't remodeling or adding to the ranch, he would clear brush and tend the 19 miles of trails that ran throughout the 688 acres of the property. Now let's go on inside."

As we moved across the patio toward the front door of the ranch, I noticed a round table with a leathery top and four matching high backed chairs arranged around it. Marilyn noted my interest, and she spoke up quickly. "This is an exact replica of the table where, on a very misty morning here in the mountains, President Reagan signed into law the largest tax cut bill in the history of the United States," she said. "You remember that you saw the actual table in the Reagan Ranch Exhibit Galleries of the Young America's Foundation where we met to begin our tour." I nodded, appreciating her answer to my unspoken question. Being careful to avoid letting any flies into the house proper, we opened the door and walked inside.

Rancho del Cielo is a small, completely unpretentious home comprised of only five rooms and two bathrooms. Its front entry opens into the first, and largest, of its rooms, the so-called porch room. Originally an L-shaped screened-in porch, the Reagans had closed in the area to enlarge the overall space of the house. In addition they had added a fireplace to provide heat during the cold weather seasons. This site, like some of the most authentically preserved presidential homes Carol and I have had the privilege of visiting (John Adams's "Peace Field," Warren Harding's home in Marion, Ohio, and Harry Truman's home in Independence, Missouri, come immediately to mind) is filled with the President's actual possessions.

Upon entering this room, I was immediately drawn to the floor to ceiling bookcase on the wall facing the front door. It holds over two hundred volumes that the President enjoyed reading, including works by a wide range of authors, from Winston Churchill and Louis L'Amour to Theodore Roosevelt and Horatio Alger. There was even a copy of a children's book he had read and loved as a boy in Dixon, Illinois, a book that had inspired him to live a life of service, *That Printer of Udell's* by Harold Wright Bell. This was a library with an appeal to both the scholarly and the casual reader. It provided a snapshot of what President Reagan had found interesting and valuable to know. He was a man who could—and did—read the latest espionage thriller and then turn to works on politics, on history, or on the taming of the old American West. He was happy to display them all. Some were titles that had simply entertained him. Others had both deepened and expanded his knowledge of the world. But they all held meaning for him and were put here unabashedly side by side.

The hearthstone before the fireplace on the opposite wall, Marilyn informed us, had been laid by the President, as had the brick-patterned linoleum tiles throughout the home. I found this stone particularly interesting. A relatively large single piece of California sandstone which had been quarried on or nearby the ranch property, it measured about five feet long by two feet deep and was nearly nine inches high. Roughhewn and massive, particularly for the space in which it was placed, the stone seemed to bring indoors the rugged, sturdy life of the mountains, trails, and hillsides visible from the room's wide windows.

Close by the fireplace was President Reagan's favorite chair. Its red and white upholstery featured an American Indian weave design. It was here, Marilyn pointed out, that the President had loved to read his books. It was also here in 1994 as the former President had sat in this very chair, that John Barletta, the Secret Service agent who was President Reagan's most frequent and valued riding companion, had regretfully told him that he would have to forgo his daily horseback rides. The Alzheimer's was causing the agents too much concern. "I felt I was telling someone I don't think he should breathe anymore," Barletta recalled in his memoir (213).

In fact much of the art adorning the walls of the ranch are portraits of some of President Reagan's most beloved horses. One particularly notable mount whose image was on display here was his early personal favorite, Little Man, a black stallion which had come from the line of Black Wax, a horse the President had ridden during his career as an actor in the movies. Below this portrait hung the image of one of Reagan's thoroughbred mares, Nancy D. It became quickly evident that horses were more than a hobby for President Reagan. They were valued friends and provided him both the means and the occasion to be alone with his thoughts and to truly experience the grandeur and freedom of his land "in the sky."

As the four of us stood talking together, I took the opportunity to ask Marilyn the question I love to pose to anyone guiding me through a presidential home: "What item or artifact here speaks to you most eloquently about the President?" She paused for a long moment, and I could see that our friend, Nancy, who had visited the ranch before, was also considering my query. They answered me almost simultaneously without ever consulting each other. "The President's bed," both of them exclaimed and laughed at the coincidence of their replies. Such an unusual—and plural—response certainly piqued my curiosity. We glanced into the cook's bedroom and then stepped into the kitchen where Carol and I enjoyed seeing the wood-grain patterned overhanging Formica countertop which reminded us of our own kitchen in St. Louis. Next we then proceeded into the living room where I noted with interest its stone fireplace with the presidential seal made of wood and nails, the gun rack, and the half of the room that contained sofas, end tables, and a television and video entertainment center. But what, I kept wondering to myself, could be so special about a bed?

The presidential bedroom was the last stop in our tour of the ranch house. Its walls were painted a bright yellow, and the entire room felt light and welcoming. The bed, actually two twin beds joined with a single white metal bed frame and headboard, was almost too big for the space allotted for it. Rectangular end tables on either side held telephones and lamps, but the room was so cramped that they had to be placed lengthwise—their drawers unable to be opened—in order to fit. A cushioned bench roughly the height of the mattress was placed at the foot of one side of the bed.

I had to admit, as pleasant as the room appeared, its furnishings hardly seemed very presidential. Marilyn could read my rather surprised expression, and she quickly explained her choice of this object. "The bed frame and white wire headboard were left by Ray and Rosalie Cornelius, the previous owners of the ranch. President Reagan's feet hung over the mattress slightly, so his solution was the bench you see positioned there at the foot of his side of the bed. His answer as to why he and the First Lady had never replaced this bed and frame had been that they 'could make do with what they had.' For me, that's classic Ronald Reagan."

On the other side of the room near the only window was a small round table and two chairs, all painted the same bright yellow of the walls. Laid on the table was a dark blue ball cap embroidered with the words "United States Mounted Secret Service" across its front. On either side of its bill were two clusters of gold braiding that had been worn down almost completely to the cloth beneath. Marilyn commented, "I paused so long to answer your question because that object was my close second choice. The President loved that cap. One day John Bartletta had noticed the worn braid on its bill, and he had suggested that the cap could be easily replaced. 'Why?' the President had replied, 'It's fine.' This is just another example of President Reagan's basic approach to life: make do with what you have; don't want what you don't need. These things give me such a clear picture of President Reagan. They're two of my favorites."

There was much more to our tour as Marilyn led us out a side door to visit the other areas of the ranch. We walked by Lake Lucky and then went into the Guest House with its painting of President Reagan's Arabian thoroughbred El Alamein in the front room and its two bed-chambers, one very masculine and one more delicately feminine in their décors. We visited the stables and tack room and took an extended drive through the ranch property in the Suburban, traveling over trails the President had often ridden on El Alamein, including a stop at a stone outcropping on which he had carved his and Nancy's initials inside a heart.

We enjoyed lunch in a building erected just above the ranch house which had served as the headquarters of the Secret Service at the time of the President's residency. And it was here that Marilyn shared what to me was one of her most significant remembrances of President Reagan.

It had occurred years earlier, when she had been involved with curating objects for the Reagan Presidential Library and Museum in Simi Valley. One of her key tasks had been to uncrate numerous boxes of official presidential gifts after the Reagans had left the White House. ("Do you remember that last scene of Raiders of the Lost Ark," she joked, "with all the crates in the impossibly large warehouse? It felt like that sometimes.")

As she had worked her way through the hundreds of mementos, gifts, and personal items stored there, she discovered that a great many admirers of the President had sent him models of the Statue of Liberty. She had decided that she would gather all these sculptures together on a shelf and have the President choose whether or not he wished to place any of them on display in his presidential library.

Marilyn had been informed that the President was coming to see how the work was proceeding, and when he entered the storage area, he asked her if she had anything particular to show to him about which he needed to make a decision. She had led him to the collection of these facsimiles of the Statue of Liberty.

"He paused and was clearly moved when he saw all the statues that people had sent to him," Marilyn told us. He had turned to her and expressed his appreciation of the display. Then he added quietly, "You know, Lady Liberty is the other lady in my life."

This story speaks directly to one of my most central questions about Ronald Reagan's place in history: Why do contemporary scholars remain so consistently baffled when citizens who are asked to rank the Presidents almost invariably include Ronald Reagan at the very top of their lists, right along with Abraham Lincoln and Franklin Roosevelt? Why is his greatness so hard for scholars to appreciate?

Perhaps the naysayers could benefit from an interesting account of Abraham Lincoln's life when he was still a lawyer in Springfield, Illinois. I believe it illustrates not only an extremely important truth about his character but also a profound lesson about what it takes to be a great leader:

> *Even as he grew older, Lincoln continued to suffer ... from spells of melancholy that troubled his friends and associates. In the midst of conversation, they observed, he would slip into one of his moody introspections, lost in himself again as he stared absently out the unwashed windows of his office, brooding over untold thoughts and secret storms. As his colleagues looked on in worried astonishment, his face would become so despondent, his eyes so full of anguish, that it would hurt to look at him. But abruptly, 'like one awakened from sleep,' Lincoln would join his visitors again —his mood swings were startling—and joke and quip until laughter lit up his cloudy face. For humor was his opiate—a device 'to whistle down sadness,' as a friend said. (Oates 99-100)*

Throughout his entire life, anyone who knew President Lincoln well could recall having witnessed similar scenes. Time and again he summoned up the will to turn from despondency and despair towards hope and geniality. Even after the tragic death of his son Willie in 1862, he was able to pull back from the brink of his sorrow to skillfully lead the nation to victory in that terrible Civil War, and he did so with his characteristic blend of humorous backwoods analogies and extraordinarily astute political acumen.

Presidents Lincoln, Roosevelt, and Reagan had each come to learn that people who persistently focus their attention on the despair and depression and horror of life create in themselves a kind of bitter contempt for anyone who refuses to accept such a lens as the only truly honest perspective on the world. For such negative thinkers, the qualities of cheerfulness, buoyancy of spirit, and optimism are at best the characteristics of those who are uninformed, disinterested, or even uncaring. For them, a dour disposition is the only sure sign of intelligence. Yet none of our greatest leaders would agree.

Ronald Reagan, like Presidents Lincoln and Roosevelt before him, was well acquainted with life's problems. He knew firsthand the challenge of poverty, its repeated uprootings and deprivations. He knew the shame of alcoholism (through the acts of his father). In his travels throughout the nation, he had seen the pressing needs of working men and women who found it hard to make ends meet. Yet, like those earlier leaders, President Reagan chose not to ruminate over these hardships. Rather they encouraged him to hold all the more firmly to his essential beliefs. These beliefs were such bedrock principles that he chose to have them carved in stone on the wall behind his final resting place:

> I know in my heart that man is good.
> That what is right will always eventually triumph.
> And there is purpose and worth to each and every life.

Aside from his great human love affair with his wife Nancy, Ronald Reagan did indeed have another "lady in [his] life." "Lady Liberty" had early on come to personify the value he believed was the most precious legacy of all human benefits: the liberty to rise up from any circumstance into which one had been born, the liberty to express freely the inherent goodness that was the heritage of every person. It was Liberty that insured the ultimate victory of "right." It was Liberty that enabled the "purpose and worth" of every free man and woman to be expressed. And, more than anything else, it was the peace and challenge of Liberty that he felt at his beloved ranch. The ground before him was a canvas of boundless opportunities, the trails defined only by his own curiosity and willingness to find them. For President Reagan, Liberty was the ultimate American value worthy of the dedication of his entire personal and political life. Her most familiar image was the great statue in the harbor of New York City. But, for the President, at least, her home address was here in the Santa Ynez Mountains at the end of a long, twisting, and even occasionally rather precarious drive up Refugio road.

View at Reagan Ranch near Santa Barbara, California

40

Afterword: Bush 41, Clinton, Bush 43

The last thirty years have certainly included a number of eventful moments in American history. President George H. W. Bush organized a coalition of nations to fight Operation Desert Storm to push the armies of Iraq out of Kuwait, then broke his campaign pledge not to raise taxes and was denied a second term in office. President Bill Clinton oversaw a period of significant economic prosperity and then suffered the humiliation of being the second President in U.S. history to be impeached by the House of Representatives. (The charge was that he had lied under oath to a Grand Jury regarding his inappropriate relationship with a White House intern. As was also the case with Andrew Johnson, the first President to be impeached, the Senate refused to remove him from office.) George W. Bush became the second son of a previous President to be elected President himself. He would initiate a "War on Terror"—which is still being waged today—after Islamic terrorists flew two passenger jets into the twin towers of the World Trade Center in downtown Manhattan. Lastly, in 2008, voters elected Barack Hussein Obama the first African-American President of the United States. He would manage, with support from Democratic majorities in both the House of Representatives and the Senate, to institute a government-mandated system of health care insurance that quickly earned the moniker "Obamacare."

Although Carol and I have visited the homes of Presidents Clinton, George H. W. Bush, and George W. Bush, no home site is currently open for President Obama. And frankly all these Presidents and their administrations are still too close to the present moment for me to be able to fully understand or fairly assess the legacies of their times in office. What this "Afterword" contains, then, is a brief taste of what I have learned thus far.

Bill Clinton

42nd President Bill Clinton (1993-2001) Birthplace in Hope, Arkansas

I remember the Bill Clinton of 1991 as a man of almost endless energy when it came to political campaigning. Above all, he loved running for office. He came across as a caring and extremely sympathetic man, someone always willing to listen to the people he met. This was a stark contrast to the sitting President, George H. W. Bush (Bush 41), who appeared to many as a man removed from the lives of ordinary citizens. Of course, Bush 41 had been Direc-

or of the CIA, Ambassador to China, Vice President for eight years, and President for four years prior to the election of 1992, but all this didn't seem to matter to voters. Clinton won the election, narrowly edging out the sitting President because of a third-party candidate, Ross Perot, who, as third-party candidates are wont to do, threw the election to the man neither he nor President Bush had wanted to win.

Carol and I have visited four Clinton sites in our travels, all of them in his native state of Arkansas. By far the most impressive is his presidential library in Little Rock. This dramatically cantilevered structure on ground near the Arkansas River contains a large number of artifacts from President Clinton's life and Presidency, including childhood

William J. Clinton Presidential Library in Little Rock, Arkansas

drawings, school yearbooks and sports jackets, his saxophone collection, the presidential limousine, and numerous pieces of correspondence he sent to, and received from, a variety of famous people. Given the circumstances of his turbulent Presidency, I found one note he wrote to late-night television host Arsenio Hall rather telling: "I like this job, but it's tough going a lot of the time, and I think I should be playing 'Heartbreak Hotel' on your show." The letter was dated January 28, 1993, less than a full week after his inauguration!

Two of the house sites for President Clinton are located in Hope, Arkansas, south of Little Rock, where he spent the first four years of his life living with his maternal grandparents while his newly widowed mother was in Louisiana becoming trained as a nurse. After she returned, she married Roger Clinton, and the young family lived for a short time in Hope before moving to Hot Springs. The house they lived in is privately owned, but a sign on its front fence identifies it as the President's childhood home. Its modest scale exemplifies clearly the working class background of the Clintons.

The Cassidy home, where Clinton's grandparents lived and raised their grandson for the first four years of his life, is now run by the National Park Service and gives a rather surprising insight into the life of young Billy. The home fronts on a highway running through Hope, and the recurring grating roar of the nearby railroad was—and still is today—a constant reminder of the Cassidy's straitened financial status. Nevertheless they were devoted to their daughter and grandson. At the time of his birth, these grandparents gave the largest room of the second floor of the house to their newly widowed daughter and her baby. As Bill grew up, they created a sunny and airy bedroom just for him right down the hall from their own. A family photograph of one of Billy's early birthdays to which nearly fifty children and their mothers were invited attests to the fact that, rather than living a lonely or forlorn life as a young child, he was loved and cared for by his grandparents with attentive affection.

A fourth Clinton site in Arkansas, the Clinton House Museum, is located in Fayetteville. This was the home that Bill purchased for Hillary in an effort to get her to marry him while they were teaching at the University of Arkansas. He was successful in both his purchase and his proposal, and he and Hillary were married in the living room of this

Clinton House Museum in Fayetteville, Arkansas

small Tudor dwelling in 1975. It contains no original furnishings as the Clintons at this time were still living very much like college students, with boards placed on cinder blocks serving as bookshelves. The couple had no television and no air-conditioning. They devoted themselves to working tirelessly to forward their careers. Still, this home enjoys its unique place in American history as being the only site in the country where a future Governor and President had married a future Senator and Secretary of State.

George H. W. Bush 41 and George W. Bush 43

41st President George H.W. Bush (1989-1993) and 43rd President George W. Bush (2001-2009): Home in Midland, Texas

George H. W. Bush and George W. Bush share the distinction of being the second father and son to have served as President of the United States. Their predecessors, John Adams and John Quincy Adams, were Massachusetts men. The Bushes regard themselves as Texans. Their presidential libraries are both located on the grounds of major Texas universities (Bush 41 at Texas A&M; Bush 43 at SMU), and both ex-Presidents maintain homes in the state. Yet this famous father and son are also possessed of distinct and noteworthy characteristics that make each readily—and even surprisingly—discernible as his own man.

George H. W. Bush (Bush 41) has always come across to me as a refined and somewhat self-effacing man. Both his heritage and his demeanor place him on the East Coast with an Ivy League background. The family home in Kennebunkport, Maine, where he pursues his lifelong love of boating, is still his favorite retreat. As a young man he served his nation as a navy flier in World War II and, in the years following his military service, he refused simply to trade on his family name or fortune in making his own way in the world.

The only Bush residence open to the public is located in Midland, Texas, where the George H. W. Bush family lived for five years from 1951 to 1955. This house enjoys the distinction of being the only location in the United States that was home to two Presidents, two Governors (George W. and his younger brother, Jeb), and a First Lady.

It is a rather typical example of the many "starter homes" that were being constructed in hundreds of neighborhoods around the country for soldiers returning from the war or from their deferred college educations and who now wished to begin their civilian lives.

The dining room and living room areas that one enters directly from the front door both feature knotty wood-paneled walls and bay windows. The rest of the home is comprised of an enclosed porch, a kitchen, three small bedrooms, and a modestly sized back yard where the children could play. The overall feel of the house is one of humble respectability, and the docents here informed us that they particularly enjoy reminding visiting school groups that this house teaches the lesson that any American can grow up to hold the highest office in the land, even someone living in a home as small as this one. Of course there are other houses in Midland where the Bushes lived as the oil business prospered. Although they are currently privately owned, they illustrate the financial progress that George H. W. Bush was making over the years that he and his family resided here.

George W. Bush (Bush 43) differs markedly from his father. Although he followed the family tradition of being educated at Yale, he is a Texan through and through. His favorite retreat is his ranch outside of Dallas in Crawfordsville, Texas. A visitor to the ranch described George W. Bush's favorite pastimes as "...jogging in 100-degree heat, fishing in his man-made lake, gunning his pickup truck over ravines and dirt roads, chopping cedar, or cooling off by jumping into a creek ..." (Walsh 257). His greatest personal achievement prior to his political career was his decision to face up to his alcoholism and to stop drinking. Early in his autobiographical memoir, *Decision Points*, he identifies the importance of that moment: "Quitting drinking was one of the toughest decisions I have ever made. Without it, none of the others [i.e. the subsequent decisions that defined his Presidency] that follow in this book would have been possible" (3).

His childhood room in the Midland house identifies clearly his youthful interests. The walls of the bedroom are finished with the same knotty wood paneling of the dining room and living room. A recessed twin bed is visible on the right as one enters the room, and a large bookcase with a projecting desk dominates its longest wall. Arrayed on its numerous shelves are a few books and a variety of toys, including cars, buses, military and cowboy toys, airplanes, and board games. Young George W. was clearly a boy's boy as his later adult activities at his ranch in Crawford are those of a man's man.

Both Bush Presidencies involved wars and economic crises. Both included failures and successes. In trying to illustrate the difference between the father and son, I will let each man's words speak for him.

George H. W. Bush Presidential Library in College Station, Texas

In the George H. W. Bush Presidential Library in College Park, Texas, the bookstore sells t shirts printed with a quotation from the President's 1991 State of the Union address. It typifies the style of his elocution: "Let future generations understand the burden and the blessings of freedom. Let them say, we stood where duty required us to stand." Reasonable words, rationally expressed.

George W. Bush's Presidential Library in Dallas, Texas, includes a massive section of partially melted steel girders from the World Trade Center. On a large screen in the same room a video is playing that shows the President's visit to Ground Zero in the days following the terrorist attack. He is speaking through a bull horn and a relief worker calls out that he cannot hear the President clearly.

Then President Bush proclaims loudly, "I can hear *you*. [the crowd cheers] The rest of the world hears you. [louder cheers now] And the people who knocked these buildings down will hear all of us soon." [thunderous cheering as the crowd begins to chant "USA USA USA"] As I look around the room, I see many faces looking up at the screen. Not a dry eye in the house.

George W. Bush Presidential Library in Dallas, Texas

List of United States Presidents

George Washington (1732–1799) 1st President (1789-1797)
John Adams (1735–1826) 2nd President (1797-1801)
Thomas Jefferson (1743–1826) 3rd President (1801-1809)
James Madison (1751–1836) 4th President (1809-1817)
James Monroe (1758–1831) 5th President (1817-1825)
John Quincy Adams (1767–1848) 6th President (1825-1829)
Andrew Jackson (1767–1845) 7th President (1829-1837)
Martin Van Buren (1782–1862) 8th President (1837-1841)
William Henry Harrison (1773–1841) 9th President (1841)
John Tyler (1790–1862) 10th President (1841-1845)
James K. Polk (1795–1849) 11th President (1845-1849)
Zachary Taylor (1784–1850) 12th President (1849-1850)
Millard Fillmore (1800–1874) 13th President (1850-1853)
Franklin Pierce (1804–1869) 14th President (1853-1857)
James Buchanan (1791–1868) 15th President (1857-1861)
Abraham Lincoln (1809–1865) 16th President (1861-1865)
Andrew Johnson (1808–1875) 17th President (1865-1869)
Ulysses S. Grant (1822–1885) 18th President (1869-1877)
Rutherford B. Hayes (1822–1893) 19th President (1877-1881)
James A. Garfield (1831–1881) 20th President (1881)
Chester A. Arthur (1829–1886) 21st President (1881-1885)
Grover Cleveland (1837–1908) 22nd President (1885-1889)
Benjamin Harrison (1833–1901) 23rd President (1889-1893)
Grover Cleveland (1837–1908) 24th President (1893-1897)
William McKinley (1843–1901) 25th President (1897-1901)
Theodore Roosevelt (1858–1919) 26th President (1901-1909)
William H. Taft (1857–1930) 27th President (1909-1913)
Woodrow Wilson (1856–1924) 28th President (1913-1921)
Warren G. Harding (1865–1923) 29th President (1921-1923)
Calvin Coolidge (1872–1933) 30th President (1923-1929)
Herbert Hoover (1874–1964) 31st President (1929-1933)

Franklin D. Roosevelt (1882–1945) 32nd President (1933-1945)
Harry S. Truman (1884–1972) 33rd President (1945-1953)
Dwight D. Eisenhower (1890–1969) 34th President (1953-1961)
John F. Kennedy (1917–1963) 35th President (1961-1963)
Lyndon B. Johnson (1908–1973) 36th President (1963-1969)
Richard M. Nixon (1913–1994) 37th President (1969-1974)
Gerald R. Ford (1913–2006) 38th President (1974-1977)
Jimmy Carter (1924–) 39th President (1977-1981)
Ronald Reagan (1911–2004) 40th President (1981-1989)
George H. W. Bush (1924–) 41st President (1989-1993)
Bill Clinton (1946–) 42nd President (1993-2001)
George W. Bush (1946–) 43rd President (2001-2009)
Barack Obama (1961–) 44th President (2009-Present)

Presidential Homes, Libraries, and Sites We Have Visited

Note: Many locations contain more than one home, a museum, and/or an additional site nearby. We recommend you call ahead for hours, special events, closures, etc.

1st President ~ George Washington
[] **George Washington Birthplace National Monument**
(804) 224-1732 Ext. 227
1732 Popes Creek Road
Colonial Beach VA 22443

[] **George Washington's Boyhood Home at Ferry Farm**
(540) 370-0732
268 Kings Highway
Fredericksburg VA 22405

[] **Mount Vernon**
(703) 780-2000
3200 Mount Vernon Memorial Highway
Alexandria VA 22121

2nd President ~ John Adams and
6th President ~ John Quincy Adams
[] **Adams National Historical Park**
(617) 770-1175
1250 Hancock St.
Quincy MA 02169

3rd President ~Thomas Jefferson

[] **Monticello**
(434) 984-9800
931 Thomas Jefferson Parkway

Charlottesville VA 22902

[] **Poplar Forest**
(434) 525-1806
P.O. Box 419
1542 Bateman Bridge Rd.
Forest VA 24551-0419

4th President ~ James Madison

[] **Montpelier**
(540) 672-2728
11350 Constitution Hwy.
Montpelier Station VA 22957

5th President ~ James Monroe

[] **Ash Lawn-Highland**
(434) 293-8000
2050 James Monroe Parkway
Charlottesville VA 22902

7th President ~ Andrew Jackson

[] **The Hermitage**
(615) 889-2941
4580 Rachel's Lane
Nashville TN 37076

8th President ~ Martin Van Buren
[] Martin Van Buren National Historic Site
Lindenwald- (518) 758-9689
1013 Old Post Road
Kinderhook NY 12106-3605

9th President ~ William H. Harrison
[] Berkeley Plantation - (804) 829-6018
12602 Harrison Landing Road
Charles City VA 23030

[] Grouseland
(812) 882-2096
3 West Scott Street
Vincennes IN 47591

10th President ~ John Tyler
[] Sherwood Forest
(804) 829-5377
14501 John Tyler Memorial Highway
Charles City VA 23030

11th President ~ James K. Polk
[] Polk Boyhood Home Marker: Along Hwy 31 N. of Columbia TN

[] James K. Polk Home and Museum
(931) 388-2354
301 West 7th Street
Columbia TN 38401

12th President ~ Zachary Taylor
[] Privately owned: 5608 Apache Road, Louisville KY 40207

13th President ~ Millard Fillmore
[] **Fillmore Log Cabin**
(315) 497-0130
1686 State Route 38
Moravia NY 13118

[] **The Millard Fillmore House**
(716) 652-4735
24 Shearer Avenue
East Aurora NY 14052

14th President ~ Franklin Pierce
[] **Franklin Pierce Homestead State Historic Site**
(603) 478-3165
301 2nd NH Turnpike
Hillsborough NH 03244

[] **The Pierce Manse**
(603) 225-4555
14 Horseshoe Pond Lane Box 425
Concord NH 03301

15th President ~ James Buchanan
[] **Wheatland**
(717) 392-4633
230 N. President Ave.
Lancaster PA 17603

16th President ~ Abraham Lincoln

[] **Abraham Lincoln Birthplace National Historic Site**
(270) 358-3137
2995 Lincoln Farm Road
Hodgenville KY 42748

[] **Lincoln Boyhood National Memorial**
(812) 937-4541
Box 1816, 3027 E. South St.
Lincoln City IN 47552

[] **Lincoln's New Salem State Historic Site** -(217) 632-4000
15588 History Lane
Petersburg IL 62675

[] **Lincoln Home National Historic Site**
(217) 492-4241
413 South Eighth Street
Springfield IL 62701-1905

[] **President Lincoln's Cottage at the Soldiers' Home**
(202) 829-0436
140 Rock Creek Church Road N.W., Washington DC 20011

[] **Abraham Lincoln Presidential Library and Museum**
(800) 610-2094
212 N. 6th Street
Springfield IL 62701

17th President ~ Andrew Johnson

[] **Andrew Johnson National Historic Site**
(423) 638-3551
101 North College Street
Greeneville TN 37743

18th President ~ Ulysses S. Grant

[] **Grant's Birthplace** (800) 283-8932
Box 2
New Richmond OH 45157 (mail)
1551 St. Rt. 232
Point Pleasant OH 45153

[] **U. S. Grant Boyhood Home**
(877) 372-8177
219 E. Grant Ave., Georgetown OH 45121

[] **Ulysses S. Grant National Historic Site**
(314) 842-1867
Whitehaven and Hardscrabble
7400 Grant Road
St. Louis MO 63123

[] **Ulysses S. Grant Home State Historic Site**
(815) 777-3310
500 Bouthillier Street
Galena IL 61036

19th President ~ Rutherford B. Hayes

[] **The Rutherford B. Hayes Presidential Center**
(419) 332-2081
Spiegel Grove
Fremont OH 43420

20th President ~ James A. Garfield

[] **James A. Garfield National Historic Site**
(440) 255-8722
8095 Mentor Avenue
Mentor OH 44060

21st President ~ Chester A. Arthur
[] President Chester A. Arthur Historic Site
(802) 828-3051 or (802) 933-8362
4588 Chester Arthur Road
Fairfield VT 05455

22nd and 24th President ~ Grover Cleveland
[] Grover Cleveland Birthplace
(973) 226-0001
207 Bloomfield Avenue
Caldwell NJ 07006

[] Privately owned: Westland 15 Hodge Road, Princeton NJ 08540

23rd President ~ Benjamin Harrison
[] President Benjamin Harrison Presidential Site
(317) 631-1888
1230 North Delaware Street
Indianapolis IN 46202

25th President ~ William McKinley
[] Saxton McKinley House
(The National First Ladies' Library)
(330) 452-0876
331 South Market Avenue
Canton OH 44702

[] McKinley Memorial, Birthplace,
and Research Center
(330) 652-1704
40. N. Main Street
Niles OH 44446

[] **William McKinley Presidential Library and Museum**
(330) 455-7043
800 McKinley Monument Drive N.W.
Canton OH 44708

26th President ~ Theodore Roosevelt
[] **Theodore Roosevelt Birthplace National Historic Site**
(212) 260-1616
28 East 20th Street
New York NY 10003

[] **Sagamore Hill National Historic Site**
(516) 922-4788
20 Sagamore Hill Road
Oyster Bay NY 11771

27th President ~ William H. Taft
[] **William Howard Taft National Historic Site**
(513) 684-3262
2038 Auburn Avenue
Cincinnati OH 45219

28th President ~ Woodrow Wilson
[] **Woodrow Wilson Birthplace Home and Presidential Library and Museum** - (540) 885-0897
20 North Coalter Street
Staunton VA 24401

[] **The President Woodrow Wilson House** - (202) 387-4062
2340 S Street NW
Washington DC 20008

29th President ~ Warren G. Harding
[] **Harding Home Presidential Site** - (740) 387-9630
380 Mount Vernon Avenue
Marion OH 43302

30th President ~ Calvin Coolidge
[] **President Calvin Coolidge State Historic Site**
(802) 672-3773
3780 Route 100A
Plymouth Notch VT 05056

[] **Calvin Coolidge Presidential Library and Museum**
(413) 587-1014
Forbes Library, 20 West Street
Northampton MA 01060

[] Privately owned: 21 Massasoit Avenue, Northampton MA 01060
[] Privately owned: The Beeches, 16 Hampton Terrace, Northampton MA 01060

31st President ~ Herbert Hoover
[] **Herbert Hoover National Historic Site**
(319) 643-2541
110 Parkside Drive
West Branch IA 52358

[] **Herbert Hoover Presidential Library and Museum**
(319) 643-5301
210 Parkside Drive
West Branch IA 52358

32nd President ~ Franklin D. Roosevelt

[] **Home of Franklin D. Roosevelt National Historic Site**
(800) FDR-VISIT
4097 Albany Post Road
Hyde Park NY 12538

[] **Roosevelt's Little White House State Historic Site**
(706) 655-5870
401 Little White House Road
Warm Springs GA 31830

33rd President ~ Harry S. Truman

[] **Harry S Truman Birthplace State Historic Site**
(417) 682-2279
1009 Truman
Lamar MO 64759

[] **Harry S. Truman National Historic Site**
(816) 254-9929
223 North Main Street
Independence MO 64050
[] **Home:** 219 N. Delaware St., Independence MO 64050
[] **Farm Home:** 12301 Blue Ridge Blvd., Grandview MO 64030

[] **Harry S. Truman Library and Museum**
(816) 268-8200 or (800) 833-1225
500 West U.S. Highway 24
Independence MO 64050

34th President ~ Dwight D. Eisenhower

[] **Eisenhower Birthplace State Historic Site**
(903) 465-8908
609 South Lamar Avenue
Denison TX 75021

[] The Eisenhower Presidential Library, Museum, and Boyhood
Home
(785) 263-6700 or (877) Ring-Ike
Box 339, 200 Southeast Fourth St.
Abilene KS 67410

[] Eisenhower National Historic Site
(717) 338-9114
1195 Baltimore Pike
Gettysburg PA 17325

35th President ~ John F. Kennedy

[] John Fitzgerald Kennedy National Historic Site
(617) 566-7937
83 Beals Street, Brookline MA 02446

[] Privately owned: Corner of Abbotsford Rd. and Naples, Brookline MA 02446

[] John F. Kennedy Presidential Library and Museum
(866) JFK-1960
Columbia Point
Boston MA 02125

36th President ~ Lyndon B. Johnson

[] LBJ State Park and Historic Site - (830) 644-2252
Box 238
Stonewall TX 78671

[] Lyndon B. Johnson National Historical Park
(830) 868-7128
P.O. Box 329
Johnson City TX 78636

[] **LBJ Presidential Library**
(512) 721-0200
2313 Red River Street
Austin TX 78705

37th President ~ Richard M. Nixon

[] **The Nixon Presidential Library and Museum**
(714) 983-9120
18001 Yorba Linda Boulevard
Yorba Linda CA 92886

38th President ~ Gerald R. Ford

[] Privately owned: 649 Union Street SE, Grand Rapids MI 49503

[] **Gerald R. Ford Presidential Museum**
(616) 254-0400
303 Pearl Street, NW
Grand Rapids MI 49504-5353

39th President ~ Jimmy Carter

[] **Jimmy Carter National Historic Site**
(229) 824-4104
300 North Bond Street
Plains GA 31780

[] **Jimmy Carter Presidential Library
and Museum**
(404) 865-7100
441 Freedom Parkway
Atlanta GA 30307-1498

40th President ~ Ronald Reagan

[] **Ronald Reagan's Birthplace**
(815) 622-8705
PO Box 344, 111-113 South Main St.
Tampico IL 61283

[] **Ronald Reagan Boyhood Home**
(815) 288-5176
816 South Hennepin Avenue
Dixon IL 61021

[] **Young America's Foundation: The Reagan Ranch Center**
(805) 957-1980
217 State St.
Santa Barbara CA 93101

[] **Ronald Reagan's "Rancho del Cielo"**
The Rancho del Cielo is privately owned and maintained by the
Young America's Foundation in Santa Barbara, CA. It is not open to
the general public. Tours are reserved for members of the Foundation, for special guests invited by the Foundation, and for young
people engaged in study and work programs at the Foundation.

[] **The Ronald Reagan Presidential Library and Museum**
(805) 577-4000
(800) 410-8354
40 Presidential Drive
Simi Valley CA 93065

41st President ~ George H. W. Bush

[] **The George W. Bush Childhood Home**
(432) 685-1112
1412 West Ohio Avenue
Midland TX 79701

[] George H. W. Bush Library and Museum
(979) 691-4000
1000 George Bush Drive West College Station TX 77845

42nd President ~ Bill Clinton
[] Clinton Birthplace Home National Historic Site
(870) 777-4455
117 South Hervey Street Hope AR 71801

[] Privately owned: 321 E. 13th St., Hope AR 71801

[] Clinton House Museum
(479) 444-0066 or (877) BIL-N-HIL
930 W. Clinton Drive Fayetteville AR 72701

[] William J. Clinton Presidential Library and Museum
(501) 374-4242
1200 President Clinton Avenue Little Rock AR 72201

43rd President ~ George W. Bush
(See The George W. Bush Childhood Home above.)

[] George W. Bush Presidential Library and Museum
(214) 346-1650
2943 SMU Boulevard Dallas TX 75205

Note: More information can be found on the websites of each **Presidential Library** and each **Presidential Home** that is open to the public. Also, on the internet, one may locate presidential biographies, election results, inaugural addresses, State of the Union speeches, etc.

A Very Select Bibliography

1. Ambrose, Stephen E. *Eisenhower: Soldier and President.* New York: Simon & Schuster, 1990.

2. Ammon, Harry. *James Monroe: The Quest for a National Identity.* Charlottesville, VA: University of Virginia Press, 1990.

3. Anderson, Judith I. "William Howard Taft" in *Buckeye Presidents: Ohioans in the White House.* Ed. Philip Weeks. Kent, OH: The Kent State University Press, 2003.

4. Anderson, Martin and Annelise Anderson. *Reagan's Secret War.* New York: Crown Publishers, 2009.

5. Axtell, James, ed. *The Educational Legacy of Woodrow Wilson: From College to Nation.* Charlottesville, VA: University of Virginia Press, 2012.

6. Barletta, John R. with Rochelle Schweizer. *Riding With Reagan: From the White House to the Ranch.* New York: Citadel Press, 2005.

7. Beschloss, Michael. *The Conquerors.* New York: Simon and Schuster, 2002.

8. -------. *Presidential Courage: Brave Leaders and How They Changed America.* New York: Simon and Schuster, 2007.

9. Bernstein, Irving. *Guns or Butter: The Presidency of Lyndon Johnson.* New York: Oxford University Press, 1996.

10. Bliss, Donald Tiffany. *Mark Twain's Tale of Today.* North Charleston, SC: CreateSpace, 2012.

11. Borneman, Walter R. *Polk: The Man Who Transformed the Presidency and America.* New York: Random House, 2008.

12. Brands, H.W. *The Man Who Saved the Union: Ulysses Grant in War and Peace.* New York: Doubleday, 2012.

13. -------. *Woodrow Wilson*. New York: Times Books, 2003.

14. Brookhiser, Richard. *Founding Father: Rediscovering George Washington*. New York: Simon and Schuster, 1996.

15. Buchanan, James. *Mr. Buchanan's Administration on the Eve of the Rebellion*. North Stratford, NH: Ayer Company Publishers, Inc., 2009.

16. Burns, Ken. *The Civil War, A Film by Ken Burns*. PBS, 1990.

17. Burstein, Andrew. *The Passions of Andrew Jackson*. New York: Alfred A. Knopf, 2003.

18. Bush, George W. *Decision Points*. New York: Crown Publishers, 2010.

19. Catton, Bruce. *Grant Moves South*. Boston: Little, Brown and Company, 1960.

20. Chace, James. "Woodrow Wilson" in "*To the Best of My Ability*": *The American Presidents*. Ed. James M. McPherson. New York: Dorling Kindersley Publishing, Inc., 2001.

21. Clinton, Catherine. "Benjamin Harrison" in "*To the Best of My Ability*": *The American Presidents*. Ed. James M. McPherson. New York: Dorling Kindersley Publishing, Inc., 2001.

22. Clotworthy, William G. *Homes and Libraries of the Presidents*. Granville, OH: The McDonald and Woodward Publishing Company, 2010.

23. Coolidge, Calvin. *The Autobiography of Calvin Coolidge*. Chatsworth, CA: National Notary Association, 1955.

24. Cowley, Robert. "Calvin Coolidge" in "*To the Best of My Ability*": *The American Presidents*. Ed. James M. McPherson. New York: Dorling Kindersley Publishing, Inc., 2001.

25. Cunliffe, Marcus. *George Washington: Man and Monument*. Mount Vernon, VA: The Mount Vernon Ladies' Association, 1998.

26. Curry, J.L.M. *Diplomatic Services of George William Erving*. Cambridge: John Wilson and Son, University Press, 1890.

27. Dallek, Robert. *Lyndon B. Johnson*. New York: Oxford University Press, 2004.

28. Donald, David Herbert. *Lincoln*. New York: Simon and Schuster, 1995.

29. D'Souza, Dinesh. *Ronald Reagan: How an Ordinary Man Became an Extraordinary Leader*. New York: Simon and Schuster, 1997.

30. Duffy, Herbert S. *William Howard Taft*. New York: Minton, Balch, and Company, 1930.

31. Eisenhower, Dwight D. *At Ease: Stories I Tell to Friends*. New York: Doubleday & Co., 1967.

32. Eisenhower, John S.D. *Zachary Taylor*. New York: Times Books, 2008.

33. Ellis, Joseph J. *American Sphinx: The Character of Thomas Jefferson*. New York: Vintage Books, 1996.

34. -------. *His Excellency: George Washington*. New York: Alfred A. Knopf, 2004.

35. Emerson, Ralph Waldo. "The American Scholar" in *Nature, Addresses, and Lectures*. Boston: Houghton, Mifflin and Company, 1892.

36. -------. "The Over-Soul" in *Essays: First Series*. Boston: Houghton, Mifflin and Company, 1892.

37. Epstein, Daniel Mark. *Lincoln and Whitman: Parallel Lives in Civil War Washington*. New York: Ballantine Books, 2004.

38. Farris, Scott. *Kennedy and Reagan: Why Their Legacies Endure*. New York: Rowman and Littlefield, 2013.

39. Finkelman, Paul. *Millard Fillmore*. New York: Times Books, 2011.

40. Fischer, David Hackett. *Washington's Crossing*. New York: Oxford University Press, 2004.

41. Fleming, Thomas. *Duel*. New York: Basic Books, Inc., 1999.

42. Flexner, James Thomas. *Washington: The Indispensabl* *Man*. Boston: Little, Brown And Company, 1974.

43. Folsom, Merrill. *Great American Mansions*. Norwalk, CT Hastings House, 2000.

44. Foote, Shelby. *The Civil War, A Narrative: Fort Sumter t* *Perryville*. New York: Vintage Books, 1986.

45. Freeman, Douglas Southall. *Lee: An Abridgement by Richar* *Harwell*. New York: Simon and Schuster, 1961.

46. Geib, George W. "Benjamin Harrison" in *Buckeye Presidents Ohioans in the White House*. Ed. Philip Weeks. Kent, OH The Kent State University Press, 2003.

47. Gibbs, Nancy and Michael Duffy. *The Presidents Club*. New York: Simon and Schuster, 2012.

48. Goodwin, Doris Kearns. *Team of Rivals: The Political Geniu* *of Abraham Lincoln*. New York: Simon and Schuster, 2005.

49. Grant, Ulysses S. *Personal Memoirs*. New York: The Moder Library, 1999.

50. Haas, Irvin. *Historic Homes of the American Presidents*. New York: Dover Publications, Inc., 1991.

51. Hagedorn, Hermann. *The Roosevelt Family of Sagamore Hill* New York: The MacMillan Company, 1954.

52. Hannaford, Peter. *Reagan's Roots: The People and Places That Shaped His Character*. Bennington, VT: Images From the Past, Inc., 2012.

53. Hawthorne, Nathaniel. *Life of Franklin Pierce*. In *Hawthorne's Works Vol 12*. New York: Houghton, Mifflin and Company, 1883.

54. Holmes, David L. *The Religion of the Founding Fathers*. Ann Arbor, MI:University of Michigan, 2003.

55. Hoogenboom, Ari. "Rutherford B. Hayes" in *Buckeye Presidents: Ohioans in the White House*. Ed. Philip Weeks. Kent, OH: The Kent State University Press, 2003.

56. Howard, Hugh. *Houses of the Presidents*. New York: Little, Brown and Company, 2012.

57. Howells, William Dean. *My Mark Twain*. Mineola, New York: Dover Publications, Inc., 1997.

58. Hyland, Jr., William G. *In Defense of Thomas Jefferson*. New York: St. Martin's Press, 2009.

59. Irving, Washington. *Life of George Washington*. New York: G. P. Putnam's Sons, 1857.

60. Kennedy, David M. *Freedom from Fear: The American People in Depression and War, 1929-1945*. New York: Oxford University Press, 1999.

61. Kessler, Ronald. *In the President's Secret Service*. New York: Broadway Paperbacks, 2009.

62. Lind, Michael. *What Lincoln Believed*. New York: Doubleday, 2004.

63. Lodwick, Ned S., compiler. *'Lys Grant*. Georgetown, OH: U.S. Grant Homestead Association, 2009.

64. McCullough, David. *1776*. New York: Simon and Schuster, 2005.

65. -------. *John Adams*. New York: Simon and Schuster, 2001.

66. -------. *Truman*. New York: Simon and Schuster, 1992.

67. McFarland, Philip. *Mark Twain and The Colonel*. Lanham, MD: Rowman & Littlefield, Inc., 2012.

68. McPherson, James M., ed. *"To the Best of My Ability": The American Presidents*. New York: Dorling Kindersley Publishing, Inc., 2001.

69. Meacham, Jon. *Thomas Jefferson: The Art of Power*. New York: Random House, 2012.

70. Millard, Candace. *Destiny of the Republic: A Tale of Madness, Medicine and The Murder of a President*. New York: Doubleday, 2011.

71. Miller, Scott. *The President and the Assassin: McKinley, Terror, and Empire at the Dawn of the American Century.* New York: Random House, 2011.

72. Morgan, H. Wayne. "William McKinley" in *Buckeye Presidents: Ohioans in the White House.* Ed. Philip Weeks. Kent OH: The Kent State University Press, 2003.

73. Nagel, Paul C. *John Quincy Adams: A Public Life, a Private Life.* Cambridge, MA: Harvard University Press, 1997.

74. Noonan, Peggy. *When Character was King: A Story of Ronald Reagan.* New York: Penguin Books, 2001.

75. Oates, Stephen B. *With Malice Toward None: A Life of Abraham Lincoln.* New York: Harper Perennial, 1977.

76. Perry, Barbara A. *Rose Kennedy: The Life and Times of a Political Matriarch.* New York: W. W. Norton and Co., Inc. 2013.

77. Petersen, Eric S., ed. *Thomas Jefferson: Light and Liberty.* New York: Modern Library, 2005.

78. Picone, Louis L. *Where the Presidents Were Born.* Atglen, PA: Schiffer Publishing, 2012.

79. Pious, Richard M. "John Tyler" in *"To the Best of My Ability": The American Presidents.* Ed. James M. McPherson. New York: Dorling Kindersley Publishing, Inc., 2001.

80. Preston, Daniel. *A Narrative of the Life of James Monroe.* Charlottesville, VA: Ash Lawn-Highland, 2001.

81. Preston, Daniel and Heidi Stello, ed. *Quotations of James Monroe on the Subjects of His Family, Friends, Private Affairs, and Public Policy.* Charlottesville, VA: Ash Lawn-Highland, 2010.

82. Randall, Willard Sterne. *George Washington: A Life.* New York: Henry Holt and Company, 1997.

83. Reagan, Ronald. *An American Life.* New York: Simon and Schuster, Inc., 1990.

84. Remini, Robert V. *Andrew Jackson*. New York: Harper/ Collins Publishers, Inc., 1999.

85. -------. *Andrew Jackson and His Indian Wars*. New York: Viking, 2001.

86. Renehan, Jr., Edward J. *The Lion's Pride: Theodore Roosevelt and His Family in Peace and War*. New York: Oxford University Press, 1998.

87. Rutland, Robert Allen. *James Madison: The Founding Father*. Columbia, MO: University of Missouri Press, 1987.

88. Schaefer, Peggy. *The Ideals Guide to Presidential Homes and Libraries*. Nashville, TN: Ideals Press, 2002.

89. Shlaes, Amity. *The Forgotten Man: A New History of the Great Depression*. New York: HarperCollins Publishers, 2007.

90. -------. *Coolidge*. New York: Harper, 2013.

91. Shaw, John B. "James A. Garfield" in *Buckeye Presidents: Ohioans in the White House*. Ed. Philip Weeks. Kent, OH: The Kent State University Press, 2003.

92. Silbey, Joel H. *Martin Van Buren and the Emergence of American Popular Politics*. New York: Bowman and Littlefield Publishers, Inc., 2002.

93. Simpson, Brooks D. "Ulysses S. Grant" in *Buckeye Presidents: Ohioans in the White House*. Ed. Philip Weeks. Kent, OH: The Kent State University Press, 2003.

94. Smith, Jean Edward. *Grant*. New York: Simon and Schuster, 2001.

95. Sosnowski, Thomas C. "Warren G. Harding" in *Buckeye Presidents: Ohioans in the White House*. Ed. Philip Weeks. Kent, OH: The Kent State University Press, 2003.

96. Stevens, Kenneth R. "William Henry Harrison" in *Buckeye Presidents: Ohioans in the White House*. Ed. Philip Weeks. Kent, OH: The Kent State University Press, 2003.

97. Stone, I.F. *The Best of I.F. Stone.* New York: Public Affairs, 2007.

98. Stone, Melville Elijah. *Fifty Years a Journalist.* New York: Doubleday, Page, and Company, 1921.

99. Trefousse, Hans L. *Andrew Johnson: A Biography.* New York: W.W. Norton & Co., 1989.

100. -------."Andrew Johnson" in *"To the Best of My Ability": The American Presidents.* Ed. James M. McPherson. New York: Dorling Kindersley Publishing, Inc., 2001.

101. Truman, Harry S. *The Autobiography of Harry S. Truman.* Columbia, MO: University of Missouri Press, 2002.

102. Twain, Mark. *Mark Twain in Eruption: Hitherto Unpublished Pages about Men and Events.* Ed. Bernard DeVoto. New York: Harper and Brothers, 1922.

103. Walsh, Kenneth T. *From Mount Vernon to Crawford.* New York: Hyperion, 2005.

104. Wead, Doug. *All the Presidents' Children: Triumph and Tragedy in the Lives of America's First Families.* New York: Atria Books, 2003.

105. Weeks, Philip, ed. *Buckeye Presidents: Ohioans in the White House.* Kent, OH: The Kent State University Press, 2003.

106. Weisberger, Bernard A. "Chester Arthur" in *"To the Best of My Ability": The American Presidents.* Ed. James M. McPherson. New York: Dorling Kindersley Publishing, Inc., 2001.

107. Wills, Garry. *James Madison.* New York: Henry Holt and Company, 2002.

108. -------. *Lincoln at Gettysburg: The Words That Remade America.* New York: Simon and Schuster, 1992.

109. Wilson, Joan Hoff. *Herbert Hoover: Forgotten Progressive.* Long Grove, IL: Waveland Press, Inc., 1992.

INDEX

Acknowledgments

No book, not even a "personal journey" such as this one, happens alone. Many helpful and wonderful people have assisted me throughout the ten-year period needed to complete and write about our travels and our many visits to the eloquent locales described throughout this book.

Of course, the most indispensable asset to me throughout this process has been my wife, Carol, our trip planner, patient editor, and, as the text illustrates on many occasions, inspired gatherer of some of the most meaningful insights recorded here. This book is dedicated to her in loving appreciation for everything she has done to bring our project to fruition.

There are many other people mentioned throughout the text who have also been tremendously helpful in providing information and unique perspectives to our travels. Carole White at Montpelier and Carolyn Holmes at Ashlawn-Highland, both now retired, were invaluable aids in learning more about the preservation of Madison's estate and the virtues of President Monroe. Nancy Purdy, Kathy Frost, and Marilyn Fisher all went above and beyond any reasonable expectation in helping Carol and me learn more about and deepen our appreciation of Ulysses Grant's boyhood, Millard Fillmore's role in American history, and the ongoing meaning and significance of Ronald Reagan's Rancho del Cielo. To Nancy Bourcier, who made the trip to the Rancho del Cielo possible, and who is arguably our most devoted reader, even the most heartfelt "Thank you" seems inadequate for her endless patience and enthusiastic support.

And, of course, there are the neap tide of docents, National Park guides, volunteers, and fellow enthusiasts who, although frequently unnamed here, gave selflessly of their time and efforts to bring these presidential sites and homes to more meaningful life. Without their efforts this book could never have come to pass, and I am extraordinarily grateful for their tireless dedication to the sites they present to travelers interested in learning more about the Presidents.

Then there are a series of friends whose criticisms, suggestions, and encouragement have provided just the right incentives to urge me to continue to work and write. To Jim Evans, my longtime teaching colleague, patient listener to chapters under construction, and fact checker, I am more indebted than I can easily say. I am also deeply appreciative of Donald L. and Christina Koch, together with the Koch Foundation, for their support and ongoing efforts to encourage my interest in sharing with others the essential value of the words and ideas of our Founding Fathers. To Angela Sage Larsen, Bruce Butterfield, Hiep Dang, and the folks at FastPencil, I extend my thanks for helping to shepherd Carol and me through the process of publishing our book. And to Donald Tiffany Bliss, and Ed and Lucy Harper, my gratitude goes out for your belief in this project and your willingness to review some of the text and provide helpful comments aimed at improving it.

Finally, to my children, my extended family, and to all my other friends and students who have shown an interest in this project, know that you have been instrumental in making the creation of this book a continuing joy. My deepest thanks and appreciation for all you have done.

About the Author

Clark Beim-Esche earned his undergraduate and graduate degrees from Northwestern University. During his over 40 years of teaching College, Secondary School, and Lifelong Learning classes, Clark has presented courses on Literature, American History, Fine Arts, and Film. In 2008, he received the Mark Twain Boyhood Home Museum Creative Teaching Award. A gifted storyteller, Clark lectures nationally and internationally on such topics as Presidential Homes, The Bill of Rights, The Declaration of Independence, Mark Twain, Fine Arts, and Film.

Information about ordering Print, E-Book, and Audio Book (read by the author) editions of **Calling on the Presidents: Tales Their Houses Tell** is available online.
www.clarkbeim-esche.vpweb.com [http://clarkbeim-esche.vpweb.com]

To send a response or request a talk for your organization, **email: callingonthepresidents@gmail.com**

CPSIA information can be obtained
at www.ICGtesting.com
Printed in the USA
FFOW02n1216100617
36602FF

9 781499 9010